SILENT SELLING

Best Practices and Effective Strategies in Visual Merchandising

Third Edition

Judith Bell
Retail Executive

Kate Ternus
Century College

Fairchild Publications, Inc.
New York

Executive Editor: Olga T. Kontzias
Production Manager: Ginger Hillman
Art Director: Adam B. Bohannon
Associate Production Editors: Elizabeth Marotta and Beth Cohen
Copyeditors: Julia Gilroy and Kathy Cleghorn

Interior Design: West's
Cover Design: Adam B. Bohannon
Illustrators: Elaine Wencl, Wencl/Creative Inc.
Craig Gustafson, Presentations Plus

Fourth Printing 2009
Third Edition, Copyright © 2006
Fairchild Publications, Inc.

Second Edition, Copyright © 2002
Fairchild Publications, Inc.

First Edition, *Silent Selling: The Complete Guide to Fashion Merchandise Presentation* by Judith A. Bell,
Copyright © 1988, 1994 by ST Publications, Inc.

Quotations from *Why We Buy* by Paco Underhill reprinted with the permission of Simon & Schuster.
Copyright © 1999 by Obat, Inc.

Library of Congress Catalog Card Number: 2005926490

ISBN: 1-56367-396-7

GST R 133004424

Printed in the United States of America

CH01, TP12

CONTENTS

Contents

Contents

Contents

Contents

PREFACE

NEW FEATURES

Ten new ideas that capture the direction in which the retail industry is moving will lead students beyond the basics of visual merchandising. Students will benefit from an understanding of experts' recent discoveries and learn valuable new techniques. With these new tools, they can learn to create and deliver professional quality presentations that will facilitate their move from the classroom to the work place.

Idea #1: Idea generation through current events

The vast number of media resources available today can be overwhelming. The best resources are named and students are encouraged to select their favorites and review them on a regular basis. The more they see, hear, and read, the more ideas they will generate.

Idea #2: Five top innovative thinkers

A summary of creative thoughts and processes from five of the best books of this decade will familiarize students with "blue sky" thinking. They will be encouraged to continue to search a variety of resources for new business reading and buzzwords throughout their careers.

Idea #3: Look, compare, and innovate!

The path to out-of-the-box thinking used throughout the text (look, compare, improve), is updated with the buzzword frequently used in retail today—"innovate," rather than "improve." The word "innovate" implies that new ideas must be more dramatic, rather than simply an improvement to the status quo.

Idea #4: Best branded environments

The importance of brand image is expanded, discussing the need to carry a store's brand from the parking lot or lease line to the fitting rooms, the back of the store, and everywhere in between. Some of the most clearly branded environments in the world are noted.

Idea #5: Emerging trends

- A new movement to *stretch-the-brand* by retailers is illustrated with a photo comparison of the Italian specialty chain Miss Sixty. Avoiding a cookie-cutter approach to store merchandising, the chain is designing a new environment for every location. Some retailers are engaged in this movement in modified ways, by providing exclusive products and services by location. Others are expanding through spin-offs, like Talbot's Men stores and Wal-Mart's Neighborhood Markets.

- Wal-Mart's dominance in the market, with projected sales of one trillion in ten years, will continue to motivate retailers to differentiate themselves to drive traffic to their stores and Websites.

- Lifestyle centers are emerging by the hundreds, providing a place where people can live, eat, and shop in the same complex. Regional indoor malls will be looking for new ways to compete.

- There has been a recent return to the extensive use of mannequins in store windows and interiors.

- A departure from the "white box" environment of the past thirty years is emerging as retailers energize their environments with murals, floor-to-ceiling graphics, and brightly colored paint.

Idea #6: Beyond the basics of color theory

The process of successfully combining an eclectic mix of colors to create unusual outfits with a stylish edge is demonstrated by full color illustrations and a list of available guides to color coordinating are included.

Idea #7: Home fashion store brand analysis

Four dominant home fashion store strategies are compared through a photo analysis. Students will learn to observe design principles and elements at work, and to discern good, better, and best merchandise presentations.

Idea #8: Signing as the store brand

Various signing styles can be compared through photographs, and students are asked to consider how well each sign fits the brand image of the store.

Idea #9: Fashion show extravaganza

Broadway style fashion shows are explored with an in-depth look at Marshall Field's annual events in Chicago and Minneapolis. Full color photographs of various stage scenes are included.

Idea #10: Workplace strategies

Summaries of new books on personal branding and working with right- and left-brain personalities will engage students in a discussion of strategies that will be invaluable in building important relationships.

ORGANIZATION

The organization consists of six parts divided into 15 chapters. Part One, Preparation for Visual Creativity, introduces the field with a unique opening chapter about thinking "out of the box," a theme that is carried throughout the book. This chapter focuses on the creative and artistic mindset of visual merchandisers. The second chapter discusses the practical application of the visual merchandiser's creative talents in the retail setting. Chapter 3 shows how design elements and principles are used to produce effective visual presentations.

Part Two, Practices and Strategies for the Selling Floor, focuses on the presentation of fashion goods, with attention to the basics of floor layout and fixtures in Chapter 4, wall setups in Chapter 5, and apparel and accessory coordination in Chapter 6. Chapter 7 discusses the presentation of home fashions. Part Three, Communicating Retail Atmospherics, shows how signing (Chapter 8) and lighting (Chapter 9) support the presentation of fashion merchandise. In Part Four, Visual Practices for Nontraditional Venues, the practices discussed in earlier chapters are applied to grocery and food service stores in Chapter 10 and to other retail outlets, including online retailers, in Chapter 11.

Three chapters comprise Part Five, Tools and Techniques for Merchandise Display. Chapter 12 features the Window Show, an on-location exhibition organized under the auspices of the Cooper-Hewitt Museum in New York, to demonstrate the magic of display windows. Basic techniques behind the magic are fully explained. Chapter 13 provides instructions for dressing mannequins, complete with step-by-step illustrations, and offers advice on using mannequins along with display fixtures to present fashion merchandise to the best advantage. In Chapter 14, the threads of earlier discussions are woven together in a description of the organization and management of the visual merchandising function. Part Six, Career Strategies, concludes the text with advice on building a career in visual merchandising. Leading practitioners tell their success stories in their own words.

FEATURES TO ENHANCE LEARNING

Throughout each chapter, special features reinforce the content of the text. The emphasis is always on practical advice from the real-world experience of industry professionals, advice that readers can apply in their own careers. Brief quotations from authoritative sources open each chapter and appear in the margins. Technical terms of the trade are highlighted in boldface in the text and defined in the margin at their first mention. Succinct tips and observations labeled "A Retail Reality" are a third type of marginal notation. They point out practical concerns that affect visual merchandisers on a daily basis. Within the text, shaded boxes call attention to safety concerns and other essential information. Diagramatic line drawings provide visual reinforcement of the verbal instructions and explanations. Photographs of cutting edge displays from stores around the world demonstrate how creative visual merchandisers use out-of-the-box thinking in their interpretations of standard strategies and practices. A twelve-page color insert shows the important role of color in merchandise presentation.

A series of end-of-chapter features offer further opportunity to relate the text to real-world experience. The first is Shoptalk, a statement in which a visual merchandising expert shares his or her observations about the aspect of the field discussed in the chapter. The three types of assignments that follow provide hands-on experience. In the Out-of-the-Box Challenge section, the challenge is to generate ideas for creative, attention-getting presentations by following author Judith Bell's look-compare-innovate procedure. This assignment is followed by a Critical Thinking activity and a Case Study.

In the Directory of Visual Merchandising Professionals at the back of the book, leaders in the field offer words of advice and inspiration. A comprehensive glossary and a list of references and resources are also provided.

ACKNOWLEDGMENTS

This textbook is for anyone who would like to learn how to think and act creatively. It is filled with letters, quotations, and photographs of people who are active in the industry today. These people are passionate about their work; they want to offer their best ideas on building careers to those who are entering the profession. They are individuals who are eager to "give back" to the industry by joining industry associations, participating on boards, speaking at seminars, planning scholarship fundraising events, and judging student design competitions. These people enjoy all that their career has to offer in this unusual, exciting, creative industry. They are eager for you to join them, and that is why they have helped us to create this text.

We would like to express our thanks to the following associations and individuals who made outstanding contributions to this textbook: NASFM, PAVE, NADI, Denny Gerdeman and Ann Rogers of Chute Gerdeman; Tom Beebe, former Creative Director, Paul Stuart; and all of the retailers, designers, manufacturers, architects, and editors who offered their quotations and letters so willingly. We thank Olga Kontzias, executive editor at Fairchild, for her guidance and generous support. The following reviewers, selected by the publisher, provided useful suggestions: Joan McCrillis, Johnson County Community College; Diane Minger, Cedar Valley College; Nancy Stanforth, Kent State University; Betty Tracy, California State Polytechnic University–Pomona; and Patricia Wilkerson, Skyline College. We also thank our illustrators, Elaine Wencl, Craig Gustafson, and also Larry Lamb for technical assistance with photographs.

From Judy Bell: Thanks to my family and friends and for their support and patience during this project; to Dan Myers, for enabling me to see a "bigger picture" in every life experience; to my agent, George Harper, for his determination and support of *Silent Selling;* and

to my creative group at Target; Michael, Jeremy, Laura, Tracy, and Cheryl, who helped to keep the office running smoothly during my work on this project. I also offer a very special thanks to my father for teaching me to work diligently and laugh daily.

From Kate Ternus: I thank my lucky stars for students—from the very first one to this semester's batch! Thanks to my dearest family who kept everything working while I was either on hold or on-line. Thanks to my mother, Dorothy Kuesel, for the floral designs—still making colorbooks for my "kids." To Tom "Full Speed Ahead!" Beebe and Steve "Image is Everything!" Platkin, my links to a rich tradition that we share with deep affection, a thousand thanks (five hundred each).

This book is dedicated to Petrena Lowthian, founder and president of Lowthian College. She always advised us to "Bash on regardless!" She still does.

PHOTO CREDITS

Chapter 1:

1.1, 1.2 Courtesy of Tiffany & Co. © Tiffany & Co. Archives 2001. Not to be published or reproduced without our prior permission. No permission for commercial use will be granted except by written license agreement.

Chapter 2:

2.1 Courtesy of Bass Pro Shops. Photo: Gayle Babcock-Butler, Rosenbury & Partners, Inc. Design: Bass Pro Shop Architects

Chapter 4:

4.5 © Peter Mauss/Esto

4.6 Courtesy of MG Concepts, Central Islip, NY

4.12 Designed by Fitzpatrick Design Group

4.30 Courtesy of Chute Gerdeman, Inc.

4.31 Designed by Yabu Pushelberg

4.32 Courtesy of R. Ceretti & Associates, Inc. Architect: Robert Ceretti A.I.A. FISP Photography: Dub Rogers Photography, N.Y.C.

Chapter 5:

5.7, 5.8 Courtesy of RTC Industries, Inc.

Chapter 7:

7.1 Courtesy of Stein Design, Design Architect: Jeffrey P. Agnes A.I.A., Stein Design, Minneapolis, MN. Design Team: Rob Shaheen, Marie Dwyer, Karl Benson, Andy Weaverling. Photographer: Jerry Swanson

7.2 Courtesy of Chiasso and Hanna Design Group

7.3 Courtesy of Chute Gerdeman, Inc.

7.4 Courtesy of R. Ceretti & Associates, Inc. Dub Rogers Photography

7.5 Courtesy of Hudson's Bay Company–Zellers Store Development. Designed by: Catherine Shaw/Jim Fiset for Zellers.

7.6 Courtesy of Chute Gerdeman, Inc.

7.7 Courtesy of Chiasso and Hanna Design Group

7.8 Courtesy of Chiasso and Hanna Design Group

7.9 Courtesy of Chute Gerdeman, Inc.

7.14, 7.15, 7.16, 7.17 Courtesy of Chute Gerdeman, Inc.

7.24 Courtesy of Dorothy Kuesel

Chapter 8:

8.1, 8.2 Courtesy of Chute Gerdeman, Inc.

8.3 Courtesy of Schafer Associates, Inc. Fedco Brand Strategy and Design: Schafer, Oak Park, IL. Fedco Photography: Andrew Bordwin, New York, NY. Woodwind and Brasswind Brand Strategy and Design: Schafer, Oak Park, IL. Woodwind & Brasswind Photography: Jamie Paggett

8.4 Courtesy of The Retail Group, Inc.

8.5 Courtesy of Schafer Associates, Inc. Fedco Brand Strategy and Design: Schafer, Oak Park, IL. Fedco Photography: Andrew Bordwin, New York, NY. Woodwind & Brasswind Brand Strategy and Design: Schafer, Oak Park, IL. Woodwind & Brasswind, Photography: Jamie Paggett

8.6 Courtesy of the Marco Design Group, Photographer: Chris Lack Photography

8.7 Courtesy of the Retail Planning Associates, Columbus, OH

8.8 Courtesy of Kiku Obata & Co. © The Mills Corporation/Kiku Obata & Co.

8.9 Courtesy of Fitch, Inc.

8.10 Courtesy of Larry's Shoes–Kay Mills, Katy, Texas; Tom Jenkins, photographer

8.11 Designed by Schafer Associates, Inc.

Chapter 9:

9.1 Courtesy of Retail Planning Associates

9.2 Courtesy of Lincoln Millwork, Inc.

Chapter 10:

10.1 Courtesy of Byerly's/Lunds © 2000 Lund Food Holdings, Inc. Byerly's Maple Grove Fashion Show for Grand Opening

10.2 Courtesy of Shook Design Group, Inc. Photo Credit: Tim Buchman

10.3 Courtesy of A&P

10.4 Courtesy of Chute Gerdemen, inc.

10.6 Courtesy of Pavlik Design Team, Ft. Lauderdale, FL. Ronald J. Pavlik–President/CEO. Sherif Ayad–Creative Director. Young Rok Park–Project Director. Patty Dominguez–Project Designer. Gina Kim–Project Manager. Sven Pavlik–Lighting Designer

10.7 Courtesy of Fitch, Inc.

10.8 Courtesy of AM Partners, Inc.

10.9 Courtesy of Communication Arts, Inc.

10.10 Courtesy of Chute Gerdeman, Inc.

10.11 Courtesy of Fiorino Design, Inc.

10.12 Courtesy of Mac's Convenience Stores, Inc. Rob d'Estrubé. Destrubé Photography, Victoria, British Columbia

10.13 Courtesy of Whole Foods Market, Minneapolis, MN, Store Team Leader, Dan Blackburn

Chapter 11:

11.1 Courtesy of Disney Publishing Worldwide

11.3 Designed by Mansour Design

11.4 Courtesy of JGA, Inc., Southfield, MI–Design Firm. Laszlo Regos Photography, Berkley, MI–Photography

11.5 Courtesy of Mithun Partners, Valerie Clark Photography

11.8 Courtesy of Target Stores, Photographer: Gerardo Somoza

Chapter 13:

13.1 Courtesy of Marsha Bentley Hale, Mannequin Museum Archive.

Portrait of Simon Doonan by John Dolan, photographer

COLORPLATES

1C Courtesy of Barneys Display Communications Department

7 Courtesy of MG Concepts, Central Islip, NY

8 Courtesy of Anna Lund

13 Courtesy of Chute Gerdeman, Inc.

14 Courtesy of Larry's Shoes

16 Courtesy of Visual Reference Publications. *Retail Ad World,* Oct. '99. www.retailreporting.com

Part One

PREPARATION FOR VISUAL CREATIVITY

Chapter 1

CREATIVE THINKING: GETTING "OUT OF THE BOX"

After completing this chapter, you should be able to

Discuss a variety of processes for creative thinking

Develop strategies for overcoming creative blocks

Identify a variety of resources for idea development

Explain the process of getting new ideas accepted

"Whatever you can do or dream
you can, begin it. Boldness has
genius, power and magic in it."
Goethe

"Everybody is talented because everybody who is human has something to express. Try not expressing anything for twenty-four hours and see what happens. You will nearly burst."

Brenda Ueland, author of
If You Want to Write

"Creativity is like a muscle. The more you exercise it, the more it grows."

Jerry Allan, professor of design, Minneapolis College of Art and Design

"Working is not grinding but a wonderful thing to do; creative power is in all of you if you just give it a little time; if you believe in it a little bit and watch it come quietly into you; if you do not keep it out by always hurrying and feeling guilty in those times when you should be lazy and happy. Or if you do not keep the creative power away by telling yourself that worst of lies—that you haven't any."

Brenda Ueland, author of
If You Want to Write

It Begins with Creativity

Visual merchandising is a creative occupation. Success in this field depends on a person's ability to infuse creativity into every part of the job. The discussion of creative thinking that launches this text should set a mood that encourages you to explore and internalize the creative retailing methods and strategies introduced in each chapter. Your ability to absorb and adapt the information presented in this book to your own practical use on the job is just as important as memorizing rules about color, fixture use, or department layouts.

Psychologist Mihaly Csikszentmihalyi, writing in *Creativity: Flow and the Psychology of Discovery and Invention*, describes creative people this way: "Creative persons differ from one another in a variety of ways, but in one respect they are unanimous: They all love what they do. It is not the hope of achieving fame or making money that drives them; rather, it is the opportunity to do the work that they enjoy doing." Consider that well over one-third of your time during your career will be spent working in your chosen profession. If you are passionate about what you do, those around you will notice and doors will open with new avenues enabling you to continually expand and grow.

The Creative Process in Visual Merchandising

In nearly every retail store there are a few people who seem to have an unusual flair for presenting merchandise. They coordinate trend-right fashion looks effortlessly, set up attractive displays without seeming to think about what they're doing, and arrange effective department layouts with precision and speed. They are highly valued employees because of their special talents. When they "set the floor," merchandise moves and profits grow.

What do these talented retailers have that others may not? They have a solid understanding of retail design principles and of company presentation standards, and they use a creative approach to merchandise presentation. Design principles and company standards can be learned, but what about creativity—that extra twist or new approach which is, in effect, a unique signature?

Creativity is not a gift that belongs only to a few individuals. It is true that some people have more creative ability than others do, but all people can further develop their creativity. What creative people do is open their minds to idea-generation through various brainstorming processes. The more often these processes are used, the easier it will be to find creative solutions to problems.

Most dictionaries use the word *productive* as a second meaning for the word *creative*. Being productive means getting results. If your creative work produces results that meet your merchandising objectives, you are on your way to developing your creativity at a professional level.

Out-of-the-Box Thinking

The term *out of the box* has found its way into today's business language as a buzzword that describes thinking creatively. Another phrase—*coloring outside the lines*—means much the same thing. "Stay inside the lines!" Remember hearing those words? Your kindergarten teacher wanted your earliest artistic efforts to conform to those of your classmates. Coloring inside the lines was your behavioral task, and development of eye–hand coordination and following rules were the teacher's learning objectives for you.

Once you had those basic skills under control, you'd be allowed to advance to more creative freehand artwork. By the time that happened, though, you may not have felt much like being creative because the desire to do unique things had been "schooled" right out of you. As a five-year-old, your wildly creative urges—curbed for the sake of orderly learning in the classroom—may have been temporarily inhibited.

As a retailer, creativity means you must color outside the lines again in order to find new solutions for merchandising problems you encounter. Being able to move beyond your usual way of thinking about things is essential in today's competitive retail environment. Look at Colorplate 1A, Sony's couch potato window. "Who would expect vegetables and technology to go together?" asked Christine Belich, Sony's executive creative director. She approaches windows as a way to "put some kind of art and culture on the street." Look at Colorplates 1B and 1C to see other examples of creative thinking.

According to Kurt Hanks and Jay Parry (*Wake Up Your Creative Genius*), "Creation isn't making something out of nothing. Instead it's organizing existing elements into new and different wholes." That should be good news, especially if you see yourself as a non-creative person. It implies that you don't have to come up with totally new ideas, provided that you do some "editing" along the way.

What is *editing*? It's a term borrowed from the newspaper industry. Newspaper editors don't normally write the stories you see in print. Instead, they assign and oversee the work of staff reporters who actually gather information, interview people, and write the news articles you read. Just before the newspaper is printed, editors inspect their reporters' stories and edit, or fine-tune, them for content, accuracy, grammar, spelling, and length.

Sometimes reporters feel their original story is ruined by editing, but most will admit that editorial changes—shortening a sentence here, changing a word there—make the resulting story or article clearer, tighter, and better overall. This is similar to the process that takes place when visual merchandisers modify ideas they've gotten from other retail sources. Presentations become more focused, more dynamic, and more effective. New (and better) ideas can come from the ideas of others.

> "Being clever is the key, but it's much more than just putting merchandise in the window. Display needs to reflect the company's philosophy to make a true brand statement, yet do it in a way that makes the CEO smile. Even more than that, it has to be compelling, so that shoppers simply have to have the product."
>
> Christine Belich, executive creative director, Sony

O'Brien's View of Creative Problem Solving

Tim O'Brien, corporate trainer and columnist for Knight Ridder's *Tribune News*, offers five ideas for looking at old problems in new ways. In a syndicated article titled "The Value of Foolish Questions: Develop New Approaches to Problem Solving," he writes:

List and counter list. When you have a problem to resolve, quickly list the first five ideas that come to mind for solving the situation. Now write out five approaches that are the opposite of the first five you wrote down. Do any of them make sense? Do any of them sound more possible than the first group? What about combining the two approaches—is there any merit to this?

Use both sides of your brain. First, think about the situation in analytical terms only. Then, think about it from an emotional point of view. Does either of these approaches lend more insight than the other? Again, what about a balanced approach, using the strong points from both sides?

Convene a panel of experts. You can do this in two ways. You can actually invite several people to brainstorm or mastermind with you about the problem. Or, you can assemble an imaginary group of the geniuses from history. Then ask the real group for ideas. Or, ask yourself, "How would Sir Isaac Newton solve this problem? What would Madame Curie have done in this situation?" Allow your mind to flow with thoughts influenced by your impression of these major figures of the past. This can produce unique insights.

Be a consultant. Approach the challenge as if you are a hired consultant. Assemble the facts. Ask questions of yourself and others involved. Identify the causes. Determine the desired outcome, define the solution. Based on this information, list the techniques to use that will lead to the final goal.

Ask children how they would solve the problem. Then sit back and let them tell you. This can be an amazingly fun and revealing exercise. What we want to do is to generate creative solutions. And, that often takes a free flowing imagination. And when you ask a child, you've gone to the source of imagination. They don't even know there is a box to be inside, unless it's a refrigerator box that's now a fort.

The first and only rule to remember when trying these suggestions is: There are no rules. Anything and everything is appropriate in the thinking stage. Don't limit yourself to what you're familiar with. In fact, that is the point of this exercise. Break out beyond the self-imposed bounds you've placed on yourself. Add your own ideas to help you think young and fresh, and you now have the tools to see problems and challenges as opportunities. Just get started, and then, never quit.

Bell's Approach: Look, Compare, Innovate

To text author Judith Bell, thinking out of the box consists of three simple action steps that can jump-start creativity and enable you to explore, edit, and expand on current ideas and practices.

The first step is to *look at what your retail competition is doing.* If you see that your retail competitors are doing something right with their store's merchandise presentation strategies and techniques, you will have a head start on doing something even better with your own.

How will you know what works for your competitors? You might watch their customers and note how they react to displays in those stores. You can observe which displays appear to be ignored and which seem to have "stopping power."

The second step to thinking out of the box is to *compare.* Once you gather ideas from your competition, you're ready to compare them with your own company's presentations. For example, you might compare a presentation at your competitor's store entrance with the presentation at your own store entrance. You might observe whether the competitor used any mannequins or props to draw customers into and through the store. You'd read the directional signing and determine if it assisted customers to locate departments. You'd read signing on merchandise fixtures and ask yourself whether it seemed to encourage customers to make buying decisions. You'd ask yourself about the effectiveness of the merchandise displays. You'd ask if merchandise presentation overall seemed to give customers fresh ideas about how fashion or home apparel products could be combined or coordinated. You'd make note of what types of lighting were used to spotlight items or add to the overall atmosphere of the store. You'd wonder about the general feeling of the store—if it "felt good" to be in the store or if specific merchandise areas invited you to stay and browse.

The third step, *innovate,* will be much easier as a result of your observations and comparisons, because it's in this phase of the out-of-the-box process that you become an editor. You start planning your store's next merchandise presentations based on effective things you've seen elsewhere. However, instead of just copying what you've seen, you'll put your own spin, or interpretation, on the strategy or technique. You'll be able to look at the original competitive presentation and analyze it—compare it to an ideal display (evaluate its strengths and weaknesses)—and, finally, innovate by creating some new alternatives to the original.

A Retail Reality
Retail stopping power makes casual passers-by focus attention on the visual presentation and really consider the merchandise. Once focused, they become potential customers and the presentation becomes a "silent seller."

Bell's Thinking Out of the Box

1. *Look.* Visit two or more competing stores and look at the merchandise presentations.

2. *Compare.* Compare the merchandise presentations.

3. *Innovate.* Combine the best presentation techniques from competing stores with those in your own store, and modify them to create a unique presentation that fits your store's brand image.

The SCAMPER Model

You often see visual merchandisers carrying toolboxes as they go about their duties. They may need rubber mallets, screwdrivers, pins, and wrenches—the mechanical tools of their trade—as they set up shelving and fixtures, hang signs, and dress mannequins. What you won't see is the "mental toolbox" that visual merchandisers reach into for inspiration every day—the creative tools that they've acquired as they've developed professionally.

In retailing, the creative thinking process can follow several useful problem-solving models. You've already learned about two in this chapter. The important thing is finding the out-of-the-box method that works for you.

Some visual merchandisers use Robert Eberle's creative thinking model SCAMPER (a mnemonic for ways to brainstorm for an unusual solution) to solve the merchandising problem at hand. This model for creative thinking offers seven options to give your thinking a creative boost. These options, which are listed below, are explained as follows:

SCAMPER Model

- **S**ubstitute
- **C**ombine
- **A**dapt
- **M**odify, minify, magnify
- **P**ut to other uses
- **E**liminate
- **R**everse or rearrange

(Eberle, Robert. *SCAMPER: Games for Imagination Development.* 1977. DOK Publishers, Buffalo, N.Y.)

Substituting strategies involves exchanging one expected element of a visual idea for another. It might mean applying an accessorizing strategy from the fashion department to items in the home furnishings area. A fully accessorized fashion mannequin might wear several layers of fashionable clothing, plus jewelry, hosiery, shoes, hat, and handbag. To use a substituting strategy in the home furnishings area, you might "borrow" the fashion strategy to create a formal-occasion table top in the housewares department. Showing fine linens (tablecloth, placemats, and napkins), place settings of fine china, crystal stemware, silver service, candles, candleholders, a centerpiece, and handwritten place cards in sterling holders for each guest at the table creates a strong home fashion statement.

Combining strategies may mean seating a pair of elegantly dressed and fully accessorized mannequins at the table mentioned above. Substitute Valentine cards for the place cards and the scene is set for a romantic Valentine's Day dinner party for two. The fashion and home furnishings tie-in also gives you a presentation with **cross-merchandising** impact.

Adapting strategies will find the visual merchandiser taking the rainbow-hued progression of colored merchandise used often on women's fashion department walls and applying it to a wall of bedding or bath linens, a display of shower curtains, or an assortment of children's toys. Or, adapting might involve using a stepladder, paint buckets, and brushes, as props to display half a dozen pairs of brightly tinted tennis shoes. You simply take an item intended for one use and adapt its purpose to suit your sales presentation.

Cross-merchandising refers to moving merchandise across traditional department or classification lines to combine elements in a single department or display. For example, books of poetry, romantic novels, candles, bath salts, terry cloth robes, and oversized bath towels could be brought together in a single display.

Modifying strategies—magnifying (making something larger) or minifying (making something smaller)—provide an imaginative counterpoint to otherwise routine presentations of any merchandise. One effective display employed a GI Joe doll to prop a jewelry display window featuring cultured pearl necklaces. The doll, dressed in full scuba diving gear, appeared to be swimming underwater (the backdrop and sides of the window were covered in sea-blue fabric). The pearl necklaces became a trail of bubbles streaming toward the surface of the water in which the doll swam. Using the miniature figure made the small pearls seem much larger and more important in scale than they would have been in a conventional display window. That's an example of minifying. Using a gigantic golf ball and wooden tee in a men's sports clothing display surely attracts attention—if for no other reason than making shoppers take a second look at what magnifying a prop 50 times does to perspective and scale. That second look is the visual merchandiser's opportunity to focus customer attention on merchandise.

Putting to other uses is a strategy that finds the visual merchandiser dressing a mannequin in a crisp white apron but inverting a stock pot on its head in place of the chef's traditional white toque. This is a fun, eye-catching way to focus shopper attention on a cooking vessel. The pot's general shape and undeniable link to the professional cook could make shoppers stop and rethink their cookware choices! The unexpected "other use" can be entertaining, thought provoking, and attention getting—three good elements to employ in any display.

The *eliminating strategy* is an amazingly useful tool to prevent a creative visual merchandiser from becoming too clever. It is always a good idea to "quit while you're ahead" in a presentation. In the stockpot example, you could easily get carried away with the fun of it all and keep on reaching for even more obvious tie-ins to the chef concept. It might be tempting to dangle cookie cutters from the mannequin's ears as another kitchen-related accessory, but it would be far better to use restraint and retain the impact of the inverted cooking pot.

The *reversing* or *rearranging strategy* is another method of presenting merchandise in an unexpected way. Mannequins that normally stand on their feet can stand on their heads (if you have a sturdy and reliable way to suspend them from the ceiling grid in a display window). Things normally arranged from smallest to largest can be reversed in order. Mannequins dressed back-to-front can stop traffic. You can have a great time devising new ways to do the opposite of what's expected.

Best Practices and Practical Applications

Retailers worldwide use creative thinking strategies. Some very competitive (and successful) retailers actually hire individuals whose principal assignment is to look at what other retailers are doing and develop new presentation concepts based on industry trends and the best current practices.

Highly professional visual merchandising managers make local comparison shopping a regular part of their working week, with occasional trips to different locations in the country to look at the latest store **prototypes.** Visual merchandisers, at any point in their careers (from window design specialist to vice president) must use their powers of observation to build professional skills and creative muscle. In all cases, the ability to look, compare, and innovate should really be part of any visual merchandiser's formal job description.

As you begin this course, visit your favorite store's direct and indirect competitors. If you currently work for an independent "junior fashion" store in a local mall, you'll want to keep an eye on other junior shops in the mall. In today's fast-paced junior fashion market, you'll also want to shop for presentation ideas in national chains like the Gap, Old Navy, Express, J.Crew, and Abercrombie & Fitch, if they are located in your community. You al-

"Creative people are playful people. It's literally impossible to create effectively, and consistently, if we're unable to let ourselves play. Why? Because creativity and play need each other."

Kurt Hanks and Jay Parry, *Wake Up Your Creative Genius*

A **prototype** is the original model on which later types are based. For example, before rolling out a dozen retail stores, a prototype is built so that design features may be tested and refined if necessary. The same process is used in the development of custom merchandise fixtures and visual fixtures.

ways want to know what the leading specialty and department stores in the retail industry are doing, whether they are your direct competitors or not. Recognized leaders are usually the trendsetters for product presentation.

It is also a good strategy to keep in touch with noncompeting stores that have interesting themes, décor, or merchandise. If your store carries only junior apparel, for example, you may find ideas at stores like Bath & Body Works, Steve Madden, and Urban Outfitters that feature other products targeted to the junior customer.

One-of-a-kind stores often provide a wealth of creative ideas. They can quickly develop and implement new ideas without dealing with the top-down bureaucracy that sometimes slows change in a larger corporation. The one-of-a-kind store can often quickly change direction and react more immediately to a developing retail merchandise trend. You may find more highly innovative ideas for merchandise presentation there than anywhere else. Once you make store observations part of your retail routine, you can begin to compare and improve upon the techniques you see to create new and more effective methods of presentation for yourself and your employer.

A One-of-a-Kind Creative Merchandiser

Gene Moore, vice president and display director at Tiffany & Co. for nearly 40 years, made an art form of creative thought in his company's world famous store. When he died in November of 1998, he left a rich legacy of window design that included wit, brilliant merchandising savvy, and notoriously unconventional methods for getting people to stop and enjoy his visual merchandising creations. In fact, Moore's windows themselves became tourist destinations.

In a *Women's Wear Daily* tribute to Gene Moore, writer Sharon Edelson wrote, "While the jewels on display at Tiffany's were precious, Moore's window designs were not. He injected his work with unexpected juxtapositions [pairing unrelated or unusual visual elements]; a diamond resting on a piece of lettuce, or a brooch embedded in a watermelon made of gumdrops." According to the article, "nothing was sacred to Moore."

Text author Kate Ternus remembers a series of Moore's winter windows featuring diamond-studded snowflake pins. (See Figure 1.1.) He propped the store's small shadow box window with artist's drawing boards, barber scissors, and folded construction paper—all done in stark white against a powder blue background—to show the grade school student's method of folding paper into tight little triangles and then snipping away pieces to create one-of-a-kind snowflake designs. Anyone who'd been to an American grade school knew immediately what the windows were all about. Moore let the paper snippets fall to the window's floor and pinned a half-finished, partly folded paper snowflake to the board. After you'd taken all that in, you noticed a single diamond snowflake pin—the artist's still life model—artlessly stuck to the top of the drawing board—as if a third-grader might have such an elegantly jeweled model to work from!

People viewing the window chuckled as they stood there and commented to one another about how clever the displays were. Ternus thought they were more than clever. She thought they were inspired. What else would make absolute strangers speak to one another on a New York City sidewalk?

Ternus couldn't afford tuition to study visual merchandising, so she studied Moore's windows. She was out there for every window change. It was an amazing way to learn, and he was a superb teacher. Later in her career, they corresponded. He was pleased to know he'd helped her and flattered to have been thought of as the best.

Another Moore admirer was quoted in the memorial article: "Gene Moore's boundless humor and creativity gave anyone who passed by his windows a smile, a surprise, or a mo-

Figure 1.1 Gene Moore's snowflake window used simple creative elements to tell an elegant wintertime tale about Tiffany's diamonds.

Figure 1.2 In this Tiffany window by Gene Moore, a flower brooch blossoms beside a planter.

ment's pause," said William R. Chaney, chairman of Tiffany's. "His talent gave people a wonderful window on Tiffany's. He was a magician, pure and simple." (See Figure 1.2.)

According to writer Edelson, "Moore saw his talent a bit differently. 'I'm crazy,' he told a *Newsday* reporter in 1990. 'I don't know how else to explain it. But I'm glad I'm crazy.'"

"What else could account for his prolific output?" asked Edelson. "Over the course of his career with Tiffany's, Moore designed about 5,000 windows." Although Gene Moore made many contributions as a designer for the arts—designing major projects for art museums, dance companies, theater—and, in 1988, his own jewelry designs for Tiffany, "his first love was windows," says Edelson. "Prior to his arrival on the display scene, store windows were fairly lifeless."

In the same *Women's Wear Daily* article, Edelson interviewed Simon Doonan, creative director for Barneys New York. He recalled that Moore used to say, "Windows should be polite because they talk to strangers." Doonan, however, disagreed with Moore's comment. "That belies the real oomph that went into his work," he said. "When you look at the body of his work, he was a total innovator. He was the first to use objects like hammers and broken glass with high-end merchandise, and the first to bring artists like Andy Warhol into the window display arena."

Additional Creative Resources

Don't limit yourself to visiting retailers to find ideas for what's new and exciting in current practice. You have many additional sources of information available—as close as your computer, mailbox, book store, or public library. For example, some retail stores even offer tours on the Internet, virtually walking you through their entire store. An Internet visit to **www.storewindows.com** features photographs of display windows and interviews with industry movers and shakers from all over the world.

Subscribing to monthly trade magazines is an excellent way to "visit" other retailers and compare. The magazines *Display and Design Ideas* and *Visual Merchandising and Store Design* can keep you updated on the latest visual techniques and fixturing trends because they are focused on retail design and presentation professionals. In addition to detailing current trends and strategies, these publications offer the addresses of hundreds of fixturing and display manufacturers nationwide. They also offer information on seasonal market weeks in New York and Chicago, where manufacturers and representatives gather to display their products each year.

To see international stores without the travel expense, subscribe to the German *Style Guide* (**www.style-guide.biz**) magazine. It offers beautiful full-color photographs of the latest in-store design and presentation. Another excellent international resource is **www. echochamber.com**. To subscribe to this free service, simply register your name, address, and place of employment or school at the Website. Their home page reads: "We love retail. We travel the world in search of the greatest stores. We feed retailers and designers with the latest trends. Welcome to a snapshot of what we have found and what we think."

Closer to home, other resources for visual merchandising ideas are community events and local traditions. You can get ideas for retail signs from parade banners, ideas for lighting from theater productions, and inspiration for retail themes from seasonal events. Tapping into local celebrations, ethnic and cultural events, plus local lore or historical information can also trigger ideas for creative retail visual tie-ins. You can find visual ideas everywhere and anywhere, so it is important to be open and receptive to inspiration in any form.

Books and movies (new and old) will show you what the world looks like today and what it looked like in the past. They can tell you what people wore, what they looked like, and how they lived. Because fashion is cyclical in nature—and what goes around comes around—a working knowledge of fashion history and lifestyles from other eras can be a treasury of adaptable ideas. Don't overlook college-level elective history courses, art history courses, fashion history courses, and other valuable insights into the past from which you can develop a view for the future by looking, comparing, and innovating!

Sometimes the best preparation for the visual merchandising of "retro looks" (the retrospective view from previous decades or eras) is cultivating friends from your grandparents' generation. They'll tell you stories about fashions, values, and lifestyles from their youth that will put the present into better perspective for you. Ask to see their scrapbooks and copies of old magazines. Photographs from prior generations will give you valuable visual information about why, how, and when people wore the fashions of the day.

Knowledge of current events and cultural trends can also trigger creative solutions. *The New York Times* Style section, published on Sundays, features articles on consumer trends, photographs of in-the-street fashions, and the hottest new products from New York City shops. *The Wall Street Journal* offers the latest buzz in business, plus articles on new gadgets and technologies. *USA Today* runs surveys called "USA Today Snapshots" on the cover page of each section that can be helpful in determining consumer insight. *Newsweek* and *Time* magazines are packed with in-depth articles about the major news stories. Television news programs like CNN are well worth tuning in every day. On Sunday mornings, *This Week, Face the Nation,* and *CBS News Sunday Morning,* all provide an excellent overview of the week's events, along with the opportunity to see and hear the people in the news. Review these resources and others, choose your favorites and build them into your routine. The more you see, hear, and read, the more ideas you will generate.

Five Top Innovative Thinkers

"Successful innovators," says business writer Peter Drucker, "use both the right side and the left side of their brains. They look at figures, and they look at people. They work out analytically what the innovation has to be to satisfy an opportunity."

As a visual merchandiser, it is critical to have a vision that includes not only what you will create, but also the business implications of that creation. Your goal in any presentation of merchandise is ultimately to sell products, and that goal should always be foremost in your mind. An artistic approach to visual merchandising will be much more effective if balanced with a business approach. Knowledge of the latest information on both creative thinking techniques and business strategies will not only help you to innovate, but it will prepare you for management positions. Whether working for a small specialty store or for a major corporate retailer, you will advance more rapidly if you have a point-of-view that focuses your creative activities on a productive end result.

To help you develop a well-rounded style, you can find a list of Business Best Sellers in The *New York Times* Sunday business section. An even more comprehensive list is available through **www.forbes.com**. Click on "lists" and pull up "Business Books of the Long Boom," for the top twenty best books in the past twenty years. When you look over these lists and have a basic knowledge of the titles that are most current, it is also interesting to spend time browsing through the business section in a Barnes&Noble or another large bookstore. This is a practice that is wise to continue throughout your career. The insight you will gain and the techniques you will learn will help you to think outside the box and become a true innovator.

A summary of five books from some of today's top innovative thinkers follows. Four are business books, and one is a children's book. It is included as a reminder that you should look at a wide variety of resources as you explore innovative thought.

A brilliant book that exudes excitement on every page is *It's Not the Big that Eat the Small . . . it's the FAST that Eat the Slow* by Jason Jennings and Laurence Haughton. New technology and global communication have resulted in a world in which everything is moving faster, including the marketplace. For those who wish to embrace the aggressive pace, the book lays out strategies to help them think and move faster than their competition. Anticipating trends is a key ingredient and nine ways to spot them are discussed, including listening to music, using the internet, and *reading* the streets. "The H&M design staff never attend fashion shows. Instead, they hang out in the pubs, bars, and clubs, attend sporting contests, watch parents with their children, go to rock concerts, eat in restaurants, and study the streets for their next season's line of merchandise."

A chapter on innovation talks about THINK© (THe Innovation NetworK) at Charles Schwab's Intranet Website. The site has four zones, one of which is called Idea Central, where ideas are accepted from everyone in the company. Those who submit an idea are asked to answer questions that determine whether their new concept fits with Schwab's guiding principles. Questions include: who would support the idea, who would it upset, will it reinvent the business, and will it create and nurture a spirit of innovation?

It is easy to see how the methodology used in a financial service firm can be applied to retailing, or any other type of business. The book has a far reach and is best described by one reviewer, Guy Kawasaki, "This book is jammed with tactics for eliminating speed bumps along the road to changing the world."

Another book that discusses the rapid-fire pace of the workplace, takes a different slant on the subject and offers a system to manage personal energy both on and off the job. *The Power of Full Engagement* by Jim Loehr and Tony Schwartz is a scientific approach that was developed during twenty-five years of working with many of the world's greatest athletes. At the core of the approach is The Corporate Athlete® Training System, which has a wide range of users, from dozens of Fortune 500 Companies to stay-at-home moms. The system focuses not on time management, but on energy management, helping individuals to establish rituals that can actually generate energy and allow them to consistently perform at the highest level. It also recognizes the importance of both activity and nonactivity: "Periods of recovery are intrinsic to creativity . . . sounds become music in the spaces between the notes, just as words are created by the spaces between the letters. It is in the spaces between work that love, friendship, depth and dimension are created."

A book filled with puzzles and quizzes that will engage and stretch your imagination is *Mega Creativity—Five steps to thinking like a Genius* by Andrei G. Aleinikov. The main premise is that everyone is innovative and that you can learn to increase your skill to a level more powerful than someone with natural genius. The author describes his book in this way: "This book is for those who dare to dream and dare to act, those who revolve the earth, those who are shakers and makers. Mega Creativity offers you a new way of thinking as well as methods for expanding your mind, giving you the power to create more powerful and more plentiful ideas. The process is easy and difficult at the same time. However, the system works—it has been tested on audiences all over the world, and these people have learned to expand their creativity."

Another book that stands out among a multitude of books on creativity is *The Art of Innovation* by Tom Kelley. Whereas many other books simply *teach* innovation, Tom Kelley actually *does* innovation every day as general manager of IDEO. With a staff of over 300, IDEO is the world's leading design firm, famous for their development of the Apple mouse, and the handheld Palm. *The Art of Innovation* gives the reader a sneak peek at the company's strategies and secrets behind developing a consistent chain of cutting-edge products.

One of the strongest emerging themes in the book is the importance of teamwork: "If you distrust the power of teamwork, consider this fact. Even the most legendary individual inventor is often a team in disguise. In six scant years, for example, Thomas Edison generated an astounding four hundred patents, producing innovations in the telegraph, telephone, phonograph, and lightbulb—*with the help of a fourteen-man team.*"

Another highlight is a five-step method that is refined for the specific needs of each project in progress. One step repeats the action cited earlier by H&M in the staff's pursuit of new ideas for the design of fashion apparel and accessories in pubs and bars. "Observe real people in real-life situations to find out what makes them tick: what confuses them, what they like, what they hate, where they have latent needs not addressed by current products and services."

The Horse and the Iron Ball by Jerry and Georgina Allan is a dramatically illustrated book for children and students of any age. It describes the history of the universe by powerfully connecting two different things, a horse and an iron ball. The authors take the reader on a journey from the origins of time, as they examine the composition of the cosmos, revealing that all things are related, linked by the stardust of our ancient past. This book stretches the reader's imagination and delivers an ending that leaves a sense of wonder and opens the mind to new possibilities.

Guidelines for Implementing Ideas on the Job

If you are employed by an independent retailer, you may have a measure of flexibility to follow your own instincts and try new presentation ideas. If you are working for a multiple-unit retailer, (e.g., The Limited, Banana Republic, Old Navy), you must maintain the company's guidelines for presentation.

There is a good reason for following company guidelines correctly in every store. Formal guidelines are established to create a consistent image of the store throughout the chain. This is particularly true of **flagship stores,** where the overall appearance of the store is its main identifier in the eyes of its targeted customer. (See Figures 1.3A and 1.3B.) Some flagship stores actually become destinations—people simply *have to* visit them. In fact, "destination retailing" has become a concept in itself. Promoters at Bloomington,

A **flagship store** displays the highest ideals of a company's brand image. Every detail from fitting room hooks to floor coverings reflect the company's brand. Stores built after the "flagship" is developed are usually modified for cost effectiveness. Examples of flagship stores are Niketown in Chicago, Prada in Soho, New York City, and both Levi's and Old Navy in San Francisco.

Figure 1.3A   Levi's flagship store, San Francisco.

Figure 1.3B   Old Navy flagship store, San Francisco.

Minnesota's Mall of America can attest to the number of international flights and national tour buses that bring guests to shop in its hundreds of retail stores, play in its indoor amusement park, and dine at its many unusual restaurants.

Multiple-unit retailers expend great effort (in marketing research and budgeted dollars) to be certain that overall store and selling space designs, merchandise presentations, and displays are efficient for store staff to install and safe for customers, have visual impact, feature the merchandise effectively, project the desired company image, and contribute to sales and profit.

No matter which of their stores shoppers enter, the multiple-unit retailer wants shoppers to feel familiar with the store layout so that their shopping experience feels easy and familiar. Providing a consistent store identity to shoppers has the effect of reassuring their belief that they will receive the same quality product and service regardless of store location.

Even in one-of-a-kind stores, merchandise presentation should have continuity; but in this instance continuity refers to consistency between merchandise presentation and the store's brand image. For example, a store with a country image, making use of hand-crafted wooden tables and reed baskets to feature its products, would not want to introduce gold-leafed French Provincial fixtures to its décor mix. Inconsistent messages do not inspire confidence on the part of the shopper. When the shopping scene is confusing or conflicting, shoppers tend to evaporate.

Also keep in mind that the idea you think is brilliant may not be. That's when it's time to practice critical thinking. Be willing to evaluate your ideas as objectively as you possibly can. To be objective, you have to stop listening to your ego.

"The time invariably comes," according to Hanks and Parry, "when you need to stop collecting ideas and start judging them. All good ideas must be evaluated under the harsh light of critical thinking. The difference between just a good idea and a creative success is the ability to judge an idea and then to apply it. However, the judgment shouldn't be totally cold and uncreative," they add. "Creativity is as important in judging an idea as it is in coming up with one in the first place."

Building and Sustaining a Creative Work Environment
● ●

In a retail environment, it's not enough to have creative ideas, or even to be supportive of others' creativity. You must also be able to prevent idea stoppers. *Idea stoppers*, according to management consultant Karl Albrecht (author of *The Creative Corporation*), are critical statements (he calls them verbal bullets) that shoot down creative ideas. Comments like, "We've already tried that," and "I don't see anything wrong with the way we're doing it now," or "Are you kidding?" are negative—Albrecht says they're "toxic"—statements that are guaranteed to stifle creativity. Think about it. Would you have enough courage to offer another idea after being put down like that? Wouldn't you rather develop a reputation for being what Albrecht calls an *idea helper*—a person who is open-minded, who actively listens, and who writes down every idea for later use?

People may assume that you are naturally creative because your job title says visual merchandiser. With effort and dedication, you can live up to those expectations. Albrecht believes that creative thinking abilities are learned, not inherited. He also says that anyone can think creatively "once you know how to go about it and once you decide you want to." He cites five characteristics that make the difference for innovative and creative thinking:

● Mental flexibility—being free of preconceived interpretations and fixed opinions.

● Option thinking—willingness to give problems further thought and having a reluctance to jump on the first idea that seems to be a solution.

● Big-picture thinking—taking the "helicopter view" and rising above the landscape of everyday ideas to see all the factors involved at once.

● Skill in explaining and selling ideas—being able to develop a concept and connect the facts and ideas involved so that others can understand and accept them.

● Intellectual courage—willingness to advocate an idea or a course of action that you believe in, but which is unpopular with your peers.

As a visual merchandiser, you are in an ideal position to be one of Albrecht's idea helpers—not only because you're constantly searching for new ideas yourself, but because the company needs to hear and use creative ideas from all its employees in order to remain competitive. If the only thing constant in retailing is change, then only those individuals best equipped to respond well to change will maintain their employability within a retail organization.

As an idea helper, you don't need to agree with every idea that's presented. But just as there are statements that are idea stoppers that devalue ideas (or the people who offer them), there are statements that can facilitate an exchange of ideas. Prefacing your ideas or the ideas of those around you with comments like, "I'd like to get your help on an idea I'm trying to work out" or "Before we make a decision, let's review all our options" can help

A Retail Reality
You may have to wait to find just the right time to make creative suggestions. Even when a company has strict presentation standards that may seem to stifle all visual merchandising creativity, it is still worthwhile for staff members to present their best creative ideas. If ten people offer ideas, one or two that couldn't stand alone might be edited, combined, or changed (SCAMPERed) to become one totally brilliant idea. Sometimes good ideas do not gain acceptance initially, but when presented at a later time or to a new audience, they may be more enthusiastically received.

"Don't be tainted by any preconceived notions that you are introduced to. Start every project fresh as a new challenge or change from the norm. It can always be toned down."

Greg Gorman, principal, creative services, GMG Design, Inc.

"Creativity is so delicate a flower that praise tends to make it bloom, while discouragement often nips it in the bud. Any one of us will put out more and better ideas if our efforts are appreciated."

Alex F. Osborn

15

those around you to react more open-mindedly to any ideas—including your own. In *The Creative Corporation* Albrecht says the ideal is "someone who realizes that ideas, in and of themselves, are fundamentally valuable; they represent intellectual wealth. In contrast to the idea killer, the idea helper actually helps other people have and express new ideas."

Shoptalk
Thinking Out of the Box

By Judith Bell

Early in my career as a visual merchandising director for a chain of women's apparel specialty stores, a vice-president of the company made an unusual request. He asked me to look at our competitors, decide which had the most inviting presentation at their store entrance, and then *copy it* in our stores. I had a difficult time with the idea of copying someone else's ideas; not only did I want our stores to be fashion leaders, I knew that the presentation must fit our own brand image. But I made a trip to Southdale Shopping Center in Minneapolis to see what I could learn. Many of women's specialty stores had positioned a table with value-priced sweaters in their entrance. I watched as nearly every female customer who passed by the store stopped at the table to look at the sweaters. Many also entered the store.

I compared those presentations to what we were featuring in our store entrances: two-way and four-way basic chrome fixtures with full-price fashions. These same types of fixtures filled the store, in addition to many simple round racks. I thought about how eye-catching the tables in front of our competitor's stores were because they were different from the basic fixtures in the store. I also thought about the appeal of showing a value item purchased in-depth at the entrance to the store to engage the customers' interest as they passed by.

With those two ideas in mind, I met with a fixture manufacturer and, together, we designed a unique fixture for the store entrance. It fit the stores' brand image, was flexible and could handle both folded and hanging products, and fit into my budget. Next, I met with a few of the company's merchants to discuss moving value product to this new fixture and then worked with them to write signing copy. I presented the concept to the VP who had requested the action, and he approved a two-month test in a few stores. I was glad I had decided not to interpret his request to *copy* our competitors' presentations too literally, and instead, took the opportunity to innovate. What was the end of the story? Sales went off the charts, and we ordered the new fixtures for every store in the company!

After this experience, I was sold on the idea of looking at the competition before developing any new idea. The inspiration was invaluable. I still use the process of looking, compar-

ing, and innovating every day of my career. I have broadened my base of research to include the Internet, the media, restaurants, and a wide variety of resources. I always begin with a direct look at my competition. I believe that in order to lead, you must be aware of what everyone else is doing. And I never, ever copy!

Out-of-the-Box Challenge
1 Comparison Shopping for Advertised Items

Directions: (1) Collect newspaper or magazine ads from at least two different stores that sell similar (or identical) items. (2) Visit the two stores and draw a sketch of the advertised items featured in each store's presentation. (3) Answer the following questions for each store.

Look

1. Are the advertised items easy to locate within the store?
2. Are the advertised items signed?
3. Are the displays neat and orderly?
4. Are the displays exciting or eye-catching? Why? Why not?

Compare

1. Which store's presentation do you like best and why?
2. Can you predict which presentation will sell the most merchandise? Explain why you think it will be more effective.

Innovate

1. What could you do to innovate each of the presentations?
2. Once you've added your own innovations, how much of the original idea will still be evident?
3. Did you use any of the SCAMPER model's elements to edit the original ideas? Explain which element(s) you used. Describe your creative results.

2 Shopping Style Comparison

Directions: Customers respond differently to various types of information offered in the displays and merchandise presentations they see. This exercise is about reaching a target customer through visual presentations of merchandise.

Look

Interview three to five different people (try to vary ages, gender, and occupation or lifestyles) and find out what information they expect from a visual merchandising presentation in a store. Be sure to include descriptive information about the person you are interviewing (e.g., the person's sex, age, interests, occupation). Here are some sample questions for your investigative interviews:

1. Do you notice merchandise displays when you shop?
2. How do you use merchandise displays to help you make buying decisions?
3. When you shop, what type of information do you look for in displays?
4. How would you feel if retailers didn't present their merchandise in any other way than storing it on shelves and hangers? Would other nondecorative approach affect your decision to buy?
5. Do you have any "pet peeves" about merchandise presentation methods currently used in your favorite stores?

Compare

Summarize the results and analyze what they mean in terms of shopping behavior and response to visual merchandising techniques.

Innovate

Based on your findings, what general recommendations can you make about creating more effective merchandise displays?

Critical Thinking

Activity 1

1. With a group of classmates, take turns naming chores that you routinely avoid or put off.
2. List the chores on a flip chart or blackboard.
3. Move down the list, one item at a time, and ask: "Is there anyone here who likes to do this task?"
4. Ask that person to describe why he or she likes (or at least doesn't mind) the listed chore.
5. Ask that person to describe how he or she goes about doing the chore.
6. Once you've had a chance to share your insights about your likes and dislikes, ask the group to describe a philosophy that explains why one person's worst task may be another's easiest.
7. Analyze the results. What seem to be the key elements for taking a positive approach to all tasks? Would you describe the elements your group identified as creative ways of looking at a task or situation?

Activity 2

1. Go to the library or an Internet bookstore site (for example **http://www.amazon.com** or **http://www.barnesandnoble.com**) and do a search for books or magazine articles on creativity or creative thinking.
2. Write down the titles of five books or articles.
3. Select three titles and identify the general objectives of each book (Internet books may be reviewed, or at least have brief descriptions so that you can get an idea about their contents).
4. Choose one title that most stimulates your interest, visit your college or local library, and sign out the book. Write a one-page report on the key concepts. (If the Internet titles are not available in your college or local library, the librarian may be able to access at least a full text copy of a book chapter or article that interests you.)

Case Study

Looking, Comparing, and Innovating

The Situation: Phase One

Her first day on the job, visual merchandiser Jane Bartlett is notified by Susan Howard, the Millville store manager, that each of the company's six metro area specialty stores will receive 150 hand-knit sweaters in the following day's shipment. Susan tells Jane that the sweaters are an important fashion item and that customers have been asking for them.

Until Jane was hired to travel between the six stores, Susan had done the visual merchandising for her busy store. She loved doing the store's creative work and often spent more time doing displays than she did doing managerial paperwork. It was corporate headquarters' idea to hire a visual merchandiser to free store managers from merchandising tasks so that they could handle their administrative duties and meet important paperwork deadlines. The company's other objective was establishing a consistent store brand image in the metro area.

Susan still thinks that hiring Jane was unnecessary. She lets Jane know that she will need to be convinced that a full-time visual person will make a difference to her store's sales figures. "I'm expecting to see a creative and exciting presentation for those sweaters, Jane," says Susan. It's clear to Jane that she needs to prove to Susan that her ideas and methods can add consistency and value to the store's current presentation strategies.

Discussion Questions: Phase One

1. How do you think Jane should *begin the process* of delivering a creative and exciting merchandise presentation that will satisfy her supervisor?

2. What does Jane need to find out about her competition? To what elements of their retail operation should she pay particular attention?

3. How can Jane be confident that her presentations will have an impact on sales?

The Situation: Phase Two

Jane used the look, compare, innovate method and toured her store's most direct competitor, another upscale specialty store. She found their sweaters neatly stacked on shelves in the first wall section to the right of the store entrance. The massive presentation of sweaters made a dramatic impact and anyone passing by the store would be likely to notice them.

In a department store, Jane found sweaters in several different areas of the casual department. A few were shown on a fixture with denim jeans in the rear of the department; some were shown with casual pants in the front of the department; and there was one sweater shown under a coat on a wall presentation.

The outfits that were coordinated with the sweaters were unusual and exciting, but because the sweaters were integrated throughout the department, she thought it would be difficult to find the right size for a customer. Jane also noticed that one fixture holding sweaters had a conversational sign telling how special yarns were used in the sweater for added warmth.

Jane compared the presentations she had observed in the two competing stores. She decided she would get the great-est impact in her store by positioning all of the sweaters in one area, as she had seen in the first store. She liked the idea of featuring coordinating items with the sweaters to create multiple sales as she had seen in the second store. Jane also thought teaching shoppers about special product features with a conversational sign was a good idea.

In her own store, Jane decided to position the sweaters near the entrance to the store. This was a departure from the norm; casual apparel was normally merchandised toward the back of the store, and gifts were normally positioned in the front. She believed the prime selling space at the entrance should be used to feature "hot items," and the sweaters definitely qualified. She stocked the sweaters on a four-tiered table, featuring one size (small, medium, large) per shelf. This left the top shelf open, and that is where Jane took advantage of her store's gift strategy.

She presented each sweater in an open, tissue-lined gift box along with a coordinating shirt. The sweaters came in bright colors, so she found some small gift books with brightly colored covers, and matching bookmarks. She placed one in each box, and tied a string of bright raffia around the sweaters and books. Then she added a conversational sign to the shelf.

Discussion Questions: Phase Two

1. List at least three things that you think Jane did right.

2. If you were in Jane's position, how would you "sell" your presentation strategy to the store manager?

Chapter 2

WHAT IS VISUAL MERCHANDISING?

After completing this chapter, you should be able to

Define visual merchandising

Explain how customers process visual merchandising messages

Describe how retailers communicate through visual images

Explain how visual merchandising efforts educate customers

Identify why visual merchandising efforts increase sales

Explain how visual merchandising efforts support retailing trends

"Visual merchandisers create the in-store environment that supports the retailer's marketing and merchandising strategies. They set the mood; highlight the merchandise; and invite, attract, welcome, and inform shoppers. They also, somewhat more subtly, make the store a wonderful, joyous place to be."
Steve Kaufman, editor, *VM + SD* magazine

The phrase **mom-and-pop** stores comes from early retailing when many retailers were in family businesses and often lived in apartments above their stores. Today, it refers to small, independent retailers.

A **target market** is an identified (targeted) segment of the population that research indicates is a good "fit" for a retailer's product or service offerings. This is the group at which the retailer aims all the store's promotional communication efforts.

A **promotional mix** is a combination of communication tools— advertising, in-store marketing, special events, and personal selling—that tells targeted customers about a store and its merchandise.

"Visual merchandisers are the creative conscience in communicating the product and brand with detail and flair that excites consumers and differentiates your company from others. They must understand the business objectives and go to places others have never been, as visual merchandisers live in and create the environment every day.**"**

Tony Mancini, Sr. vice president, global retail store development, Walt Disney Imagineering and Walt Disney Parks and Resorts

Visual Merchandising Supports Sales

Visual merchandising, once called "display," has evolved from its origins as a store's decorative arts department to its current status as a sales-supportive entity, which impacts store design, store signing, departmental merchandise placement and display, store atmospherics, and store brand image. Where once the display department was charged with "making pretty," the visual merchandising department is now challenged with "making sales." In a large corporate retail operation, it is generally part of the retail advertising and in-store marketing department. In **mom-and-pop** stores, sales staff or freelance visual merchandisers may do the visual merchandising tasks.

For a working definition of *visual merchandising*, you could refer to a dictionary and find that the adjective *visual* relates to images that are taken into the brain by way of the eye. One meaning for the verb form *merchandising* is "promoting the sale of certain commodities." In other words, visual merchandising could be defined as the process of promoting the sale of products by producing mental images that urge potential customers to make purchases.

Martin Pegler, longtime "dean of displaymen" and prolific writer on topics related to visual merchandising, store planning, and layout, titled one of his books *Show and Sell*, which says volumes about the business of getting people to look at and buy merchandise.

The title of this text, *Silent Selling*, gives you another short but useful definition for visual merchandising. Effective visual merchandising techniques establish and maintain the store's physical (and mental) image in the customer's mind, providing support for the rest of the store's selling effort. In other words, merchandise should be displayed and signed so effectively that it can sell itself, without the assistance of a sales associate.

Visual Merchandising Supports Retail Strategies

Successful stores have mission statements that describe how they will serve their **target markets.** They also have vision and goal statements that describe their ambitions—how they see their stores moving forward. In addition, they have strategies for reaching the goals and realizing their vision by utilizing a mixture of promotional methods. Their challenge is letting their target customer know who they are, what they stand for, and what they plan to do. Clear communication is the key to success.

A store's total **promotional mix** is a combination of communication tools—advertising, in-store marketing, special events, and personal selling—that tells targeted customers about merchandise. If each part of the mix accomplishes its goal, potential customers will be drawn to the store for a closer look.

Advertising tells customers that a store's merchandise is different, better, less expensive, or more fashionable than products offered by other retailers. When those ad-reading, commercial-viewing customers arrive at a store, they expect to see whatever it is that the advertising has communicated to them—in a setting that matches the promise of the advertising. The visual merchandiser's job is to make the advertised promise of a pleasant and productive shopping experience come true.

Visual merchandisers physically carry out a store's promotional selling strategies by
● Designing and executing window and interior displays that support advertising goals
● Installing promotional signing for in-store selling
● Producing workable departmental layouts and interior décor
● Devising merchandise fixture layouts for day-to-day operations

- Placing and presenting merchandise on walls and fixtures
- Working as team members with the store's promotional staff

Visual Merchandising Communicates with Customers

Communication has three basic elements: the sender, the message, and the receiver. Unless all three elements are present, communication does not occur. If you call 911 and no one answers your call, for example, communication has not taken place. (See Figure 2.1.)

If a retailer buys advertising space in a paper that is never delivered to the customer's doorstep, how productive do you think the ad will be? If a discount retailer designs an elegant storefront that discourages bargain-hunters and annoys upscale customers once they have entered, has the design message reached the *right* customer?

The retailer is the message sender. The retailer's store, its interior design and selling floor layout, **atmospherics,** merchandise presentation, plus the store's selling services are the unique merchandising message. The retailer has chosen a specific person to send this message to—in hopes of attracting that targeted individual to shop in the store. If that person is open to receiving the message and responds by coming to the store and making

A Retail Reality
Atmospheric elements influence how shoppers feel about *being in* and *staying in* a retail space. The longer they stay in the store, the more likely they are to buy.

Atmospherics is a word coined by retailers to describe the elements (lighting effects, sound levels, aromas, etc.) that appeal to our five senses and contribute to the overall environment of a store.

Figure 2.1 A store exterior that clearly communicates with its core customer and differentiates itself from other retailers; Bass Pro Shops, Outdoor World, Concord, N.C.

Strip malls are made up of side-by-side stores with parking lots immediately outside their doors. Some strip malls may have enclosed walkways, but they are not configured under one large roof as conventional covered malls are.

A store's **brand image** is the retailer's identity in shoppers' minds. It encompasses not only merchandise brands and types but also store environment, reputation, and service. In some cases, the retailer employs the store's name or another exclusive title on its private-label merchandise; for example, Bloomingdale's "Bloomies" label, Macy's "INC.," or Sear's "Craftsman."

purchases, then communication is complete and can be judged successful. That's the retailer's communication goal—attracting customers and making sales.

Every tangible (see-able, hear-able, smell-able, touch-able) aspect of a store sends a message to shoppers. Whether a store is a stand-alone structure, next to other stores in a **strip mall,** or side by side with other stores in an indoor mall, the store's exterior must have a physical appearance that will identify it to its intended market segment and differentiate it from its neighbors. The store's exterior must effectively communicate its message to the customer.

Visual Merchandising Communicates Retail Brand Image

Retail **brand image** is a combination of tangible and intangible factors that describe what a shopper thinks about his or her relationship with a favorite store. Brand image describes not only how the store looks but also how it acts toward its customers. Target, for example, has "guests" rather than customers; Wal-Mart stations "greeters" inside its doors to offer carts and pleasant, personal, welcoming messages. What type of brand image do you think those retailers are trying to establish in their customers' minds?

A store's brand image is generally driven by the retailer's mission statement—a formal expression of the retailer's purpose for operating the business. Sometimes the mission statement is posted prominently in the store and incorporated into its print advertising as a slogan or identifying phrase. The mission statement summarizes what the company and its products or services are all about, whom it hopes to serve, and how it hopes to do it.

For example, Aveda's body product stores carry this message: "Our mission at Aveda is to care for the world we live in, from the products we make, to the ways in which we give back to society. At Aveda, we strive to set an example for environmental leadership and responsibility, not just in the world of beauty, but around the world." From this statement, you might guess that the company's management wants to build customer trust in the way that its products are developed and manufactured. You could also infer that the company wants the customers to know that by purchasing Aveda products, they are also helping the environment.

A mission statement couldn't get much simpler (or shorter) than the one for Bloomingdale's. A visit to its Web page (**www.bloomingdales.com**) tells us that "Bloomingdale's mission was—and is—to seek and create." Other retail companies may have more elaborate statements, with philosophies of doing business stated in greater detail. However, the number of words in the statement is not as important as how effectively the retailer is able to get that message across to the customer.

Brand image is also portrayed by a high-end retailer's interest in developing ongoing relationships between its sales associates and its shoppers. Members of the selling staff often have "little black books" containing special clients' names, sizes, brand preferences, birthdays, etc. Just the idea that retail operations are interested in creating relationships with their customers says much about the value of brand image. Concern for reputation, responsiveness to customer needs and wants, easy-to-manage credit arrangements, convenient hours and locations, brand and service reliability, fashion leadership, and technological leadership are all intangible factors by which customers measure retail brand image.

Smart retailers choose their target customers and build stores and advertising strategies that match their customers' values and self-images. Throughout the entire store—from the lease line to the back wall and on everything in between—the environment should communicate the brand image. Every fixture, sign, and display in the store must fit the brand. The cash wrap, lighting fixtures, wall coverings, floor coverings, and even the restrooms should tell shoppers where they are. A good example of a store with a clear brand image is Niketown. Every detail, from fixtures to fitting room hooks, has an athletic feel. (See Figure 2.2.)

Fitting rooms are frequently overlooked when it comes to brand image. Often tucked away into a tiny space, they are difficult for shoppers to locate. Shoppers should never have to ask where the fitting rooms are. If they can easily see them, they may be more likely to try on an item. One successful retailer's mantra is: "The sale is one-half made when the customer is in the fitting room." Stores like Ann Taylor understand the importance of carrying their store brand image into the fitting rooms; they even call them "selling rooms." They are spacious, comfortable, and well lighted. There is no gap in décor style or quality between the sales floor and the fitting rooms.

Location of stores is also important when considering a store's brand. Have you ever seen a Victoria's Secret store adjacent to an Italian carryout restaurant in a shopping mall? Probably not. Why? Because the two entities have conflicting brand images and different atmospheric goals. It's hard to imagine shopping for luxurious lingerie in a shop filled with the aroma of its neighbor's garlic and tomato sauce. That's why Victoria's Secret is careful about selecting its locations. It wants to sell perfumes and bath products with its fine lingerie, not pizza. Retail communication is most effective when the message sent is clear and consistent with image.

Shopping centers must also pay attention to their brand image. The Seven's shopping mall in Düsseldorf is one of the best branded malls in the world. (See Figure 2.3.) Seven stories of shops, each with their own identity, all fit under one umbrella because the architecture of the mall is so distinct. In general, shoppers do not like to travel up more than two flights to reach their destination. Malls with numerous floors must employ interesting architectural details to make traveling up irresistible. Seven's Mall does its best through innovative use of lighting and design.

Figure 2.2 Notice the "branded" seating in Niketown, Chicago.

Figure 2.3 Exceptional architecture and lighting create a strong brand umbrella for shops in the Sevens shopping mall, Düsseldorf.

"Change the leaves, but keep the roots."

Author unknown

Stretching Brand Image

Most chain stores look the same from location to location. They have often been referred to as cookie-cutter stores, almost identical except for variations in size. Today this is changing in many stores, as retailers begin to *stretch* their brands and pique shoppers' interest. "Designers' new strategy for their stores marks a departure from the cookie-cutter blueprints that companies have espoused for years. 'I think it's a cultural reaction to globalization,' said Trey Laird, president and executive director of New York-based ad agency Laird + Partners. Maybe five, six, or seven years ago it seemed like there was a desire for this unified image all around the globe. But now that has become so predominant, there's sort of a reaction to it." (*WWD*, April 2003)

Miss Sixty, an Italian apparel company, is breaking the cookie-cutter mold by opening stores that fit in with the style of a particular neighborhood or mall where they are located. Miss Sixty in South Coast Plaza in Costa Mesa, California, is a sleek, modern space with fixtures inspired by Verner Panton, and shiny red vinyl floors. In Soho, New York City, Miss Sixty's floors are covered in orange carpeting and fixtures are reminiscent of the 1970s. In neighboring Nolita, Miss Sixty has a rustic, residential feel. In San Francisco, glazed blue-green flooring and reflective upper wall surfaces give the space a fluid design. Combined with the yellow–gold walls on the second level, the space reminds one of California sun and water. (See Colorplate 2.)

How can this retailer succeed by projecting one brand image with so many variations? Because their brand image is all about individuality, and that is exactly what appeals to Miss Sixty's core customer. Even though each store is different, a common thread runs through all of them, delivering a venue that surprises and delights.

Have you ever traveled to another city and passed by a familiar store just because you had the same one in the mall at home? Would you be able to pass by any of the Miss Sixty stores without checking them out? It is a more expensive venture for a retailer to design and build many different prototypes, but it clearly has an advantage over cookie-cutter stores. This strategy may work well with smaller stores, but big box environments are best with easy-to-find products in formats that do not vary by location.

Prada is another retailer that is departing from the cookie-cutter approach. Prada's chief executive Patrizio Bettelli, discusses its new strategy: "At the beginning, many criticized us. They said that to differentiate the image of the stores would destabilize the concept of the label, but now many are following the same path. The brand can be expressed in different ways." (*WWD*, January 2003)

Retailers who find that the expense of creating a new design for every store is not a viable alternative have opted for other ways to make their stores unique. They are introducing new products that are exclusive to different store locations. If you are traveling in London, you may not find the same handbag at Chanel that you saw on Madison in New York City. This puts excitement and fun back into the mix for global shoppers, who have become bored. Others are offering services that are unique by location, like Burberry's custom trench coat service and "Mad Tea Cup" café in their midtown New York City store. "In the Nineties, having a uniform image across the world was a key way in which brands built recognition and enabled customers to understand what the brand lifestyle was all about," said Claire Kent, luxury analyst at Morgan Stanley in London. "But today, consumers sometimes complain that there's not enough differentiation across cities to make shopping interesting." (*WWD*, January 2003)

Another way that retailers are making their brands unique is by expanding their offerings. For years, Coach offered handbags only in leather. In 2003, Coach began to show fabric bags in a wide variety of colors, even introducing new items like shoes, furniture, and pet food bowls. The company mission was to add fun to the assortment and stretch their brand to appeal to a wider range of shoppers. Coach also changed the store environment dramatically with new white fixtures and beautiful lighting for a light, airy feel.

On a smaller scale, Base, a one-of-a-kind store in Miami, expanded its apparel and home décor offerings to include a CD bar, because customers were always asking for the name of the recordings playing. Large or small, every retailer must be open to change, but should always maintain its core brand image.

Shopping Is a Form of Communication

The way people *act* in a certain environment is a form of communication, too. Retail merchants put the entire store on display saying symbolically: "Here's what we have to offer. Here's our pricing. What do you think?" If customers respond by making purchases, they're saying: "This is quality merchandise at great prices. We like your way of doing business."

Over the years, retailers have studied shopping patterns and have passed them down from one generation to another. Have you ever wondered why the less-expensive, generic cereal products are on the lowest shelves in some grocery stores, while the premium-priced kid-pleasing brands are on the middle shelves, and the "healthy" brands are on the top shelves? Grocers believe that the more expensive brands should be placed on the top shelf, with adult-level sightlines in mind, because they are the decision makers on these brands. Products placed on middle shelves catch the attention of the younger child riding in the shopping cart and reaching out to grab at recognizable favorites. As a consequence, bottom shelves may be the least desirable spots for merchandise, but grocers know that bargain-hunters don't mind reaching down to save money.

As retailing methods have become more scientific, formal research studies, have been conducted in an attempt to quantify and formalize some of retailing's common wisdom. In these studies, experts study shoppers and their behavior. They watch how people act when they're shopping and then use the information to help retailers sell more profitably. One of the best-known researchers is Paco Underhill, founder of a company called Envirosell. Underhill's book *Why We Buy: The Science of Shopping,* details the thousands of hours he and his team of "trackers" have spent observing and recording shopping behavior.

Underhill says, "The first principle behind the science of shopping is the simplest one: There are certain physical and anatomical abilities, tendencies, limitations, and needs common to all people, and the retail environment must be tailored to these characteristics. . . . You'd think it would be easy to get everything right. Yet a huge part of what we do is uncover ways in which retail environments fail to recognize and accommodate how human machines are built and how our anatomical and physiological aspects determine what we do. . . . The implications of all this are clear: Where shoppers go, what they see, and how they respond determines the very nature of their shopping experience."

For every truism about consumer behavior, there is a corresponding retail practice that uses the common (or highly scientific) wisdom contained in it. Retailers are learning how to make profitable use of this information and shoppers are the beneficiaries. Did you know that Americans tend to shop at a store in much the same way they walk and drive—veering to the right? When was the last time you pulled out a grocery cart and turned left to start your marketing? It's almost impossible to do. Smart retailers know to set up their traffic patterns and prime merchandise layouts to facilitate this preference.

Since certain shopping behaviors are fairly predictable, retailers can make use of the knowledge. That's why clearance racks are most often found at the rear of the store or department. Retailers know that experienced shoppers habitually check for bargains, but they also want to guide them through all their regular-priced goods on their way to the markdown racks.

Did you know that it takes furniture shoppers at least 20 seconds to become acclimated to the store's layout before they're ready to do any serious "looking"? That's why most furniture stores employ an "up" system. Salespeople take turns watching the entrance of the store from a discreet distance, and then wait for those important seconds to tick by before approaching customers after they've entered the store. They are counting: "one, one thousand, two, one thousand, three, one thousand, four . . ."

Those few seconds also equate to distance traveled. When shoppers enter a fashion store, they are so busy getting a feel for the retail atmosphere, they may not be able to process any fashion messages from merchandise positioned directly inside the doors. The best way to use this space is to create entrance presentations with traffic-stopping impact. If you've shopped in a Gap or Old Navy store, you know that these strong fashion statements help shoppers pause. Without them, shoppers might move on into the store too quickly and fail to get the most important fashion message. As shoppers move the next ten feet into the store, you have their full attention.

In retailing, the expression "too close for comfort" really means *physically* too close for comfort. Americans are quite conscious (and protective) of their "personal space" and they're very uncomfortable in stores that force them to squeeze between fixtures or bump up against other shoppers. This has been a difficult concept for many retailers to grasp since they've been trained to make the most of every square foot of selling floor space. However, if shoppers are continually jostled by traffic moving through a department or down an aisle, they'll spend less time examining garments or reading labels on packaged products. They may even leave the store.

The Americans with Disabilities Act (ADA) mandates that retailers create aisles that allow wheelchairs to pass safely between fixtures. Stores that comply with this far-reaching law improve shopping experiences for all. In 20 years, about 18 percent of the American population will be at least 65 years old. People who cannot bend and stretch or see as clearly as they once did, will have special needs when they shop. Imagine what a store that does not accommodate this growing segment of the population will communicate to the shopping public. It would be wiser to listen and attend to customer preferences before they become major issues. Communication is a two-way process.

How Do Customers Process Visual Merchandising Messages?

Think about your last trip into a store that you had never shopped before. Ask yourself:

- Why did you decide to go to the store?
- Were you responding to a specific ad or were you just curious as you walked by?
- Did someone you know visit the store first and tell you positive things about his or her experience?
- What did you see as you walked up to the store's entrance?
- Did the store's exterior send you any messages about what would be inside?
- Was the view through the storefront appealing? Informative?
- When you entered, was the lighting pleasant to your eyes?
- Do you remember any particular scents or sounds?
- How welcoming did the store's interior feel once you'd stepped inside?
- Was it easy to tell what the store was selling?
- Did you get the impression that the store was selling merchandise that you'd want to buy?
- On the basis of your first impression, did you decide to explore further?
- Was it clear to you how to shop the store?
- Were you directed to or drawn to the merchandise? Bottom line, did you make a purchase?

If your answers were mostly positive, the store's visual merchandising probably played a large role in your going home with a package under your arm. There is a sequence or set of events that usually takes place for merchandise presentation to result in an actual sale. The retailer communicated something vital to you about merchandise through the store's presentation methods . . . and you got the message.

Information Processing in a Visual Merchandising Strategy

Visual merchandisers expose merchandise to potential customers, who process the information in eight stages (see box). Imagine that you're walking into a department store you haven't visited before, to shop for a new watchband. As you search for the accessory department, you notice a mannequin dressed in a casual outfit with an attractive wool tweed jacket. That's *exposure*. (See Figure 2.4.)

27

Stages in Consumer Information Processing

- Exposure
- Attention
- Comprehension
- Agreement
- Retention
- Retrieval
- Consumer decision making
- Action taken

(Shimp, T. *Advertising, Promotion, and Supplemental Aspects of Integrated Marketing Communications,* 4th ed. 1997. Fort Worth: The Dryden Press.)

If the store's visual merchandisers have presented the merchandise in a way that shows how it could be used when purchased, you might say, "If I had that jacket, I could wear it with jeans or wool slacks." That's *attention.*

If the visual merchandising message is clearly stated—by signing, by location in the department, by accessorizing, by vivid color, and by level of activity in the area—you will reach the *comprehension* stage. You may say to yourself, "The way this jacket is shown, I could wear it to work on casual Fridays. I wonder how it would look dressed up. . . ."

The next step, *agreement,* occurs if the product information you've just absorbed is credible and compatible with your values, and you mentally file it away—perhaps for future reference. If, at this point, you revert to looking for the watchband, your *retention* of the mental image of the jacket and later *retrieval* of it will be very important to the store. Will the visual merchandiser's message about the jacket stay with you after you purchase the watchband? Will you ask yourself, "Now where did I see that great tweed jacket? Oh, that's right . . . it was near the entrance. It was on a mannequin, so it should be easy to find."

Figure 2.4 "Outpost" mannequins; Neiman Marcus, Miami.

If the mental imagery of the presentation was strong enough and all the rest of the promotional elements support the *consumer decision-making process,* there will be *action taken.* If your next step was to purchase the jacket, consumer information-processing model worked for you—and the department store.

Visual Merchandising Supports Selling

In the last scenario, there was no salesperson to suggest the tweed jacket to you as a shopper. The visual merchandiser's presentation of the jacket on a mannequin made the sale. Current trends in store staffing indicate that stores have reduced the number of sales associates on the selling floor to lower operating costs. Effective visual merchandising efforts can supplement and support the sales staff of any store.

Although they will never replace an alert and attentive sales associate, successful visual merchandising techniques may keep customers involved with a display until a sales associate reaches them and completes the sales transaction. If the tweed jacket had been presented on a floor fixture with eleven other similar tweeds in assorted colors you may not have noticed it.

You were only looking for a watchband; a simple purchase priced around $19.99, but the jacket on the mannequin caught your eye. Even though you'd been momentarily sidetracked, you followed the signs to the accessories department and purchased the watchband. The next move you made was to try on the jacket. The *silent selling* of a merchandise presentation added $90 to your shopping bill—for a jacket that you sold to yourself!

According to Cotton Incorporated's Lifestyle Monitor research, "Retailers maintain that in-store displays should do the following: (1) communicate the latest trends in fashion and colors; (2) assist the customer in making a buying decision, and (3) create an exciting environment within the store. In addition, retailers are also faced with the challenge of a consumer who is spending less time shopping, making it all the more imperative that visual displays act as instruments of swift persuasion."

Visual merchandising can transform a shopper into a buyer. It can also increase the average dollar amount per sale. Effective displays teach shoppers about using multiple basic and accessory items to enhance and extend the use of their purchases. It's not uncommon to hear a shopper say "I'd like to purchase the entire outfit, just the way you have it on the mannequin." That's silent selling at its best.

A fully accessorized visual merchandising treatment educates customers when and how to wear fashion and trend items. In this way, effective merchandise presentation provides fashion direction to customers who may not trust their own fashion savvy.

Imagine gift shopping for someone whose taste is different from yours. You may not know what kind of table linens to select for a wedding gift, if the bride's china pattern is far-removed from your own preference. You may not know what kind of socks to wear with a pinstriped suit and wingtip oxfords, if you've spent most of your life in tennis shoes and jeans. Effective visual merchandising techniques can solve many buying problems for prospective customers who are looking for advice.

Shoppers don't have to have all the answers as long as the store's merchandisers do. When they can trust their favorite store's merchandisers to offer them advice, they can relax and enjoy the shopping experience. Educational and tasteful presentations can give confidence (and direction) to shoppers and save them time.

The visual merchandiser can stimulate customers' appetites for artfully presented merchandise in the same way that the gourmet cook stimulates diners' appetites for an artfully presented meal. Pick up any lifestyle magazine and look at the food in the photographs. You anticipate how good the food will taste because your senses are stimulated by the imagery on the paper.

A Retail Reality
It is possible for fewer sales personnel to manage more customers when the product presentation assists with the selling process.

A Retail Reality
Visual merchandising's effect on the presentation of goods builds add-on sales by suggesting coordinating items for the customer's selection—which creates a value-added transaction for both retailer and customer.

" . . . 50% of women surveyed said they get their ideas for clothes from store displays or window shopping. The *Monitor* is unequivocal on this point: nothing is more important to selling apparel products than visual store displays—not fashion, not catalogs, not peer pressure, not advertising, not even sales personnel."

Cotton Incorporated's Lifestyle Monitor tracking research, *Women's Wear Daily,* November 5, 1998

A Retail Reality
An add-on sale of $2.89 for a pair of socks adds more than 10 percent to a $25 purchase of knit pants. Ask people you know if they'd be happy to have a 10 percent increase in their paychecks this week . . . or if they'd like to be earning 10 percent interest on their savings accounts!

A Retail Reality
Value-added products and services are the result of a retailer's efforts to enhance those products or services with information, which allows customers to gain more satisfaction and better results from the use of their purchase.

A Retail Reality
Retail trends are often circular in direction. Today's up-to-the-minute merchandising methods and presentation strategies may be out of fashion in a matter of months, but their replacement strategies may very well come from the past instead of the future.

An effective presentation of merchandise is a virtual "recipe" for making the most of the shopper's investment. The shopper tells others about your *value-added services* . . . and the shopper comes back again and again.

How Does Visual Merchandising Support Retailing Trends?

A fashion apparel or accessory item becomes a "trend" when it is widely desired by consumers. Visual merchandisers have the tools to draw attention to the item and make it easy for shoppers to locate. Product placement, mannequins, props, signing, and lighting may all play a role in highlighting trend merchandise. Every retailer wants to be the first, the best, the leader. The visual merchandiser is the invisible force that is doing a lot of the pushing behind the trend.

Store interiors have changed, presentation methods have changed, and shopping has changed. In the 1980s, trend reports indicated that interior store layout and wall and fixture merchandising had more impact on sales than store windows did. Many specialty retailers removed traditional streetside theatrical display windows and opened up the entire main floor to public view. Windows that once blocked the pedestrian's view of the inside of the store now created an opportunity to view the store's entire shopping assortment. Windows became an invitation for passers-by to enter for a closer look. The visual merchandiser's concern changed from "Are our windows dramatic?" to "Are the windows *clean*?" Store interiors became their new focus.

Consumerism, another trend, meant that customers wanted the opportunity to thoroughly inspect products before making a purchase. In the case of expensive or technical products, they wanted demonstrations to determine if all of their requirements were going to be met. Lamps needed electrical power, television screens needed moving images, and stereos needed soundproof demo booths.

The barriers of showcase selling also had to come down if retailers were going to reduce selling costs and stay competitive in a growing market. For economic and competitive reasons, stores began to move in the direction of self-service. There are fewer salespeople now than in the past on the floor to remove merchandise from a display case and hand it to a customer or demonstrate an appliance.

Visual merchandisers were challenged to find new ways to put shoppers in touch with merchandise assortments. Improved selling fixtures were fabricated, and store furnishings became more functional as selling tools. Layouts changed to facilitate customer interactions with merchandise. Signing directed traffic and told customers about merchandise on self-service fixtures. Graphics on the walls set moods and explained lifestyles.

As lifestyles continually changed and new trends accelerated in all areas of shoppers' lives, retailing had to anticipate the changes quickly and provide the latest trend-right merchandise. Competitive retailers added the task of trend forecasting to their merchandise buyers' and visual merchandisers' job descriptions.

Visual merchandisers have had to become experts at anticipating and responding to lifestyle trends. They study how their target customers live their lives. They try to understand what shoppers want in new products and how shoppers use the products they buy. They must interpret the trends within the store's physical setting so that people know what's important *today*. Stores must be poised to change and then change again. Smart merchandisers are always looking ahead for tomorrow's strategy, because they want to be there ahead of the competition. See **www.echochamber.com** for international retail trends.

An interesting recent direction in retail strategies is the trend away from enclosed shopping malls to upscale, open-air **lifestyle centers**. Beautifully landscaped and located in affluent areas, lifestyle centers appeal to time-starved shoppers who want to park closer to their favorite specialty stores and restaurants rather than in the sprawling parking lots of traditional indoor malls. Lifestyle centers include many of the same specialty shops of the enclosed mall but often do not have department store anchors. The Grove in Los Angeles and Bal Harbor in Miami are excellent examples. The Village of Merrick Park in Coral Gables, Florida, is another open-air lifestyle center. It opened in 2002 with gorgeous landscaping and architectural design, and adjacent condominiums that are all part of the complex. Shopping is right outside your own doorstep! (See Figure 2.5.)

The emergence of lifestyle centers may come as a result of a lifestyle trend—a certain dissatisfaction with the anonymity of a work life spent in a cubicle with a computer on the desk and few human interactions in the business day. As more individuals choose to work from their homes, there is even less human interaction. People long for a neighborhood shopping district "where everyone knows your name."

And what could fit better inside a lifestyle center than a new *lifestyle store*? *Post-Gazette* staff writer Teresa F. Lindeman reported in an October 2003 article: "In an era of supersized everything, from clothes to even fries and frozen meals, Kaufmann's yesterday unveiled what it hopes will woo more of the shopping public—a store that's smaller than the norm. At 140,000 square feet, it is one of eight so-called "lifestyle" stores that St. Louis-based May has built in the last year or so, but the first for Kaufmann's group. Because they are smaller and cheaper to build—the new stores fit more easily into open-air shopping centers or tight urban markets where development opportunities might come now that mall construction has slowed."

Nonstore retailing is a trend that is going to affect visual merchandising. There are hundreds of home shopping opportunities beamed into your living room 24 hours a day on your television. Infomercials don't have storefronts. They don't need them when merchandise is a phone call away.

Specialty shopping by mail-order catalogs is another retail trend that reflects today's lifestyles. People who have less time will take short cuts, even if they have to spend money to have their purchases brought to their doorsteps. A new generation of retailers is count-

Lifestyle centers have an open-air configuration of at least 50,000 square feet of retail space occupied by upscale specialty store chains. Retail categories most commonly represented are apparel, home goods, books, and music. They have one or more table-service restaurants, and sometimes include a multiplex cinema.
Source: International Council of Shopping Centers

Figure 2.5 Open-air lifestyle center; Village of Merrick Park, Miami.

ing on it. The Internet offers books, movies, music, clothing, medicine, food, business services, electronic products, housewares, automobiles, airline tickets—you name it, it's probably there.

While these trends in retailing present a tremendous challenge to in-store retailers, they also present opportunities for visual merchandisers seeking employment opportunities in a growing field. The merchandise on the electronic shopper's television screen or computer monitor has to be presented well even if it is not in a store. Who arranges the assorted goods for the camera? The goods are arranged by a visual merchandiser whose title may be different but whose duties remain essentially the same. They are called *stylists,* but what they do is prepare and present merchandise.

Shoptalk
• •

"The Way Things Were"

By Kate Ternus

Thirty-five short years ago, I stepped off a department store escalator into a new world. I had just left a sales job in handbags and leather goods to become a displayman for the same company. Never mind that I'm a female—anyone working in the display department then was called a displayman. I began as a helper—fetching, carrying, and cleaning up after the master displaymen. Advancement was a years-long process. It felt good to be part of a rich tradition, and I absolutely loved my work.

Starting out, I dressed mannequins for the ten fashion windows that lined one of the first pedestrian malls ever built in a large metro area. There were often more than 30 fiberglass figures to deck out and accessorize each week. I was scared most of the time. Fashion had never been my "thing." Suddenly, I was handling designer garments that cost more than my car and college tuition put together. I worked with one eye on the latest copy of *Vogue* because, when it came to fashion, I was the dummy, not the mannequin. It was my theater design background that got me the job, not my fashion savvy.

Every week brought a complete theme and merchandise change and a challenge to make the latest window merchandise exciting and provocative. Our team had to come up with a completely new visual idea to carry out the advertising department's theme. No repeating. Ever. Our store was the city's fashion leader. It still is. But that's about the only thing that has stayed the same.

Windows use to be the driving force of merchandise presentation (although we didn't call it that until later). We felt sorry for the poor drones who had to do interior displays. They could only try to echo our brilliant window themes using our retired mannequins and cast-off props. Windows were higher on the food chain than interiors. Once a week, we covered our display windows with canvas curtains, turned off the spotlights, and made magic. Later, one huge pane at a time, we pulled the canvas away to unveil our next offering for the fashion conscious pedestrian. Ta-dah!

Our crew was always encouraged to be creative. The vice president of promotion was a brilliant guy. His office door (and his mind) was always open. He once hired a bus to take us—plus the advertising group—off to a suburban theater for a midday movie. Imagine being paid to watch the Beatles' *Yellow Submarine* during a workday! He thought we could use a creative boost and wanted us to see how others were "pushing the envelope" as we say today.

Alas, vice presidents eventually move on. When our favorite did, retail life went on . . . but it was different, and we weren't sure we liked it. The new guy was an envelope-pusher, too, but he called his act "cutting edge." Instead of having shoppers out on the sidewalk ogling the windows and wondering about what might be inside the store, this guy wanted people outside to actually see inside. Imagine that! He had a name for his new concept, too—*merchandise presentation.*

Guess what happened next. One by one and then two by two, our wonderful, dramatic, closed-off, mini-theater of mall windows disappeared! Where our great window dramas had been supreme, glass took over. Sheets of glass. Plain. Flat. Clear.

Mr. Cutting Edge decreed, "The whole store is now going to be a display. People buy things they can not only see but also touch." Guess who ruled then. The drones.

Guess who had their pick of our expensive window mannequins. The drones. Only they weren't drones any more. They were *interior visual merchandisers.* Along with all our good mannequins, the drones got new titles. We began to wish we'd been nicer to them when they were drones. They paid us back, big time!

We whined, "What about all this . . . uh . . . space . . . in the store interior? What are you people going to do with this space, all this . . . uh, stuff . . . and all these . . . fixtures?"

We whimpered, "And what are we going to do now?" Mr. Cutting Edge had all the answers. "Help the interior people," he said. We helped.

We learned to treat a department and its merchandise as a total presentation. We became "story" tellers. "ROY G BV became our new buzz best friend (Red, Orange, Yellow, Green, Blue, Violet). We told color stories. A rainbow spectrum of merchandise marched along walls and around circular fixtures.

We told merchandise "stories." Display platforms at the heads of escalators became fashion "editorials" telling the same thematic stories that windows once told. We presented tennis togs with sporting accessories. Holiday gifts with holiday clothing. Floral prints with gardening tools and signs inviting shoppers to the Eighth Floor Auditorium's Annual Flower Show.

Oh. The auditorium—that was Mr. Cutting Edge's answer to our old-hat windows. "Why let people look into a window and walk on past the store?" he asked. The man actually built a spectacular events showcase on the store's top floor and then invited shoppers to escalate up through eight floors of appealingly presented goods on the way to superlative retail-related entertainment. Imagine that!

For a while there, I thought Mr. Cutting Edge had gone over the edge. But he was right on the money, as usual, and auditorium events attracted people in droves . . . with money in hand and merchandise on their minds. When I got over pouting about losing "my" windows, the store became a larger and more creative display arena than I'd ever imagined. Most days, I couldn't wait to get to work. In the quarter century since then, I've worked for a half-dozen other major retailers, and I've been through more retail change and renovation than most people have had hot breakfasts. I learned to let go and enjoy what I could learn from Mr. Cutting Edge, and it's been a fine career.

Good wishes for a fine career of your own!

Out-of-the-Box Challenge
Comparison Shopping

Look

1. Look at three stores that are selling the same style of sweater in the latest new trend. Draw a sketch of each presentation.

Compare

2. Compare the three presentations.

Innovate

3. Use the ideas to create and sketch a new version of the presentation. Include a sign and new fixture as part of your idea.

4. Mount the four sketches on a black presentation board. Your new, improved idea should be a larger sketch than the three that you saw in the competition.

5. Present your idea to the rest of the class.

Critical Thinking
Play 20 Questions

1. What is your own working definition of visual merchandising?

2. Think back to your last shopping trip to your favorite store and describe the feeling you had as you entered. Consider all your senses. What made you feel that you'd arrived at a place where you'd really like to shop?

3. What does the term *atmospherics* refer to?

4. When you visited your favorite store, did you notice a mission statement posted anywhere? Do you know what the company's mission is?

5. Think about communication. Identify the retailer's unwritten "message" to you as you approached the store. Did you understand the message? Did the message match your image of yourself as the store's customer?

6. Describe your mental image or profile of yourself as a shopper.

7. What kinds of images would a retailer use to design a store especially to fit you and your ideas about your personal image?

8. How do you know that your favorite store is "your" store? What did this retailer seem to know about you?

9. List as many physical, visual, or atmospheric elements as you can recall about your favorite store that seem to match your image of yourself.

10. Recall and describe a shopping situation where you went through all the steps of the consumer information processing model described in this chapter.

11. How do you feel about there being fewer salespeople available to help you in stores where you shop?

12. When you shop for new fashions, do you pay attention to the ways in which merchandise is displayed and accessorized? Why or why not?

13. How can you tell if a store is giving you good "visual advice" about the products offered for sale in its displays?

14. What influences you to buy items that aren't on your predetermined shopping list? Does it happen often? What seems to trigger an unplanned purchase?

15. Think back to a shopping trip where you bought more than the one item on your list. What was the price of the single item you intended to buy? How much did the extra item add to your bill? Did you mind spending more than you'd planned? Why? Why not?

16. Discuss how your favorite store's visual presentation teaches you about the store's merchandise.

17. Ask an older person (at least one generation older than you are) to tell you how the look and function of retail stores have changed over time. Ask that person to compare shopping when he or she was younger to today's retailing methods. List as many changes as you can.

18. Visit an electronic retailing Website and list the variety of products you can find. Explain how one makes an electronic purchase.

19. Describe how the merchandise or service available for sale on the Website is displayed on the screen. Explain how this technique compares to the in-store presentations.

20. Which retail store that you've shopped at that has the clearest brand image from front to back? Which catalogue? Which retail Internet Website?

Bonus Question

What kinds of employment opportunities can you forecast for a well-trained visual merchandiser in the coming decade?

Case Study
●●●●●●●●●●●●●●●●●●●●●●●●●●●●●●●●●
Store Image and Visual Continuity

The Situation

Ben is a selling associate who works for a national department store chain that targets the middle-income suburban family. The store's retail image is one of affordable but trend-right fashion for all members of the family. Ben's selling department carries workday casual clothing for men—assorted sweaters, dress slacks, casual woven shirts, knit polo shirts, and some accessories. The overall fashion statement is fairly conservative, and the store's presentation style has been detailed in the company's Corporate Display Guidelines. Visual merchandisers implement new wall and selling floor planograms (layouts) sent from corporate headquarters every 10 days.

Ben likes to watch visual merchandising specialists at work. It looks like an exciting job, with freedom to do different activities throughout the store instead of having to stay in one department. In fact, he hopes to work in the visual department one day. Ben's only current display responsibility is to make sure that a coordinated outfit is shown on the front of every feature fixture in his area.

One evening, when business was slow, Ben noticed that the display forms on the side wall of his selling area featured merchandise that was nearly sold out. Although he needed to complete his own assigned tasks, and wall presentation was the responsibility of the visual merchandising specialist, Ben decided to change the display. Ben reasoned that this show of initiative would demonstrate to the store manager that he was ready to move into the next available visual merchandising position.

First he removed the display forms and outfits from the wall. Then, using a visual merchandising technique he'd seen once in a store window that he'd liked, Ben tied monofilament to hangers and began to "fly" the garments high on the wall over the selling fixtures. The project took over 2 hours, and he didn't have time to complete his assigned tasks. In addition, he lost his balance and almost fell off the ladder near a shopper's child.

When he was finished, Ben was pleased with himself. He thought his presentation was much more interesting than anything he'd seen set up by the department's visual specialist. Besides, Ben told himself, the specialist seemed to do all of his work with one eye on the Guidelines for Display section in the company's policy and procedure manual. How creative was that?

The next morning, Ben enthusiastically showed his display to the store manager and the visual specialist. To emphasize how challenging the project had been, he even described how he'd almost fallen off the ladder. The manager and the specialist were not pleased. The store manager told Ben that he'd overstepped his responsibilities and violated company guidelines for presentation. Then he directed the visual merchandiser to replace Ben's display immediately. Ben was crushed.

Discussion Questions

1. Did Ben really do something wrong?

2. Why do you think the store manager was upset with him?

3. What's so important about the style of display in the department?

4. Isn't having sold-down merchandise off the wall more important than who actually does a display?

5. Could Ben have communicated his interest in a visual position more appropriately? How?

Chapter 3

CORE DESIGN STRATEGIES

After completing this chapter, you should be able to

Identify the elements and principles of design used to create a welcoming store environment

Create harmonious color schemes for effective wall and fixture presentations

Describe the atmospheric elements and design strategies that enhance store environment and strengthen store brand or image

"Creating dreams means producing beauty
of an artistic caliber. Yet, unlike the beauty
of art, this beauty is not about extremes
or a revolution in originality. The goal here
is not to glorify the creator, but to elate
the customer."
Gian Luigi Longinotti-Buitoni,
Selling Dreams: How to Make Any Product Irresistible

"The success of the retail architect's design hinges on the work of the visual merchandisers. They are responsible for capturing the architect's vision for the store and implementing it through their choice of fashion, color, props, lighting and focal points. The creativity and hard work of the visual merchandiser are the linchpins of effective store design."

Wayne Visbeen, president of Visbeen Associates, Inc.

A Retail Reality
Atmospherics should be the result of strategic planning by store owners and managers. Opening and stocking a store is too expensive and competitive to leave any element of store design to chance.

Multiple sales are transactions where two or more items have been purchased. For example, a shopper buys a single CD plus a carrying case.

Étagères are tall furniture units with open shelves. Originally used only as pieces of furniture in homes, these elegant cases adapt well as display fixtures.

The Visual Merchandiser Is a Design Strategist

What creates a store environment that invites you to enter and encourages you to stay and browse? By the end of this chapter you will know that it is a store design that effectively utilizes basic principles and elements drawn from the art world—color, balance, rhythm, emphasis, and proportion—to create a welcoming place where shoppers can purchase goods and services.

You'll also know that it's the visual merchandiser—carrying out the design concept and strategic plans created by the store's management team—who actually makes the store and its merchandise come to life. Once the carpenters, electricians, and painters leave and the fixtures and merchandise arrive, the visual merchandiser does the important work that will make the store's blueprinted promise into a retail reality. What the visual merchandiser adds to the basic design is a concept known to retail practitioners as atmospherics. It is a strategic tool that, used effectively, gives the retail operation personality and brand image.

Atmospherics as a Merchandising Strategy

Basic design concepts used throughout a store create a strong foundation for a successful retail business. Atmospherics, décor, and layout strategies that appeal to our five senses, can be "layered" into the basic shell of the store to enhance the shopping environment and build the brand image of the store. *Layering* means including multiple sensory elements to achieve a particular atmosphere for the store environment—simultaneous use of sight, sound, touch, taste, and smell. Layers of atmospherics can actually alter the perception of time for shoppers, encouraging them to become so comfortable and pleasantly stimulated in the shopping environment that time becomes less important than it might otherwise be. They may browse longer, see and touch more products, and become more inclined to make purchases.

Atmospherics borrow practices and techniques from the artists' realm. Every element in a store's makeup—from the display of a single garment to an expansive presentation featuring an entire wall of coordinates—uses some or all of the principles and elements of design. Where painters choose colors, shapes, lines, and textures to create works of art, visual merchandisers choose colors, shapes, lines, and textures to create store environments. Their use of these creative tools ensures that selling floors will be organized, easy-to-shop, and filled with eye-catching, merchandise-centered displays that will attract shoppers and encourage **multiple sales.**

If you've shopped in a Victoria's Secret store, you know something about atmospherics. When you enter the store, you see color and texture everywhere—from the silk fabrics of intimate apparel to lavishly printed wallpaper to painted moldings and elegantly carved **étagères.** The soft lighting is easy on your eyes, similar to the type of lighting that is used in your home. You notice a subtle fragrance in the air and hear sweet classical music. How long does it take before you begin to touch the fabric of the merchandise? Was it on the first table as you entered the store?

Victoria's Secret does an excellent job of appealing to four of our five senses: sight, smell, hearing, and touch. It could also appeal to our sense of taste by developing and sampling a line of small indulgences—chocolates and sweets, for example. Doing so would create a complete sensory experience for shoppers and also expand the retailer's private-label brand and its value to customers.

A retailer that does it all is Eatsies, a small specialty grocery store, with national locations. In Eatsies, you are surrounded by old-fashioned market style presentations of fresh produce, freshly baked breads, cakes, and rich desserts. Opera music rings through the space, and wonderful scents are everywhere. Mouthwatering samples are offered at every

Figure 3.1 Professional chefs provide service from the deli counter at Eatsies.

counter. Professional chefs serve steaming plates of pasta with spicy sauces from the deli counter. You can pick up a take-out order or enjoy your meal in their pleasant dining area. Colorfully hand-lettered messages on chalkboards throughout the store are fun and always make you smile. Every one of your five senses is stimulated in this unique retail environment where atmospherics are as important as products. (See Figure 3.1.)

Art is a sensory experience. We are moved by paint on canvas, touched by sculpted shapes, stirred by musical notes, soothed by silken textures. Watch a creative chef prepare a meal that looks enticing, smells wonderful, and tastes sublime, and you know that even food preparation can be elevated to an art form. Your senses tell you so. Use of basic design principles that pay attention to our five senses forms the basis of store design and atmospherics.

To begin to understand how design elements are applied to a store environment, we will identify several and look at examples of how they are used in merchandise presentation. Practical applications of design principles are explored in more depth in later chapters.

Design Elements and Principles

In visual merchandising, design is about the way we arrange products, signing, props, and so on, to create a shopping environment that is pleasing to the eye. We work with various elements—color, for instance—to bring unity, or a sense of wholeness and completeness, to our design work.

Unity is one of the principles or goals of design. The others are *harmony, repetition, balance, rhythm* (movement), *contrast,* and *emphasis.* For merchandising, we also use *surprise.* To achieve the design goals, we use tools or elements of design—color, texture, proportion, size, shape, direction, line, sequence, tension.

Using a design element like size (an oversized prop) may alter the apparent size of a product on display and make it seem small in contrast. The change in the proportions of the items in the display will establish the presentation's emphasis (a principle or goal). However, if all of the elements used in the design of the display come together to create a harmonious whole, then the principle of unity has been served.

For example, you might use a 6-foot-long golf club and a golf ball that's 6 inches in diameter as props for a window display featuring a dozen pairs of golf shoes (repetition) from one manufacturer. The disparity in size between props and product may be a bit startling to passers-by (the principle of surprise), but the whole theme of golf is the unifying principle that brings it together to send a congruent message to window shoppers.

Principles of Design	Design Elements
Unity	Color
Harmony	Texture
Repetition	Proportion
Balance	Direction
Rhythm (movement)	Size
Contrast	Shape
Emphasis	Line
Surprise	Sequence
	Tension

Color as a Merchandising Strategy

The first and most critical of the design elements is color. It is important to realize that color is a private experience. That is, you may tell someone that the sky is blue or the grass is green, but you don't actually know that the shade of blue *you* see is the same precise shade that another person with normal color vision sees. Human physiology and the viewing environment determine what each of us perceives at any given time and place. Nevertheless, scientists have agreed that the relationships between colors can be shown in the form of a *color wheel,* using yellow, red, and blue (primary colors), at the 12 o'clock, 4 o'clock, and 8 o'clock positions. (See Colorplate 3.) Moving clockwise around the circle, you'll see that the colors blend and change gradually from one to the next. Colors will range from yellow to yellow-orange to orange to red-orange to red, for example.

Red, yellow, and blue are called *primary colors,* and orange, green, and violet are called *secondary colors* because they are formed by combining the primaries. Red and yellow merge to become orange; yellow and blue become green; blue and red become violet. If you mix the primary colors with the secondary colors, you'll form *tertiary* (third-level) combinations like yellow/green and blue/violet.

M. Grumbacher, Inc., has a very useful product that it calls a *Color Computer*—a cardboard "color harmony wheel" that illustrates very clearly how colors are formed and how they relate to each other. You may want to buy one from an art supply retailer for your professional use. Grumbacher's Internet site is: **www.sanfordcorp.com/grumbacher.**

You will need to know some additional color-related terms because grouping merchandise by color is a common practice, and a particular language is used when discussing color. For example, red, yellow, green, and blue are *chromatic* (highly colored). Black, white, and gray are *achromatic* (the exact opposite of highly colored). *Shades* of a color are made by adding varying amounts of black or gray. *Tints* are created by adding white to a basic color. *Value* is the amount of lightness or darkness in a color. *Hue* is another word for the name of a color—red, blue, brown, and so on. In everyday speech, *hue* is used as a synonym for *color,* but technically, the term *color* refers to the combination of hue, value, and *intensity* (brightness).

Color Schemes

There are many ways to coordinate colors in eye-pleasing arrangements or color schemes. Grumbacher's two-sided Color Computer calls these schemes *color harmonies.* The most basic color schemes or color harmonies are based on six variations of the color wheel. (See Colorplate 3.)

1. *Complementary* schemes consist of two colors that are directly opposite each other on the color wheel. Example: yellow and violet.

2. *Split-complementary* schemes consist of three colors—one central color plus the two colors on either side of its complement. Example: yellow with red-violet and blue-violet.

3. *Double-complementary* schemes consist of four colors—two colors plus their complements. Example: yellow with violet plus green with red.

4. *Triadic* schemes consist of three colors that are equidistant from one another on the color wheel (they form a triangle when you look at the wheel). Example: orange, green, and violet.

5. *Analogous* schemes (color families) consist of two or more colors that are next to each other (adjacent) on the color wheel. Example: yellow with yellow-green.

6. *Monochromatic* schemes consist of a single color in different values and intensities (more white or gray blended into the basic color). Example: navy blue with medium blue and light blue.

These schemes are your color tools in display and presentation. Even if your store is too small to have a full-time trend-merchandising department, you will notice that store merchandise is arriving in a seasonal color scheme. In this situation, it may be up to you to combine merchandise items on the selling floor, on fixtures, and on walls in ways that make the merchandise look attractive to customers.

Much common wisdom has evolved from the study of color. Some colors (related to red, yellow, and orange) are said to be "warm," while the blues, greens, and some purple shades are spoken of as "cool" colors. In the language of color they make a statement. They call up feelings that don't have to be said aloud; they're simply understood because we share common experiences as humans.

Warm colors are said to be aggressive, reminding us of fire and sun. They pop out at us to make strong color statements. However, if red is the color of passion, blue speaks to us of cool restraint. Cooler shades like the blues and greens are said to be recessive, relaxed, and calm, reminding us of clear skies and grassy meadows at a distance. The idea that warm colors advance and cool colors recede comes from the color theory that makes it possible to create the illusion of depth in a painting.

Color as a Communication Tool

Color has a spoken language of its own. We often use colorful terms to add emphasis and flavor to our thoughts. Expressions like "true blue" suggests loyalty; "royal purple" suggests a color once worn only by kings, queens, and members of their courts; "seeing red" denotes angry feelings; white stands for purity; and black represents depression or mourning. However, remember that's how particular colors relate in Western cultures. Other cultures may apply different significance to certain colors. For example, yellow may be a cheerful color in the United States, but in another culture it may have a different significance. Needless to say, visual merchandisers and store designers working for international chains must be aware of these factors.

Colors may take on names of their own over time. This generally occurs through association with something that people who share a language recognize as universal. Prussian blue comes from dye color used in making that country's national military uniform. Wedgwood blue takes its name from a characteristic gray-blue glaze used to create the famous English pottery with classic white figures and shapes around its circumference. Chartreuse is both the name of a yellow-green color and the name of a well-known tinted liqueur.

In the late 1960s, a popular maroon color was paired with navy for several seasons in both men's and women's fashion. Each season, that same color was given a new name. One season it was called wild onion, another year it was called burgundy, in another year it was called beet root. This is how copywriters gave a fresh impression to a color that had a long selling cycle.

Color is a powerful visual element. It can set mood, emphasize features, and highlight a product. In print advertising, research indicates that color increases an ad's attention-getting and recall powers. Certain color combinations have been used for so long that seeing them makes us automatically think of a specific season or occasion—red and green at Christmas; black and orange at Halloween; red and pink for Valentine's Day; or red, white, and blue for Independence Day. However, color can be fickle, too. One fashion season's "in" color can be "out" in the next.

Color in Store Décor

Stores that build a color trend into their store's décor may find themselves looking dated in a very short time—probably before the décor itself is even paid for. Most design practitioners urge caution when selecting storewide color schemes.

Greg Gorman, store designer and author of *The Visual Merchandising and Store Design Workbook,* suggests that initial store design should use an overall neutral palette that can be "punched up" with colorful accents in key presentation areas within the store or department. For example, colored acrylic bins could be utilized for folded products on white walls to complement the coloration of each seasonal merchandise shift but won't lock the store into a single overall color presentation.

Another school of thought on color in store décor emerged in 2002. Most store environments had been "white boxes" for more than 20 years, but suddenly retailers began to energize their stores with all manner of wall coverings, murals, and bright colored paint. Issey Miyake features a colorful, exotic, floor-to-ceiling mural in its Tribeca store. Miu Miu, Swiss Army, Puma, BCBG, and scores of others in New York City painted many of their walls bright red. Paul & Joe on Bond Street in New York City installed black boards and decorated them with colored-chalk illustrations. As fashion apparel and accessories became more neutral in color, retailers infused energy into their selling environments with a wide variety of finishes and textures on their walls, floors, and fixtures.

Color as a Fashion Merchandising Strategy

Retailers promote different color schemes each season. They may introduce new shades of a currently popular color or select an entirely different *palette* (selection of colors). Standard colors may be combined in unusual ways. These color schemes should be featured in highly visible areas of the store, like store entrances, department entrances, along aisles, in windows, or on interior displays, so that customers can find them easily. If the colors are part of a national trend, or have been aggressively promoted through advertising, customers will be looking for them.

Once customers have entered a store, the next visual merchandising challenge is to draw them through the entire store to the back walls. Experience tells us that, on average, customers pass through only the first third of the store and then exit unless something happens to entice them to stay. If merchandise displays with colorful impact are used throughout the store, it is more likely that the customer will be drawn from one area to the next. The more merchandise customers are able to see and touch, the more likely they are to make purchases. Color is one strategy to help you accomplish this critical merchandising goal.

Fashion merchandise within a store is generally divided into departments, and it is important to note that color trends are not limited to clothing. A department store may have a dress department, an accessory department, several sportswear departments, men's wear and children's wear departments, plus gift and housewares departments. Each merchandise category will have its own seasonal differences along with unique fashion and color trends.

In smaller shops, merchandise is often segmented in some way to provide easier shopping. In a gift shop, for example, you might find sections containing candles and candleholders grouped on shelves, or greeting cards, calendars or small books gathered together in central locations. These are *functional groupings.* You might also find a particular brand of gifts grouped in an area. These are *branded groupings.* In other key display areas of the same store, unrelated items might be grouped to create a **color story.** One place where this is particularly effective is in an antique shop where a variety of odds and ends are pulled together to form a merchandise grouping by color. You might see a corner featuring green depression glass dishes, enameled spatterware pots and pans, hand-painted luncheon cloths, silken lampshades, and embroidered bed linens displayed together in a green story. In another corner, you might find items drawn together by their red, white, and blue accents.

The self-explanatory terms to cover these merchandising techniques is *color-coordinated grouping* or *color-keyed product statement.* Color-keyed groupings provide ease of selection for customers who may not have time to research magazines for current color trends and often do not have confidence in their ability to coordinate colors effectively. Look at Colorplate 4 to see examples of fashions and housewares grouped by color.

Color story A colorcoordinated or colorkeyed product grouping that shows how to use a season's trend colors.

The How-to of Color Coordination

When text author Judy Bell was developing training materials for a chain of specialty stores where she was employed as a visual director, she developed a set of color guidelines that set merchandising policy for all stores to use in uniform fashion. The following step-by-step directions give you her practical guidelines for merchandising by color in today's retail operations:

1. Divide the colors of product into groups, according to their color **intensity.** There are seven common color groups. (See Colorplate 5.)

Intensity is the degree of saturation of a color.

- brights—the clearest, most vivid primary color intensities
- pastels—colors with added white to lighten and soften their effect
- midtones—not bright and not pastel, just in-between values
- jeweltones—royal colors
- muted/dusty—midtones with added gray
- earthtones—the colors of the earth: sand, rust, brown
- neutrals—colors that blend with every color group

2. Combine the colors within each group to create color schemes. Colors of the same intensity blend together harmoniously. For example, look at the flower arrangement in Colorplate 6A. Flowers in several bright colors are combined in a pleasing arrangement.

3. Do not combine colors from the various groups together, except for neutrals. Neutral colors can be combined with colors from any of the various color groups. Look at the flower arrangement in Colorplate 6B. Flowers in bright colors have been combined with a pastel—pink. The colors do not blend harmoniously; they are not of the same intensity.

Color Systems

There are two color-related professional organizations with Websites that you should know about and visit. The decisions they make will affect your work in many ways. The Color Marketing Group (CMG) is a not-for-profit, international association of more than 1500 color designers involved in the use of color as it applies to the profitable marketing of goods and services. Its members are qualified color designers who interpret, create, forecast, and select colors for manufactured products. They can be found at **www.colormarketing.org.** At the Website of the second organization, Pantone, Inc., you will find information about color along with a discussion of the company's role in developing and marketing products for the accurate communication of color for color-conscious industries like textiles, plastics, graphic arts, and film and video technology. You will find them at **www.pantone.com.**

Balance as a Merchandising Strategy

In the art world—and that includes merchandise presentation—the term *composition* means balancing various elements in an artful format. In the same way that artists plan the composition and design of their works, visual merchandisers compose and design retail space using garment rods, shelves, and other specialized display fixtures to present merchandise on walls and floor fixtures in stores. Visual merchandisers combine everything they know about art and business to plan how fixtures will be placed on selling floors and how walls will be set with merchandise. They seek a harmonious and eye-pleasing balance of elements in their store design. Among the artistic techniques they use are formal and informal balance.

In visual merchandising, *balance* can be defined as an equality of optical weight and importance that creates a unified presentation. Imagine two children on a seesaw. If each child weighs the same, they have no problem moving up and down. That's *formal balance*—two items of equal size or weight balanced equidistant from a center point. It is also called *symmetry*. *Informal balance* is *asymmetrical* (meaning "away from symmetry"). To understand informal balance, think about what happens when the children on the seesaw are not the same weight. Faced with a physics problem of this nature, children seem to understand instinctively that the heavier child will have to move closer to the center point of the seesaw, and the lighter one can stay at one end. To your eye, the two children may not appear to be balanced, but by adjusting their weight distribution, they can enjoy the seesaw because they've struck an informal (but workable) balance.

To employ formal balance in a home furnishings display, you might place a mirror in the exact center of a mantelpiece and split a pair of identical candles at an equal distance from the mirror's edges. As the name suggests, displays employing formal balance are rather conservative and restrained in nature. Some visual merchandisers say that formal balance is rigid, or at least static—suggesting little movement. You may also think of it as a disciplined approach. Formal balance is simple to learn and easy to use consistently. It's a way to keep wall displays organized and to maintain uniformity. In windows, unless you want to portray an elegant, restrained mood for the merchandise, informal balance may be a better choice. Keep these strategies in mind when selecting items for a display composition employing balance techniques. You'll want to be certain that the mood you're setting is appropriate to the merchandise message.

Optical weight is how important, large, or heavy an object appears to be versus how much it really weighs or how large it is in actual scale.

In visual merchandising, you can accomplish informal balance by grouping a variety of objects that have the same **optical weight** on two sides of a center line. (See Figure 3.2.) Even though the items are not the same on each side of the line, they appear to have the same weight, achieving an informal balance. This is a less restrained visual strategy, and it will allow you more freedom to express movement and activity in merchandising terms. With practice, you will train your eyes to guesstimate the size and importance of the items to be displayed by balancing the optical weights of the various items or objects used in your composition.

To understand formal balance on something as large as a store wall, draw an imaginary line down the center of the section to be merchandised, dividing this space into equal-sized

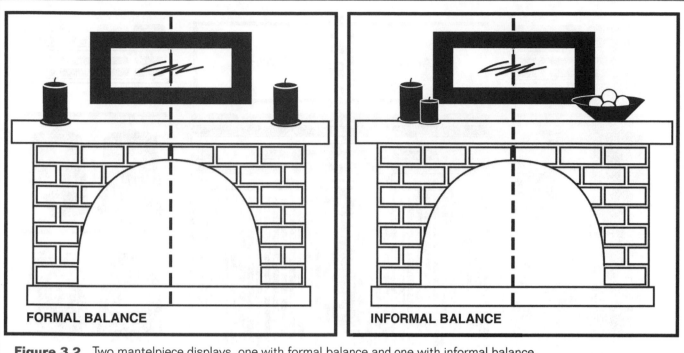

Figure 3.2 Two mantelpiece displays, one with formal balance and one with informal balance.

sections. Use an identical merchandise treatment on either side. If you display four shirts on **face-out** hanging fixtures on one half of the space, you must do the same on the other half. If you hang pants on a four-foot **garment rod** on one side of the line, you must do the same on the other side of the line. Look at formal balance at work on a section of wall in Figure 3.3 to see exactly how it's done.

In the top portion of Figure 3.4, which illustrates informal balance, the setup is not the same on both sides of the line, but the same amount of space is merchandised. This gives the *appearance* of balance even when the items are in an asymmetrical arrangement. The incorrect example (at the bottom) shows what happens when the two sides are not balanced. If a store has a long run of walls, you can add interest to the overall effect by alternating formally and informally balanced sections.

Other examples of balance include

- An entire store layout that appears to have evenly distributed focal points when viewed from the store entrance
- A single round table with even rows of sweaters stacked around its circumference

A **face-out** is a piece of hardware for hanging merchandise so that the full front of the item is visible. It can be a straight arm or a slanted arm for a "waterfall" effect.

A **garment rod** is a length of round or flat metal tubing (crossbar) that fits into wall-mounted brackets and is used to hold rows of garments on hangers. Garment rods are generally cut in 4-foot lengths to allow flexibility in wall design and to avoid overloading.

Rhythm as a Merchandising Strategy

Musicians aren't the only ones who use rhythm in their art. Just as you find yourself tapping your foot to a compelling drum beat, your displays can impart feelings of movement and rhythm to those who see them. In visual merchandising, rhythm can be defined as a sense of visual movement from item to item and element to element in a single display or presentation of an entire department. This movement can come as a result of the effects of lines, shapes, or colors as well as varying heights, lines, and forms used in the overall display's design. Rhythm does not require mechanical animation. Instead, it relies on the viewer's eye following the patterns established by the composition of the design.

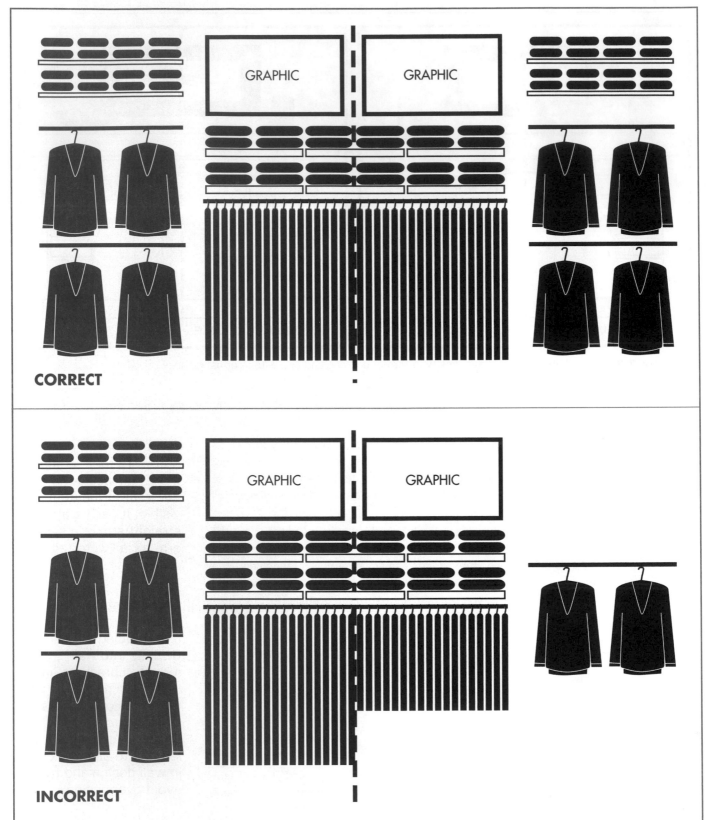

CORRECT

INCORRECT

Figure 3.3 A fashion apparel wall presentation. In the correct example, formal balance is achieved by creating a mirror image of garments on both sides of a center line. This does not occur in the incorrect example.

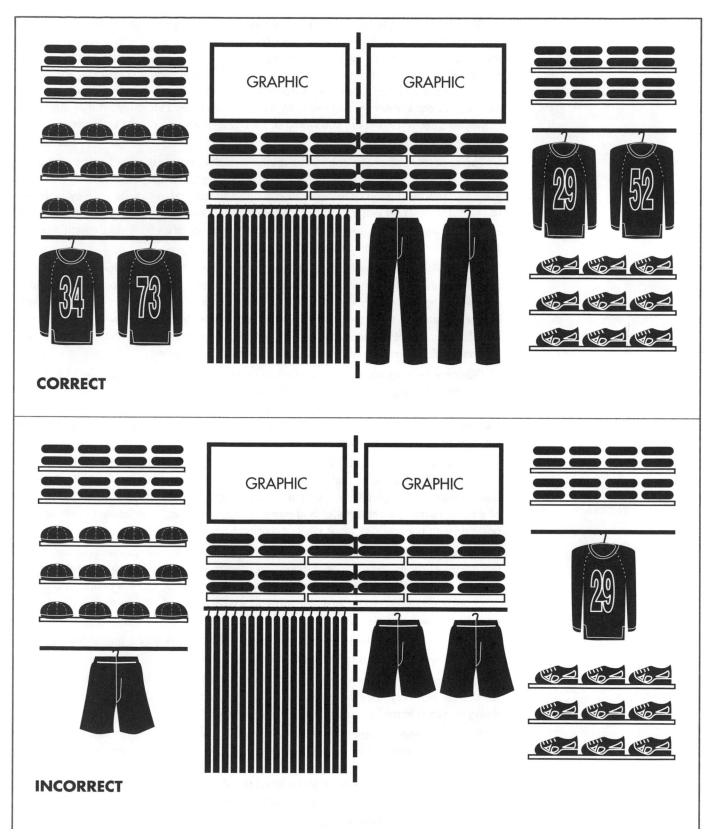

CORRECT

INCORRECT

Figure 3.4 A fashion apparel wall presentation. In the correct example, informal balance is achieved because an equal amount of space is filled on either side of a center line. This does not occur in the incorrect example.

Rhythm can be understood by taking a panoramic look at a specialty store from the front entrance. If you notice a "sea" of fixtures of the same height (without any signing to break the horizon), the optical flow of rhythm would be absent. To create visual rhythm, heights of fixtures can be varied. An even stronger sense of rhythm can be created by adding displays or graphics to the tops of key fixtures in a department or shop. If you drew an imaginary dot-to-dot line connecting low to high points looking at a store layout that effectively conveyed a sense of rhythm, you would see a zigzag pattern. Look at Colorplate 7 for an example of a store with brilliant rhythm.

The strategic use of *line* can lend a rhythmic feeling to any display or area where you want to suggest activity and movement. Use of line—graphic stripes or arrows—can create a very active rhythm or feeling within a retail space that will guide your eye into and through it. Line is an integral part of rhythm in the composition of a visual presentation. Used effectively, linear elements direct or guide the shopper's visual trip through an entire selling area or stand-alone display.

Vertical lines send a message of dignity, strength, and height. Chicago's Niketown entrance features a three-story vertical spiral mobile of plaster figures doing various active sports—riding mountain bikes, shooting baskets, and so on. In architecture, a few strategically *repeated* vertical structural columns hold up entire buildings. People who "walk tall" are society's models for ideal posture. In fact, the taller the fashion model or mannequin, the more refined and elegant the garment shown appears to be.

Diagonal lines speak of action and make us think of rockets launching, jets taking off, and arrows starting their arcs through the air. These could be effective mood-makers in sporting goods, active sportswear, and toy departments. Zigzagging lines are diagonals that are so active that they're almost frenzied. Think of cartoon lightning bolts or the spiking lines of an electrocardiogram and you have the idea of zigzag activity.

Horizontal lines are much more restful than verticals and diagonals. They remind us of landscapes and seascapes that seem to go on forever. The status quo (a state of equilibrium) is represented graphically as a flat line. A designer who wants to downplay the height of a room to make it feel smaller and more intimate, will "cut" the unwanted vertical impression with horizontal color borders or architectural moldings.

Curved lines—which speak of graceful, relaxed, and carefree movement—can establish a sense of femininity in a department devoted to women's intimate apparel, fine jewelry, cosmetics, a bridal shop, or a maternity wear department. Curves added to checkout counters and fixtures in a department soften the total effect of otherwise masculine, hard-edged construction materials.

Study the photographs for displays in Figure 3.5. You will notice that the lines lend a sense of direction (action) to the area where they're used.

Repetition of certain design elements can create a special sense of visual rhythm in retail design. Not only does the eye travel along the paths of repeated items, the merchandising message is reinforced again and again as well.

Sometimes the *sequence,* or order, in which you place items in a display, from smallest to largest, for instance, helps visual merchandisers tell merchandise stories, too. If size or progression from largest to smallest, for instance, informs the shopper about the importance of product size, this rank ordering leads the shoppers' eyes through the presentation and helps them decide which items will best serve their needs.

Examples of repetitive or sequential rhythm include

- A grouping of three mannequins dressed in jackets of the same style and color with different accessories to give each basic jacket a unique look

- An assortment of various sizes of a particular manufacturer's luggage line ranked from smallest carry-on to steamer trunk

Figure 3.5 Strategic use of line lends a sense of direction and rhythm to various display areas.

A Horizontal and vertical lines; Express, Miami.

B Curved lines; Good Guys, Los Angeles.

C Diagonal lines; Express, Columbus.

- A series of signs or banners suspended from the ceiling or angled out from columns lining the main aisle of a store

Proportion as a Merchandising Strategy

Proportion can be defined as a relationship between the apparent size, mass, scale, or optical weight of two or more objects. In a visual presentation, proportion could relate to an oversized prop used with normal-sized merchandise. Or, it could describe the contrast (extreme difference in scale) between large and small items in a display window.

Proportion has its place in fashion coordination, too. Imagine dressing an elegant mannequin in a black chiffon cocktail dress with a soft knee-length skirt and then accessorizing the costume with a heavy shoe with a chunky heel. Not only is the style of shoe inappropriate, the proportion of shoe to gown is also incorrect. A light strap high heel is an appropriate choice of shoe, in the correct proportion.

How would you know that? Even if you weren't an instinctive "fashion person," you could certainly rely on your built-in sense of proportion to tell you that something was out of order. A current fashion magazine may help you choose the best fashion accessories until you are more confident in your fashion savvy. This is true of home furnishings or other hard goods as well. Magazines like *Elle, W,* and *Metropolitan Home* can be tremendous resources for you.

Other examples of proportion include

- A furniture showroom featuring a display with an oversized loveseat, two companion chairs, and the appropriately scaled end tables

- A fashion wall section featuring assorted woolen jackets faced out over a garment rod of coordinated twill skirts

Texture as a Merchandising Strategy

"Look but don't touch." You probably heard this often as a child because children experience the world through all of their senses—even when it makes their parents nervous. In *Why We Buy,* in the chapter titled "The Sensual Shopper," researcher Paco Underhill says, "The purest example of human shopping I know of can be seen by watching a child go through life touching absolutely *everything.* You're watching that child shop for information, for understanding, for knowledge, for experience, for sensation." He adds that shopping is "more than what we call the 'grab and go'—you need cornflakes, you go to the cornflakes, you grab the cornflakes, and *haveaniceday.* The kind of activity I mean involves experiencing that portion of the world that has been deemed for sale, using our senses—sight, touch, smell, taste, hearing—as the basis for choosing this or rejecting that."

Today more than ever, people buy things based on trial and touch. If a product's tactile qualities are its most important feature, shoppers must know for themselves how the product feels. Think about all the plastic-wrapped packages of merchandise you see broken open on store shelves. People want to touch merchandise. And while some textures are easy to visualize, some require hands-on experience. In fact, Underhill's research found that some new Americans who hadn't grown up with U.S.–style brand advertising for lotions, soaps, and shampoos "tore into the boxes or opened the bottles to test the viscosity and scent of the products."

Think of all this in terms of customer response. As Underhill points out: "Touch and trial are more important than ever to the world of shopping because of changes in how stores function. Once upon a time store owners and salespeople were our guides to the merchandise they sold. They were knowledgeable enough, and there were enough of them, to act as the shopper's intermediary to the world of things . . . when space was clearly divided between shoppers and staff."

Today's **open sell** merchandise presentations put almost everything out on the selling floor with few if any salespeople between shoppers and previously untouchable merchandise. Shoppers have come to expect access to samples when packaging becomes the final barrier. The strategic use of accessible presentation and décor that makes use of the textural element are more important than ever to creating a welcoming, sales-supportive atmosphere in the retail store.

It is important to realize that texture can be seen as well as touched. How store designers and planners use textural contrasts in store décor determines overall environmental "mood" and can influence the appearance of merchandise as well. In artistic and aesthetic terms, texture can absorb or reflect light, provide contrasts that enhance the features of merchandise, help set mood, and actually invite a shopper to touch merchandise. Remember, the more contact shoppers have with certain types of merchandise, the more likely it is that they will buy.

Textural congruity is important. Rough-hewn wooden walls and fixture surfaces may be an appropriate backdrop for a shop featuring equipment for sports and outdoor activities, but they might bewilder shoppers looking for fine china and stemware. Texture shouldn't be used for its own sake unless it makes good sense when paired with merchandise. Of course, there are times when a textural choice can create great contrast and focus attention on differences. If irony or humor is part of your company's visual merchandising plan, then strong contrast statements may be very appropriate. Tiffany's Gene Moore was a master of visual irony when he combined exquisite jewelry pieces with the most unlikely props. (See Figures 1.1 and 1.2.)

Display and décor materials convey meaning. Slick, shiny surfaces making use of modern, angular lines reflect light and suggest products like high-tech electronics, streamlined home furnishings, updated home accessory products, automotive products, and youthful, forward-looking fashions.

Texture can set the mood and set the stage, too. Wall coverings in a store selling high-quality products related to sound and music could suggest the professional ambiance of the recording studio where extraneous sound is absorbed by thick acoustical padding. Here, the combination of form and function are important in selection of décor elements because these textures speak to shoppers and tell them what to expect from the merchandise housed in the music store environment.

Sumptuous textural elements that might set a private club mood in a traditional men's business attire department might include: richly wood-paneled walls and floors, ornate moldings, oak beams, deep armchairs in slightly worn-looking leather coverings, heavy drapes, discreet displays on library tables, polished brass hardware, and thick carpeting. The same treatment could be a total turnoff to young males shopping for casual weekend wear. More appropriate textural elements for this younger target market might be brushed metal tables, gleaming gym floor finishes, and scoreboard signing.

Open sell is fixturing that makes most merchandise (even items traditionally kept in locked cases) accessible to shoppers without assistance of salespeople.

A Retail Reality
Be sure that your textural attempts are in harmony with your company's visual policies before you invest time and resources in anything radically different from what's usual for your store.

A Retail Reality
The smooth and friction-free surfaces of modern décor materials may suggest action, but they are also fingerprint magnets. Every surface will reflect great amounts of light and spotlight your house-keeping habits as well.

Harmony as a Merchandising Strategy
●●

In the texture examples, one of the most important factors is selecting décor elements that are compatible with the merchandise for sale. Taken together, the examples also illustrate the principle of harmony—the careful selection of complementary, interwoven elements that create an unified whole.

Harmony is an "artful" element, creating visible unity on many levels. That is a serious challenge to visual merchandisers because it is so easy to forget that the single department they're working in is part of an entire store, or that the single display they're constructing is part of an entire department. You must keep the store's brand image and merchandising goals in mind the entire time you're working. Resist the temptation to create little islands of blinding brilliance that pay homage to your own cleverness as a visual merchandiser because storewide design and presentation harmony will suffer if you don't.

This doesn't mean that there is no room for creative expression in your work. In fact, the really effective creative person will find ways to insert humorous, surprising, or ironic elements in displays that are accent notes to the retailer's everyday presentation.

Emphasis as a Merchandising Strategy

The final principle, *emphasis,* is presented last for a reason. Any of the art principles and design elements discussed so far can be manipulated to emphasize specific items or focus attention on certain areas of your store—but no matter what you're presenting, your strategy must be merchandise-centered.

When you employ the principle of emphasis, you are deciding which feature of the merchandise you will highlight. What you choose to emphasize will depend on what you want to communicate to the customer. If it's the importance of a new fashion color, then you would need to use more of that color than any other in composing your presentation. You can also emphasize merchandise by dramatic use of lighting, by effective use of signing and graphics, and by strategic placement of merchandise on fixtures—all of which are discussed at greater length in coming chapters.

Design composition is important. You have great power to influence purchasing decisions when you use your imagination and technical skills to direct shoppers' attention and get them involved with your merchandise. Tasks this important require advance planning. Every display should begin with a sketch. Every floor change should start with a **planogram.** If you're not an accomplished sketch artist, you can draw simple squares and circles to compose your design—plotting out focal points and checking that you've "spotlighted" the necessary items.

You'll see the principle of emphasis at work in most specialty stores at the entrance or **leaseline.** Merchandising tables and other selling fixtures will feature items that have been purchased in depth (several items per size, style, and color), showing the store's commitment to their sales potential. This show of strength in a given merchandise category is an emphasis strategy. It tells customers that the item, category, or trend is one the store believes in.

One of the best examples of using emphasis as a visual merchandising strategy is Old Navy's "Item of the Week," which is always dramatically signed and adequately stocked to generate profitable sales. It is like an "exclamation point" that not only emphasizes certain categories of merchandise but also serves to slow shoppers down long enough to see the display that functions as a huge billboard for the latest trend merchandise. The strategy behind the first display that shoppers see is to focus attention and prepare the customer to shop in the store.

Another effective "traffic stopping" strategy that emphasizes products revolves around bringing elements of *tension* or *surprise* into presentations. By adding the unexpected—clown masks on mannequins faces, for instance—customers can be stopped in their tracks to notice a sportswear display. Once they get over the surprise at the attention-getting device, they will give the mannequins' fashion apparel a second look, too. Tying a national read-a-book campaign to a precariously balanced tower of new hardcover books from The *New York Times* best-seller list could create tension—making shoppers wonder whether the tower is going to topple. Books would be emphasized without the addition of a single prop. All you'd need is an effective sign announcing the list and the tie-in reading campaign (and a tube of glue to keep the stack stable).

Planograms are drawings that show how merchandise and selling fixtures should be placed on selling floors, wall sections, or freestanding displays and window displays. They are planning tools that make it possible to communicate consistent store layout and décor directives to multiple locations thereby creating a strong retailer identity.

In mall merchandising, the **leaseline** is the boundary line where store space begins and the mall's common area ends.

Other examples of emphasis include

- Store interior mannequin displays that feature strong merchandise category or color stories
- Wall presentations with oversized graphics that underline the most salable items in the store or individual department
- An interesting belt used as an accent on a single outfit
- Tables in home fashion stores that feature seasonal trends: for example, a Christmas-theme table with everything you'd need to bake gingerbread cookies, from basic ingredients to mixing bowls to cookie cutters and bakeware plus the serveware (trays, platters, etc.) to deliver the cookies to holiday guests

A Retail Reality
Customers become annoyed when merchandise displayed on mannequins or forms is not stocked in *depth* (several items per size, style, and color). If limited selections are "selling down" quickly, the display should be changed just as quickly . . . or not set up in the first place.

Shoptalk
• •

By Jim Smart
president of Smart Associates, Minneapolis

Somewhere along the way to my goal of becoming a famous theatrical designer, I became enchanted with the workings of the retail "stage." I know just when it happened, too. It was when I walked into a major department store and saw how the creative staff (I didn't know that name then) "directed" us around the store and got us to see and buy the things they wanted us to see and buy. I suddenly wanted to be part of that, too.

With available technology and the sophistication of today's market, it is now possible to include as many theatrical elements in the design for a retail store or restaurant as once only went into something like a huge Broadway spectacular. The goal of the theatrical designer in a successful production is to engulf each audience member in the total atmosphere of the play. Utilizing all of that person's senses does that. The first sense is vision—stimulated by color, movement, and light. Done well, effective store design can have the same effect on a customer as the incredible moment in *Chorus Line* when the full chorus in gold hats and tailcoats turns toward the stage apron, singing "One, singular sensation. . . ."

We call it atmospherics. Of course, the retail or restaurant setting is a little more permanent than a stage show, and there are many other factors that come into play—safety and energy codes, issues pertaining to the Americans with Disabilities Act, and budgets.

When our firm jumps into a new project, we start with a "no rules" approach. That is, we are interested in who our client's customers are, what the practical needs of the space are, what kinds of things and feelings will appeal to the desired customer base, and, most importantly, what will bring them back. We find that not worrying about the "rules" at this stage is helpful in identifying just what the atmosphere should feel like, look like, and smell like. This first phase is called the *programming phase*.

When all of the information about the project is gathered and the brainstorming is completed, we produce the drawings necessary to convey our ideas to our client. This is called the *schematic design phase*.

Once we feel that we're on the right path—capturing the essence of the personality of the space—we go back to look at those very important guidelines and rules. We must be sure that our client's space is safe, complies with all related building codes, and can pay for itself. This is the *design development phase*.

When our client has reviewed the work produced to this point and agrees with our direction, we produce the construction documentation needed to build the project, including plans and elevations, lighting designs, the millwork designs, plus any other technical specifications, budget projections, and construction timetables.

Throughout each phase, one thing that never leaves our minds is the budget. The other even more important thing is atmospherics. We never take our eyes off the goal of our design. It is all too easy to start to focus on details and fail to see the larger picture while marching through the phases of a design project. We accomplish this by having a project manager whose job is to handle all communications with the client and the general contractor as well as any city building officials who may enter the picture. This project manager keeps copious notes and is always ready to "defend" the design on any front.

All of this is important because we must provide our client's customers with an atmosphere that is conducive to the business of the space, whether it's shopping, dining, golfing, or buying services. Now and then a client will say, "Personally, I don't like that color." We try to find a tactful way to reply; "We don't care." If that sounds harsh, it isn't meant to be—but it underscores the point that we are vitally concerned about what the client's *customers* will like. In fact, we research their reactions and preferences in the early (programming) phase to sense what will get them to return and return again because when that happens, we know we have a successful project and a happy client.

If you were to ask me about the most important part of a designer's job, I would have to say *listening*. If we go off into outer space thinking that we know more than our clients know, we are certain to fail. It is only through listening carefully to the needs and desires of both client and customer that an effective project is produced.

So there it is—my view of the designer's role in creating that "one singular sensation"—that you know as atmospherics.

Out-of-the-Box Challenge

1 Creating a Color Collage

Directions: Collect an assortment of old fashion and home furnishings magazines (preferably publications that feature a large proportion of colorful ads) that you wouldn't mind cutting up. Two weeks' worth of mail-order catalogs and gardening and seed catalogs are good (and inexpensive) sources for color photographs. Then proceed as follows to create a collage:

1. **Look** through the magazines and catalogs until you find items in pure, primary colors—red, yellow, and blue. You may find a sweater in one color, an umbrella in another, and a coil of garden hose for the third. Cut these items out and reserve for future use.

2. **Look** for photographs that have items in the secondary colors—green, orange, and violet. Cut these items out and set aside.

3. **Look** for photographs that have items in the tertiary colors. Cut these examples out and set them aside.

4. **Assemble** your colorful clippings in a color wheel format that shows the progression from one variation of a color to the next. Do not glue them down at this point.

5. **Compare** your preliminary arrangement with the example shown in Colorplate 8.

6. **Innovate** on the example as you create your own color collage. On a separate sheet of paper or cardboard, mount the photographs to form a color wheel collage of overlapping shades and objects.

2 Magazine Project

Directions: Imagine that magazine advertisements are merchandise displays in store windows. Since photo stylists use the principles and elements of art in the same ways that you would if you were constructing merchandise displays, you should be able to identify examples that show each one at work to sell merchandise. Proceed to analyze the ads as follows:

1. **Look** for photographic examples of

Balance	Line
Proportion	Direction
Repetition	Color
Harmony	Texture
Emphasis	Shape
Rhythm	Tension or surprise

2. **Compare** your findings to illustrations in this text. Do you see the shapes and lines suggested by the definitions in the chapter? With a marking pen, draw lines and arrows or circles to identify the elements. Label each principle or element.

3. **Innovate** by suggesting ways in which ideas from the photographic examples could be adapted to a retail display.

3 Atmospherics

Directions: Visit your favorite store to study its atmospherics.

Look

Look at the store through "new eyes." List the atmospheric elements that impress your senses. Ask yourself:

1. How does the store "greet" visitors?

2. Is there a traffic-stopping display at the entrance?

3. What merchandise was featured at the entrance? Did it invite you to shop the store in more depth? Why? Why not?

Compare

Summarize your impressions and analyze what they mean in terms of your shopping behavior and your response to the visual merchandising techniques this retailer has used to create this shopping environment.

Innovate

Briefly list things that this retailer could do to create a more welcoming and favorable shopping atmosphere for customers.

Critical Thinking

Build an Artist's Palette of Colors

Directions (Figure 3.6): This activity requires a red, a yellow, and a blue crayon (second choice: colored pencils or a simple set of children's paints). Marking pens are not appropriate for this exercise. Once you've completed this assignment

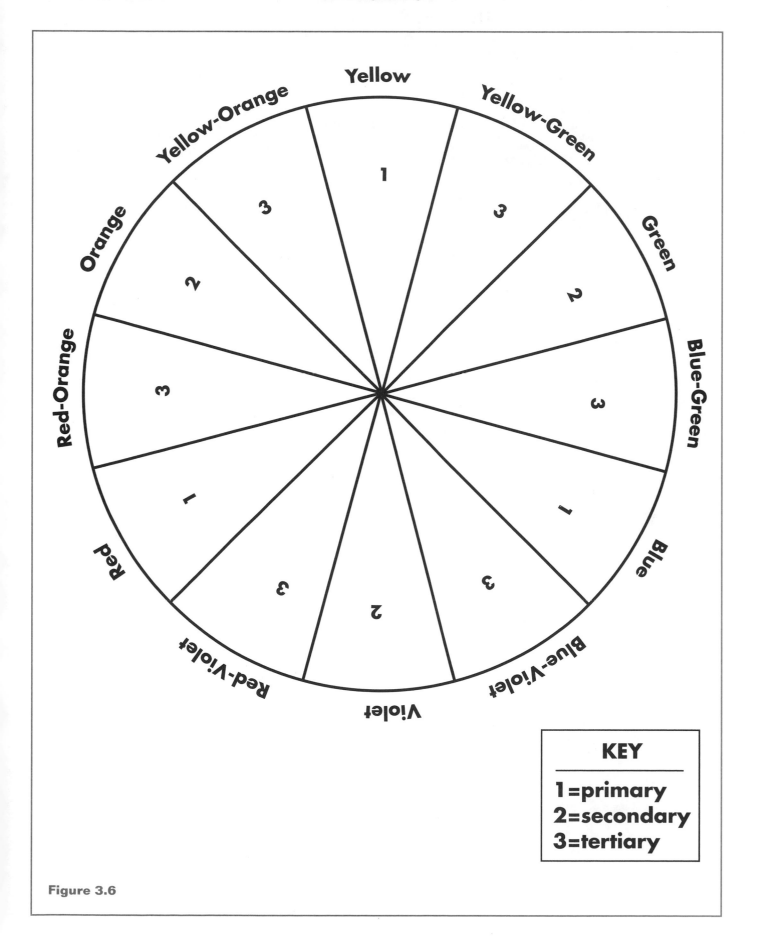

Figure 3.6

successfully, you will understand where the rainbow of colors originates. You may want to practice on another sheet of paper, or in the margins of this workbook, to get the exact shades you want for this activity.

1. In the circle in Figure 3.6, fill in the spaces marked for the *primary* colors with your crayons or pencils. Be lavish with your applications. Lay down rich, solid-looking colors.

2. Now, in the spaces between the primaries—marked *secondary* colors—create orange, green, and violet by blending the primaries. As you color, red and yellow layered over each other will mix to form orange. Blue and yellow will mix to form green. Blue and red will form violet.

3. In the spaces marked *tertiary*, still using only red, green, and yellow, create the third-level, or tertiary, colors, of red-orange, yellow-orange, yellow-green, blue-green, blue-violet, and red-violet. You may need to practice on another sheet of paper or in the margins of this workbook.

Case Study
Creating a Store Environment

The Situation

"Scooters" is the name of a children's clothing and gift store that is about to open on a city block that also has a natural food co-op, a pharmacy, and a pet store. The store is located in the "first ring" of a large Arizona city, about 5 miles from the central business district near several small parks, a YMCA, and two grade schools—one is a combination of all-kindergarten and extended-hour day care, the other is an elementary school for grades 1–5.

Siblings Mike, Ron, and Mary Rodrigues have decided to open a retail store catering to young families moving back into the city. The older residents in the neighborhood are moving to apartments or the retirement communities that abound in the area. The three grew up here and are delighted to see the neighborhood "turn" and welcome families who are rehabilitating older homes for their growing families.

The basic services in the area are ideal—a foresighted response by the city and school district to the changing demographics. The only drawback that the owners can see is metered on-street parking, although there are six parking spaces directly behind the store that can be signed for store parking only.

While the "Scooters" owners have managed the financial aspects of their start-up without too much trouble, they are not exactly in agreement about how the store should look and what

its physical image should be. In fact, Mary's name for the store—Scooters—was drawn from a hat after they failed to agree about the name and the overall look of the store. They have agreed to hire a consultant to guide them through the design of the store.

The store's exterior is tan stucco with a traditional southwestern red tile roof. Its interior is 40 × 60 with an additional 40 × 20 "backroom" space, including a bathroom that is accessible to the public. The second floor is equally large, with office/storage space in the 40 × 20 back area. Their plan is to sell clothing for infants, toddlers, and boys and girls up to size 12 on the main floor; and toys, books, and gifts on the second floor. Their principal differentiating factor will be pricing. The owners want their store to have an upscale environment, but they plan to sell at 30–40 percent off normal retail by purchasing off-price, promotional, and end-lot goods in the market. They want the environment to be playful and demonstrate to shoppers (adults and children) that Scooters understands what young families like, want, and need.

Your Challenge

Assume that you are the design consultant hired by the Rodrigues family to get them started on their store's image and appearance.

- Identify some of the *atmospheric elements* you think will impart the feeling that you have heard the owners describe for their store. "Borrow" elements from children's furniture, fixtures, large-scaled toys, and play equipment; cutting and pasting from magazines, catalogs, and brochures.

- Choose an appropriate *color scheme* for the store exterior and interior walls and floor. Collect paint chips or sample cards from a decorating or hardware store, or simply cut and paste colorful elements from magazine pictures to help visualize your choices. Be prepared to explain why the color scheme will enhance Scooters's brand image and support the other atmospheric elements you have chosen.

- Design a colored *graphic element* that would be appropriate for an exterior sign and that could be carried onto the store's interior walls. It could be a simple figure from a child's coloring book, a cartoon, pictures of toys, elements of a game, or anything that brings to mind the colors, activities, and happiness of a carefree childhood. Be prepared to explain how this graphic element captures Scooters's brand image and how it will support the store's atmosphere both outside and inside the store.

- Present the case to your instructor or to your classmates in a role-play situation.

Part Two

PRACTICES AND STRATEGIES FOR THE SELLING FLOOR

Chapter 4

LAYOUT AND FIXTURES FOR FASHION APPAREL

After completing this chapter, you should be able to

Identify the different types of retail stores

Demonstrate how and why floor department layouts are planned

Categorize a wide variety of floor and wall fixtures

Present garments and accessories on fixtures

"Visual excitement is truly achieved once
the key focal areas of the 'box' are
determined and then occupied with
stimulating and attractive fixtures. They
become the merchandising tools and
partners with products and signage . . . for
a successful design that increases sales
and word-of-mouth marketing."
**Greg M. Gorman, principal,
Creative Services, GMG Design, Inc.**

Creating Retail Atmosphere

Think of a retail store as a "box" that's enclosed by ceiling, walls, windows, and floor. The strategic design of the store involves its exterior aspect (storefront and surroundings) and its interior (walls, floors, windows, doors, signing, lighting, furniture, and fixtures), merchandise and fixture arrangement on the selling floor, and displays. The total effect of these elements creates a statement about what shoppers will find in the box—retail atmosphere.

Effective store designs link store atmospherics and management's merchandising philosophies to offer a pleasant, productive shopping experience. The retail store should always be more than a place for a shopper to exchange money for products. It should also be the best place to inspect and interact with products—trying before buying. Nothing about a store's design or layout should interfere with that process. When shoppers leave retail stores with products they have purchased, they may not realize that they have "bought" the entire retail experience as well, but that's what really happens.

Edward Hare, president of Hare Enterprises, Inc., a West Coast fixture designer and manufacturer, offers an interesting definition of what's inside the box: "It's function with an illusion—it's nothing more than a Hollywood set." This is a notion shared by Gian Luigi Longinotti-Buitoni in *Selling Dreams: How to Make Any Product Irresistible.* He believes that successful dream sellers should create products and services that convey intense emotions. They should also do everything possible to enhance customers' perceptions of added value. For example, if they believe there is more to a store than a building and merchandise, they will happily shop there and pay whatever prices are asked. Buitoni's term for the marketing of dreams is "dreamketing." He says: "The dreamketer should ensure that the company's communication, distribution, special events, and any type of customer relations consistently support the brand's mission to build that dream in the customer's mind."

Fixturing, or furnishing, stores is an aesthetic and financial challenge for successful retailers. They want their stores to be attractive and effectively communicate their unique messages about their stores' brand image and merchandise to shoppers, yet they want to do it economically. An expensive store design does not guarantee an effective store environment.

Effective store design places merchandise and customer service at the heart of the effort. At the same time, it presents the store in a way that differentiates it from competing stores. The store's visual message to the customer must be fit in with everything else the store does to communicate its brand image to the shopping public. For example, if the retail store employs a warm, friendly approach in its print advertising copy, then the shopper will expect the physical store to feel warm and friendly, too. This implies that store owners and managers have a plan—a retail strategy.

A Retail Reality: Every square foot of a store must be profitable. Often retail space is leased, and rent is based on sales per square foot. When total sales ($) are divided by leased square footage (store length × store width), the merchant is able to determine productivity or sales per square foot. This figure can be broken down to measure earnings by classification or department as well.

Types of Retail Stores

There are at least ten retail store categories describing the way stores may be designed, organized, or operated: department, specialty, boutique, discount, dollar stores, hypermarket, outlet, warehouse, thrift stores, and pop-up stores.

Department stores consist of many departments, each devoted to a specific category (product classification). In terms of square footage, these are large stores that offer a broad variety of products and cater to an equally wide range of customers. To merchandise this expansive a selection of goods and services, the department store retailer uses many styles of specialty and custom fixtures designed to showcase each category. The size of the typical department store—Bloomingdale's and Macy's, for instance—is going to depend on the size of its basic floorplan. Multiply length times width for the main floor selling space footage and then multiply again by the number of similar-sized selling floors above the main floor.

Specialty stores have a limited number of departments or merchandise categories, and generally have a smaller footprint (Gap, Banana Republic, Abercrombie & Fitch). A small specialty store in a mall could range from 1500 to 3000 square feet. A medium- to large-sized specialty store might range from 4000 to 6000 square feet. A free-standing specialty store in a strip mall could range from 1500 to 25,000 square feet or more.

The specialty store's product selection is, as the term implies, more specialized than that of a department store and usually caters to a narrower range of customers. The specialty retailer often uses unique fixtures and seeks to project a more exclusive store image based on price and status.

Boutiques are small specialty shops featuring assorted items that fit specific merchandising themes or appeal to a specialized clientele. You'll find entire blocks of boutiques in areas like Manhattan's Greenwich Village or on Castro Street in San Francisco. The term *boutique* may also be used to describe cross-merchandising within a department store, when retailers bring items from several departments together for a special promotion (a tropical cruisewear shop, for example, which features swimsuits, sandals, beach towels, and suntan lotion.)

Discount stores have many departments and a wide range of products at discounted prices that appeal to a wide variety of customers. They utilize mostly no-frills metal gondola fixtures (long ranks of shelving or pegboard) that hold a great deal of merchandise. Discount stores may also utilize custom-made fixtures or vendor-supplied fixtures in a few departments (Target, Kmart, Wal-Mart.) It isn't unusual for a free-standing discount store to be 80,000 to 150,000 square feet.

Dollar stores vary in size from less than 500 square feet to 6000 square feet. All items fit into a specific price range. Bill's Dollar stores price everything at one dollar, whereas in Dollar General and Family Dollar, prices range from one to twenty dollars per item.

Hypermarkets (hybrid markets and superstores) are concepts borrowed from European retailing. Carrefour, which originated in France more than 30 years ago, is the first and most famous example of this mega-merchandising concept. Several merchandising categories are housed under one *very* large roof—softlines (apparel and health and beauty aids) and hardlines (home, gardening, automotive, sporting goods)—along with a grocery store. These one-stop shopping destinations can be as large as 200,000 square feet.

Outlet stores are either stand-alone stores or small stores located in outlet malls. They use fixtures similar to those found in specialty stores, but merchandise presentation sometimes has less visual impact because stock quantities may be broken, (incomplete color, style, and size assortments). Some of the newest outlet stores, however, have presentations and fixtures that would rival mainstream specialty stores. The largest outlet stores are filled with capacity fixtures for massive clearance presentations. The outlet store may sell catalog overstocks; manufacturers' irregulars or overstocks; or a combination of out-of-season items, special purchases, and stock consolidations from retailers who are reducing postseason inventory or from those who are going out of business. Marshall's, T.J.Maxx, Lands' End, Guess?, Ralph Lauren, and Brooks Brothers, among other retailers, operate outlet stores.

Warehouse stores—built to house massive quantities of goods on grids of industrial shelving and pallets—offer no-frills shopping at reduced prices (Sam's Club, Costco). Fashion goods may or may not be part of the stores' offerings. These stores are large, plain, and fluorescent-lit, and they have a decidedly industrial ambiance. Fitting rooms, if they have them at all, may be utilitarian, separated only by gender. Shopping carts are oversized and, in some instances, are low, flat carts large enough to handle furniture items or heavy cases of goods. Some warehouse stores don't even furnish bags to carry smaller purchases, assuming shoppers will make case-lot purchases rather than buy single items.

Thrift stores are often operated by nonprofit organizations such as the Salvation Army as fund-raising and employment training ventures. They often resemble garage sales with

A **grid layout** is a linear design for a selling floor where fixtures are arranged to form vertical and horizontal aisles throughout the store.

In store presentation, **sight line** refers to the area a person can see from a particular vantage point—the view at the end of an aisle or at the top or bottom of an escalator, for example.

The **free-flow layout** has selling fixtures arranged in loosely grouped, informal, nonlinear formations to encourage browsing.

A **racetrack layout** exposes shoppers to a great deal of merchandise as they follow a perimeter traffic aisle with departments on the right and left of the circular, square, rectangular or oval "racetrack."

In a **soft aisle layout,** fixtures are arranged in groups, creating natural aisles without any change in the floor covering to designate a separate aisle space.

A **minimal floor layout,** almost gallerylike in its simplicity, shows small selections of handcrafted or very exclusive merchandise.

wildly assorted merchandise categories—from clothing in all sizes to small appliances to furniture and books. Their products are all donated by private citizens or business organizations. Some operations are more sophisticated than others. You may see traditional fixtures, décor, traffic patterns, and standard checkout arrangements, with displays of seasonal categories. In other stores, you'll see a blend of makeshift shelving and traditional fixtures. This is no-frills merchandising. Merchandise categories expand and shrink according to unpredictable donations of goods. As a result, most stores are decorated and fixtured with flexibility in mind.

Pop-up stores are temporary concepts that blend retail with event marketing. They launch new product lines or promote existing stores. For example, Meow Mix opened a cafe for kitties in Manhattan for two weeks and Target docked a boat in New York City filled with products during the holidays.

Store Layouts

Over time, retailers have evolved several basic floor plans to move shoppers past fixtures of merchandise in their stores. Early on, their aim was to efficiently expose the maximum number of shoppers to the maximum amount of merchandise in the minimum amount of space and time. Today, selling space, traffic control, and sales productivity still matter, but an increasing number of retailers are paying attention to shopper comfort and store aesthetics as well.

The **grid layout**, as the name implies, is a linear design with fixtures arranged on parallel aisles. Fixtures are positioned in a checkerboard pattern, with vertical and horizontal aisles that run throughout the store. There may also be one primary aisle and several secondary aisles, depending on the total square footage of the store. This layout is efficient in terms of space use, allows orderly stocking, helps shoppers see (and reach) a great number of items easily, is simple and predictable to navigate, and is efficient to maintain. The grid layout creates natural **sight lines,** which lead to focal points at the ends of aisles. The customers' attention naturally focuses on these areas, so visual merchandisers can take advantage of this, creating displays that act as "interior windows." (See Figure 4.1.)

The **free-flow layout,** shown in Figure 4.2, is the opposite of the grid pattern. Merchandise fixtures are arranged in a number of interesting formations to encourage browsing. There may be several round racks grouped loosely around a central cash–wrap desk, and merchandise tables interspersed with four-way fixtures along a department's exposure to an aisle. The critical factor is providing enough room between fixtures to allow traffic to flow smoothly. Shoppers will not linger at a fixture if another shopper is nudging past them or trying to maneuver a baby stroller between tightly packed tables. The free-flow layout also encourages shoppers to easily move from one department into another, increasing exposure to other categories of merchandise.

A **racetrack layout** features a traffic aisle that loops around the store's perimeter. (See Figure 4.3.) There are departments on the right and left of the circular, square, rectangular, or oval track, and this layout exposes shoppers to a great deal of merchandise. You often see this layout employed in a discount or department store. Overhead directional signing and departmental graphics provide visual cues to the location of other departments, helping shoppers to plan their shopping trip throughout the store.

In the **soft aisle layout,** fixtures are arranged into groups, sometimes with a 5-foot aisle along merchandised wall sections. (See Figure 4.4.) This technique encourages customers to shop the walls and to move easily around the entire store. Walls are considered to be the most important sales generating locations in the store in this layout strategy.

The **minimal layout,** as the name implies, is almost gallerylike in its simplicity. In fact, the merchandise may sometimes be wearable art—handcrafted, designer-made, in one-of-

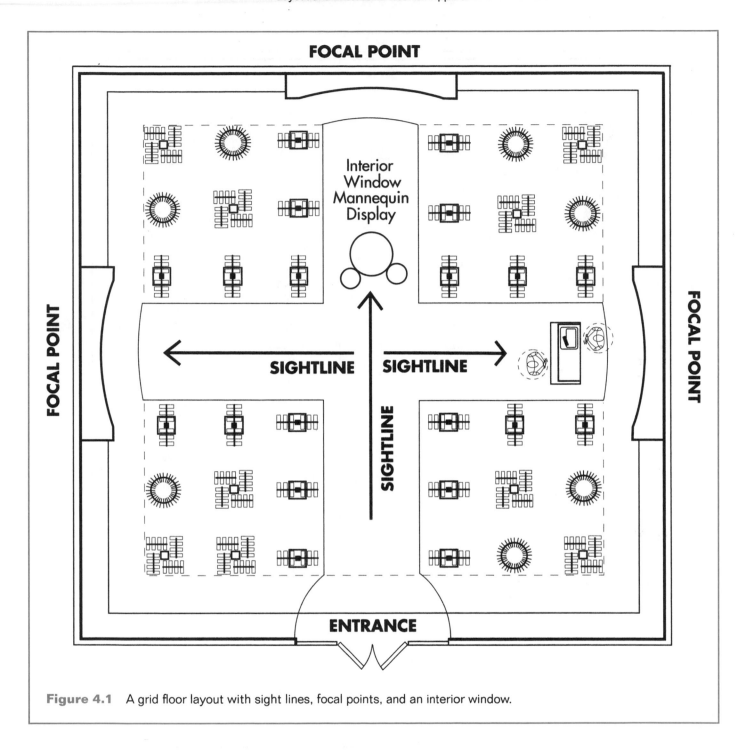

Figure 4.1 A grid floor layout with sight lines, focal points, and an interior window.

a-kind fabrications. More often, however, this layout is used in very high end retail stores with designer merchandise (Dolce and Gabana, Soho, New York City). Borrowing from the artistic school of aesthetic minimalism, products are presented dramatically on the walls of the store—much like art objects—with a minimal use of selling fixtures on the floor. This allows for wide-open spaces in the center of the store, where customers may stand and survey the entire offering of the collection before they approach the merchandise for a closer look. The minimal layout option requires dramatic merchandise, simple display strategies, and effective sales associates. (See Figure 4.5.)

The **combination floor layout** employs the best features of standard layouts in one overall plan that suits the retailer's specific strategy. A department store may use a mini-

A **combination floor layout** employs the best features of several selling floor layouts in an overall plan that suits a retailer's specific strategy.

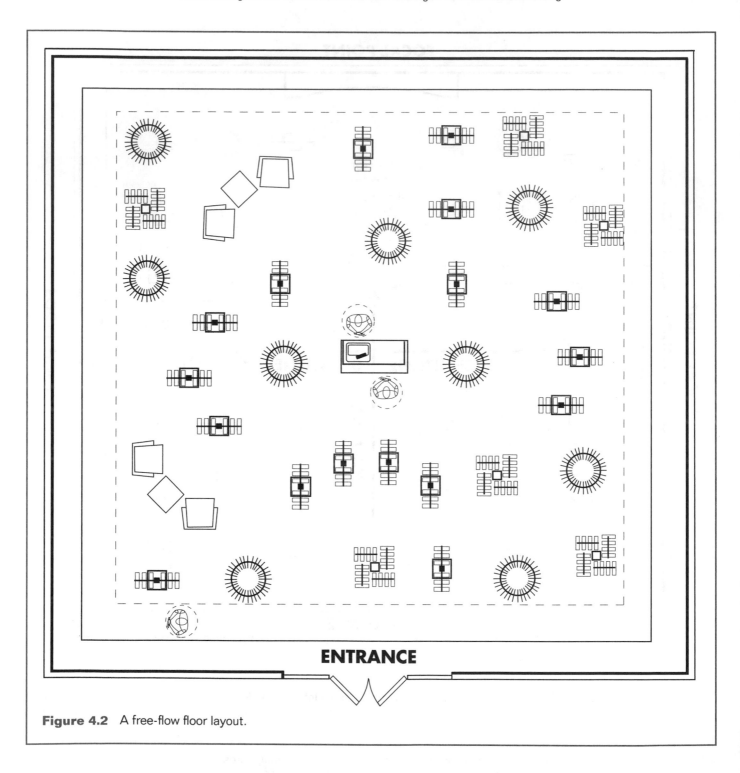

ENTRANCE

Figure 4.2 A free-flow floor layout.

mal layout for its more upscale departments, and a free-flow layout for its junior sportswear department. (See Figure 4.6.)

A specialty store may combine a free-flow layout in the first third of the store and a grid layout for a clearance department in the rear of the store.

Guidelines for Universal Access

In a chapter of *Why We Buy* titled "Shop Like a Man," Paco Underhill reports testing a new concept for a denim jeans area at a department store whose merchandising goal targeted

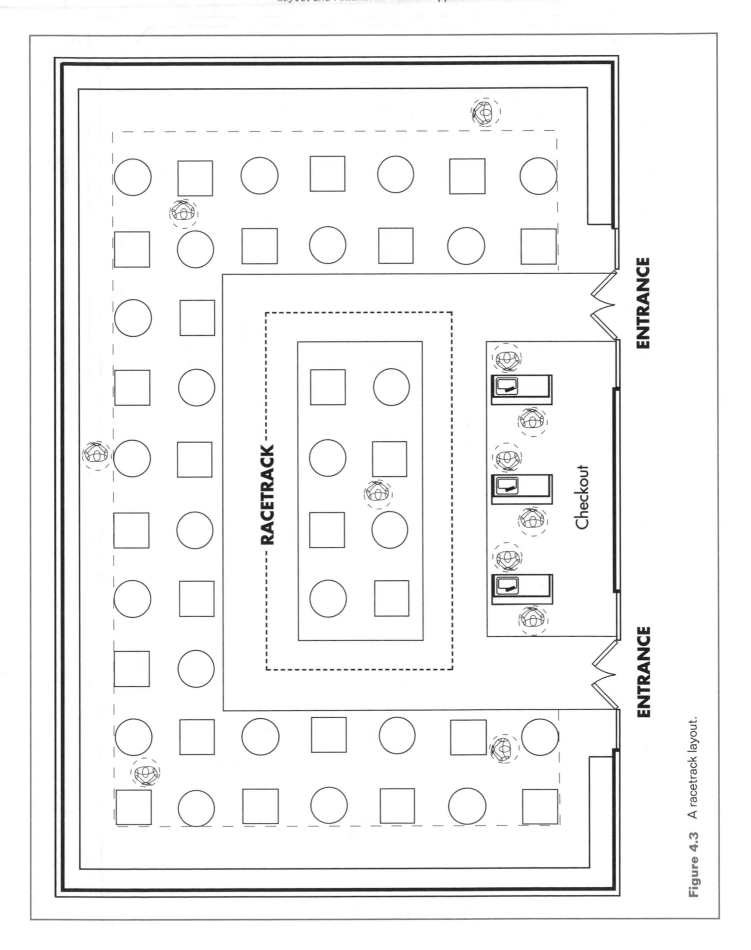

Figure 4.3 A racetrack layout.

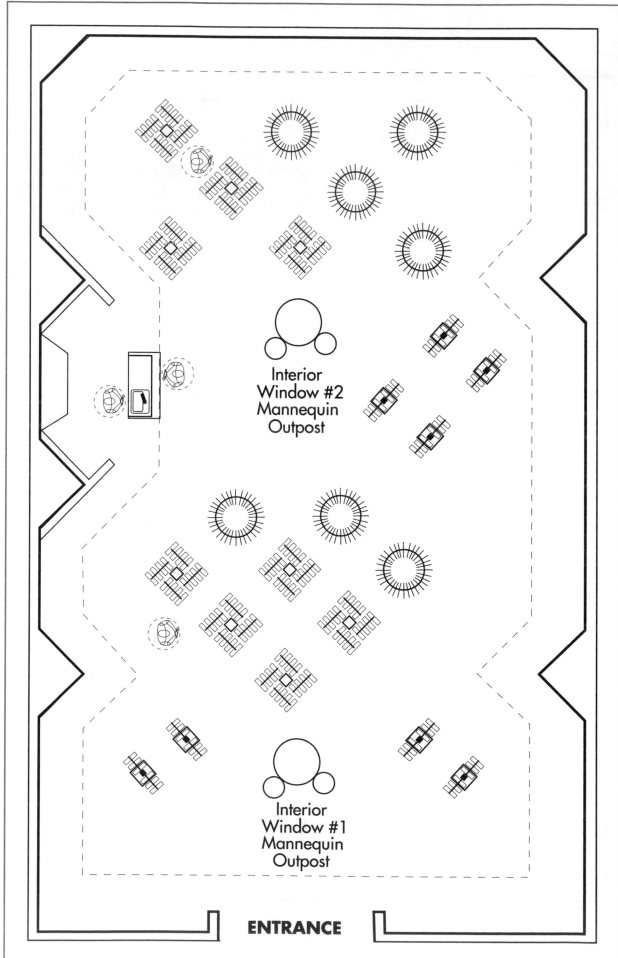

Interior
Window #2
Mannequin
Outpost

Interior
Window #1
Mannequin
Outpost

ENTRANCE

Figure 4.4 A soft aisle floor layout with fixture groupings and 5-foot aisles along perimeter walls. Notice focal wall locations and two interior windows.

Figure 4.5 A minimal floor layout in Trufaux, Soho, New York City.

men in their twenties and thirties. On video, researchers captured the image of a young man pushing a baby stroller walking down a main aisle with his wife. When they arrived at the denim jeans department, the tape showed that he couldn't maneuver the stroller through a maze of close-set floor fixtures. Underhill says, "He did what most people would do in that situation. He skipped the pants."

A great deal of retailing's collective selling floor is still off-limits to too many shoppers—a problem largely solved when retailers comply with both the spirit and the letter of regulations spelled out in the Americans with Disabilities Act (ADA) or design their stores to follow the principles of *universal design,* as established by the design center at the North Carolina State University (**www.design.ncsu/cud**).

Retailers may need to discuss these issues with architectural or store planning consultants who know the rules for access to public spaces and can interpret these requirements efficiently and accurately. Another option would entail consultation with an architect who embraces and practices the principles of universal design.

The mission of universal design is to "simplify life for everyone by making products, communications, and the built environment (retail stores, for example) more usable by as many people as possible at little or no extra cost. Universal design benefits people of all ages and abilities."

Two principles of universal design speak to selling floor spaces: Principle one relates to "equitable use" and says that a design should be "useful and marketable to people with

Figure 4.6 A combination floor layout in Levi's, Macy's Herald Square, New York City.

diverse abilities." The goal of principle two is to design building elements and furnishings of an appropriate size and space for approach, reach, manipulation, and use regardless of user's body size, posture, or mobility. Its guidelines include

- Providing a clear line of sight to important elements for any seated or standing user
- Making reach to all components comfortable for any seated or standing user
- Accommodating variations in hand and grip size
- Providing adequate space for the use of assistive devices or personal assistance

Layouts within Selling Departments

All of the store layouts discussed can be either permanent or nonpermanent. *Permanent layouts* indicate that the location of departmental selling areas within a store seldom changes. Since department stores are large, often with three or more floors, it is costly to move entire departments. Even more important, customers can become confused if their favorite shopping areas constantly shift from floor to floor.

Discount stores do not usually change department locations, but they may expand or contract categories according to sales trends. A 24-foot gondola fixture with camping gear and apparel could expand to two 24-foot gondola runs during camping season. There are usually two or three traditional "swing spaces" in discount stores, and customers soon adapt to the seasonal shift when this week's lawn and garden section becomes next month's back-to-school department. Effective directional and informational signing helps orient customers to the location of seasonal merchandise.

Several types of specialty stores maintain permanent floor layouts:

- Designer stores catering to customers who visit regularly to purchase specific brands or designer fashions. In stores featuring just one designer or brand, there are often shoes, handbags, accessories, fragrances, and cosmetics, in addition to fashion apparel. "Home bases" for these accessory departments are often designed into the architecture of the store and not easily shifted to other locations.

- Career stores for men, women, or both, where suits, career separates, and shoes are the most important items featured. This merchandise is always positioned at the entrance and front of the store. Accessories, casual wear, and coats are located toward the middle and rear of the store. Ann Taylor is an example of such a store.

- Specialty stores with merchandise for both men and women rely on permanent layouts. Shoppers would become confused if these departments shifted location without notice. Examples are Banana Republic, Gap, J.Crew, Club Monaco, and Express.

Nonpermanent layouts imply that changes do occur. Some small- to medium-sized specialty stores and outlet stores change the locations of departments according to trends and seasonal changes. These retailers consider the front third of the store to be the prime selling space, and they take advantage of the stores' manageable size to rotate their product offerings routinely.

Seasonal rotation of stock allows stores to present

- A "fresh face" to shoppers, implying that the store is very responsive to new and exciting fashion developments
- Current season or trend merchandise in cutting edge merchandising schemes that inform and invite
- Preseason merchandise at special prices in prime store locations, allowing store buyers to take an early "reading" on which items to buy in depth for the rest of the season

A Retail Reality:
Merchants base floor layout moves on sales data from previous years, so they can evaluate dollar results of merchandise in prime selling space. If a specific merchandise classification did well in one floor location last year, it may make sense to present it there again. If a classification (specific merchandise category) did not perform well in that area, sales data can point the decision makers to another location.

Presenting Current Season Merchandise

In the specialty store merchandising example that follows, the first third of the store features products that customers are currently seeking. In the floor layout shown in Figure 4.7 for March and April, the career department is positioned on the right side of the store at the entrance. This is prime selling space, and since shoppers are looking for new spring suits in March and April, it seems wise to present career wear at the front of the store. There's a bonus to this move—passersby may see the presentation from outside as they approach the store and come in to shop.

In Figure 4.7, you see dresses located next to the career department. Here's the strategy—if a customer is unable to make a selection in the career department, she may notice an appealing dress in the neighboring area and be drawn further into the store's selling space. This explains why selling areas must be laid out in a logical progression, often referred to as **adjacencies.**

Look at Figure 4.7 again. Casual spring sweaters, shirts, and pants are also important during March and April, so they are placed at the front of the store. For this merchant, presenting both casual and career categories at the front of the store may appeal to a wider range of shoppers. It's a workable plan because the merchant has a broad storefront. However, a store with a narrow front would present just a single merchandise category or fashion trend statement in prime selling space, positioning remaining departments in order of importance (based on sales history).

You can see how the floor layout might change for the next time period, May to June, by looking at the layout in Figure 4.8. Lightweight casual wear dominates the entire front of the store, anticipating the warmer season. Many remaining items from early spring career, dress, and coat categories have been shifted to the store's clearance area. In mid-June, fall merchandise begins to flow in and is positioned at the rear of the store. In mid-July, it will be moved to the front of the store to kick off back-to-school shopping.

Adjacencies are thoughtfully planned layouts that position same "end use" products next to each other. A logical adjacency, for example, would be shoes and hosiery positioned side by side.

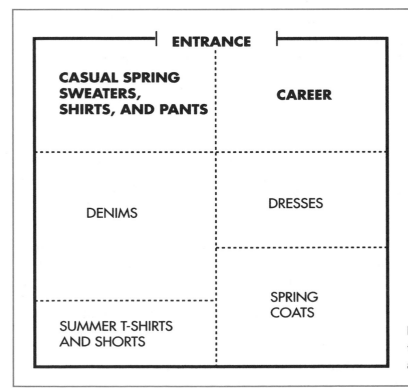

Figure 4.7 A specialty store selling floor layout for March and April. This layout is nonpermanent, and would change seasonally.

Figure 4.8 A specialty store selling floor layout for May to June. Notice how it changes from the March to April layout.

Presenting Preseason and Test Merchandise

The retail fashion cycle that drives sales and departmental presentations is a bell-shaped curve. The fashion cycle begins with a nearly flat line that represents "incoming" or "test" merchandise. Buyers introduce items in small quantities to the department in order to determine how shoppers will respond to them before they commit to larger orders. As shoppers react, the test merchandise is either cleared out—signaling a poor response—or reordered in greater depth. If reordered, the item is expected to rise in popularity with correspondingly solid regular-priced sales (*prepeak* in the cycle). As sales increase, you will see the item *peak*. At this point the item's popularity with customers is firmly established, and sales are brisk. When everyone who wanted the item has made a purchase, the item's rate of sale will gradually (or quickly) diminish. This is known as the *postpeak* stage, where merchandise is marked down and cleared out of the department, so that new fashion goods can move in. (See Figure 4.9.) The fashion cycle is an important consideration when planning an item's position on the selling floor.

The front third of the store may be used to present preseason or test merchandise. Several fixtures of wool coats may be positioned strategically in the store's center front during the hottest months of the year for a preseason sale. Coats are offered at sale prices to pace-setting, fashion-forward customers who like to shop early for the newest fall and winter styles. By tracking sales results, this strategy allows store buyers to decide which styles, colors, and brands to reorder in greater depth for upcoming fall and winter selling seasons when the fashion-followers do their shopping. Naturally, the visual merchandising department has a role to play in this process by providing sales support with signing, graphics, or mannequin displays.

Individual Department Layouts

When merchandising a department or a specific merchandise category within department stores and specialty stores, each separate selling area is treated much like an individual

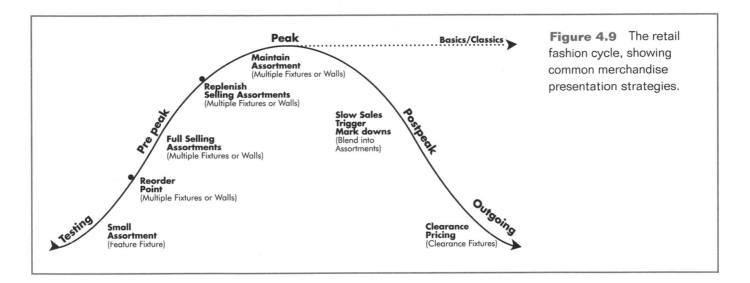

Figure 4.9 The retail fashion cycle, showing common merchandise presentation strategies.

store—especially when identifying prime selling space. Each department can be divided into five areas: trend, test, shops, basics, and key items. However, all five areas aren't always represented in every department.

Trend areas feature merchandise that has been accepted by shoppers as "hot" or current fashion. Items have been purchased in depth. The trend area may use display props, mannequins or forms, and large graphics to support the most exciting items. In Figure 4.10, the trend department is positioned along the main aisle of the store to take advantage of customer traffic. In Figure 4.11, the specialty store does not have a main aisle, so current trend products are featured at the front of the department.

The *test area* is set aside to sample merchandise representing items or styles the department's buyer believes will soon become popular with shoppers. To determine whether shoppers agree, the buyer brings in small quantities of goods to test shopper reaction and watches sales figures for these items closely. If customer response is strong, the buyer may make a larger purchase and greater dollar investment. Test merchandise is usually presented on **feature fixtures,** such as two-way or four-way selling racks.

Shops are created when similar types of merchandise are bought in depth (sufficient to fill six to ten selling fixtures) and are pulled together into one area of a department. To illustrate, the T-shirt dress shop in Figure 4.10 features T-shirt dresses pulled out of regu-

Feature fixtures typically hold smaller merchandise assortments, allowing presentation of a single style (on a two-way) or a coordinate grouping (on a four-way). They are intended to spotlight items rather than show full category assortments.

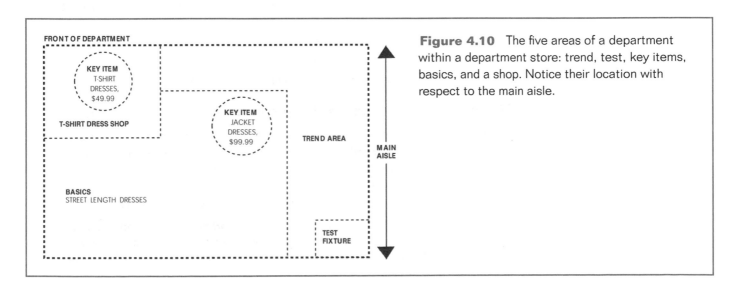

Figure 4.10 The five areas of a department within a department store: trend, test, key items, basics, and a shop. Notice their location with respect to the main aisle.

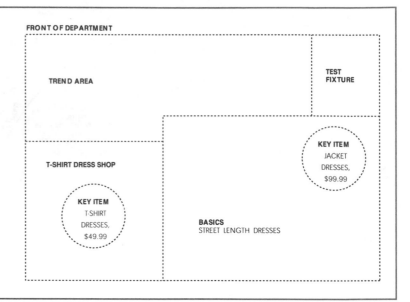

Figure 4.11 The five areas of a department within a specialty store: trend, test, key items, basics, and a shop. This store does not have a main aisle. Notice how this selling floor layout varies from that of Figure 4.10, which does have a main aisle.

lar dress stocks from several different vendors and presented at the front of the dress department. Products can also be pulled together by brand name to create a small shop within a department. Large quantities of a single brand name (10 to 20 fixtures of DKNY, for instance) could create an entire department.

Basics—the bulk of the stock in any department—are a department's core merchandise. The legs of basic denim jeans may be slim one season and then wide the next, but the denim jean classification stays the same. These items can be placed toward the back of a store or selling department because shoppers looking for basics will move into the area to find what they want. Other examples of basics include khaki pants, short sleeve T-shirts, and turtlenecks.

Key items are proven sellers that have been purchased in depth for the department and offered at a competitive price. They can be found in trend or basic areas and in shops. Key items are presented on fixtures that can hold large quantities of product, like tables, round racks, or shelving in a wall area. Key items often carry a store's private label. Rather than purchasing items in the traditional garment market, buyers purchase goods directly from manufacturers. The advantages of direct buying for key items are

● The store creates its own specifications and has the items modified to better fit the needs of its customer.

● The store creates its own unique brand name and has an opportunity to develop it to fit the image of target customers.

● The store is able to offer the items to customers at a lower price.

Merchandise Placement Guidelines

There is a step-by-step process to help you place fashion merchandise on selling fixtures so that people can quickly and easily find the styles they want. When merchandising methods are consistent throughout all the departments in your store, shoppers will be able to follow your lead and "work the racks" or "read" the shelves exactly as you hope they will. When this happens, shoppers turn into customers. Here are the four steps:

1. *Separate fashions by "end use" within each department.* For example, a dress department may carry dresses for several different end uses—casual, career, evening, and formal wear. These different dress classifications should be presented on separate fixtures.

2. *Separate fashions by fabrication.* Each classification of merchandise should also be separated by fabrication. Casual jumpers may be offered in both linen and cotton, and these fabrications must be presented separately.

3. *Separate fashions by style.* Casual cotton dresses, for example, may be offered in jumper styles, and low-waisted styles. These two styles should be presented on separate fixtures, or at least on separate arms of the same fixture.

   A cotton T-shirt dress may come in both short- and long-sleeve styles. Although the dresses could be presented on the same fixture because their end use and fabrication are the same, they should be placed on separate arms of the fixture. Short-sleeved sweaters and long-sleeved sweaters should not be presented together on the same garment rod in a wall area. Capri length pants would not be presented on the same garment rod as long trousers, nor would walking shorts and active shorts. In addition to different hem lengths, these "bottoms" have different end uses.

   Exception: Items that are coordinated by the manufacturer to be sold together as a group, may be merchandised together on the same fixture. The fact that these items have been designed to work together in a wardrobe may allow you to follow the designer's lead. You would still group the items by style; all sleeveless tops together, all shorts together, all jackets or sweaters together.

4. *Separate fashions by color group.* All fashions can be separated into one of the seven groups of color (see Colorplate 5). For example, T-shirt dresses that are offered in both brights and pastels must be presented on separate fixtures for the greatest degree of color impact. Remember that neutrals can be presented separately or combined with any of the other color groups.

How to Sort Merchandise

End use

Fabrication

Style

Color

Clearance Merchandise

Clearance merchandise consists of products that have been permanently marked down for quick sale. These items may be handled in several ways

- Clearance items may be pulled together at the rear of each department. For example, clearance suits may be positioned on one or more fixtures at the rear of the career department.

- Clearance merchandise from all departments may be pulled into one area of the store to form a permanent clearance department. This catch-all clearance department should be positioned in the rear of the store. Think about the Gap and Banana Republic. Customers will routinely check the clearance department for bargains as they shop. Retailers like Saks and Neiman Marcus take this process a step further— moving their clearance collections to separate "clearance floors."

- Clearance merchandise in specialty stores may be pulled to the front of the store for traditional major clearance events in January or early July.

- Some chain retailers consolidate clearance merchandise into a few larger stores (with high traffic or ideal bargain shopper demographics), send it to a company-owned outlet store, or remove their own tags and sell the lot to an outlet store.

Clearance Presentation Guidelines

While clearance merchandise no longer merits major promotional effort, it remains a company asset until sold. The visual merchandiser's role is to present clearance goods effectively enough to sell them at their highest possible clearance price so that the company can

A Retail Reality:
Display signs must be accurate and correspond to what's being presented, or customers will be confused (or angry) about what seem to be careless or deceptive sale policies. Stores generally honor mistaken prices or sale terms—an unnecessary embarrassment and financial loss. Customer service is a visual merchandising responsibility, too.

Price points are the actual *numbers* ($12.99) used on signs to inform shoppers of prices.

"Ask leading retailers about purchasing store fixtures and they invariably point to three important criteria: cost, quality, and service. Although price of the fixture is always of concern, the real priority seems to be cost effectiveness. Retailers want to spend the least amount of money possible but still meet project expectations."

Karen Doodeman, director of marketing, National Association of Store Fixture Manufacturers (NASFM)

reinvest the dollars in newer, more appealing merchandise. The following guidelines will ensure that optimum presentation is achieved:

1. *Present clearance merchandise on floor fixtures only.* Clearance product with broken styles and color assortment cannot result in a fresh, exciting wall presentation; wall space is best used for new stock. The exception is when clearance merchandise is presented on an entirely separate clearance floor. There, you may utilize the entire space—walls and floor.

2. *Never feature clearance merchandise on mannequins or in displays.* These are your premium silent selling tools and must be reserved for only the newest products. In addition, clearance merchandise must be *immediately available* to shoppers, never out of reach on display.

3. *Present clearance goods on large fixtures,* such as round racks, superquads (extra large four-way racks with arms that may be extended) or rolling rack fixtures. Clearance tables for foldable goods are very effective because there is a general perception among shoppers that clearance tables hold the best bargains.

4. *Sort clearance garments by size* (with sizing rings or hangers with built-in size tabs) *and then by color within each size range* so that shoppers can readily see what is available. Example: Size 5 (red shirts, yellow shirts, and blue shirts) followed by size 7 (red shirts, yellow shirts, green shirts, and blue shirts).

5. *Always clearly sign clearance merchandise* with **price points,** percentages-off, or at least a clearance sign.

6. *Make selling floor maintenance a routine aspect of any clearance presentation.* Clearance merchandise gets handled (and mishandled) continuously as shoppers look for bargains. Store staff must check clearance areas frequently, straightening sale racks, refolding table goods, checking for damaged goods and lost tickets, etc. These are aesthetic as well as security issues that tell customers how your company feels about its image, its merchandise, and its atmosphere. Customers should see clearance merchandise as an added benefit to doing business with your store. Even when merchandise is marked down, you should be adding value to it through your presentation.

Store Fixtures

A wide variety of fixtures is available for the presentation of products. Like the furniture in your home, each fixture type has a useful purpose (holding quantities of merchandise) and a decorative purpose (reinforcing retail décor decisions). Store fixtures include

- Conventional metal fixtures
- Furniture fixtures
- "Found" objects
- Vendor fixtures
- Custom fixtures

Purchasing the store's fixtures is a long-term and expensive investment—much like furnishing a home. Just as you wouldn't buy a new sofa simply because you've had one for a while, visual merchandisers expect the store fixtures they select to perform effectively and efficiently for as long as possible. They must choose carefully, taking purpose, function, and durability into consideration along with style and fabrication.

Capacity, Feature, and Signature Fixtures

In addition to the various types of fixtures retailers may choose from, each fixture category can be further differentiated by its end use.

- **Capacity fixtures** hold large quantities—usually showing one style of a product bought in depth, like several dozen sweatshirts, in assorted sizes from S to XXL, trimmed with a variety of colorful cartoon characters. Because capacity fixtures are the largest floor fixtures in the store, they should be positioned primarily in the rear of a department or store layout.

- **Feature fixtures** are designed to hold fewer items and are used to highlight category groupings or smaller coordinate groups. You might see a four-way fixture with a dozen cotton sweaters in bright yarns paired with matching polo shirts and walking shorts. Feature fixtures bring together coordinated outfits to make shopping easier. They are best used as lead-in fixtures to any department, but may also be interspersed throughout a department to add interest and variation to the layout.

- **Signature fixtures** are one-of-a-kind units that are positioned at the entrance to a store or department. Their unusual, unique design is created specifically to attract shoppers' attention. The signature fixture's design must reflect the brand image of the store, both in fabrication and style. (See Figures 4.12 and 4.13.)

A **capacity fixture** holds large quantities of merchandise, usually showing a single style in several colors and in a complete range of sizes.

A **signature fixture** is an attention-getting, one-of-a-kind unit positioned at the entrance to a store or department that reflects the store's brand image.

Conventional Metal Floor Fixtures

Simple metal fixtures like round racks and T-stands have been used in retail stores throughout the twentieth century. Their design forms the basis from which custom fixtures are created, so it is important to have a solid understanding of their function. Early fixtures were fabricated in chrome, and they are still widely used today. In the 1980s and 1990s, some retailers used brushed bright black, brushed satin black, and even white finishes. Today, brushed stainless steel and buffed satin are often preferred for their softer, less reflective look, which is easier to maintain because fingerprints are less visible.

Round Racks

A **round rack** (rounder) is a capacity fixture. Its chief function is stocking basic items that have been purchased in depth. Round racks are also used to stock broken assortments (*broken* refers to assortments with missing sizes, styles, and colors after sell down) and clearance merchandise. This fixture is available in several diameters and adjustable heights so that dresses and slacks can be presented with their hems an adequate distance from the floor. (See Figure 4.14.)

A **round rack** (rounder) is a capacity fixture fabricated in several diameters and adjustable heights for stocking basic apparel items.

Figure 4.12 A signature in Ulta Cosmetics & Salon, Las Colinas, Irving, Texas.

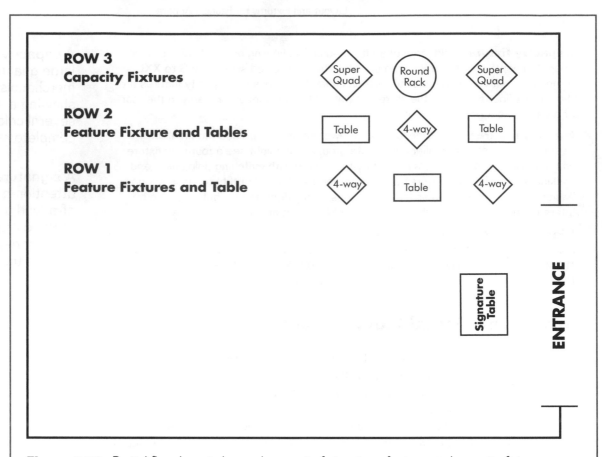

Figure 4.13 Partial floor layout shows placement of signature, feature, and capacity fixtures leading to wall. Lower, smaller fixtures are in front two rows; taller, larger fixtures, in back.

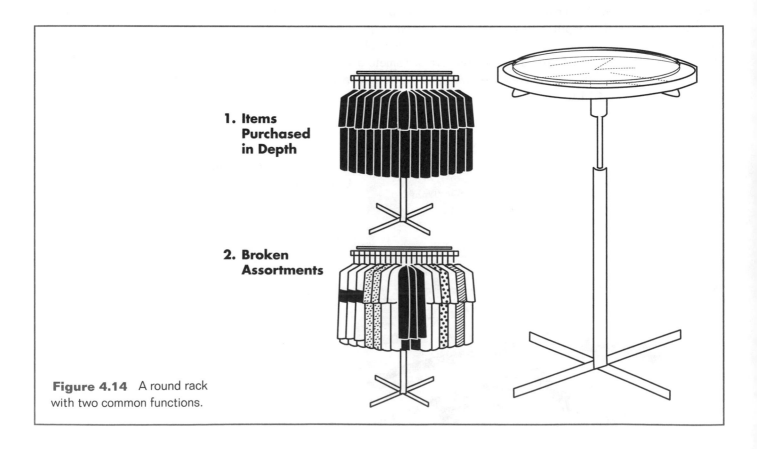

Figure 4.14 A round rack with two common functions.

You can easily determine fixture fill for a round rack by measuring the circumference. A 36-inch diameter round rack is 118 inches in circumference. It can comfortably hold 118 tops or bottoms. A 42-inch diameter round rack is 136 inches in circumference, and it could hold 136 tops or bottoms. If garments are thinner, like T-shirts, the quantities increase; if they are thicker, like winter coats, the capacity will decrease.

Presentation Guidelines for Round Racks

1. Round racks should *not* be positioned at the store entrance or along aisles except during special promotional and clearance events. At those times it may be effective to line them up along the aisles or down the center of the store.

2. Sleeve lengths and hem lengths should be the same on the entire fixture, unless the rack is being used for clearance merchandise.

3. A single rack should hold products from just one of the seven color groups, for the best presentation. Neutrals may be combined with any group.

4. Arrange colors in a sequence that follows the natural color order of the rainbow— red, orange, yellow, green, blue, violet. Begin the color sequence at the nine o'clock position as you stand in front of a round rack and work *counterclockwise*. If there are neutral colors, they should be added so that they follow the rainbow assortment, and range from lightest to darkest tints.

An easy way to remember the rainbow sequence is with the mnemonic device *Roy G. Bv* (the *Bv* can be pronounced "Biv"), which stands for red, orange, yellow, green, blue, violet. The mnemonic may be used as a training tool to ensure that there is continuity in the color arrangement of merchandise on fixtures in any size retail organization. Roy can function as an "invisible visual merchandiser," in charge of all color decisions! (See Figure 4.15.)

A Retail Reality:
Fixtures should never be so overstocked that shoppers have difficulty previewing items. A simple way to determine fixture fill (the quantity of merchandise a fixture will hold) is to measure the length of the fixture arm or garment rod. You can hang one item per inch of its length—a 12-inch arm holds 12 garments. If items are thinner, like T-shirts, you may be able to add more pieces. If the items are thicker, the arm may hold fewer pieces.

Figure 4.15 An easy way to remember color flow with the mnemonic device, Roy G. Bv.

All color schemes are based on relationships to the basic rainbow colors described by Roy G. Bv, except for neutrals. See Colorplate 5. In the pastel color group, pastel pink relates to bright red, peach relates to bright orange, pastel yellow relates to bright yellow, and so on. Even looking at the earth tones, you'll see that wine relates to red, rust relates to orange, gold relates to yellow, and so on.

Some presentation guides advise arranging colors from light to dark. However, perception and interpretation of color values is an individual thing, so a light-to-dark guideline offers no guarantee of storewide color continuity. One of the biggest drawbacks to a light to dark color sequence allows bright schemes, jewel tones, midtones, and pastels to be mixed on a rack—at the expense of strong color impact. If the store you work in recommends the light-to-dark coloration format, you will need to use it; but if you have a choice, we believe that rainbow colorization is easier and will provide more impact in your fashion presentations.

If the round rack is used for clearance merchandise, first size the items, then colorize within each size. Example: size 5—red, yellow, blue; size 7—red, yellow blue; size 9—red, yellow, blue. The smallest size, 5, should be positioned on the side of the fixture that faces the front of the department and then sized from there, working to your right (counter-clockwise).

The round rack has one variation—the trilevel round rack. (See Figure 4.16.) This fixture has three levels that are all height-adjustable. It's an ideal fixture to separate garments with differing sleeve lengths or show a group of top and bottom coordinates. Each of the three sections provides 39 inches of hanging capacity, so the trilevel could hold 117 garments (1 inch per garment). The lowest level of the trilevel round rack should always face the front of the department or an aisle. Like the round rack, this capacity fixture should be positioned primarily toward the rear of any department.

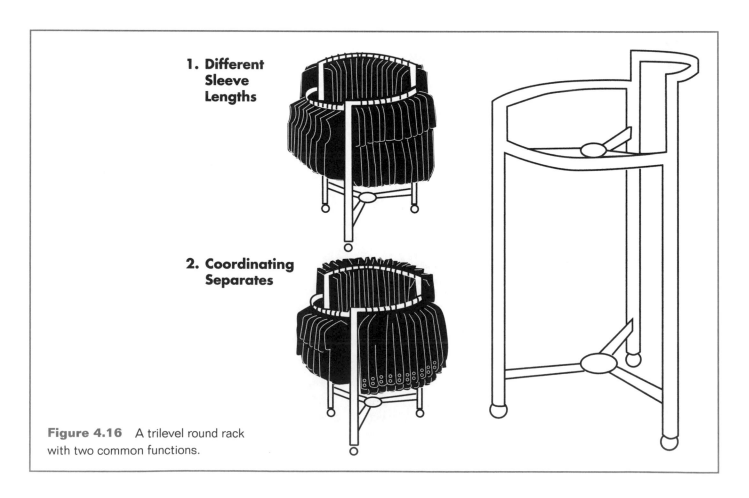

1. Different Sleeve Lengths

2. Coordinating Separates

Figure 4.16 A trilevel round rack with two common functions.

Superquads

The **superquad** is a four-armed capacity fixture designed to hold basic items that have been purchased in depth. (See Figure 4.17.) It allows display of items with different sleeve or hem lengths and works extremely well to feature coordinate groupings composed of pants, skirts, blouses, and sweaters or jackets. The superquad is useful to show broken or unrelated assortments and can be used for a collection of clearance merchandise, as well.

The arms of a superquad can be set at a variety of heights. One technique is to start low in the front of the fixture, setting each level a few inches higher as you move around the fixture, from left to right. Another method is to set the arms with tops higher than the arms with bottoms. This is a natural look, because that's the way tops and bottoms are worn. The arms of a superquad should be colorized from left to right. Begin with the arm that is in the 9 o'clock position and move counterclockwise around the fixture. (See Figure 4.18.)

Gondolas

In a plan view (view from above), **gondolas** resemble the Roman numeral one or capital letter I. (See Figure 4.19.) The ends of the gondola are called **endcaps.** A gondola's length can range from as short as 48 inches in a small specialty store to 60 feet or more in a superstore. Approachable from all four sides, these versatile capacity fixtures are used by discount stores to house basic merchandise like socks and intimate apparel—usually faced-out on pegs. Foldable and boxed merchandise can be stacked on gondola shelves. Large gondolas must be disassembled in order to be moved. Consequently, floor layouts seldom change. Specialty stores use shorter gondolas that often have locking wheels or casters so that they're easy to move when resetting the selling floor. Gondolas can be colorized from left to right, using Roy G. Bv. Product should be arranged with smaller items on the top shelves, moving to larger items on the bottom shelves.

A **superquad** is a four-armed capacity fixture with an adjustable height feature for showing items purchased in depth or coordinate groupings of pants, skirts, blouses, and sweaters or jackets.

A **gondola** is a versatile four-sided capacity fixture that may be shelved for folding or stackable products, and is occasionally set with garment rods to show apparel on hangers.

Endcaps are valuable display and stocking spaces at the ends of gondola fixtures. They may be used to feature a sampling of the merchandise on either side of the gondola, for new merchandise offerings, for value-priced products, or for advertised specials. They may be either pegged or shelved.

1. Different Sleeve Lengths

2. Coordinating Separates

Figure 4.17 A superquad with two common functions.

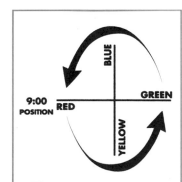

Figure 4.18

Directional color flow with a superquad fixture. Notice the color flow begins at the 9:00 position. This technique may be used with any floor fixture.

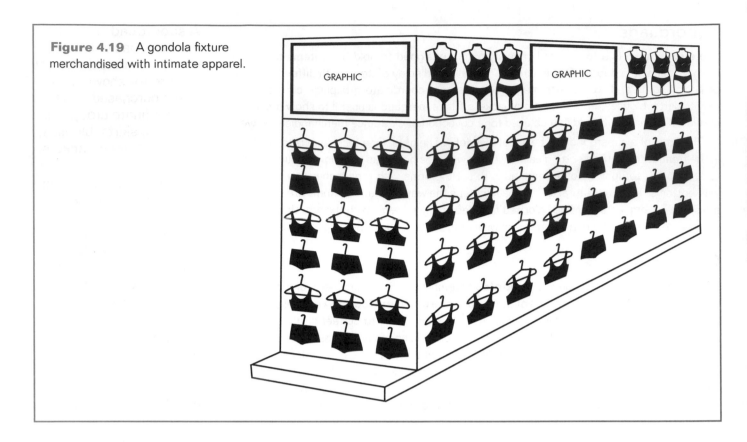

Figure 4.19 A gondola fixture merchandised with intimate apparel.

Bins and Cubes

Bins and cubes are interchangeable terms, although many retailers define cubes as containers that are open on their sides and define bins as containers that are open from their tops. You might see tilted bins used for bulk items like candy or filled with nuts and bolts in a hardware store, while cubes are reserved for use in fashion stores as wall treatments or in stand-alone floor fixtures.

When used as selling floor fixtures holding folded fashion merchandise, cubes are permanently stacked on gondola bases and ranked in pairs so that they are "shoppable" from both sides. It isn't unusual to find entire walls of folded basics arrayed in banks of cubes. The visual impact of a cubed wall with a rainbow array of goods stacked from ceiling to floor is tremendous. It tells shoppers that the store has a wide selection of merchandise.

Basic fashion items that come in several colors and straightforward sizing sell well from cube fixtures. A floor fixture with basic turtlenecks in four colors and three sizes is shown in Figure 4.20. This is an extremely adaptable fixture from a merchandising point of view—systematic and uniform. The cubes you see in the denim presentation (Figure 4.21) can be merchandised by fabric finishes, colors (stone-washed to black), waist and inseam sizes, and leg styles. Similarly, the shirts in Figure 4.22 are presented by size and color. That's exactly the kind of versatility retailers need from a fixture.

Guidelines for Fashion Cubes

1. Arrange Roy G. Bv colors vertically. Begin with one vertical column of red, followed by one column each of orange, yellow, green, blue, and violet. Work from left to right. (See Figure 4.20.) If stock quantities are too low to support an entire vertical column, use vertical colorization in at least the top two or three cubes that are most visible in the department.

2. Size the cubes with the smallest size at the top moving down to the largest sizes.

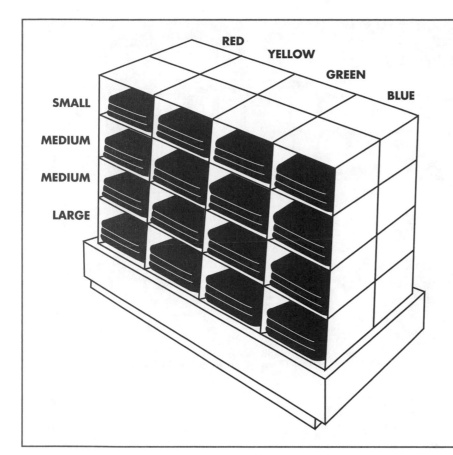

Figure 4.20 A floor fixture of stacked cubes merchandised with basic turtlenecks in three sizes and four colors.

SMALL

MEDIUM

MEDIUM

LARGE

RED

YELLOW

GREEN

BLUE

Figure 4.21 A floor fixture with jeans in cubes, arranged by fabric finishes, color, size, and leg style.

Stone Washed Denim	Deep Blue Denim	Khaki	Black
29x30 29x30 29x30	29x30 29x30 29x30	29x30 29x30 29x30	29x30 29x30 29x30
Straight Leg	Straight Leg	Tapered Leg	Tapered Leg
30x30 30x32 31x30	30x30 30x32 31x30	30x30 30x32 31x30	30x30 30x32 31x30
32x32 33x32 33x30	32x32 33x32 33x30	32x32 33x32 33x30	32x32 33x32 33x30
34x32 34x34 35x30	34x32 34x34 35x30	34x32 34x34 35x30	34x32 34x34 35x30

Figure 4.22 The display of men's shirts at H&M in Chicago makes it easy for customers to find the sizes and colors they want.

Conventional Floor Feature Fixtures

There are several styles of conventional floor feature fixtures, but those used most commonly in retail stores today are **two-ways** (T-stands), and **four-ways** (costumers). They are used to feature small quantities of trend merchandise, test merchandise, and coordinates and separates that are being presented as coordinated outfits. Feature fixtures present coordinated fashion looks that will build multiple sales—an opportunity for silent selling. Shoppers look to feature fixtures for fashion advice. In a way, you're selecting the best for shoppers to see and try. (See Figure 4.23.)

Presentation Guidelines for Feature Fixtures

Standard two-way (T-stand) and four-way feature fixtures may have either straight arms or slant (waterfall) arms providing flexible configurations for merchandisers. Additional arms may be added to double or triple hang intimate apparel or children's wear. On some fixtures, the fixtures' arm styles are interchangeable; others are fixed. In either case, the following guidelines will ensure the best use of these fixtures:

1. *Use feature fixtures to highlight only the newest and most exciting items in stock.* Basic items like turtlenecks should not be presented on a feature fixture.

2. *Present a single color story on each fixture.* Choose just one of the seven color groups (Colorplate 5) for a single fixture. Neutrals may be combined with any color group. Look at Colorplates 9A and 9B. In the incorrect example, the pastels and

A **two-way fixture,** also called a T-stand, is a two-armed hanging fixture used to feature small quantities (12–24 items) of trend apparel or test merchandise.

A **four-way fixture,** also called a costumer, features a hanging coordinate group or a small (24–48 items) quantity of separates presented as coordinated outfits.

brights presented together on the fixture are out of harmony. In the correct example, products are from the same bright color group. The result is a pleasing, well-coordinated pairing that makes fashion sense. If you're working with a coordinate group, you will need to show the grouping as presented by the manufacturer (regardless of what you think a proper color scheme should be).

3. *Use feature fixtures to hold products from similar merchandising classifications that have the same end uses.* You would never feature career suits on two arms of a four-way fixture along with two arms of shorts and T-shirts.

4. For maximum visual impact, *use two-way and four-way fixtures to feature only* one style of garment per single arm faceout; only one color of garment per single arm faceout; and only one fabrication per single arm faceout. For example, an arm with six red cardigan sweaters is correct. An arm with three red cardigan sweaters and three yellow cardigan sweaters is incorrect.

5. *Use feature fixtures to show outfits,* that is, tops and bottoms that coordinate. This device facilitates silent selling, creating opportunities for multiple sales.

6. *Reset feature fixtures with new items weekly or biweekly.*

7. *Position feature fixtures in front of the store and along major aisles.* If there are no major aisles, they should be positioned at the front of each department.

8. *Adjust feature fixtures heights* as needed. To determine the correct fixture height, the product on the fixture should be hung at a height that reflects the way a customer might wear it. For example, pant hemlines should be set about 3 inches from the floor. Set any higher, the pants do not look natural. Knee length dresses should skim about 17 inches from the floor. Midcalf hems could be shown lower; perhaps 8–12 inches from the floor. In any case, garment hems should *never* touch the floor. All other fixtures in the store should be adjusted to reflect hemline uniformity. Keep in mind that tops should be hung on arms that are set several inches higher than arms with pants.

9. *Present pants only on straight arms, never slant arms.* This is because slant arms would have to be set too high to accommodate the cascading leg lengths.

A Retail Reality:
Stores come in all sizes and all budgets. If you read that you should never mix colors on a T-stand and *your* store buys in large quantities—the rule stands. It's a current "best practice." If your store buys only four sweaters per style and color, you're going to have to adapt the rule to fit your unique situation. This is true for all "rules" in this text—reality must prevail.

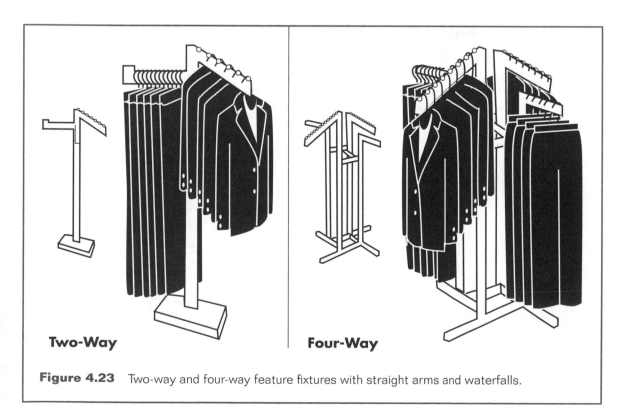

Two-Way   **Four-Way**

Figure 4.23   Two-way and four-way feature fixtures with straight arms and waterfalls.

Conventional Wall Capacity Fixtures
• •

Garment Rods and Crossbars

Round garment rods and flat metal crossbars are basic fixtures used to show large quantities of goods on hangers in walls. For continuity, only one style should be used throughout a store.

Garment rods and crossbars are secured to walls by inserting them into wall standards with 14-inch brackets. These wall standards are mounted at regular intervals—from 2 to 4 feet apart depending on the span of the wall and its structural underpinnings. The entire assembly is sometimes referred to as a *wall system*. (See Figure 4.24.)

A rubber mallet is essential for inserting brackets into wall standards. A gentle tap with a rubber mallet will secure the bracket and prevent the unsightly nicks that will occur with use of an ordinary hammer. Ends of the rods or bars are always "capped" with special snap-in hardware inserts to prevent merchandise from sliding off as shoppers push hangers back and forth. The mallet is a useful tool for tapping snap-in caps into place and later removing them.

Some garment rods and crossbars have caps already welded in place; with others, caps are separate accessories. Removable snap-in caps allow the merchandiser to join lengths of rod or bar with adapters to create longer wall presentations. Rods and crossbars can be purchased in several lengths (2–12 feet) and combined as needed. They can be a store's least expensive and most versatile fixturing device. However, they must be properly installed and supported every few feet for safety—protecting both merchandise and shoppers.

In addition to being used to hang merchandise, a crossbar can be applied to spans between wall system standards as a "bridge" when merchandisers want to use waterfalls and straight arms in spaces that don't have enough standards in the desired places. To secure the crossbar to wall standards, you'd use 3-inch brackets (rather than the 14-inch brackets used when products are hung "shoulder-out"). Once in place, waterfalls and straight arms can be slipped over the crossbar and positioned exactly where the merchandiser wants them. (See Figure 4.25.)

Slatwall and Gridwall

There are two other common wall system options known as **slatwall** and **gridwall.** With the slatwall system, a series of painted wood or laminate-covered horizontally grooved panels is applied directly to a wall. They look somewhat like wooden siding on a home. Gridwall is a series of wire panels fabricated in a variety of gridlike patterns permanently fastened to store walls by brackets and screws. Both slatwall and gridwall systems require a

A **slatwall** is a wall system of horizontal backer panels with evenly spaced slots that accept brackets and display accessories with special slatwall fittings.

A **gridwall** is a wall system of metal wire, which accepts brackets and display accessories with special gridwall fittings.

Figure 4.24   A wall system utilizing a garment rod.

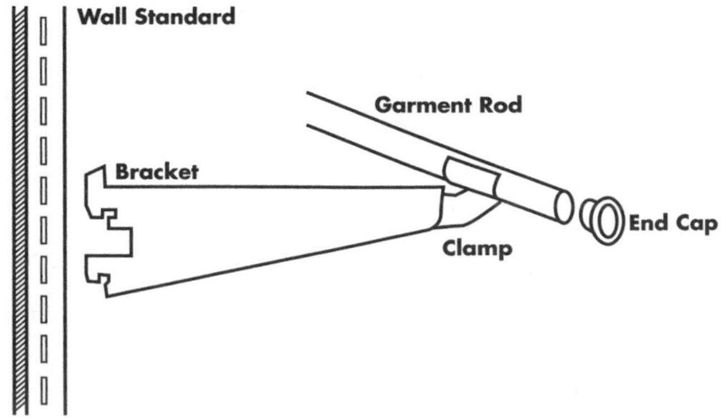

Wall Standard

Garment Rod

Bracket

End Cap

Clamp

unique type of hardware bracket on each garment rod, crossbar, straight arm, or waterfall. (See Figure 4.26.)

Wall System Accessories

Additional wall system fixturing options include specialized fixture accessories like six 12-inch pegs that hold prepackaged items on cards (i.e., packages of shoelaces, packs of socks, shrink-packed cosmetic products), handbag hooks, plus a variety of shoe, hat, and belt displayers. New designs in wall system accessories appear in trade magazines and catalogs every year. (See Figure 4.27.)

Shelving

Glass, wood, or colored plastic laminate shelving holds folded products like sweaters and jeans or accessories like handbags and hats. Shelves are generally 2 to 4 feet in length and are secured to wall standards with sturdy metal brackets. The number of brackets used per span of shelving will depend on the weight of the product load. Safety is the critical factor. Some retailers add transparent plastic edge moldings to keep items from slipping off accidentally. They may also add a plastic channel to the shelf edge for size and pricing information. Both gridwall and slatwall will accept shelving when the proper brackets are employed.

When presenting merchandise on wall system shelving, many retailers reserve the top shelves to feature displays of merchandise in combination with wall graphics. This practice adds eye-catching variety and height to the back of the departmental "skyline." It also en-

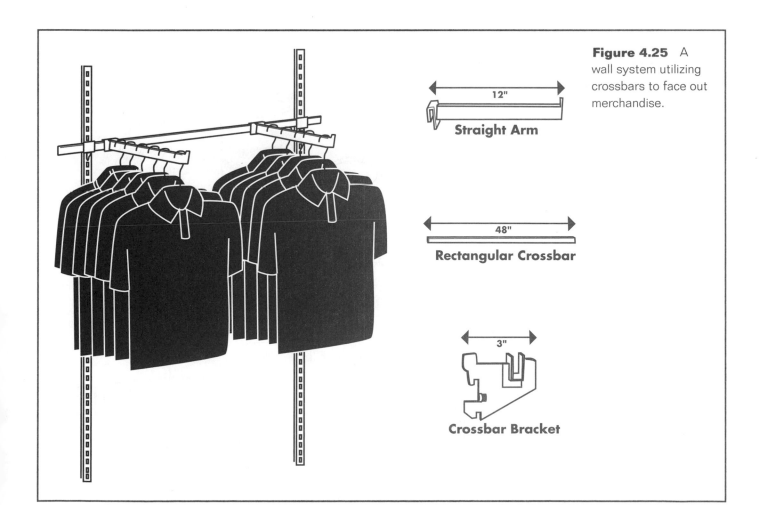

Figure 4.25 A wall system utilizing crossbars to face out merchandise.

12"
Straight Arm

48"
Rectangular Crossbar

3"
Crossbar Bracket

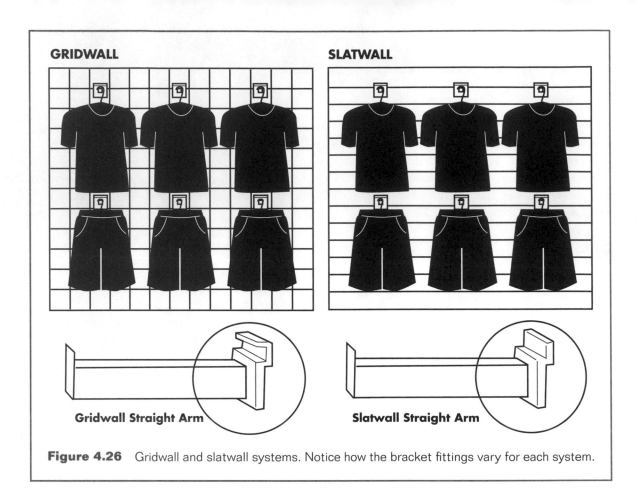

Figure 4.26 Gridwall and slatwall systems. Notice how the bracket fittings vary for each system.

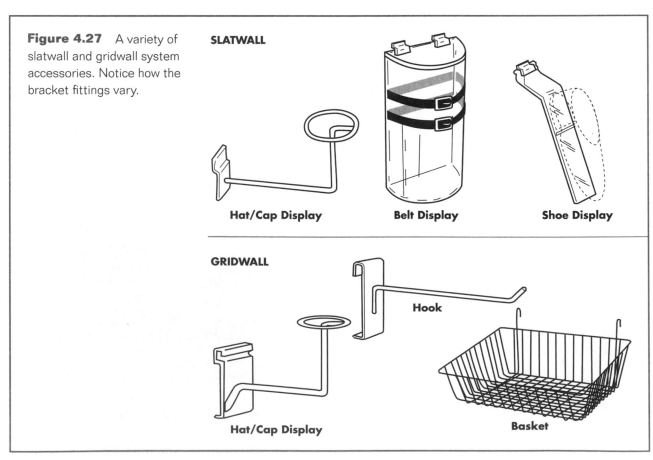

Figure 4.27 A variety of slatwall and gridwall system accessories. Notice how the bracket fittings vary.

hances shoppers' views from the front of the store or edge of the department, drawing them farther in to inspect merchandise.

Conventional Wall Feature Fixtures
Waterfalls

Waterfall fixtures (slant arms) display products on a wall, facing outward, so that the full front of the garment is visible. (See Figure 4.28.) This device employs 5 to 12 decorative (and functional) knobs or "stops" to space garments on hangers evenly. The waterfall is best used to feature tops, jackets, suits, or dresses. Pants and skirts do not merchandise well on waterfalls because the hanger tops are so prominent—all you see at fixture level is a cascade of plastic. When bottoms are shown as a straight-armed accompaniment to waterfalls of tops, their hangers are much less obvious.

A **waterfall** is an angled display arm affixed to a wall standard, slatwall or gridwall system, or a T-stand (two-way or four-way), or other selling floor fixture to show a cascade of hanging merchandise.

Straight Arms

Straight arms serve the same purpose as waterfalls—to make the full front of a single garment visible to shoppers. They are available in square and rectangular versions, in addition to round tubing. Either tops or bottoms may be featured on straight arms.

Straight arms are available with different styles of fittings so that they fit into gridwall and slatwall standards or clip over crossbars. (See Figure 4.29.)

A **straight arm** is a perpendicular display arm affixed to a wall standard, slatwall, or gridwall system or a T-stand or other selling floor fixture to show a small quantity of hanging merchandise.

Furniture Fixtures and Antiques

Furniture like hutches, desks, curio cabinets, tables, and armoires can be used as merchandising fixtures. (See Figure 4.30.) Also called *case pieces* or *case goods,* residential

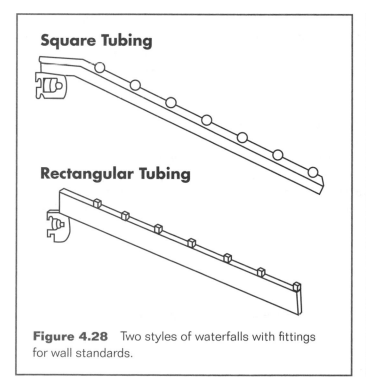

Figure 4.28 Two styles of waterfalls with fittings for wall standards.

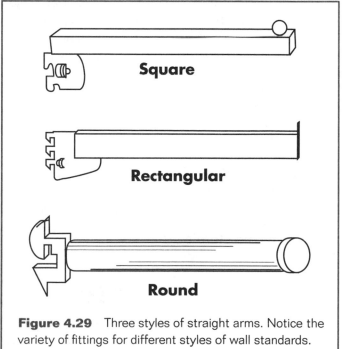

Figure 4.29 Three styles of straight arms. Notice the variety of fittings for different styles of wall standards.

Figure 4.30 Notice how retro-modern style furniture is used both as a fixture and an atmospheric element in UP Footgear, Grandville, Michigan.

A Retail Reality:
There should never be a conflict between focus on merchandise and focus on fixtures or display devices. When everything is working correctly, shoppers should always be more aware of the merchandise than the means of showing it. Store layout, atmospherics, fixture designs, or displays should never be more powerful than the message of the store's merchandise.

furnishings as fixtures may be "borrowed" from any design era, period, or style—from French provincial elegance to 1960s American sitcom. The only requirement is that each piece must fit the brand image of the store.

Antique furniture pieces may find new lives as capacity, feature, or premier fixtures. Shoppers enjoy seeing traditional furnishings put to new or unexpected uses (See the SCAMPER model, Chapter One). The addition of decorative and functional hardware to the inside doors of an old armoire, for example, can create a clever merchandising fixture for a jewelry presentation. Picture a marble-topped gentleman's dresser with several drawers pulled out at random filled with artfully rolled-up silk ties.

Furniture fixtures may also be used exclusively as display props, creating focal points and highlighting special products. They may serve a dual purpose and actually be a part of the store's merchandise inventory. For example, an antique armoire filled with ancient bed linens, lace doilies, and pillows may be for sale as well. The cupboard sells the linens and the linens sell the cupboard. Finally, it's also possible that furniture pieces may be used as nonmerchandising atmospheric elements—to add to the store's overall ambiance. The furniture fixtures in ABC Carpet in New York City, for example, perform all four functions, fixture, display, merchandise inventory, and ambiance.

Tables

The single most important fixture in the retail industry is the table. Tables of some type greet shoppers at the entrances to most stores or departments. Such display tables may be permanent fixtures or temporary installations with a mission. They can be circular and skirted to the floor, rectangular and as substantial as any fine wooden furniture, or a multilevel grouping of nested serving tables.

A table is an ideal introductory fixture because it has a low profile. It shows merchandise effectively at the front of a department while providing clear sight lines into the rest of the area—where more merchandise is presented.

Tables set out in midaisle also offer a great way to test or feature new items or offer regular products at special prices, enticing passers-by to stop and shop on impulse. Sale tables are effective during clearance periods because customers are conditioned to finding bargains on temporary tables. However, do not overuse the bargain table device. If you do, your bargain table strategy will lose impact and credibility with shoppers.

Special sale table tops that look like shallow boxes on legs are called "jumble" or "dump" tables because they will hold all types of sale items that might normally slide in all directions when shoppers sort through them. Stores that have tracked sales results for products presented on tables versus round racks have often found that tables are more productive. Perhaps it's the possibility of discovering a treasure that draws shoppers to them. Tables that look "jumbled" and "shopped" must be sorted, inspected for lost tickets or damage from rough handling, and rearranged periodically to keep the area attractive-looking and to assist shoppers in their search for legitimate values.

"Found" Objects as Fixtures

There is another source of store fixtures that bears mention in this section—*found objects*, such as wooden packing crates, antique trunks, wooden barrels, buckets, and washtubs, 1950s kitchen tables and chairs, even sections of car or truck bodies. Large and substantial, these items may fit very well into certain stores' atmospheric or thematic plans.

Found object fixtures are not for everybody . . . and probably not for an entire store. Used strictly as accent pieces, they can add that magical element of whimsy or surprise that every designer delights in using—a signature statement. However, fixtures like these must fit the store's atmospheric intent, and overuse may limit their appeal. The principal benefits of found objects as fixtures are their novelty, price, and disposability. Since they're not as expensive as conventional store furnishings, found objects are easy to discard when they are no longer effective as merchandising tools.

Vendor Fixtures and Shops

Merchandise manufacturers sometimes supply retailers with fixtures that are designed specifically for their company's products. They may even offer to provide the store with décor elements, signing, and fixtures to create an entire shop for their brand. By doing this, manufacturers hope to control how their products are presented and thereby strengthen their brand image.

This business arrangement may look like a bargain to retailers because they do not have to pay for the shops, but they must also accept the fact that they may have to give control of that new shop's appearance and merchandising over to the vendor. Accepting such an arrangement may compromise (or at least challenge) the store's brand image. The retailer also faces the possibility that competitors may have identical shops in their stores.

These are issues to consider carefully before entering into a shop fixture agreement with a vendor. On a smaller scale, these same issues apply to accepting even smaller vendor countertop or floor-standing merchandising units (selling fixtures that hold merchandise and bear the manufacturer's logo, signing style, and other brand identity marks).

Custom Fixtures

Intense retail competition has led to the development of a custom fixture industry that enables retailers to create exclusive store images through one-of-a-kind fixture fabrications. The industry wide retail trend today favors use of custom fixtures throughout a store. (See Figures 4.31 and 4.32.) Small retailers who cannot incur the expense of an entire store filled with custom fixtures could consider positioning a few special fixtures in the most visible areas of their store. This would include the store entrance and the entrance to each department.

To develop custom fixtures, retailers work with design teams from their own companies or from outside sources (the term *outsourcing* refers to work performed by another company). Fixture manufacturers interested in producing the custom fixtures may also participate and even offer the services of their own in-house designers. This can be particularly helpful in translating the retail team's design ideal into practical terms for the eventual manufacturing process. The design phase of the project may be handled as a separate project for a fee, or the manufacturer may provide this service at no charge, if the company is assured that it will be awarded the contract to build the fixtures.

Once a design team is selected, store executives and designers discuss and sketch "concepts" (ideas) for fixtures that will reinforce the company's brand image. They must also agree on the materials that will be used to build the fixtures. When making this type of decision, it is critical to look at the total store environment with all of its décor elements, wall coverings, floor coverings, and so on. The materials that are selected for fixtures must complement the entire retail environment. Fixtures should also be designed as a coordinated group. For example, if the materials agreed upon are brushed metal and cherry wood, some fixtures in the grouping could be brushed metal, some could be cherry wood, and some could be a combination of both materials. It would not be a good design decision to add an additional fixture of maple wood, because it would not fit in with the group.

In the next phase, the best of the teams' design concepts are converted to dimensional computer drawings, and they may be modeled in small-scale mock-ups. If designs are approved, full-scale prototype fixtures are built, tested on-site if possible, and then modified as necessary. The accepted prototype design is then sent to two or three manufacturers for **bidding.** Selection of a manufacturer is a decision which should not be based solely on price. The manufacturing plant and production staff must also be the right size, equipped to handle the quantity of fixtures needed and able to meet a very specific delivery schedule. This is especially important to large retail organizations. Key considerations—as important as any price quotation—are trust, communication, reliability, and quality. This allows the retail team time to stay on top of the entire process and react accordingly should a manufacturer run into production or delivery problems and not be able to fulfill the contract by the due date. The retailer must be kept up-to-date with progress reports.

Karen Doodeman, director of marketing for the National Association of Store Fixture Manufacturers (NASFM) offers insight and advice on the purchase of fixtures. "It's no secret. There is a right way and a wrong way to purchase store fixtures, and the wrong choices

A **bid** is an estimate of manufacturing costs to produce a fixture or perform a service and a formal offer to do so. Once the bid, and all its terms, have been accepted, a contract is awarded. This formal agreement between the buyer and the manufacturer becomes the official basis for actual production, delivery schedule, and terms of payment.

90

Figure 4.31 Custom design fixtures, XXXY, Toronto, Ontario, Canada.

can cost you a great deal of time and your company a lot of money. Store fixtures can represent as much as 60 percent or more of the cost of a new store or store remodel. Whether the fixtures are part of a vendor shop program that may only last 12 to 18 months or perimeter fixtures that will be used for a number of years, proper selection is crucial.

"Purchasing store fixtures requires due diligence in selecting the best vendor for your company's specific needs. Get to know your vendors strengths and weaknesses by work-

Figure 4.32 Custom design fixtures, Zara, New York City.

A Retail Reality:
Generally, the price of a fixture decreases as the number ordered increases.

A Retail Reality:
Retailers must also estimate tax, handling, and freight charges for fixtures to arrive at their destination. Manufacturers often do not include these added expenses in their estimates unless requested to do so.

"NASFM—What's in a name? Founded in 1956, the National Association of Store Fixture Manufacturers, or NASFM, was created to raise the professional, ethical, and educational standards of the store fixture manufacturing industry. NASFM represents 400 store fixture manufacturers throughout the world and over 250 industry suppliers. Its members combined produce more than 80 percent of the store fixtures manufactured throughout the U.S. and Canada.**"**

www.nasfm.org

ing with them closely. Then consider backup vendors for weak areas, such as specialty fixturing or jobs that require different production levels or materials.

"Keep your competitive edge. Visit trade shows like Global Shop to see what's new in the industry. It's also a good idea to meet periodically with your team of designers and manufacturers to brainstorm new concepts and take advantage of new materials and techniques that might give you a leg up on the competition."

Custom Fixture Guidelines

1. *Design the style of the fixture to fit into the existing store environment.* For example, a high-tech fixture from Niketown would not be appropriate for a store like Bass Pro Shop (see Figure 2.1), which has a decidedly rustic environment.

2. *Fabricate the fixture in materials and styles currently in use in the industry.* The useful life span of custom fixtures is about 8 years, at which point they begin to look dated. This span shrinks even more rapidly as customers are continually exposed to newer concepts in competing retail environments. In other words, do not choose a look that your competitors already have.

3. *Design the fixture to hold the type of product that will be shown on the fixture.* Designers should test any design with the intended merchandise to avoid the need for revisions after the fixture has been fabricated in its final form.

4. *Design the fixture to be compatible with the type of hardware accessories already used by the store.* Store designers must be aware of the type and number of shelves, bins, crossbars, and face-outs that the store already uses in day-to-day merchandising. It can be very expensive and time consuming to have to stock two sets of hardware for a store's fixtures.

Safety Concern!

Check the prototype fixture for safety. Is it stable when filled with products? Are there any sharp edges? Can the fixture be moved easily to help protect associates from back strain when resetting the floor? Large corporations often have a safety department that will inspect new fixtures. Records should be kept of their comments and suggestions, along with their signed approvals. This will be helpful if accidents do happen.

NASFM

NASFM, the National Association of Store Fixture Manufacturers, can help you to learn about trends and stay up-to-date with the store fixturing industry in a variety of ways. Its Website (**www.nasfm.org**) offers resource information for fixture buyers, innovations in fixturing, a glossary of fixture terminology, and a list of related links, including Websites for magazines like *Display and Design Ideas, VM + SD,* and *Chain Store Age.* You can also learn about Global Shop, the largest annual store design and in-store marketing show in the world, which is sponsored by NASFM.

The NASFM Website explains why it is prudent to work with its members and their affiliates on fixtures purchases: "As a retail buyer, you want more than a woodworker or a metal worker, you want a seasoned professional who understands the demands of your project. You want a company that has access to the tools and experience which enables it to perform under pressure. By virtue of its membership in the industry's only fixturing association, a NASFM member displays its commitment to the marketplace. Each member has agreed to observe the association's Code of Ethics and technical specifications. NASFM members are focused on constant improvement. They attend seminars and conferences to learn about new technologies, materials, and practices that make them better retail partners."

Fixturing the Accessory Department

There are many merchandise classifications in fashion accessory departments—hats, jewelry, scarves, belts, gloves, handbags, hosiery, socks, and shoes. From a customer service point of view, availability of accessories adds value to the store's fashion presentations.

The best location for an accessory department is adjacent to fitting rooms, so that sales associates can easily select a variety of coordinating accessory pieces for customers who are trying on clothes. This is simple to accomplish in specialty stores, but department stores typically have very large accessory areas that may not be located on the same floor as clothing departments. If adjacency isn't possible, department store sales associates in clothing departments should check accessory departments regularly to see what is in stock, so they can suggest fashionable add-ons that will complement garment purchases.

Accessory Presentation Guidelines

1. *Separate merchandise by end use.* For example, earrings could be separated into casual wear, career wear, and formal wear categories.

2. *Divide each accessory classification by fabrication.* Items in different fabrications (material used to make the product) should be presented on separate fixtures, if possible, or at least on different sides of one fixture. For example, earrings could be placed on a triangular jewelry spinner presenting two sides of wooden earrings and one side of shell earrings. (See Figure 4.33.)

3. *Divide the items by style within each fabrication.* For example, wooden earrings on one side of an earring spinner could be assorted and presented by style—round wooden earrings and square wooden earrings. Notice that the earrings are also arranged from small styles to large styles. (See Figure 4.33.)

   On a wall section, you might show canvas handbags on face-outs and assort them by style—shoulder bags and totes. These handbags would also be arranged from small to large. (See Figure 4.34.)

4. *Within each style, separate the items by color group.* Present a single color group on each side of a fixture. (See Figure 4.33.) Bright earrings are presented on one side of the jewelry spinner, pastels on another side. Keep in mind that it would be even better to present just one color group for the entire fixture. Now look at Figure 4.34. Bright and neutral color canvas bags are presented together in a wall area. Each section of wall should feature just one color group with neutrals; never mix two color groups like brights and pastels together on a section of the wall.

   Within each color group, present the same colors together vertically. Colors may also be arranged according to Roy G. Bv for all color groups, simply deleting colors that are not in stock at that time. Neutrals follow the other color groups. (See Figures 4.33 and 4.34.) Both earrings and handbags are colorized vertically.

> ### Exceptions to Accessory Presentation Guidelines
>
> In reality, many events may limit how closely you'll be able to follow the accessory presentation guidelines presented here. In smaller shops, for example, store buyers may not purchase earrings in large enough quantities for you to use a vertical colorization strategy. In that case, you could work in horizontal rows—starting, for example, on row 1 with three pairs of red earrings, three pairs of yellow; then following on row 2 with three pairs of blue earrings, and three pairs of purple.
>
> Another guideline exception can occur when earrings purchased from different manufacturers arrive on earring cards in varying sizes and shapes. Mixing these cards on the same side of a fixture may make it appear to be disorganized. In that case, the display will be more effective if you separate the earrings—first by type of card, and then by end use, fabrication, style, and so on. (See Figure 4.35.)

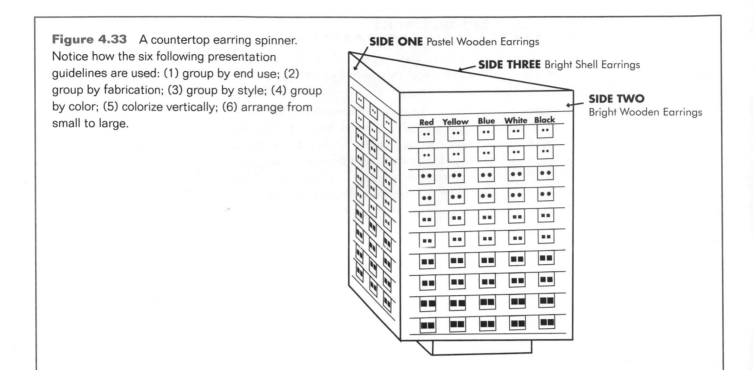

Figure 4.33 A countertop earring spinner. Notice how the six following presentation guidelines are used: (1) group by end use; (2) group by fabrication; (3) group by style; (4) group by color; (5) colorize vertically; (6) arrange from small to large.

SIDE ONE Pastel Wooden Earrings

SIDE THREE Bright Shell Earrings

SIDE TWO
Bright Wooden Earrings

Red	Yellow	Blue	White	Black

Figure 4.34 A minislatwall presentation with canvas handbags in bright and neutral colors. Notice how the six presentation guidelines are followed.

RED	YELLOW	GREEN	BLUE	BLACK

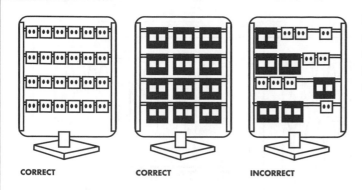

Figure 4.35 An earring presentation on the countertop fixtures. Notice how organized the earrings appear in the correct examples, as opposed to the incorrect examples, where different styles of earring cards are mixed.

5. *Arrange all accessory items in straight rows, keeping items of similar length together.* (See Figures 4.36 and 4.37.)

6. *Present accessories as sets whenever possible.* (See Figure 4.38.) This teaches shoppers how to put accessories together in current fashion looks and encourages multiple purchases. You can group and coordinate (*a*) hats, scarves, gloves, and handbags; (*b*) belts, scarves, and handbags; and (*c*) earrings, necklaces, and bracelets.

   Accessory presentations must be maintained during **sell-down.** Ideally, there will be new items coming into the department at regular intervals during the season. In the meantime, closely monitor sales activity and consolidate or remerchandise frequently to keep the fixture filled. See this as a professional challenge to rethink and make broken assortments seem new again. Actually, shifting items within the accessory area can give your regular weekly shoppers the impression that you have just brought new merchandise into the department. Follow the guidelines whenever you can to create dynamic presentations that make shopping and selection easier for your customers.

Sell-down, also called sell-through, is a retail term for the period during which an item or grouping is on the selling floor, from introduction at full price through the markdown stage.

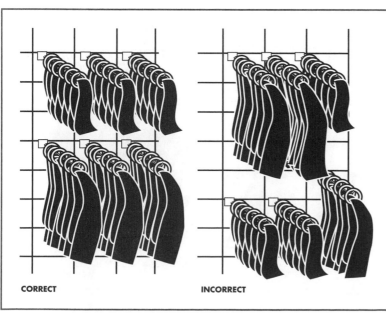

Figure 4.36 A scarf presentation on gridwall. In the correct example, scarves are presented with the same lengths together in each row. In the incorrect example, scarf lengths are mixed.

Figure 4.37 A necklace presentation on acrylic display boards on a mini slatwall. In the correct example, necklace chains are presented from short to long lengths, with just one length per row. In the incorrect example, necklace lengths are mixed.

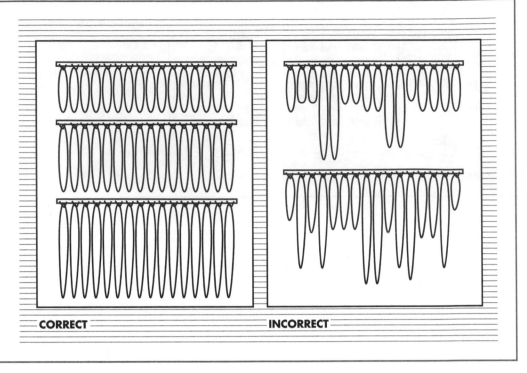

CORRECT   INCORRECT

Accessory Showcase Presentation

Accessory showcases are frequently used to secure accessory items with high "shrink" potential—smaller, more expensive items that might tempt shoplifters. Showcases like these are often locked or their openings will face the inside of a counter island staffed by a sales associate.

Figure 4.38 A countertop acrylic slant board with a presentation of mix-and-match earrings, neckwear, and bracelets.

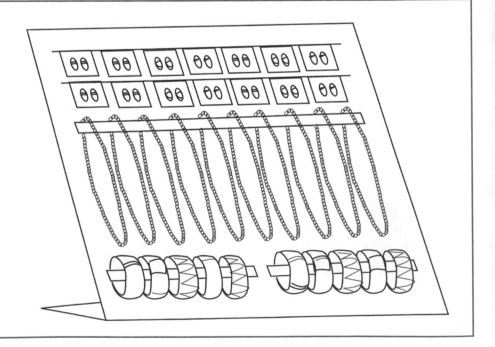

Showcased products may be presented in several ways:

- Massed stock presentations of single classifications such as a case showing only exclusive watches
- Massed presentation of items or coordinated sets from a single designer (Monet jewelry or Ralph Lauren fragrances)
- General presentation of a variety of jewelry items from several vendors
- Display presentations featuring a few selected items which are often "propped" or signed. For example, as a promotion for a special event in the scarf department, you might set up a selection of designer scarves paired with scarf pins. To tie the merchandise to the event, you might prop the display with a scattering of promotional booklets the designer will be giving away at the event. Then you'd complete the display with a sign featuring time and date plus the designer's logo. This type of presentation isn't used very often since the "value" of showcase space has increased with the demand for productivity from every square inch of store space.

Merchandising a showcase fixture should follow the basic accessory guidelines already outlined in this chapter—separating products by end use, fabrication, style, and color. Showcase product presentation should also rely on the basic design principles and elements that you'd use in a larger display area—emphasis, balance, rhythm, and proportion. (See Figures 4.39 and 4.40.) Can you identify the specific design principles and elements that are used in the two illustrations?

A Retail Reality:
Neglected fixtures with "shopped" assortments communicate to potential shoplifters that the store and its staff don't care what happens to their merchandise. The same is true of dusty, fingerprinted fixtures, shopworn or unticketed items, and so on. These are exactly the kinds of indicators that prompt dishonest shoppers to look for opportunities to steal. If the "store" doesn't care, why should they?

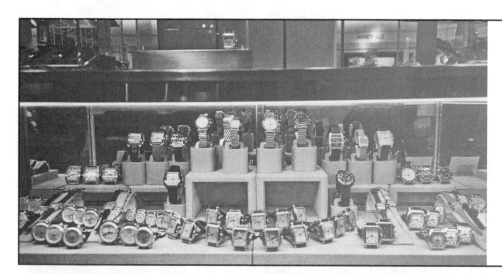

Figure 4.39 A presentation of watches in a showcase; Nordstrom, Chicago.

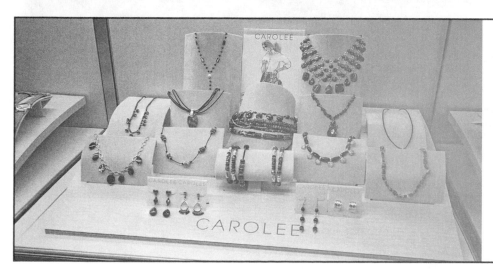

Figure 4.40 A presentation of jewelry in a showcase; Marshall Field's, Chicago.

"This concept [open sell] provides clients with a great deal of experiential freedom in making their selections. The ability to let clients sample the product in an environment of quiet persuasion, which balances beauty and efficiency, and helps streamline the shopping experience, is the driving force behind Sephora's store designs.**"**

Barbara Emerson, director, store planning and design, Sephora

Open-Sell Accessory Fixtures

The most recent development in accessory fixturing is the trend toward open sell. Encouraging inspection while protecting merchandise is a challenge for the coming decade. Fixture manufacturers and retailers are working together to devise fixtures that allow shoppers to inspect and try on accessory items previously kept in secure cases, including items with high theft potential. (See Figure 4.41.) The Swatch watch fixture features bands that are attached in only one place, allowing shoppers to actually handle and try on watches without assistance.

While most retailers agree that open sell is cost-effective in terms of lowered staffing costs and increased gross sales, they are afraid that shrinkage rates will increase exponentially as well. Nevertheless, they are facing the challenge and are continuing to experiment with creative solutions that will remove "barriers" between customers and merchandise.

Spence, a fine jewelry store with locations in the United States, Canada, and Belgium, fills its open cases with samples of rings made of brass and glass that customers may try on at will. The cases are glass covered on top, with open fronts, maintaining an elegant look that is suitable for their line of products, which consists mainly of diamond and gemstone rings. After making a selection, customers can request that the item be custom made in a price range that is comfortable for them.

Figure 4.41 This open sell fixture of watches allows shoppers to slip their wrists under the watchbands without actually removing the watches from the fixture.

Bloomingdale's has a different version of open sell, placing showcases back-to-back with access from the front. The cases are locked, and the assistance of a sales associate is required, but the need to communicate from behind a counter is eliminated.

Sephora was the first retailer to set itself apart and open a store without the traditional enclosed counters that require sales assistance. An entirely new way to shop for beauty was developed and every product was immediately accessible to consumers. Aura Science was another interesting open sell strategy. (See Figure 4.42.)

Specialized Accessory Fixtures

Accessory products are best presented on specialized fixtures and display forms. To achieve enough visual mass and optical weight to be seen from a distance, the smallest fixtures may be used inside glass cases or placed on jewelry countertops or shelves in wall areas. Some of the smaller styles of fixtures that are available include

- Plastic (clear or colored) or metal earring spinners (two-, three-, or four-sided fixtures on variable-height pedestals that turn on ball bearings), eyeglass spinners, and so on
- Earring boards and necklace boards with easel stands
- Multiarmed necklace bars on pedestals, two-bar necklace and bracelet stands, and scarf stands
- Hat stands
- Handbag stands
- Display baskets and trays in metal and clear plastic fabrications
- Clear or colored plastic cubes and risers
- Wall face-outs and pegs

Figure 4.42 An open sell strategy called Aura Science was tested by The Limited Corporation and Shiseido.

Virtually any countertop fixture can be enlarged or elongated to become a floor-standing accessory fixture. The advantage is being able to show more merchandise in a limited amount of square footage on the selling floor rather than on a countertop. The drawback to a selling floor filled with floor-standing fixtures is visual clutter. If too many free-standing spinners take over an accessory department's aisles, they may block sight lines to the rest of the accessory department. You must also allow adequate aisle space for people to pass between spinning fixtures without putting the fixtures in motion. Shopper-friendly floor layout is just as important as great-looking fixtures. If people don't stay in a department because they feel crowded and uncomfortable, they can't shop and they won't buy.

Shoptalk

Retail Feng Shui: A Modern Approach to an Ancient Practice

By Linda Cahan

principal, Cahan & Company (excerpt from *Women's Wear Daily*)

"Feng Shui is everywhere. Donna's doing it, Martha's thinking about it, Calvin has heard of it, and you are either aware of it or wondering if it's #10 on the take-out menu.

I learned about Feng Shui in 1991 from a friend who looked at my visual design experience, added it up with my metaphysical interests, and presented me with a concept that's been around for centuries—in China. When I started reading about Feng Shui, I couldn't stop. I realized that all the work I've been doing has a name and a long history. Using the principles of Feng Shui in my work has strengthened my designs and added greater success to the stores I've worked on over the years. It also makes sense—and that appeals to me the most!

Feng Shui translates to "wind" and "water" and is the ancient Chinese system of creating harmonious environments to achieve prosperity, balance, happiness, and good health.

This harmony is achieved through an awareness of energy flow, the balance of the natural elements of wood, fire, earth, water, and metal, the correct placement of objects in an interior space, and the balance of yin and yang. Not easy—but not as complicated as it sounds!

It all starts with energy. Energy must flow comfortably in your store. *Bad* energy is when the energy is rushing down an aisle, through a store, into the back wall or out the stockroom door. *Bad* energy is also trapped in L-shaped areas, angled spaces, under stairwells, around columns and compressed under beams or architecturally lowered ceilings. Energy flow is a basic component of creating positive Feng Shui in your store. Of course, first on your energy flow list is a good HVAC system! An awareness of how energy flows requires looking and sensing your store with an open mind and a fresh view.

To view your store with Feng Shui "eyes," walk up to your store and look into its eyes—the windows. What are they saying to potential customers? Are they awake, alert, clear, bright, and have strong focal points? Or, are they dirty, clouded, unfocused, and confused? Your windows tell the world who and what you are. In Feng Shui, these represent the soul of your store.

Next, stand at your entrance. There are seven exercises you can use to evaluate Feng Shui as you move through a store. Here is one of them:

Exercise #1 is to experience how you want to walk through the space. Do you move instinctively to your left (the past, accumulation, messiness, and profit) or to the right (your future, the transformation from strangers into customers/friends)? The left side of the store is powerful for lower-priced or sale items, while the right side is the best place for powerful focal points and full-priced merchandise.

Feng Shui is a highly complicated study and only a sample of its ideas are discussed here. If you want to learn more about Feng Shui, there are some excellent books available by authors such as Sarah Rossbach, Denise Linn, William Spear, and many others. Good energy to you all!

Out-of-the-Box Challenge

Premier Fixtures

Look

Visit five stores in a shopping mall and describe or sketch the fixture in the store entrance. Try to find as many stores as possible with fixtures that are unique.

Compare

Compare the fixtures. Which fixtures caught your eye? Were there any that were so appealing you decided to shop in the store? How were the fixtures signed? What did the signs say?

Innovate

How would you improve your favorite fixture?

Critical Thinking

Activity 1

Visit several display fixture manufacturers' or distributors' Internet sites. Select the one you like best and describe the range of products available today. Try a site like A Virtual Display Mall (**www.avdm.com**) or do a Web search for "retail store display fixtures." You can also find Websites in current ads found in magazines like *Visual Merchandising and Store Design* and *Display and Design Ideas*.

Activity 2

Imagine that you have an opportunity to open a moderately priced, contemporary, women's clothing shop in your neighborhood. Your space (30' × 30' selling floor) is in a thriving strip center that has excellent traffic every day of the week. The landlord is going to install slatwall all around the selling floor as part of the lease agreement. The front of the store is mostly glass. Think about the merchandise categories you would offer. With an opening fixture budget of $6000, what kind of "furniture" could you afford to buy for your store? Refer to Activity 1 for prices. List the type and number of fixtures you would purchase. Explain why you chose each piece.

Activity 3

Visit three stores in a mall that are different sizes: small, medium, and large. Ask the store manager whether they can tell you the square footage of the store. List the names of the stores and their square footages. This exercise will help you to get a sense of square-footage space, and your list will be a useful frame of reference for the future.

Activity 4

Using the fixtures and instructions from Figure 4.43A, create a new planogram (Figure 4.43B) that correctly positions selling fixtures in a workable free-flow traffic pattern that accommodates the merchandise hung on the store's perimeter walls and the three mannequins in the store's open window and provides enough walking space between fixtures so that shoppers will be able to move between them and look at merchandise comfortably.

Case Study

Designing a Signature Fixture for Accessories

The Situation

Ken Sinclair owns both a bridal photography and consulting business and a thriving floral business. He has leased the main floor of a large, older building that once housed a variety store in a picturesque midwestern college town. Most of the ornate Main Street storefronts were built of red brick around 1900 with charming architectural features and flower boxes.

Ken is pleased with the photo studio space his landlord allowed him to build at the rear of the shop, but he was frustrated with the large open area that greets floral customers and photography clients when they enter his business. He thinks it is too open and lacks the more intimate atmosphere he wants to bridge his photography and bridal consulting space and his floral shop.

Ken has an idea that he is certain will transform the front of his business into a sales-generating area for the smaller bridal accessory items that he was not displaying very effectively at the present. In addition to the usual picture frames and photo albums, he also sells guest books, toasting glasses, cake-toppers and cutters, ice buckets, centerpieces, vases, mirrors, cake cutters, unity candles, and small mementos for members of bridal parties.

Ken thinks that a signature fixture could make a statement about his two businesses, display the accessory items in his inventory and encourage impulse shopping. He envisions something eye-catching and original—a supersized, multitiered wedding cake!

Discussion Questions

1. Ken is obviously thinking outside the box. Is his idea a good one for his store long term? Explain why you agree or disagree with his thinking.

2. What might the wedding cake idea add to the atmospherics in Ken's store?

3. Would a fixture like the one Ken's suggesting differentiate his business from others?

4. Do you visualize a traditional tiered and frosted cake or something more abstract, just suggesting a wedding cake?

5. Do you see this as an open-sell fixture?

6. What advantages would there be to placing such a fixture adjacent to Ken's waiting area? What disadvantages?

Your Challenge

Ken hires you as the designer for his signature fixture concept. Proceed as follows:

● Sketch a prototype fixture that might fit Ken's specifications.

● Describe dimensions for both a floor-standing fixture and a fixture that might be placed on a large, round, skirted table.

● Think of a way to cross-merchandise both of Ken's businesses and incorporate your ideas into the fixture design. Show your ideas in the sketch.

● Present your ideas in your classroom setting or one-on-one with your instructor playing Ken's role. Explain how your prototype will work and how it will benefit both of Ken's businesses as well as enhance the store's atmosphere and its image overall.

Key

Back Bar to Cashwrap

Cashwrap Desk

4-Way	2-Way	Round Rack

Templates   1/4 inch = 1 foot

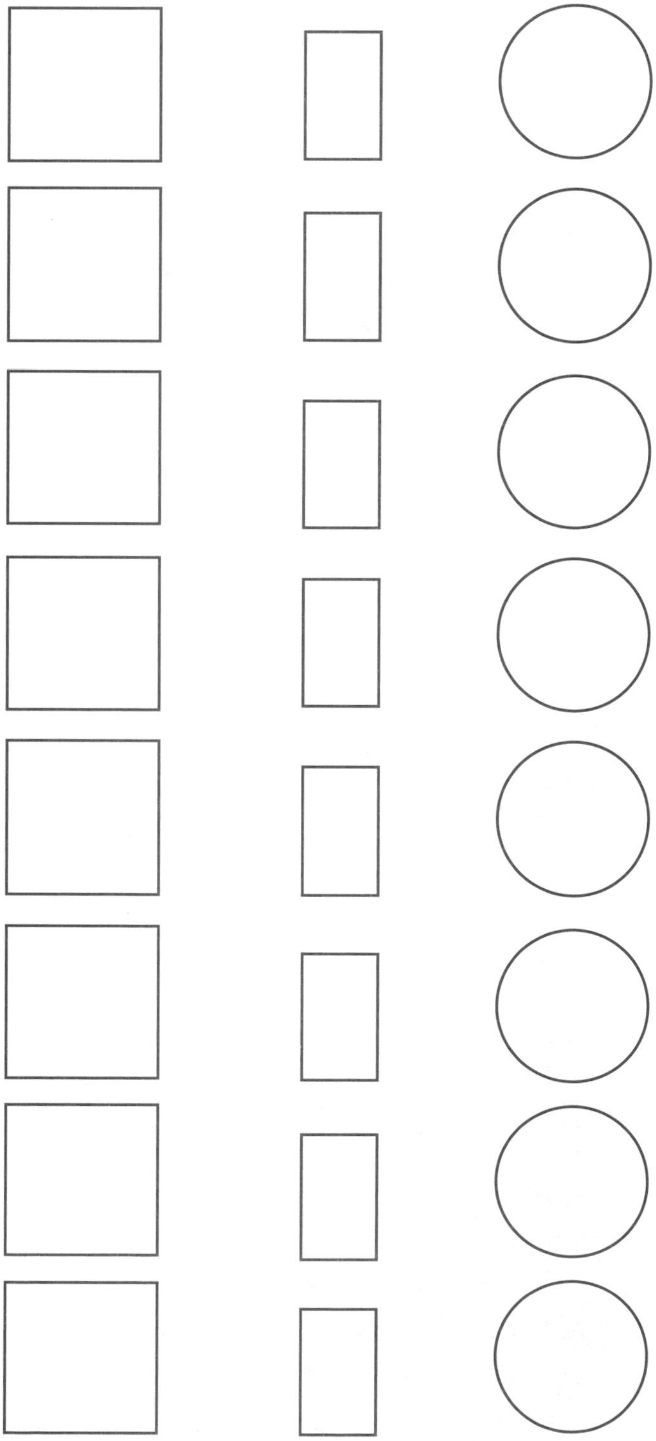

Use these templates of common floor fixtures (scale is 1/4 inch to 1 foot) in your floor layout. There may be more fixtures here than you can use in a correct layout.

- Plan one fixture for every 100 square feet on blank floor plan 4.44 B.

- Fixtures must be at least 3 feet apart.

- Assume that the perimeter walls are merchandised and that hanging merchandise extends 2 feet from the walls. Add an additional 3 feet to allow for walking space between wall areas and the first row of floor fixtures.

Figure 4.43A   (Use with Activity 4)

Office

Fitting Room **Fitting Room**

Mannequins

Window

Entrance

1/4 inch = 1 foot

Figure 4.43B (Use with Activity 4)

Chapter Five

FASHION APPAREL WALL SETUPS

After completing this chapter, you should be able to

Explain the importance of wall presentations as selling tools

Analyze the impact of walls on customer traffic patterns and sales

Create dramatic wall presentations using a variety of fixtures, signs, visual props, and mannequin alternatives

"Walls create different
experiences in retail spaces and
help communicate what you want
your consumers to see."
Tony Mancini, Sr. vice president,
global retail store development,
Walt Disney Imagineering
and Walt Disney Parks and Resorts

Walls as Retail Selling Tools

Walls are the largest selling tool and one of the most important fixtures in the retailer's overall selling strategy. Effective use of store walls as selling tools meets several visual merchandising objectives. They capture shoppers' attention as they enter the retail space. The wall displays draw shoppers farther into the store, exposing them to as much merchandise as possible. Wall presentations communicate fashion information, and they encourage multiple purchases. Clearly, the more attractive merchandise shoppers see, the higher the probability they will buy.

Store walls act as **way-finding** tools guiding shoppers to products they have come to see and buy. Reflecting product categories featured on adjacent selling floors, walls serve as *merchandise locators*. To reinforce these important merchandising messages, retailers often use lifestyle graphics that offer both product category and trend direction. Graphic elements must be placed high enough on walls to be visible from store entrances and aisles. If the arrangement of selling floor fixtures provides clear sight lines leading up to the walls, effective wall signing will inform shoppers about the categories of merchandise featured on the walls below and in areas nearby. Wall signing is particularly useful to "call out" brand, size, gender, or a category of merchandise.

In addition to attracting shopper attention and moving people through the store, walls form the retail background, supporting store brand image by strategic use of a variety of interesting wall surfaces, paint colors, and wallpapers that reinforce the retailer's atmospheric intent.

Architecturally, *perimeter walls* (outer walls) define the store's overall shape and support its basic construction. Perimeter walls are commonly divided and then merchandised by sections ranging in size from 4 to 60 feet (depending on the type of store). Inside the store space, strategically placed *interior walls* guide traffic, separate merchandising departments, and increase merchandisers' ability to present products. These interior structures (sometimes called *T-walls* or *divider walls*) are also useful in defining and separating specific selling spaces and enclosing fitting rooms, restrooms, offices, and storage areas. Because they can be merchandised on both sides, interior walls are very important in department stores. They may be built to meet the ceiling, or may rise only part way. Whatever their construction or location, because of their large size, walls generally provide visual merchandisers with opportunities to create some of the most dramatic presentations in the store.

Walls as Destinations

If merchandise is presented effectively on the walls of a store, the walls will become *destinations*. Store planners can design traffic patterns that move shoppers toward the store's side and back walls—as opposed to leading them directly down an aisle (traffic lane) or stopping them in the front third of the selling space. Dispersing traffic into selling departments and drawing shoppers toward merchandised walls offers several strategic advantages that will have a positive impact on sales:

- Shoppers will be exposed to and inspect more merchandise.
- Once out of main traffic patterns, shoppers are more likely to spend time browsing through the store's entire merchandise assortment.
- Once they've made their way to see the merchandise on the walls, customers will return to the main aisles. On that return trip, they will see merchandise housed on the back side of floor fixtures.

Way-finding is a term used by architects to describe any tools that help customers to "find their way" through a store. Signs positioned in highly visible areas—on walls or hanging from the ceiling—are examples of way-finding strategies.

A Retail Reality:
As a profit-minded retailer, your goal is to make the most effective use of every square foot of your store. Using store walls—from floor to ceiling—to communicate with shoppers will make profitable use of every cubic foot (length × width × height).

A Retail Reality:
Merchandisers frequently overlook back-to-front merchandising opportunities. Stand with your back to a selling department's wall and develop merchandising strategies for shoppers who are returning to the main aisles after visiting merchandise arrayed on the walls.

Walls as Store Fixtures

Since walls are the tallest store fixtures, visual merchandisers should be concerned with the height of the topmost shelves and displays. While they want shoppers to see merchandise on the walls, they would not want them to reach above their heads to pull down products. Safety and service are the prime concerns.

Stocking shelves several tiers high and then signing them with directions to seek help can provide opportunities for sales associates to work with shoppers and develop additional sales. Of course, that strategy implies that sales assistance is going to be *readily available.* If that is not the case, visual merchandisers must be certain that shelved merchandise is accessible to *most* customers.

You may prefer that a shelf of sweater styles on bust forms is not accessible to shoppers. Perhaps you've placed them there strictly for display. You will need to ask these questions, "Is there adequate selling stock of the displayed sweaters shelved below the display? Are the sweaters easy to reach? Are they sized?" If not, adjust the shelves to a height that the average customer can reach and add sizing to channels on shelf edges, or apply sizing stickers directly to the front folds of the sweaters.

Some retailers claim to be self-service stores, but they routinely place products out of reach. Other store chains place waterfall face-outs of sweaters and tops well over 10 feet from the floor on walls. Rather than providing the service of sales associates to assist shoppers, they place 5-foot extension poles in a few locations around the store. Typically the poles are difficult to locate because they quickly become hidden among the merchandise on garment rods or face-outs after shoppers have used them.

The Visual Merchandising Tool Kit

Visual merchandisers have a multitude of tools to work with as they create exciting wall presentations. Like most craftspeople, they may not use every tool at their disposal for each task they do. Carpenters may use hammers and measuring tapes all the time, but they carry other tools just in case they're needed. Visual merchandisers will use their "basic tools"—themes, art principles, and elements of design—for every wall they set up. Other tools, like wall fixtures, mannequin alternatives, props, and lighting techniques will be used on an as-needed basis. What follows is a discussion of the way each of these tools contributes to the development of wall presentations that sell.

Wall Dividers

The primary function of wall dividers is separating a long wall into shorter, clearly defined sections. Dividers may be permanent, like architectural columns, or semipermanent like paints and textured wall coverings. Nonpermanent dividers, like outriggers and detachable panels for displaying coordinated outfits, may be repositioned as merchandise categories expand and contract. Whatever the style, these sections can effectively create departments or shops within a store and, combined with directional signing, make it easy for customers to quickly locate the products they want to see.

The materials used for dividers and wall surfaces can shape the store's atmospherics and enhance its physical image. For example, galvanized metal **outrigger** panels could be very appropriate wall enhancements for the sports apparel store—clean and spare. Polished oak panels with ornate moldings would add elegance to an upscale specialty store's image and create a more intimate mood.

Many times stores that were not initially designed with dividers are **retrofitted** with these elements to break up wall space. Whenever dividers are installed, it is important to

A Retail Reality:
Anything that frustrates shoppers risks sending them away annoyed and empty-handed. If your store must shelve duplicate products overhead on the selling floor, every size and style must be readily accessible on the fixtures below.

A Retail Reality:
A holiday shopper was overheard to say: "If I'd wanted to work in this store, I would have gone to Personnel to apply for a job instead of coming here to shop." With that, she put down the self-service pole she'd been using to find her size from a three-tiered wall presentation of blouses and left the department. This shopper did not become a customer.

Outriggers are decorative or functional elements mounted to a wall at right angles in order to define, separate, and frame categories of merchandise presented on shelves or display fixtures.

Retrofitting is the act of adding architectural features, fixtures or other elements after the original structure is completed.

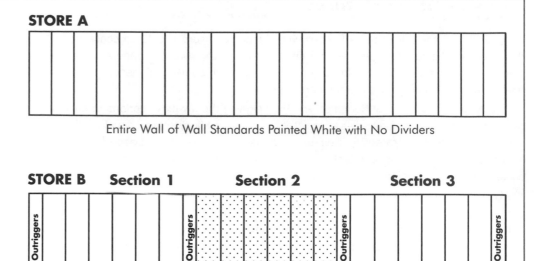

Figure 5.1 In store A there is no variation—just one long expanse of wall standards. In store B outriggers and perforated metal panels divide the wall into sections.

select materials that fit both store brand image and merchandise. If the materials are not compatible, the designer sends a confusing message to shoppers.

Dividers are also used to break up longer wall spans by adding elements of visual interest. In Figure 5.1, Store A's walls have no architectural dividers. The result is a featureless wall treatment that lacks merchandising impact. In contrast, Store B has added outriggers and perforated metal panels to divide the lengthy span and add an element of visual interest, emphasizing the center wall section.

Look again at Figure 5.1. The wall in Store B has been divided into three sections. With the outriggers in place, each section can be merchandised to create three separate color and fashion statements. In stores with large quantities of merchandise, the center outriggers could be removed, and one large statement could span all three areas. Flexible outriggers offer merchandisers the option of using as much space as they need to develop presentations for varying stock levels.

A **soffit** is a long ledge, permanent arch, or box reaching down from a store's ceiling to its top shelves or usable wall space. It is often used to mask nondecorative (functional) lighting fixtures that serve to illuminate merchandise displayed on store walls.

Architectural **soffit** treatments—long ledges, permanent arches, or shadow boxes reaching down from a store's ceiling to its top shelves or usable wall space—can limit merchandising flexibility. If the soffit treatment is an arch stretching out over several wall sections in a store, the best practice is to treat the entire area under it as one section. Even though an arch doesn't reach the floor, it communicates a "shoplike" feeling to that area.

Compare the two wall presentations in Figure 5.2. Which presentation do you think is stronger? In the correct example, three sections of casual merchandise presented under a single architectural band make a dramatic fashion statement. In the incorrect example, the combination of casual and formal wear shown under the same band results in a wall presentation that would be confusing to a shopper.

Decorative Lighting Fixtures

Decorative lighting fixtures are an excellent way to add warmth, interest, and "personality" to wall treatments. Basically atmospheric in nature, decorative lighting should not be the only method of lighting used. There are decorative fixtures to fit any store's image. They can add warmth to the cooler, fluorescent tones of general lighting in large retail spaces and highlight fashion colors without distortion. They may range from small-scale feminine

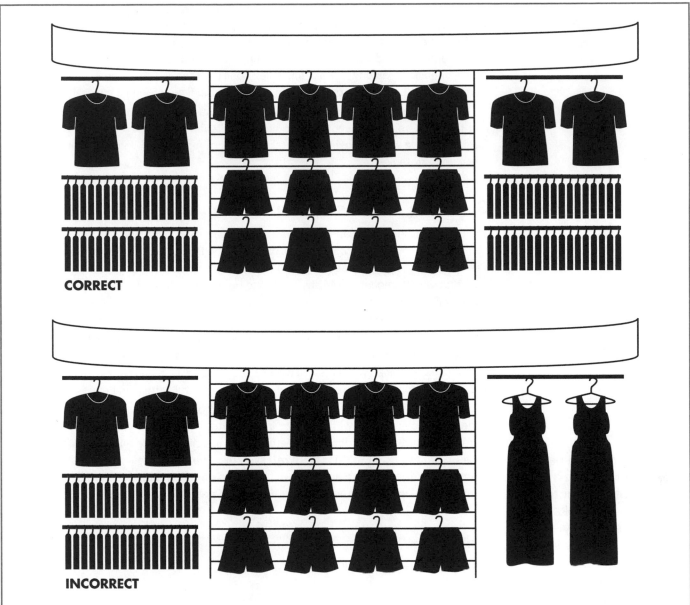

Figure 5.2 Wall presentations under a single soffit. In the correct example, only casual merchandise is presented, which makes one fashion statement. In the incorrect example, the combination of formal wear with casual merchandise results in a confusing message.

fixtures, with beaded or fabric lamp shades, to industrial photography fixtures and high-tech theater lights.

Lighting Techniques for Walls

Merchandised walls are lit separately from the store's overall illumination. An ideal store design will set track lighting into the ceiling 5 or 6 feet away from a merchandised wall. The goal is accent lighting that highlights merchandise on a department's perimeter walls. A combination of general (floodlight) and specific (spotlight) lamps give merchandisers flexibility to vary visual presentations. When the store's initial construction does not include track lighting for perimeter walls, accent lighting fixtures can augment the general lighting plan.

Accent lighting is, by definition, more dramatic than general store illumination. It is meant to set displayed merchandise apart in visual "hot spots," according to Greg Gorman's *Visual Merchandising and Store Design Workbook*. He says that accent lighting provides focus, orientation, and visual impact supporting merchandise presentation: "Accent lighting allows specific areas on the walls and sales floor to stand out from the rest of the general illumination. When used properly, it can control traffic flow through a space."

Typically merchandisers set floodlights to illuminate products on walls with general light and then use adjustable spotlights to accent merchandise displayed on mannequins and forms or shown with props. In Chapter 9, you'll learn more about lighting techniques, practices, and strategies.

Selecting Fixtures for Wall Presentations

Imagine this retail "wallscape": Two rows of ten waterfalls, with neutral-colored linen jackets, for a span of 20 feet. Monotonous. Now imagine this: a 12-foot wall featuring the same linen jackets hanging shoulder-out on 12 feet of garment rod. At a 1-inch per garment fill rate, that would amount to 144 shoulders and right sleeves in a row—with no relief in sight. Bland wall treatments like these do not make effective use of any of the selling opportunities that walls provide.

Fortunately, visual merchandisers have a much more interesting set of tools to enhance their stores' wallscapes. A variety of wall system fixtures, graphics, props, or mannequin alternatives combined with artistic elements like balance, line, and color can create tremendous visual interest and product appeal. Compare the wall setups in Figure 5.3.

There are many kinds of wall fixtures. Every issue of the visual merchandising industry's trade magazines is filled with ads showing the latest wall fixture offerings. Fixture manufacturers' catalogs show dozens of merchandise-specific fixtures and presentation accessories for slatwall, gridwall, and **pegwall** systems. The key to creating interesting wall presentations is using these elements in multiples. To create an interesting wall presentation, you should select at least two or three different types of fixtures (see the wall fixture tool kit below).

A **pegwall** system has backer panels with a gridwork of holes into which pegwall hooks and other specialty fixtures may be inserted.

A Retail Reality: The term *story* underlines the merchandiser's role as communicator. Telling a merchandise story communicates the retailer's trend awareness, marketing expertise, and fashion leadership. A color story highlights a color that is important to current fashion. A fabric story might introduce a new textile product.

Wall Fixture Tool Kit

1. Face-outs: straight arm
2. Face-outs: waterfall
3. Garment rods
4. Product shelves
5. Bins
6. Display shelves

Selecting Merchandise for Wall Presentations

As you prepare to setup a new wall section, your first step will be to survey the entire selection of stock within the department. In the same way that you select merchandise for a single fixture, use the technique of sorting merchandise by end use, fabrication, style, and color. Choose a single end use, or "story," for the section you are merchandising. *Do not combine different end-use items on one wall section.*

If the department's stock consists of a new fashion career story of feminine silk blouses and linen skirts, and another career story of jackets and skirts with a menswear fabrication, choose only *one* of these stories for the section. This effective practice makes selec-

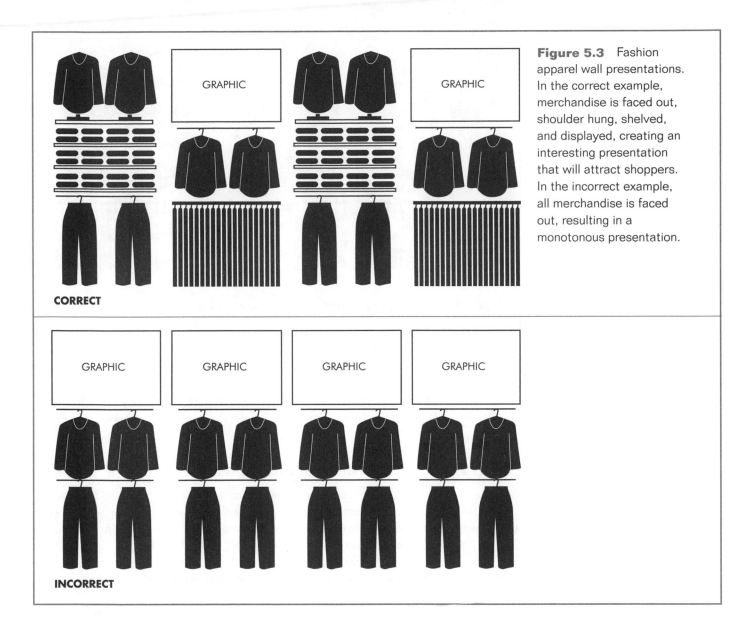

Figure 5.3 Fashion apparel wall presentations. In the correct example, merchandise is faced out, shoulder hung, shelved, and displayed, creating an interesting presentation that will attract shoppers. In the incorrect example, all merchandise is faced out, resulting in a monotonous presentation.

tion easier for shoppers because it provides a variety of pieces to mix and match. Another example of two separate fashion stories might include a group of coordinated summer shorts and T-shirts and a collection of summer sun dresses.

If the product you've chosen to highlight on the wall is available in colors from several different color groups, *choose only one color group per wall section.* See Colorplate 10. If you are setting up a major wall presentation of clothing that comes in several colors (also called **colorways**), you might want to select the bright colors for the wall. If you couldn't fit all the bright fashions in the wall section, you could present them on a floor fixture directly in front of the wall. Any remaining items or accessories that didn't fit into the color-keyed sections could be pulled together on floor fixtures nearby. This wall strategy provides a silent salesperson to help shoppers find a variety of easily coordinated clothing items.

Another way to create a dramatic wall presentation with color is to use repetition. This technique requires large quantities of a single style of merchandise but has high visual impact. You could span an entire wall section with a Roy G. Bv assortment of basic polo shirts

Colorways are the assorted colors or groups of colors a manufacturer has chosen for its line of fashion products. A manufacturer's representative might tell a store buyer that a polished cotton skirt comes in three different colorways: jewel-toned solids, pastel floral prints, and earth-toned plaids.

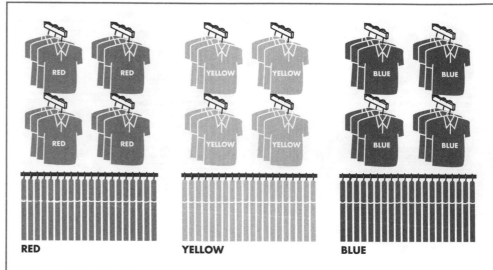

Figure 5.4 A wall presentation with dramatic impact achieved by color repetition.

to communicate that your store not only believes in the fashion ability of the polo shirt, it also has one to coordinate with virtually every pair of casual pants in a shopper's wardrobe. (See Figure 5.4.)

Using Balance in Wall Presentations

When you set up a wall section, the arrangement of merchandise and fixtures must be artfully balanced to create a pleasing composition and a natural sense of order while offering ease of selection to shoppers. In Chapter 3, you learned about formal and informal balance. *Choose just one type of balance for each wall section.* Look at Figures 5.5 through 5.8 for examples of formal and informal balance. Compare the four presentations to see how effectively balance has been used to create interest and differentiation.

Figure 5.5 A wall presentation using formal balance by Vitrashop, a fixture designer/manufacturer in Germany.

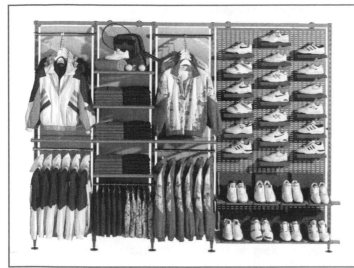

Figure 5.6 A wall presentation by Vitrashop using informal balance.

Signing and Graphics in Wall Presentations

In *Why We Buy*, author Paco Underhill says that the addition of signs to a store's interior means that it is no longer a store. "It's a three dimensional TV commercial. It's a walk-in container for words and thoughts and messages and ideas. People step inside this container," he says, "and it tells them things. If everything's working right, the things they are told will grab their attention and induce them to look and shop and buy and maybe return another day to shop and buy some more." In his discussion of signs, he emphasizes that you "can't waste a chance to tell shoppers something you want them to know."

If sight lines are uncluttered, shoppers will see most of the store's upper walls—all the more reason to use them to draw shoppers into the departments they border. Large signs

Figure 5.7 A wall presentation using informal balance from Nike Kit O Parts.

Figure 5.8 A wall presentation using informal balance from Nike Kit O Parts.

employed on the upper reaches of department walls can identify department locations, express seasonal themes, call out gender or brands for merchandise below, or draw attention to special product features.

Poster to billboard size photographs can replace mannequins, showing models in fashionable, coordinated outfits. They can update shoppers with trend information by highlighting the latest colors, product styles, and fashion designs. They can communicate lifestyle information by showing how garments are to be worn in real-life settings. Any number of sizes and shapes of graphics can be mounted at various heights on upper walls to tell important merchandise stories. This is another practice that makes full use of the store's cubic footage, thus increasing productivity.

For wall signs to be effective, they must be legible from a distance. Do you want incoming shoppers to see them? Do you want shoppers to be able to see them from the opposite side of the store or just from the main aisle? The best way to determine ideal locations for ceiling and soffit signs is to test them *inside the store.* Use your own eyes and then the eyes of others. Try tall and short people, try young people and older people, and try people who wear glasses and people who don't. Ask them to tell you what they can see. Ask them to read your sign copy to you. Are the signs and graphics appropriately sized? Are they easy to read? Are photos crisp, clear, and easy to view from a distance? Are their meanings clear?

In addition to printed signs and photographs, departmental signs can be made of multidimensional materials like wood, plastic, foam, fabric, or neon. Foam lettering is light, inexpensive, and can be custom-sculpted or die-cut into virtually any type font from Arial to Zelda. Neon lettering is probably the most expensive to produce, but it may be particularly useful in drawing attention to back walls or "hidden" areas.

Larger signs and graphic posters employing bold, uncomplicated symbols, pictures, and print styles work best for upper walls because they can be read more easily from a distance by most shoppers. Print messages in general must be very brief. Shoppers will usually not take the time to read lengthy sign copy. Chapter 8 has more detailed information on signs in general and specific signing strategies.

Mannequins and Mannequin Alternatives in Wall Presentations

Choose mannequins or mannequin alternatives that best fit the image of the merchandise selected for the wall section. If you plan to feature junior fashions on a wall, a mannequin alternative that appeals to the junior customer might be a wire form with neck, shoulders, waist, and hips that can wear a top and bottom. Or it could be a neon colored plastic form for swimsuits. Whatever you choose, all materials used should be consistent. For example, traditional wooden display hangers should not be combined with brushed metal mannequin alternatives. A brushed metal display hanger would be a better choice here.

You might also put a full-scale junior mannequin on a floor platform against a wall, or you might place a seated mannequin on a large shelf unit bracketed to a merchandised wall section. Since the figure would wear the same styles that are shown in depth on the wall, shoppers would see for themselves how the coordinated garments look on a figure. However, you'd certainly want to check your store's guidelines to see if this is an acceptable display practice, since mannequins are generally presented as lead-ins to departments, rather than in wall areas.

Safety Concern!

When placing mannequins on wall shelving units, make certain that every precaution is taken so that they will not pose any safety hazards. Check that shelf brackets are strong enough to hold the weight of the mannequin. Next, you may need to run a length of wire around the mannequin's waist (under the garments) and attach it to a wall standard or a short bracket for added security. All your safety mechanisms must be entirely invisible to the customer.

Visual Merchandising Props in Wall Presentations

A well-chosen **prop** can be the element that separates great merchandise presentations from those that are mediocre. Any props used must fit the image of the product that is being presented, in addition to the brand image of the store. For example, a basket of apples could be an appropriate prop choice for a wall featuring tops in apple print fabrics.

The "less is more" rule applies to props for wall displays. Use no more than two props per wall section (plus a sign) or the wall will appear "busy." Imagine you are setting up a wall featuring off-white crepe georgette tops, skirts, and jackets. An understated shelf setup might consist of a framed print of calla lilies propped against an ivory-toned vase of fresh or silk calla lilies.

Props may include a wide range of items, but those used most commonly today are live flowers, silk flowers, framed prints, vases, antique objects, original art, and gift boxes with the company logo. (See Figure 5.9.)

Guidelines for Wall Setups

Specifics may vary among retailers, but what follows represents current best practices for wall setups across the industry.

1. *Merchandise tops above bottoms.* This is how garments are worn, so a top-above-bottom presentation will seem natural to the shopper. A possible exception to this guideline applies to children's or young junior fashions where you can achieve a playful look by hanging bottoms over tops, as shown in Figure 5.10. It is also useful when bottoms have trimmings, oversized pockets, or other special features. Although this presentation may be appealing for children's or juniors' fashions, it would be inappropriate for adult fashions.

2. *Hang pants so that the pant leg hem is about 3 inches from the floor.* Merchandise should never be allowed to touch the floor. This is not an appealing look from a housekeeping point of view and can also result in shopworn items. At the same time, if pants are hung too high on a wall, you will eliminate the opportunity to

Props (stage properties) are items or objects other than painted scenery and actors' costumes that are used on a stage set. The term has migrated to the visual vocabulary to mean decorative items or objects other than merchandise and signs used in a display.

A Retail Reality: "Prop-happy" visual merchandisers who use too many props fail to focus attention on the merchandise. Shoppers should never wonder: "What's for sale, merchandise or props?"

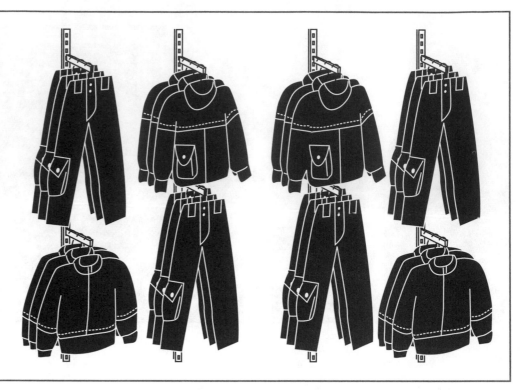

Figure 5.10 A junior department wall presentation where attention is drawn to unusual pocketed pants by hanging them above jackets.

"Who says art and culture can't be part of the shopping experience—when blended carefully it can both enhance a presentation and add value."

Ignaz Gorischek, vice president, visual planning and presentation, Neiman Marcus

merchandise a top above it. Effective displays of tops and bottoms result in multiple sales for retailers and offer value-added purchases to customers. (See Figure 5.11.)

3. *Position waterfalls, straight arms, and garment rods so you can see at least 5 inches of space between tops and bottoms.* (See Figure 5.12.) Too much space between garments will make the wall look understocked. It may also mean that garments are positioned higher on the wall, out of shoppers' reach.

4. *Feature coordinated tops and bottoms on every wall section.* A wall section featuring only T-shirts does not encourage multiple sales. Since the goal of presentation is to increase sales, visual merchandisers must take every opportunity to show customers complete outfits. Adding related accessories like hats, scarves, handbags, and shoes will further enhance wall presentations and support even greater sales opportunities. In an occasional exception, a wall may be used to feature all tops, as shown in Figure 5.4, if large quantities of product are available.

5. *Hanging garments with similar sleeve lengths together on garment rods results in a cleaner and more appealing presentation.* Varying sleeve lengths can be presented together on less visible floor fixtures if necessary. (See Figure 5.13.)

6. *Keep bottom styles separated.* Do not mix pant, skirt, or shorts styles on the same garment rod. Mixing styles confuses shoppers who are looking for their sizes within a particular style. For example, mixing pants with cuffs and pants without cuffs on the same garment rod is not a good practice—nor is mixing pants with and without belts.

7. *Present just one style and one color of an item per face-out.* Featuring a single color per face-out results in a clean, easy-to-shop presentation.

8. *Keep the average customer's height in mind when positioning menswear items on a wall.* Don't assume that men are taller than women or that they will be able to reach merchandise hung higher on walls. Hanging a long-tailed shirt or sweater above hanging pants will put the shirt out of comfortable reach for either gender. Unless there are selling associates available to assist shoppers, a better strategy would be shelving folded shirts or sweaters over the hanging pants. (See Figure 5.14.)

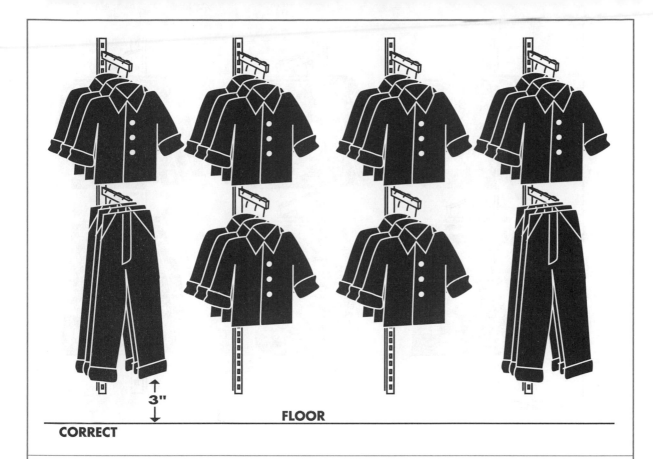

3"

FLOOR

CORRECT

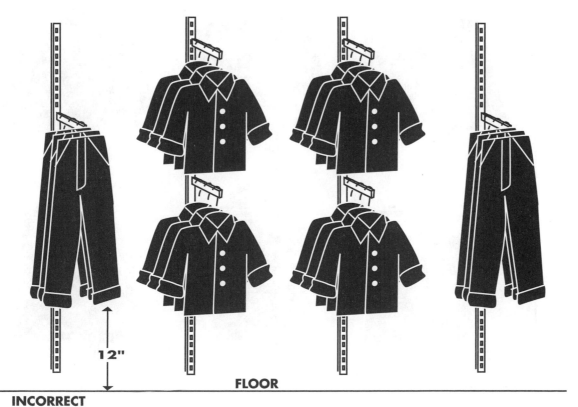

12"

FLOOR

INCORRECT

Figure 5.11 A fashion apparel wall presentation of casual tops and pants. In the correct example, pant hems hang approximately 3 inches from the floor. In the incorrect example, the pant hems are 12 inches from the floor. Not only does this appear unnatural, there is not enough room to hang tops above pants, and valuable selling space is wasted.

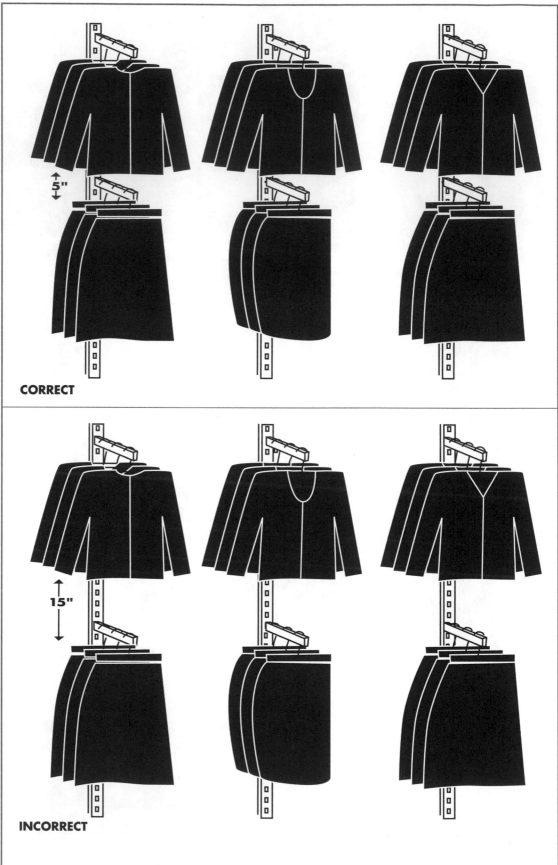

CORRECT

INCORRECT

Figure 5.12 A fashion apparel wall presentation of women's suits. In the correct example, there is about 5 inches of space between jackets and skirts. In the incorrect example, there is about 15 inches of space, which appears unnatural.

120

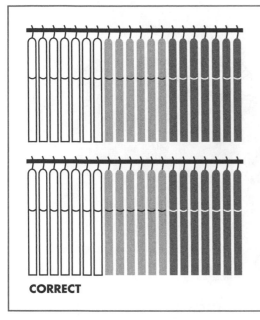
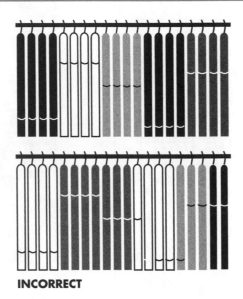

CORRECT   **INCORRECT**

Figure 5.13 A wall presentation of sweaters. An appealing, easy-to-shop presentation is achieved in the correct example, where sweaters with the same sleeve lengths are presented. In the incorrect example sleeve lengths are mixed, resulting in a confusing presentation.

9. *Do not size products on garment rods in walls with sizing rings.* Sizing products mixes colors and patterns together, and merchandise looks as if it has been marked down for clearance. Since products stocked on store walls are viewed from distances, items should be merchandised for maximum visual impact—first pulled together by end use and fabrication, next arranged by style, and then sized without sizing rings. (See Figure 5.15.)

   An exception to this guideline is when there are large quantities of the same style and color of product—a 4-foot section of khaki pants, for example. Then sizing rings may be used, working from left to right and from small to large.

10. *Hangers should be hooked over bars and rods in the direction that makes them easier for shoppers to remove.* Since most people are right-handed, hangers should be hung so that they can be removed from the right, or lifted *toward* the shopper. (See Figure 5.16.)

Folding Techniques for Shelved Products

Sweaters and Shirts

Fold sweaters or shirts on shelves in a consistent manner. There are a number of folding techniques, but just one technique should be implemented in any one wall area. Most stores

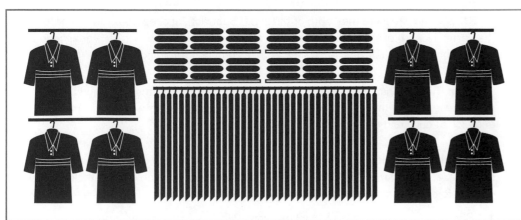

Figure 5.14 A menswear wall presentation, where T-shirts are folded on shelves over pants rather than shoulder hung, so that they are easy to reach for the average customer.

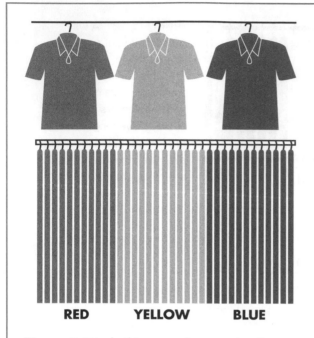

RED   YELLOW   BLUE

Figure 5.15 In this women's apparel wall presentation, one style of pants is presented. The pants are colorized and then sized within each color without sizing rings.

Figure 5.16 Hangers are hooked over this waterfall so that they may be removed from the right, since most shoppers are right-handed.

have chosen a uniform folding style and have made it a company wide standard. Two of the more common techniques are illustrated in Figures 5.17 and 5.18. Directions for creating folding boards to ensure that all items are folded in the same dimensions follow. The vertical armfold is best for light- to medium-weight sweaters, and the horizontal armfold works well with heavy, hand knit style sweaters.

Folding Boards

You will need a folding board to implement either of these techniques. Diagrams of the folding technique can be screen-printed or mounted on the board to reinforce storewide uniformity. Folding boards may be made of styrene, Fome-core, Plexiglas, or any art board with a smooth finish. The smooth finish makes it easier to remove the board after the folding process is completed. The following steps will help you construct a folding board in proper dimensions for any size shelving. (See Figures 5.19 and 5.20.)

Step One: Measure the depth of the shelf. Subtract 2 inches from this figure to obtain the vertical length of the folding board. By subtracting, you allow for the variance in thickness of fabrics. A shelf that is 14 inches deep requires a folding board that is 12 inches deep.

Step Two: Measure the length of the shelf. Divide the length by the number of stacks to be presented on the shelf, allowing 1 to 2 inches of space between each product stack and also at each end of the shelf.

Vertical Arm Folding Board

Example: A shelf that is 48 inches long by 14 inches deep is to hold four stacks. The vertical arm folding board will be 11 inches wide and 12 inches deep. The calculation follows:

1. Board depth is 12 inches (14 inches minus 2 inches for fabric thickness).

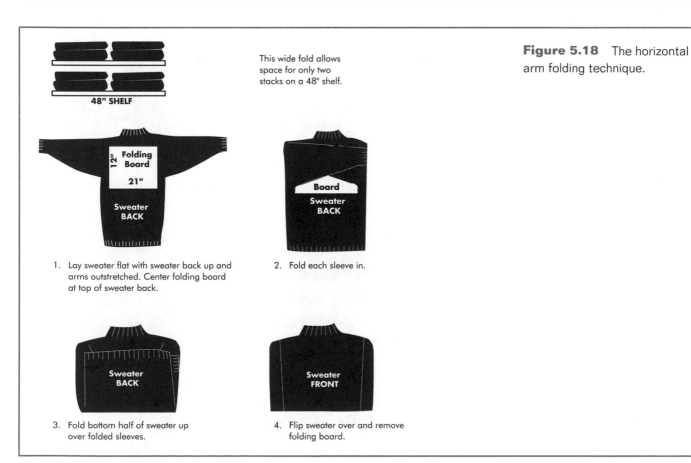

Figure 5.17 The vertical arm folding technique.

This narrow fold allows space for four stacks of sweaters on a 48" shelf.

48" SHELF

1. Lay sweater flat with sweater back up and arms outstretched. Center folding board at top of sweater back.

2. Fold left sleeve over board.

3. Fold sleeve down vertically so that the sleeve BACK is up.

4. Repeat with right sleeve.

5. Fold bottom half of sweater up over folded sleeves.

6. Flip sweater over and remove folding board.

Figure 5.18 The horizontal arm folding technique.

This wide fold allows space for only two stacks on a 48" shelf.

48" SHELF

1. Lay sweater flat with sweater back up and arms outstretched. Center folding board at top of sweater back.

2. Fold each sleeve in.

3. Fold bottom half of sweater up over folded sleeves.

4. Flip sweater over and remove folding board.

123

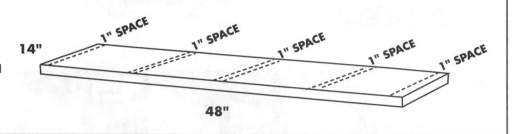

Figure 5.19 Spacing on a 14- x 48-inch shelf for the vertical arm folding technique. Five 1-inch spaces are allowed for separating sweater stacks and at the edges of the shelf.

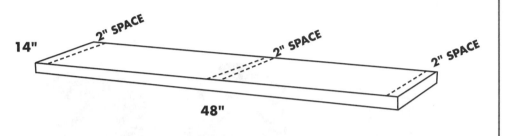

Figure 5.20 Spacing on a 14- x 48-inch shelf for the horizontal arm folding technique. Three 2-inch spaces are allowed for separating sweater stacks and at the edges of the shelf.

2. Board width is 11 inches, as follows:

From the 48 inches in the shelf length deduct 5 inches (three 1-inch spaces between the four stacks + 1 inch at each end of the shelf).

This gives you 43 inches of available space.

Divide 43 by 4 (43 ÷ 4 = 10.75) and round the answer to 11 inches.

Horizontal Arm Folding Board

Example: A shelf that is 48 inches long by 14 inches deep is to hold two stacks. The horizontal arm folding board will be 21 inches wide and 12 inches deep. The calculation follows:

1. Board depth is 12 inches (14 inches minus 2 inches for fabric thickness).

2. Board width is 21 inches, as follows:

From the 48-inch shelf length deduct 6 inches (one 2-inch space between items + 2 inches of space at each end of the shelf).

This gives you 42 inches of available space.

Divide 42 inches by 2 (42 ÷ 2 = 21).

Note: if 21 inches is too wide for the sweater, simply add more space at the shelf edges and between sweaters.

Jeans and Pants

Fold jeans and pants presented on shelves in a consistent manner. Proper folding techniques will give a higher-quality look to the product. Figure 5.21 illustrates one commonly used folding technique.

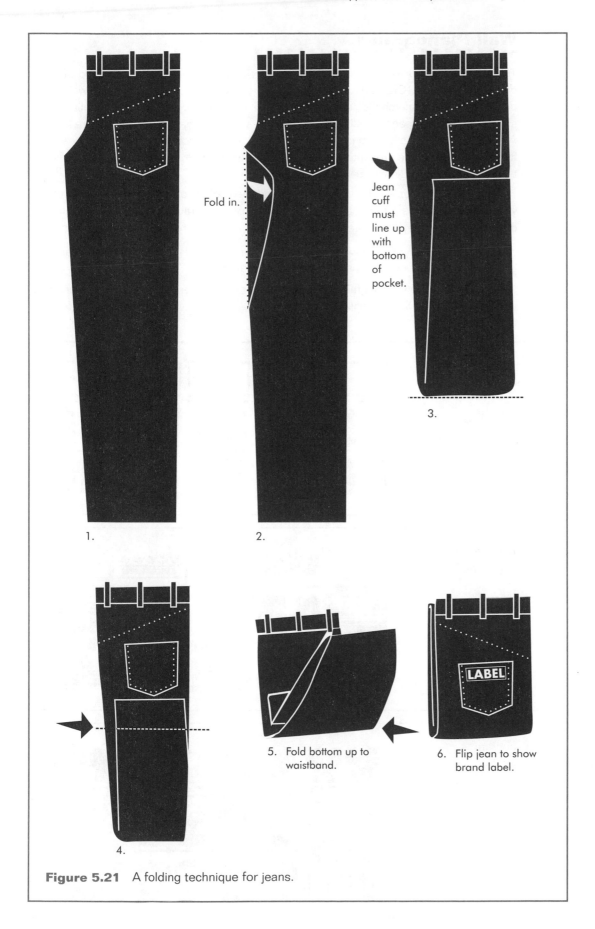

Fold in.

Jean cuff must line up with bottom of pocket.

3.

1.

2.

5. Fold bottom up to waistband.

LABEL

6. Flip jean to show brand label.

4.

Figure 5.21 A folding technique for jeans.

Wall Planograms

The planogram, or illustrated layout of products, is a chain store's best method of visual quality assurance. Created and distributed from company headquarters, well-drawn planograms guide merchandisers to present fashion uniformly. Planograms facilitate consistent fashion messages in all of the company's stores no matter where they are located. A good corporate planogram can be an efficient long-distance teaching tool, as well. The five basic planograms presented in Figures 5.22 through 5.26 are ideal examples of artistic balance and coordinated selling strategies.

Just as many people keep journals to remind themselves of important life experiences, visual merchandisers often keep physical records of memorable in-store presentations or display windows they've created. There are several excellent reasons to get into this habit:

- In a field where you are rewarded for innovation, a record of previous efforts can spur you to create new looks, new merchandise treatments.

- Planograms are meaningful portfolio pieces for job-seekers who need to demonstrate the depth of their retail experience.

Figure 5.22 A 20-foot wall planogram presenting women's sweaters, pants, and handbags.

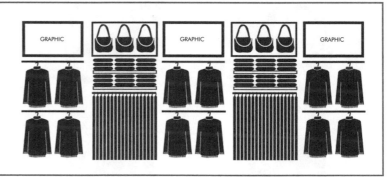

Figure 5.23 A 20-foot wall planogram presenting women's sweatshirts and pants with props; tulips in planters.

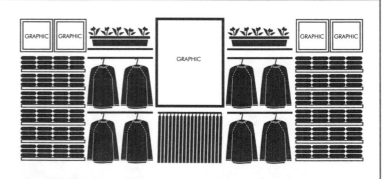

Figure 5.24 A 16-foot wall planogram presenting women's T-shirts and shorts.

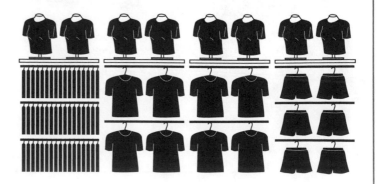

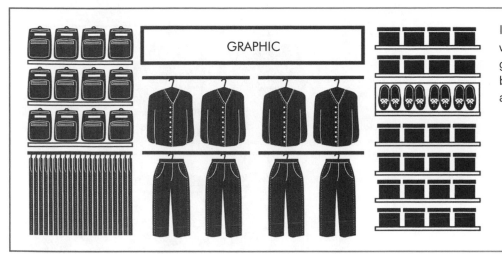

Figure 5.25 A 16-foot wall planogram presenting girls' cardigans, pants, backpacks, and shoes for a back-to-school theme.

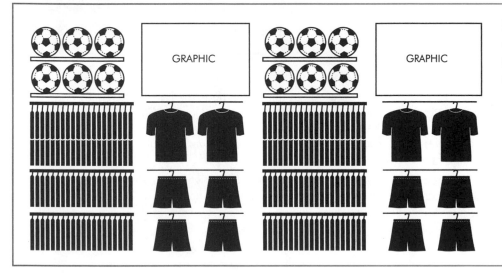

Figure 5.26 A 16-foot wall planogram presenting shorts and T-shirts with a soccer theme.

● Employers look for people who can do more than carry out planograms. They look for people who can design them and communicate standards for competitive presentation to others.

Working a planogram and creating a planogram are two kinds of applied, or hands-on, experience. Starting out, you'll probably need to go through the motions of actually setting up each wall before sketching it on paper. Later on, hours of practice plus familiarity with store guidelines will allow you to draw planograms without actually setting up the display on a wall.

Creating Wall Planograms

By following the simple steps listed in this section, you'll be able to formulate your own planograms for any fashion merchandise wall:

1. Choose a fashion grouping with the same end use, fabrication, style, and color story.

2. Start your composition with a blank wall section. Remove all previous fixtures such as straight arms and flat bars from the wall section.

3. Gather one piece of each item from the merchandise you have selected. If you are going to setup a manufacturer's coordinate grouping, you might pull one hanger with each blouse, knit top, skirt, pant, sweater, vest, or jacket from the coordinate group.

"Plan and then leave yourself open for discovery."

Arnold Newman, photographer known for his environmental portraiture of celebrity figures.

A Retail Reality:
Wall planograms look best when face-outs and shoulder hangings are combined. As product sells down, shoulder-hung areas may be temporarily converted to face-outs until more product arrives or there is time to reset the entire wall.

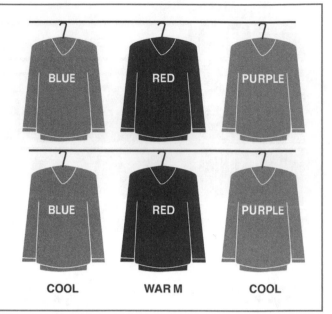

Figure 5.27 A wall presentation using a cool-warm-cool color arrangement.

4. Rather than installing hardware at this stage, hook the hangers temporarily onto the wall standard or gridwall in a balanced setup. Use the Roy G. Bv color chart as you work out the composition, or use a warm–cool color technique. For example, arrange colors in a cool, warm, cool, or warm, cool, warm configuration. (See Figure 5.27.)

5. Add props, graphics, signs, or mannequin alternatives if they are appropriate enhancements to the merchandise. Strive for balanced optical weight, good proportions, interesting lines, and so on.

6. Step back and evaluate the composition of the new wall section. Review the planogram examples and wall presentation guidelines offered earlier in this chapter. If you deviated from the suggested formats, consider reworking the wall.

7. Once you are satisfied with your composition plan, sketch a planogram that shows placement of each item.

8. Remove the preliminary single units of merchandise from the wall and install the correct fixtures in their places.

9. Replace the initial coordinate pieces and fill in behind them with the remaining stock in that style and color. Arrange from smallest size in front to the largest at the back of the straight arm or waterfall.

10. Make note of any signing, graphic, or prop specifications for this presentation on the planogram form. This becomes your historical record. Your wall planogram can then be easily replicated if headquarters sends it to other stores. This record will also prevent you from duplicating something you've done before, or it will help you do it again if you choose to repeat a successful presentation.

Safety Concern!

When you setup a wall presentation, you will be using a variety of wall fixtures, like straight arms, garment rods, brackets, and shelves. As you work, it is a good practice to place all fixtures in a cart rather than on the floor where shoppers or store associates may trip over them. Some retail stores have designed carts specifically for storing and holding fixtures. If a cart is not available, lay fixtures on the floor as close to the wall as possible, so that they are out of traffic aisles.

Creating a Wall Setup

1. Clear wall of previous fixtures and merchandise.

2. Choose a fashion story based on end use, fabrication, style, and color.

3. Select single items from the fashion story. Hook hangers temporarily into wall standards.

4. Arrange product in a balanced composition, using Roy G. Bv, a warm/cool/warm or cool/warm/cool arrangement.

5. Work props or signs into the composition.

6. Observe, evaluate, and reset if necessary.

7. Sketch a planogram.

8. Replace preliminary merchandise items with appropriate fixtures.

9. Fill fixtures with merchandise according to completed planogram.

10. Secure any signing, graphic, or props.

Priority Wall Areas

Now that you have a basic understanding of all of the tools that are available for creating impressive wall presentations, you should also know the location of the three most important walls within a store. Standing at the store entrance, the walls in your immediate range of vision will be the back wall of the store, and any walls visible at angles to your left and right. (See Figure 5.28.) These are the *priority walls* where you'll want to create the

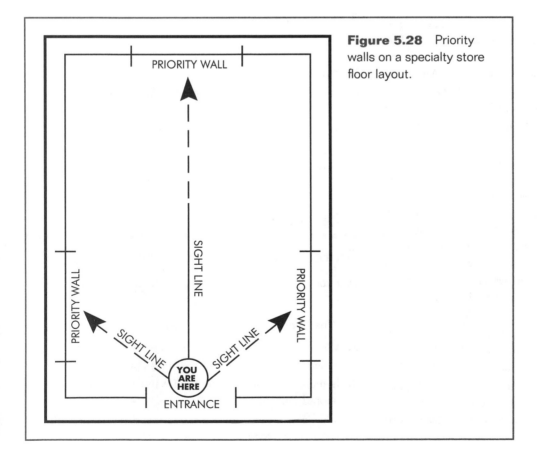

Figure 5.28 Priority walls on a specialty store floor layout.

most excitement and "theater" in the store. In addition to presenting masses of appealing merchandise on a variety of wall fixtures, priority walls are the perfect place to employ communication devices like neon signs, graphic lightboxes, plasma or laser screens, and interactive kiosks. Visit a retailer geared to the youth market to discover how influential an entire wall featuring monitors playing musical videos can be. Priority walls have the potential to become virtual magnets, attracting shoppers to enter and move throughout the store.

Shoptalk
Opportunities in Wall Areas of a Store

By Tony Mancini, vice president, global retail store development, Walt Disney Imagineering and Walt Disney Parks and Resorts

Walls of a store always conjure up a lot of passionate discussion among many people within retail organizations, and usually there are two different schools of thought. Some people think they are important, and others don't believe in them at all! What would an environment be without walls—a spaceless, nondefined area with no focus at all.

Walls create different experiences in retail spaces and help communicate what you want your consumers to see. They could define an area, make a space intimate, and draw your eye into long narrow areas that seem miles away. Walls don't always have to be chock-full of merchandise either as they can communicate brand, presentation, way-finding or be back-lit. It all depends on what you, as a retailer, want to communicate about your business.

The most important component is flexibility. I believe it is the seamless blend of architecture, lighting, composition, and presentation of merchandise graphics and signage. They communicate a lifestyle. It's also important to think about how you segment product and stores as to not confuse consumers about what you want them to focus on. Defining the intentions up front during design is critical to the outcome. Equally important to walls are the floor fixturing systems that are usually in front of them. If you create fixtures that block walls, suddenly the importance of that wall is compromised.

I always look at stores in the fourth dimension. That is, to look beyond the obvious to imagine all elements holistically and how they interface with one another, not interfere.

A retail environment creates a sense of experience. A place of believability, one that you want your consumers to feel great about and to recognize there is differentiation between your brand and someone else's.

Out-of-the-Box Challenge
Comparison Shopping—Store Walls

Look
Visit two stores that cater to similar types of shopper. Look at a merchandised wall section in each store. Make a quick sketch of each wall to help you make comparisons later.

1. Does the wall section tell a single story based on end use, fabrication, and style? What is it?

2. Does the wall section tell a single color story? What is it?

3. Is the wall section artfully balanced? What type of balance is used?

Compare
In which store would you rather shop? Explain why.

Innovate
How would you use innovation in the wall presentations that you observed in each store?

Critical Thinking
Store Analysis

Visit your favorite clothing store. If the store is a department store, choose your favorite department.

1. What types of wall fixtures are used?

2. What types of architectural dividers are used on the walls?

3. Is there a special ceiling or soffit treatment that creates shops? Describe it.

4. Are visual merchandising mannequins, mannequin alternatives, or props used on the walls? Describe them.

5. What types of decorative lighting devices are used to focus attention on the walls?

6. What types of signs are used? Where are they located on the wall?

7. Does the store make use of graphics on the walls? Describe them and tell who the target shopper might be.

8. How do all of the above features contribute to the store's image?

9. Did any of the things you've observed in the wall treatments detract from a consistent store image?

Discussion Questions

1. Why is it useful for a merchandiser to divide perimeter walls into sections?

2. Why is it useful for a merchandiser to divide the store with interior walls?

3. What impact does balance have on the effect of wall setups?

4. When is it permissible to treat separates as if they were part of a coordinate group on a wall?

5. Why is it necessary to feature tops and bottoms in each wall section?

6. Describe why it makes retail sense to show accessories on a wall with a coordinate grouping.

7. Name three merchandising strategies that are supported by dispersing traffic throughout a store and drawing customers to a department's back walls.

8. When is a consistent or systematic approach to wall treatments especially useful to a visual merchandiser?

Activities

Hands-on Planograms

Use Figures 5.29A and 5.29B to create your own planograms.

Case Study

Merchandising Walls Effectively

The Situation: Phase One

Judy Evenson has just started her own visual merchandising business as an independent contractor in a Chicago suburb. There are a number of other visual merchandisers marketing similar businesses, and the competition is keen.

To differentiate her business from those of her competitors, Judy advertises her expertise in creating exciting wall presentations. As a part of her marketing strategy, she has arranged to speak at a monthly mall meeting for a group of suburban mall store managers. Judy shows slides of wall presentations she has created at other malls, and she offers a few basic tips to the managers in her audience. She collects business cards from the managers for a drawing that awards a free wall setup to the winner. Karen Solimar is a winner at one of these drawings.

Discussion Question

Besides speaking at this mall meeting, what else can Judy do to market her business to the people who did not win the free setup? Think outside the box.

The Situation: Phase Two

Karen, the winning manager, is from a store that carries both women's executive wear and workday casual apparel, in a moderate price range. After talking to her, Judy learns that Karen not only owns the store but also purchases all of its merchandise. Even though Karen is excited to have Judy reset one of the walls in her store, she seems a bit uncertain about the outcome. Karen is accustomed to doing all of the presentation work herself and, frankly, she thinks she's very good at it.

Judy senses Karen's hesitation. Judy knows she must satisfy Karen because the success of this job is critical in developing future visual merchandising accounts in the mall. She must find a way to gain Karen's confidence and her enthusiastic support. They agree to meet in Karen's store on the following Monday.

When Judy analyzes Karen's current wall setups, she finds that several critical visual elements are missing from the displays and that Karen is not using any of the techniques presented in the recent workshop. In Judy's opinion, Karen's current wall treatment, featuring only tops, is colorless and monotonous. Furthermore, some of the displayed tops are suitable for executive wear and some are clearly casual—sending a mixed end-use message to shoppers.

Judy notices that Karen has used no props or mannequin alternatives to enhance the wall or any of her other presentations in the store. When she asks about them, Karen tells her that she doesn't think props are important. "If the merchandise doesn't speak for itself," Karen says, "I don't think adding props will help." She then adds, "I don't sell props, I sell clothes."

The outcome of this job for Karen will affect Judy's future business. She knows that she is working with a store manager who is uncertain about her (Judy's) abilities and is likely to feel threatened by any negative comments on her present display efforts. To make it even more difficult, Judy sees nothing on hand, not even a sign, to enhance any presentation she does right now.

Discussion Questions

1. How might Judy approach the subject of adding props, graphics, signing, or any other elements in her "demo" wall treatment for Karen's store?

2. Is there any additional activity that could help Judy gain Karen's confidence?

3. What can Judy do to create a new, exciting presentation on a wall featuring nothing but tops? What can she do without any props?

The Situation: Phase Three

Concerned that Karen was missing multiple sales by showing tops without coordinating bottoms and accessories, Judy and Karen toured competing stores in the mall. As they walked, Judy pointed out the number of complete outfits presented in those stores. They actually counted the number of outfits displayed per store as they walked the mall. One of the stores with considerable shopper traffic featured 25 outfits.

Judy made note of Karen's favorite presentations and when they returned to her store, Judy used these ideas in addition to some of her own and sketched a few options for the wall presentation.

They decided to present a workday casual theme on the wall because that group had the most coordinating pieces, with a large number of natural tones. In the center of the wall, Judy arranged coordinating scarves on one shelf, and handbags on the shelf below. She balanced the wall with complete outfits faced out on either side of the shelf. Judy added another shelf over the scarves and handbags, and asked Karen if she could bring in five inexpensive flower vases from her own prop collection to place on the shelf. Karen agreed, and they scheduled a time to meet at the mall's floral store where, together, they chose a simple arrangement for each vase—a single gerbera daisy and a few stems of beargrass for each vase. Once they were arranged on the wall, Judy adjusted the lighting to enhance the entire wall presentation.

Karen was visibly excited about the outcome. Judy suggested that Karen has her staff track the number of pieces sold in each sale, now that the wall featured complete outfits. She also offered to write up a proposal with several phases to get the entire store in shape. Karen agreed to consider it. On the drive home, Judy congratulated herself for handling a potentially sticky situation and made a mental note to check back with Karen in a few days to see how sales were going. Judy was confident that Karen was going to see a tangible improvement in sales . . . and that she was going to land that contract to update the rest of Karen's store.

Your Challenge

● Sketch a planogram that represents your version of the strategies that Judy put to work in Karen's store. If you need a technical boost, page through the text for planogram elements that you can trace for this project.

● Choose a color story for the wall presentation you've just read about and add it to the planogram.

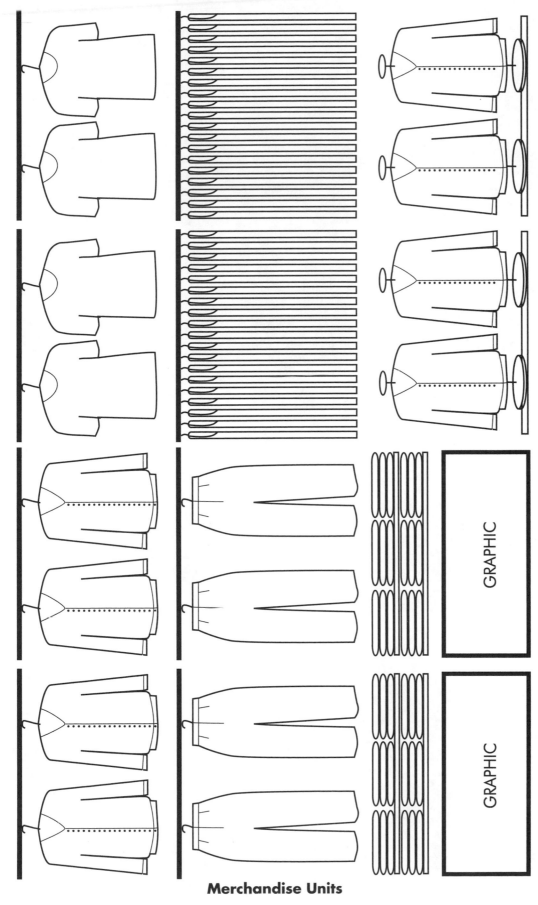

Merchandise Units

Figure 5.29A

133

Blank Wall

Figure 5.29B

135

Chapter 6

FASHION APPAREL AND ACCESSORY COORDINATION

After completing this chapter, you should be able to

Coordinate fashions by end use, fabrication, style, and color

Dress a display hanger with a coordinated outfit

Identify resources to expand your knowledge of current fashion trends

"The tuck of the scarf, the twist
of the belt, the swagger of the
handbag—the expert visual
coordinator knows how to create
'gotta have that too' excitement.
Accessory coordination is the
secret to multiple sales."
RoxAnna A. Sway, editor,
Display & Design Ideas **magazine**

Fashion customers depend on their favorite retailers to have the newest merchandise—in the right colors, fabrics, sizes, and prices. They also expect merchandise to be grouped together by the activity for which it will be worn. When the selling floor is set and the fixtures are filled with trend-right apparel, you may think that the only thing missing is a store filled with shoppers—but there is some very important unfinished business.

How will shoppers begin to visualize themselves wearing the garments they find on the department's racks and hangers? Who will help them pull entire outfits together before they enter fitting rooms? Who will advise them about accessories? Visual merchandisers!

With fewer sales associates on the floor in recent years, shoppers have come to rely on visual merchandisers to bring garments and accessories together in ready-to-buy fashion looks. With that in mind, what is the final step to preparing the store for business? The creation by the visual merchandiser of displays showing distinctive fashion looks accessorized with taste and style that make the merchandise practically sell itself—in multiple units. This retail strategy offers value-added and highly visual services that shoppers really appreciate—fashion know-how, wardrobing guidance, time-saving tips, and simplified shopping.

Fashion coordination takes place in every fashion department—on mannequins, forms, and display hangers—wherever there are opportunities to bring apparel and accessories together for shoppers' benefit. Some visual merchandisers call these coordinated presentations *outfits*, some call them *capsules* or *costumes*, some use the term *display coordinates*, some call them *trend looks*. The terminology isn't nearly as important as the net effect—bringing clothing, accessories, and shoppers together.

Like display techniques, fashion savvy can be learned. By following the guidelines in this chapter; practicing until outfit coordination seems like second nature, you'll soon become an expert and ready to train less-experienced associates. New associates often add their own "creative fashion touches," leading to some amazing fashion *faux pas*. You'll need tact and expertise to explain the importance of the end-use concept plus the other strategies that you'll learn in this chapter. Assure yourself that you can learn effective fashion coordination and presentation techniques—and that you will be able to also teach them to others.

A **fashion editorial** is a display in a strategic location within a store; it reflects a retailer's support for merchandise and trends in the form of a strong fashion statement. Editorials are always positioned in high traffic areas like store entrances, department entrances, escalator platforms, main aisles, and at the ends of aisles on sight lines. Other names used by retailers for these locations include strike-points, hot zones, focals, and interior windows.

Selecting Merchandise for Display

While the fashion coordination guidelines in this chapter may lead you to believe that you have a great deal of freedom about what to select for display, many choices may have already been made for you. A large percentage of today's merchandise arrives at the store already organized in coordinated groupings by manufacturers. In addition, when buyers from department stores and specialty chains return from the market, they work closely with the advertising department to plan and schedule fashion ads, department activities, and fashion events around their purchases. Visual merchandising directors commit window space, in-store **fashion editorial** space, and departmental feature presentations to specific items. Selling department merchandisers or managers allocate wall and feature fixture space to new arrivals. They develop floor plans to accommodate them. Planograms may arrive from central headquarters, and your coordination responsibilities may include carrying out these predetermined plans.

Store buyers also purchase "unrelated separates." This is your opportunity to set walls and fixtures with apparel that hasn't already been prescribed, or whose coordination has not been dictated. Learning to coordinate outfits by end use, fabrication, style, and color will give you the tools you need to increase your own coordinating skills and a method to teach others.

Coordinating by End Use

Just as fashion apparel is separated by end use on walls and fixtures and within selling departments, each coordinated outfit you put together in a department will be composed with end use in mind.

Begin by asking: "Will all of the items I'm coordinating for this display will be worn to work on a regular day or a business casual day? Would a shopper wear these garments and accessories to a dinner in a fine restaurant or for a quick snack in a neighborhood café? Here's the rule: *Whatever the nature of an event, casual or formal, fashion garments and all of their accessories must be end-use appropriate.* Shoppers are depending on you for advice and fashion leadership.

Department stores usually do not mix in the same selling area apparel that is designed to be worn for different occasions. Most fashion departments are separate entities with architectural features like divider walls and varying floor coverings to make their physical separations distinct. Generally, department store associates must remain in their assigned selling areas and are not free to carry items from one department to another—especially from floor to floor. Items with different end uses are therefore less likely to be paired up in an outfit in a department store.

In specialty stores, departments are often adjacent—without many formal boundaries. it is much easier to carry items between areas while coordinating the elements of a fashion purchase—and it is also much easier for a fashion faux pas to occur. Even though sales associates may be familiar with the merchandise in their own areas, they may not be aware of trend direction in other selling areas. (See Figure 6.1.)

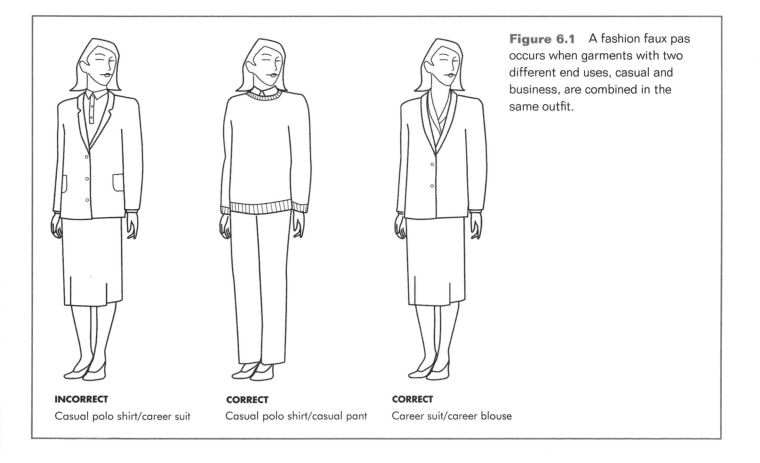

Figure 6.1 A fashion faux pas occurs when garments with two different end uses, casual and business, are combined in the same outfit.

INCORRECT
Casual polo shirt/career suit

CORRECT
Casual polo shirt/casual pant

CORRECT
Career suit/career blouse

139

Coordinating by Fabrication

Outfits must be coordinated with fabrications that complement each other. One way to determine this is to think about whether they are intended for the same end use. A lightweight gauze shirt would work well with a linen suit if the shirt is a dressier style. If it had an embroidered trim, it might be better paired with a casual pant or jean. Another way to learn about how fabrics are coordinated is to look at the outfits that are displayed in your favorite stores. Next, to expand your range of knowledge about fabrication blending, look at the outfits in stores where you do not normally shop.

Coordinating by Style

Fashion apparel can be divided into two distinct style categories: *classic* looks and *trend* looks. When you put fashion merchandise together for display on a wall hanger or selling floor fixture, your choices should reflect *just one* of these categories. If you are featuring a classic polo shirt on a face-out, match it with classic casual pants. If you are featuring an oversized trend polo shirt on a mannequin alternative, match it with the appropriate trend pant. Accompanying accessories should also enhance the single theme. (See Figure 6.2.)

Coordinating by Color

After determining end use, fabrication, and style of an outfit, you must consider a color. If you are pulling together an outfit from a manufacturer's coordinated grouping, your job will be easy. Manufacturers have already planned an assortment of pieces like shirts, jackets, sweaters, vests, skirts, and pants fabricated from dyed-to-match fabrics and yarns or paired with carefully selected woven and printed patterns. Your work is virtually done for you.

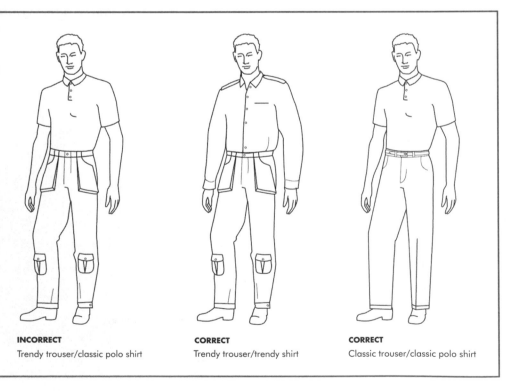

Figure 6.2 A fashion faux pas is created when garments with two different styles, classic and trend, are combined in the same outfit.

INCORRECT
Trendy trouser/classic polo shirt

CORRECT
Trendy trouser/trendy shirt

CORRECT
Classic trouser/classic polo shirt

Creating a coordinated look from unrelated separates is more challenging. You may find it helpful to refer to the color wheels in Colorplate 3. Another approach might be to choose garments based on the color groupings in Colorplate 5.

How to Color-Coordinate Fashion Looks

Step 1: Select just one color group (or color intensity) for any one outfit. (Use the color groups in Colorplate 5.)

Step 2: Add neutral color(s) in additional garments or accessories if you wish.

Step 3: Repeat some or all of the colors in additional garments or accessories.

Pay close attention to the third step—repetition. Colors that are repeated must *match!* Mismatched colors stand out and distort an overall color scheme. If you are looking for pants to coordinate with a multicolored sweater featuring tints of pastel pink, pastel blue, and *off-white,* the coordinating pant must also be *off-white.* White pants would be inappropriate, in the same way that red and wine would not work together, even though they are both shades of red.

The same is true for accessories. If you want to accessorize a mannequin with gold earrings, the necklace you choose could be a gold chain or colored beads mixed with tiny gold chain links. You would not want to choose a silver chain. If the earrings feature a combination of gold and silver, however, you could select a gold or silver chain necklace—or use multiples of each.

Colorplate 11 shows how easily garments may be color-coordinated by using the design element of repetition. The patterned shirt is used as a **pivot piece** for the entire outfit. Colors found in the shirt are repeated in the pants and all the accessories. Note that it isn't necessary to repeat every single color found in a patterned piece, just the dominant ones. If the pivot piece has only tiny specks of yellow in a print or plaid, for example, you shouldn't repeat it.

A **pivot piece** is the dominant item in that it dictates the direction (end use, fabrication, style, and color) for all subsequent pieces used in a coordinated outfit.

Advanced Color Coordinating

The color coordination techniques explained above require that all colors combined are the same intensity. For example, pastel pink can be paired with another pastel like green, for an aesthetically pleasing combination.

To create an unusual outfit, you can give the color theory a twist by combining colors from different groups. This is seldom seen in fashion stores, because it is a little more difficult to accomplish, but it is a fun way to differentiate products that are almost identical in various stores.

First choose colors from two separate groups. For example:

● Pastel pink polo shirt

● Bright green cotton sweater

Then repeat the colors in accessories like a casual scarf and earrings. Complete the outfit with neutral khaki slacks, chocolate brown casual shoes and handbag. See Colorplate 11.

Simple repetition of core colors is the key to making this technique work, but it must be combined with a sense of taste and style. There are several books available with a wide variety of color pairings. These resources can help you to think outside-the-box as you coordinate outfits in your displays. Most of these books are available at **www.stmediagroup.com/stbooks**.

● *Showing Your Colors – A Designer's Guide to Coordinating Your Wardrobe* by Jeanne Allen, Chronicle Books, San Francisco

- *Color Harmony* by Hideaki Chijiiwa, Rockport Publishers, Gloucester, MA.
- *Color Harmony 2* by Bride M. Whelan, Rockport Publishers, Gloucester, MA.
- *Color Harmony Jewels* by Martha Gill, Rockport Publishers, Gloucester, MA.
- *Color Harmony Pastels* by Martha Gill, Rockport Publishers, Gloucester, MA.
- *Color Harmony Naturals* by Martha Gill, Rockport publishers, Gloucester, MA.
- *The Designers Guide to Color Combinations* by Leslie Cabarga, North Light Books, Cincinnati
- *Color Harmony Workbook—A Workbook and Guide to Creative Color Combinations* by Lesa Sawahata, Rockport publishers, Gloucester, MA.
- *PANTONE© Guide to Communicating with Color* by Leatrice Eiseman, Grafix Press, Sarasota

Color Coordinating with the Basic Color Wheels

The basic color wheels in Colorplate 3 offer endless possibilities for color coordinating. When working with bold combinations like bright purple and yellow, it is more pleasing to use one of the two as an accent, rather than in equal amounts. Too much bold color can make an outfit more appropriate for the stage than the street.

Monochromatic schemes are beautiful, but are seldom seen. It may take a trip to several departments in a store to pull all of the pieces together for a single monochromatic outfit. The added effort will allow you to offer your customers a unique outfit that they won't see everywhere they go. Your expertise will draw them back again and again. Experiment with all of the color wheels and make notes of your favorite combinations. It will take practice, but is a very valued skill when mastered. See Colorplate 3.

Seasonal Color Schemes

When you're coordinating outfits, it is best to avoid color combinations that are associated with holidays. For one thing, these color combinations are clichés—done and overdone until there's no doubt about the season they represent. What holiday do you think of when you see bright red and green clothing? How about an orange and black outfit? What image do you see in your mind's eye when you see lavender, yellow, and pink combined? Retail-oriented Americans will probably think of Christmas, Halloween, and Easter. Shoppers are not likely to purchase outfits in these color combinations; especially red with green and orange with black. Even though it may seem like a fun approach, your major emphasis should be focused on *fashion*. To do otherwise may waste effort and valuable selling space on outfits that will never sell.

An exception to the rule would be if your company purchased novelty seasonal items; for example, holiday sweatshirts with green Christmas trees and red ornaments. In that case, select a neutral bottom and let the patterned sweatshirt be the dominant piece in the outfit.

Coordinating Patterned Pieces

Fabric patterns come in all shapes and sizes—from large buffalo checks to plaids to tiny herringbone tweeds. The easiest way to coordinate patterns within one outfit is to *combine one small pattern with one large pattern*. As a rule, the dominant colors in both patterns should match. You could blend a medium stripe with a small floral print or combine tiny

142

Figure 6.3 Notice how large and small patterns are combined in these two examples. The dominant colors in both garments must match to achieve a well-coordinated fashion look.

CORRECT   **CORRECT**

checks with a large abstract figure, provided that their main color schemes are compatible. (See Figure 6.3.)

You may have heard that stripes and prints should never be mixed. Visual merchandising is about interpreting fashion trends and creating a fashion image for your store. If designers are mixing their patterns, you may certainly do the same. Shoppers will notice what you've put together—and may opt to purchase exactly what you've coordinated or decide to go with a more conservative version of your look. The choice is theirs. Your job is to create attention-getting, fashion-forward visual presentations that shoppers can edit.

Coordinating Brand Names

Many fashion apparel items have prominent brand names embroidered or stamped on them. Feature only one brand name per outfit. A Tommy Hilfiger T-shirt might coordinate with a Nike jacket and Patagonia shorts when you consider the end use, fabrication, style, and color criteria mentioned earlier. The question is, should you bring all of those brand names together in one outfit? Never. Fragmented identity is not a look you'd want to promote to shoppers who depend on your fashion direction. In fact, many designer brand agreements stipulate exclusivity for their product presentation.

Coordinating by Trend

Fashion trends often seem contrary to the guidelines you've just learned. You might think that bright purple and pastel pink should never be combined in an outfit, but an emerging

A Retail Reality:
You'll soon train your fashion coordinator's eye if you rely on current magazines and videos for fashion direction. Cutting-edge looks from top apparel and accessory designers will teach you about important fashion trends that will soon reach the mass market.

143

trend shown in the media may dictate use of that very combination. Media-driven fashion trends frequently break rules and override accepted guidelines.

We've said that fashion items with different end uses should never be combined. That's the rule. Here comes the exception: A fashion trend may combine items with different end uses to achieve an innovative look. One season's hot trend might involve taking a dressier top—a black angora sweater with iridescent buttons, for example—and pairing it with denim jeans. Forward-looking "fashionistas" would call this *dressing down*. A more conservative customer might disregard the "edgy" new trend, pair the identical sweater with a slim crepe skirt, wear it to dinner in a fine restaurant, and call it *dressing up*. That's the great thing about fashion. Customers can do whatever they like with their purchases. However, if the prevailing trend pairs the sweater and jeans, present it this way in the store.

Dressing a Coordinate Display Hanger

Most retail stores have invested in special hangers for displaying coordinated tops and bottoms together as one unit. The hanger functions as a mannequin alternative and is dressed as if it were a human torso. It may be a simple flat wire hanger or a decorative hanger with the retailer's name imprinted on it, or it may even include a molded chest or bust form. Hangers may have conventional hooks or custom hooks (a loop of cable wire for example) that will easily fit over a face-out. Some may come with hooks that are compatible with a store's slatwall, gridwall, or other wall systems. A display hanger for coordinates has an extension that holds a bar for draping a pair of pants or clips that will hold skirts or shorts where a person's normal waistline would be. Do not use a coordinate hanger from stock because the waistline will be three inches below the shoulder—hardly a fashion look!

Display hangers are sometimes used as "solo" presentations in wall displays and are often featured as the front items on waterfall and straight-arm fixtures. The hanger should always emphasize the items featured on that particular wall section or fixture. In fact, that's the entire purpose of composing an outfit on a hanger—to give shoppers an idea about how garments will look when pulled together as an outfit. Why try to sell only one item when you can just as easily sell two or more?

The following steps will guide you through the process of dressing a display hanger:

Step One. Select an outfit from the fixture on which the display hanger will be placed. Use only the items that are on the fixture.

As you select the items for your outfit, do not add layers of clothing that would not realistically be worn together. Even though two colors of polo shirts would brighten up an outfit, customers won't buy two polo shirts and wear them at the same time. Attention-getting devices are effective in a store window or on a high ledge display but should not be used for an outfit hanger on the selling floor.

Step Two. Dress the display hanger. If you are showing a pant, fold it over the pant bar on the hanger. If you are showing a skirt or short, you may wish to tuck the top in, showing the waist of the bottom. If there are belt loops, add a belt. Belt loops should not remain empty. As a fashion expert, it is important that you show a completely finished look to your customers and also take advantage of the opportunity for multiple sales.

Step Three. Steam the outfit with a professional steamer to remove wrinkles. Display garments must *always* be steamed. Follow the instructions on the steamer to fill and preheat the unit. Hang the display hanger fully dressed, on the steamer hook.

Glide the steamer gently over the fabric. You may also prefer to reach inside the garment and pull the steamer head against the fabric. The steam will come through the garment toward you and the pressure you exert from behind the fabric may help you get better results. For stubborn wrinkles, tug on the bottom hem of the garment to gently stretch the fabric while you are steaming it. (See Figure 6.4.)

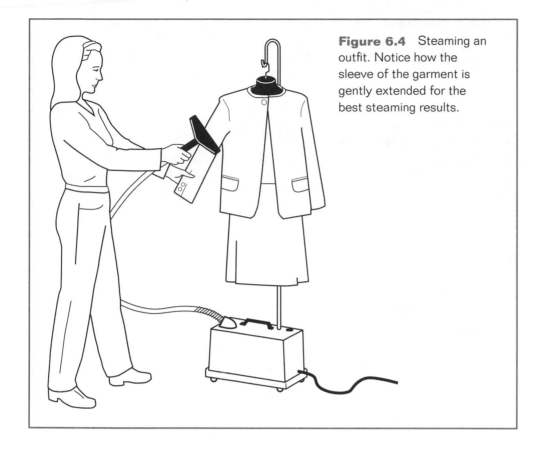

Figure 6.4 Steaming an outfit. Notice how the sleeve of the garment is gently extended for the best steaming results.

Safety Concern!

All steaming techniques must be done with extreme caution; the steam is very hot.

When steaming knits, lay sweaters flat on a towel. Don't hang them until they are completely dry. Knits—particularly those made of heavier yarns—will stretch too much if you steam them thoroughly while they are on hangers. Always be careful not to damage garments as you prepare them for display.

Step Four. Place the display hanger with the steamed outfit on the display hook provided on the fixture, or if there is none, face it out on a straight arm or waterfall.

Coordination Resources

As a small store visual merchandiser, you may be expected to take the lead in determining how fashions are coordinated in your store. Many smaller specialty operations depend on communicating a one-of-a-kind fashion message to their target clientele. They want to differentiate themselves from their competitors.

If you are employed by a larger retail corporation, you may receive information detailing precisely how fashion apparel items should be presented. These bulletins or messages from headquarters are intended to keep corporate image and overall merchandising style uniform from store to store. Familiarize yourself with corporate presentation practices, so that the fashion looks you coordinate match those presented by other units in the chain.

When working for any retail organization, large or small, expand your awareness of current fashion trends. Before you begin your research, identify the store's target customer. If the store's customer base is composed of 35- to 55-year-old executive level males, your research should focus on that type of customer. This can be a "reach" if you're a 30-year-old female from a blue-collar background, worried about making a car payment. If you are in your twenties and would rather be pulling trendy outfits together, you may have to put your personal preferences aside to learn about your employer's customer's needs . . . or find an edgy store that's looking for help.

Fashion magazines and catalogs are probably the easiest and least expensive resources to use because you can clip out or highlight the fashion ideas that you might like to use for inspiration. Many newspapers run regular fashion columns and feature stories about national and local trends or publish seasonal fashion magazines, such as *Fashions of the Times* or the Sunday *Style* section from *The New York Times.* Fashion shows will expose you to the latest fashions and accessory trends. Watch for styles of shoes and hosiery or boots as the models move down the runway; it is usually easy to pick up on strong trends as you repeatedly see certain accessory styles—flats with anklets, or strap heels with nude hosiery, and so on. You can see clips from the most recent fashion shows worldwide on the Internet at **www.firstview.com.** MTV, E! and other cable channels are rich sources of international, national, and local fashion information. Popular movies and TV series often trigger fashion trends. To find out about trends for the future and to discover what is happening in the marketplace today look at *Women's Wear Daily* and the *Daily News Record.*

People-watching is another productive way to gather fashion ideas. All you have to do is choose a location based on the demographic segment you want to observe in its natural surroundings—nightclubs, coffee shops, shopping malls, or any place where people gather. If you want to learn more about acceptable dress in business settings, go to a corporate building and watch people coming and going during lunch hour. If you are working in a store that sells junior fashions, staff members who are still in high school can probably offer you ideas.

As you conduct your fashion research, look for people who are wearing unusual colors, textures, and fabric combinations. You may find that they are using familiar accessories in new ways. You may see ideas to which you can add your own creative twist. Remember to edit what you observe so that it fits your customer. Look, compare, and innovate!

Don't forget to shop the competition. In *Confessions of a Window Dresser,* Simon Doonan advises: "A window dresser would be crazy not to peruse the competition. Why not go right to the source?" In typical tongue-in-cheek fashion, Doonan says: "Plagiarism is flattering in the warm and fuzzy world of window dressing. I always feel immensely complimented if someone takes the trouble to knock off my window ideas." He adds "Other people's windows can also be a major source of counter-motivation, as in 'Shoot me if I ever do that!'" His point? Look, compare, and innovate!

Shoptalk

Trends for Fun and Fashion

By Ignaz Gorischek, vice president, visual planning and presentation, Neiman Marcus

Trends are as simple as a single item or as complicated as anything else. Of late, the latter seems to apply. Individuals used to buy into a "trend" to gain acceptance, an identity, of being one with the crowd. Consumers these days are more confident with themselves—trends are still important, but the individual twist that is added to the trend makes it your own.

I look for future trends everywhere: books, magazines, movies, art openings, parties. Trends today seem to burn brighter and faster—thanks to the many channels of communication. I dare say one could not keep up with or participate in all of the trend options we have today, but the good news is that even after the trend is not necessarily the item of the moment, it can (and should) remain a part of your personal style.

Out-of-the-Box Challenge

Trend Shopping in a Social Gathering Place

Look

Go to your favorite place for people-watching; coffee shop, shopping mall, airport, and so on. Look for three people wearing outfits that do not seem to work. Sketch the outfits.

Compare

Compare the sketches with the guidelines from this chapter, coordinating outfits by end use, fabrication, style, and color.

Innovate

Add notes to your sketches describing how you would add a new twist to the outfits.

Critical Thinking

Activity 1 Play 20 Questions

1. Describe how fashion displays within selling departments act as silent sellers.

2. Describe a display that helped you make a decision to buy both the featured garment and the accessories shown with it.

3. Describe the kind of shopper who likes shopping from a fixture that contains several coordinate elements

brought together in a grouping. What do you think that person likes about coordinate groups?

4. Do you ever mix elements from various coordinate groupings to create a unique look? If you do, describe what motivates you to do so. If you don't, describe why you're reluctant to do so.

5. Explain why we say that coordinators make "fashion statements" when they combine clothing and accessories.

6. There is a lot of competition among store employees to "prescribe and present the newest fashion items." How can a display be prescriptive?

7. What kind of fashion statement are you, your clothing, and your accessories making today?

8. When you got dressed today, did you mix end uses? Explain what you were thinking as you chose your clothing.

9. Describe a current trend style that you've seen on display recently. What is this trend's end use?

10. What is your definition of a fashion classic?

11. Explain how a basic item in a fashion department could also be considered a classic.

12. Look around the room and identify someone who has effectively used a pivot piece in putting together an outfit to wear today. How does the rest of this person's clothing relate to it?

13. Name another color cliché related to a holiday or season in addition to the four listed in the text.

14. One of the Retail Realities listed in this chapter mentioned that cutting-edge designer fashion eventually reaches the mass market. Do you think the looks get more "edgy" or more conservative as that happens? Explain your reasoning.

15. Describe a recent trend that you think has broken fashion rules. Who has embraced that trend?

16. What do you think the term — refers to?

17. Where would you recommend that an employee of your favorite clothing store go to do some people-watching research?

18. What college courses could you recommend to visual merchandisers who want to expand their background knowledge of both past and present fashion trends?

19. What would you do to edit the most popular fashion look for teenagers today and make it more acceptable to people in their late twenties?

20. What would you do to edit the most popular business dressing trend today and make it more acceptable to people in their teens?

Activity 2 Fashion Coordination Resources

1. Visit a store with a large selection of fashion magazines. Select the magazine that you consider to be the best fashion coordination resource for each of the following customer bases:

   - Generation X
   - Generation Y
   - Baby Boomers

2. Bring the magazines to class and discuss why you chose them.

3. Repeat the same exercise using shopping Websites on the Internet. Print out a few pages from each site to bring to class for discussion.

Activity 3 Coordination Collage

If you've ever looked at a fashion editorial in a magazine and wondered why the photo stylist or fashion coordinator used those particular items and accessories to make the fashion statements, here's *your* chance to be the coordinator. This activity is not gender- or age-specific.

1. Create a fashion collage composed of unrelated items. Cut out single items from magazines and catalogs to create seven new head-to-toe coordinated fashion looks. Each look should relate to one of the following end uses:

   - A professional look that's appropriate for a workplace
   - A student look that's appropriate for your campus
   - A spectator sportswear look (to be part of the audience)
   - An active sportswear look (to participate in the activity)
   - A party look
   - A dressy or elegant look
   - A trend look

2. For each new outfit, select:

   - A top
   - A bottom
   - A pair of shoes
   - A handbag, briefcase, or another appropriate bag
   - A pair of earrings or other jewelry
   - Other appropriate accessories like a hat, a watch, and so on.

   Note: if you select a dress or suit, choose an optional jacket, sweater, or blouse to create a layered look.

3. Assemble a new "body" for the collage. Compose each collage on an 81/2 x 11 sheet of typing paper or construction paper. Label the "look" you are presenting. Explain why the elements you've brought together make the outfit appropriate for each of the end uses.

   Note: Don't be alarmed if the various items are out of proportion. The idea is to have some fun coordinating unique fashion looks.

4. Present your collage collection to the class and compare your interpretations to those of your classmates. You will find that everyone has his or her own personal style and has interpreted each assigned look differently. This exercise will explain why retailers want their visual merchandisers to work within their corporate guidelines as they coordinate merchandise to be presented to customers.

Case Study

Presenting a Fashion Trend Workshop

Visual merchandisers frequently train sales associates to present the current season's fashion trends effectively in their work on the selling floor. In some instances, this training helps the employees understand the store's fashion image message more clearly so that they can express it to shoppers in their one-to-one sales presentations. In many cases, much of the merchandise presentation on the selling floor is actually done by associates—or at least maintained by them once set by visual merchandisers.

This exercise can be a solo or a group project. Either way requires prior planning. The team approach is a skill-builder. Creating teams and working with them effectively is important to your career development.

Your Challenge

Present a fashion trend workshop to your class that will bring the elements from Chapter 6 together. This is a task that visual merchandisers are sometimes asked to do in their stores.

The "merchandise" to be presented will come from your own and your classmates' wardrobes.

Step One

- Choose a gender to be represented by the clothing.
- Choose a fashion season for the garments to be presented—Spring, Fall, Holiday, or Cruise/Resort.

You could plan this project as one large group and choose a single season, or you could break into four smaller groups and do all four seasons. The more groups you have, the greater variety of coordination and presentation techniques you'll be able to experience.

With this arrangement, no one individual has to furnish every single item in order to participate. If you want more than four teams, you can always add a decade theme (1950s) or a book/movie theme *after* you've followed the standard guidelines in the next step.

Step Two

- Select a seasonal end-use theme (e.g., holiday evening wear), then a fabrication theme (e.g., shiny fabrics), then a style theme (e.g., short party dresses), then a color theme (e.g., pastels), and finally a trend theme (e.g., ruffled hemlines). Once you have those specifications identified, you can brainstorm to see what each person can contribute to the various presentations.

- Imagine that you're dressing hangers for face-out presentations on walls and selling fixtures. If you don't have display hangers in your classroom, improvise with regular hangers. Presenting a fully dressed hanger is more visually effective than draping garments over your arm or showing things on a flat tabletop.

- Plan to include several alternative tops to go with one or two bottoms—the usual ratio for coordinate groupings—if you're showing separates. Remember that you're trying to encourage multiple sales by showing enough merchandise for a wardrobe "capsule" that will give a shopper many outfit options in a single shopping trip. Even party clothes could be accessorized with elegant shawls, dressy evening coats and capes, plus shoes, hosiery, evening bags, and jewelry.

Step Three

Select a *complete* accessory treatment to enhance your presentation. Even if the items—like sandals and sunglasses—don't fit on the hanger, you should present everything you'd use if you were coordinating to dress a mannequin. This teaches selling associates valuable cross-merchandising techniques and imparts a complete fashion statement in keeping with the store's image.

Step Four

- Once your team has completed its planning, meet with the other groups to design an evaluation form to be used for all of your presentations.

- Identify the important criteria for this presentation and prepare an evaluation form. You may elect to use a scale that rates each aspect of the presentation from 0 (the element was missing from the presentation altogether) to 5 (an exemplary presentation in every way). Then, as each team presents, the other teams can rate its presentation and offer feedback. You might rate how effectively the presenters dealt with the seasonal theme, how completely they followed through with end use, style, fabrication, and color, how they accessorized, and so on.

Step Five

- Pull all of your merchandise and accessories together (clean, pressed, and on hangers in "outfits") for the presentation.

- Be ready to describe the garments and accessories using current fashion terminology and trend information. Learning the correct fabric names and use and care instructions are particularly helpful tools for selling associates. That information (plus anything you can tell them about manufacturers and current fashion trends) is appropriate for the visual merchandisers to know and share in the training session.

- Describe how you plan to present the merchandise on face outs and selling fixtures in the selling departments.

Step Six

Using the evaluation forms, plan a 5-minute postpresentation *constructive* feedback session that addresses the effectiveness of the coordination effort as well as the strengths of the presentation. Peer feedback is valuable. You may not agree with what you hear, but you can learn from it and from the process.

Chapter 7

HOME FASHION PRESENTATION

After completing this chapter, you should be able to

Identify the different types of home fashion stores

Recognize several styles of home store entrances

Coordinate home fashions by end use, fabrication, style, and color

Create tabletop and wall presentations

Identify resources to expand knowledge of current home fashion trends

"A strong home fashion visual
merchandising environment
inspires the customers to purchase
products that help satisfy their
pursuit of the good life."
**Rick Burbee, creative director,
Sears full-line stores**

"Home. Going there, staying there, and entertaining there. Designers, and then soon everyone else in the world, will discover self-expression, not just in what they wear, but suddenly—and most likely from now on—in where they wear it, and what they do when they get there."

Peter Glen in *10 Years of Peter Glen*

"High touch. People will crochet a cover for their home computers and display the quilt next to the robot. Every natural material, everything that is or looks handmade, will be prized. And this new balance between high-tech and high-touch is here to stay. There are tremendous retail implications here."

10 Years of Peter Glen

Home Fashion Stores

There was a time when *home fashion* referred only to wall coverings, paints, window treatments, and furniture. Today the steady influx of well-designed home products involves everything from pots, pans, and pepper mills for the kitchen to bedding and blankets for the bedroom. Skyrocketing national sales figures indicate that American shoppers care passionately about *all* the trappings of their lives, not merely what they wear. Williams-Sonoma, Inc. (**www.williamsonomainc.com**) says it very well: "People love their homes. They form lifelong memories and create unbreakable bonds with the rooms in which their lives unfold."

Today, fashion touches even unglamorous housekeeping items like rubber gloves, brooms, and buckets. Visit any home store or discount store and you'll see hundreds of housekeeping basics in trend colors and updated, ergonomic designs. Furthermore, it's not unusual to find commonplace household items in specialty gift stores . . . complete with coordinated themes and current trend colorways. Turn on cable television and you'll find multiple networks devoted to homes, gardens, and lifestyles.

Penelope Green of the *Star Tribune* (Minneapolis) writes, "Cleaning has come out of the broom closet. A home magazine, *Dwell,* makes its debut this month with a cover line that reads, 'The Most Beautiful Vacuum Cleaners on Earth.' And aren't they just? They range from the pink Hello Kitty Sanyo, $89.95, the Filter Queen Majestic, to a ringer for the robot on *Lost in Space,* about $1800. Cleaning has gone all high tech and looks gender neutral. You might call it indoor gardening."

People are interested in making all aspects of their daily lives—especially precious free time—more enjoyable. And that includes surrounding themselves with useful, pleasant-looking, functional household products and home furnishings. This trend has expanded the number and variety of home products sold, and the number of specialty stores dedicated to home fashion products continues to grow. A sampling of well-known retailers that specialize in fashionable home décor products today includes

- Department Stores—Macy's Cellar, Marshall Field's Marketplace, Bloomingdale's, Saks
- Specialty Stores—Crate&Barrel, Williams-Sonoma, Inc., Pottery Barn, Restoration Hardware, Smith & Hawken, Pier 1 Imports, Portico Home, Portico Bed & Bath, Conran's, Ikea, Calvin Klein, Banana Republic Home, Eddie Bauer Home, Caban.
- Discount Stores—Bed, Bath and Beyond, Linens 'n Things, Target, Wal-Mart.
- Outlet Stores—CB2

Store Entrances

From the growing list of competitors entering the field, you can see that differentiation is a major factor in positioning home fashion stores as branded entities. In brick-and-mortar retailing, differentiation begins at the front door. There, the entrance to the store or department offers home fashion retailers their first opportunity for creativity.

In the past, the specialty store entrance was approximately 16 feet wide with a standard plate glass display window on either side of the doors. In Figures 7.1 and 7.2 you see two unusual store entrances that reflect originality in home fashion store architectural design. Notice that both stores have about 6 to 10 feet of free space before shoppers reach the first floor fixture. Both approaches are open and inviting, and welcome shoppers inside before they are exposed to merchandise—space that allows shoppers to adjust to each store's environment and builds visual anticipation for the products to come.

Figure 7.1 An unusual store entrance at Cooks of Crocus Hill, Edina, Minnesota.

Figure 7.2 An unusual store entrance at Chiasso, Tyson's Corner, McLean, Virginia.

Figure 7.3 A signature fixture at the entrance to Woolworth's, South Africa.

Figure 7.4 At M.J. Décor, in New York City, architectural design elements in the ceiling combine with a center aisle to encourage traffic to move through the store.

Visual designers who position a signature fixture immediately inside the store entrance believe that the first item a shopper sees will be imprinted on memory for later retrieval. Although they need to sell merchandise, they also want to make a fashion image or value statement. This strategy is meant to draw shoppers to the fixture for closer inspection of the featured product. Shoppers may not make their product selections right away, but they will file the information away for comparison to other items in the featured categories as they travel farther into the store. (See Figure 7.3.)

Another approach to entry design presents a center aisle at the store entrance. In Figure 7.4, the aisle draws traffic through the store to its back wall. The store's skylighted ceiling pattern further encourages movement, stopping just short of the arch opening into the last section. With an intriguing layout like this, how could a shopper leave the store without exploring its entire length?

Store Layout

Store layouts in moderately priced or discount stores like Bed, Bath and Beyond, Linens 'n Things, Wal-Mart, and Target typically combine grid and racetrack layouts. A looping racetrack leads traffic past stand-alone departments in which the fixtures are arranged in a grid pattern. This layout pattern is effective for gondola fixtures ranging from 12 to 24 feet or more in length. (See Figure 7.5.)

Department stores often use a combination of grid and free-flow layouts. Look again at Figure 7.3. A symmetrical free-flow layout leads into the Woolworth homewares department. Now look at Figure 7.6 to see the fixtures positioned in a grid layout next to the wall. This is an effective combination layout that not only invites shoppers into the department, but it utilizes valuable square footage adjacent to the back wall.

Upscale specialty stores usually implement a combined soft aisle and free-flow layout. Fixtures are grouped together in clusters, with 5 to 10 feet between clusters. You'll see this layout in Williams-Sonoma and Pottery Barn stores. In Figure 7.7, Chiasso's architectural plan shows its version of a combined soft aisle and free-flow layout. Pay attention to the

Figure 7.5 Notice the racetrack that runs along Zeller's Housewares department in Burlington, Ontario, Canada.

Figure 7.6 Fixtures are arranged in a grid floor layout at Woolworth, South Africa.

store's main traffic pattern (indicated by dotted lines). Chiasso uses unusual wall fixtures to draw shoppers through the store and lead them to merchandised walls. (See Figure 7.8.)

Floor Feature Fixtures

A **riser** is any display unit used to elevate merchandise in a composition so that the overall presentation has visual interest and variety.

The most commonly used floor fixtures in home fashion stores or departments are **risers** and *tables*. These fixtures are classified as feature fixtures (see Chapter 4) because of their editorial function—which is to display the latest home fashion trends. The late retail consultant Peter Glen called these editorials *punctuation points.*

You may purchase riser units in all sizes and shapes from fixture manufacturers' catalogs. Plexiglas or polycarbonate riser cubes, towers, rounds, and rectangles are available in clear, opaque white, black, or colored finishes. Common rectangular measurements are 11 × 11 × 24, 11 × 11 × 30, and 11 × 11 × 36—sizes that provide a good base to work from and eye-pleasing height variations for display.

Wooden display cubes or rectangular risers generally have laminate surfaces for durability and ease of maintenance. White laminate finishes are the most popular, but they may

Figure 7.7 A combined soft aisle and free-flow floor layout in Chiasso's, Tyson's Corner, McLean, Virginia.

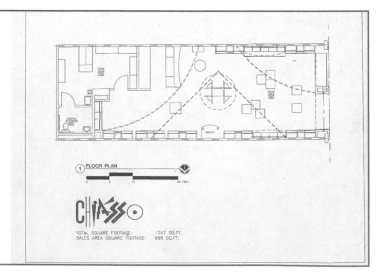

Figure 7.8 Notice the unusual wall fixtures in Chiasso, Tyson's Corner, McLean, Virginia.

also be custom-covered in everything from black and white photographs to the latest trend color prints and patterns.

You'll also find *round columns* and *pedestal risers* available in many diameters, heights, and a variety of fabrications from faux (false) marble to smooth plaster. As far as styling goes, you can order Greek columns and futuristic pedestals and just about anything in between. Since you'll use them in twos and threes, you'll want matching sets in multiple heights. Overall, they must be proportionate to the average tabletop size, so be sure that the "footprint" of each doesn't take up too much of your fixture's valuable surface space.

The more basic or neutral the riser is, the more useful it will be in working with various themes of merchandise. Most visual departments begin their riser collections with neutral or nondescript risers that will blend with a broad selection of merchandise and build from there.

Tables are also available through fixture manufacturers. They may be fabricated of metal, wood, MDF (medium-density fiberboard), or any number of other materials. They may be curved or straight, square or round; the variations are endless. Tables are widely used in retail stores, and there is a great deal of focus placed on them by manufacturers. This ac-

Figure 7.9 Nested tables at Woolworths, South Africa.

counts for the innovative designs available recently, including versions constructed of wooden frames with canvas webbing tabletops and others edged in neon colored acrylic.

Tables can be paired with risers to add height to a display and create visual interest from a distance. Williams-Sonoma combines a variety of naturally colored wooden butcher-block tables with white risers in its floor groupings. Tables are also "nested" in groupings of two to five. Figure 7.9 shows Woolworth's grouping of five nested tables.

Specialty stores often use baskets with their fixture groupings to display smaller items, such as artfully rolled hand towels, houseware gadgets, and napkin rings. Baskets add extra texture and homelike warmth to the grouping, and softening the look of hard-edged tables. They can also give a table grouping an informal outdoor "marketplace" feel. Baskets may be placed on tables or pedestal tops, or positioned under tables and pulled forward to utilize the open space between the tables' legs. A good rule of thumb to use for stocking baskets says that any time you can fit only three or four of the same item into a basket, the item is too large to be shown in a basket.

Floor Capacity Fixtures

Among the capacity fixtures (see Chapter 4) used in moderate or discount stores are basic gondolas, which may be shelved or pegged. They may be customized with colored or textured laminate finishes for an upscale look. Look again at Zeller's housewares department (Figure 7.5) where designers upgraded the appearance of a standard gondola with a custom high-gloss white finish and metallic trim.

Another way to upgrade the look of gondolas is to use colored paper, in solids or patterns, to cover Peg-Board back panels. It is best to have the paper custom-printed so that it will properly fit into each 4-foot section of gondola. This technique is especially useful when products like lamps do not fill the entire shelf space, and Peg-Board panels emerge

158

as a plain, monotonous background. Paper panels may be easily replaced to match changing product colors. If Peg-Board holes need to be accessible for hanging products, panels may be ordered with preperforated holes that may be easily punched out to insert peg hooks.

Department stores, specialty stores, and some moderate-priced home stores utilize custom-made capacity fixtures. These fixtures may be permanent or movable, if they are fitted with casters. Refer again to Figure 7.6, where both permanent and movable fixtures are shown. Casters allow the unit to be easily rolled to another location if necessary. The fixtures presenting pillowcases beside it are considered permanent, because they cannot be moved without being disassembled.

Cube sets can double as feature fixtures or capacity fixtures depending on their size, height, and how they are utilized in the selling department. Commonly grouped in odd numbers, they should never be used singly since their effectiveness comes from massed presentation. Most cubes have adjustable and removable shelves, which makes them versatile presentation tools. They fit easily around architectural columns and can transform what is usually "lost" selling space into profitable cubic footage. Sets can be stacked to create an "instant wall" treatment. Look at Figure 7.10 to see a cube configuration and how it can be effectively merchandised as self-service fixtures and displayed as department focal points at the same time.

Figure 7.10 A cube set is stacked and merchandised to turn an architectural column into productive selling space.

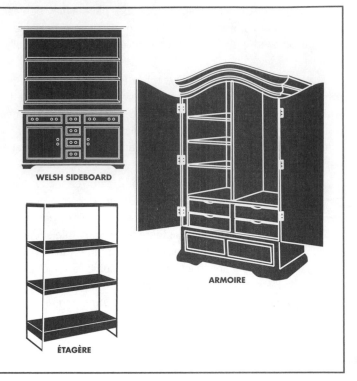

Figure 7.11 Furniture pieces like Welsh sideboards, armoires, and étagères focus visual interest on special products, adding additional merchandising space while supporting store image and atmosphere.

WELSH SIDEBOARD

ARMOIRE

ÉTAGÈRE

"Consider some exciting uses of fixtures that are *not* fixtures: A fixture has got to be admitted to be anything that houses and presents merchandise."

10 Years of Peter Glen

Furniture and Found Fixtures

It makes sense that selling floor fixtures in some home fashion stores or departments are furniture like: étagères, armoires, shelved cupboards, and tables. Étagères are open shelf units; armoires are shelved cabinets with doors (some have drawers within as well). Shelved cupboards may have shelves above and doors or drawers below a "sideboard." All are naturals to hold home fashion products—in fact, some were originally meant to do just that because early home designs did not include the built-in closets and cupboards we take so much for granted today. Figure 7.11 shows each type of cabinet.

ABC Carpet and Home is a store that is worth a visit on every trip to New York City. This multilevel home store is a visual merchandiser's dream environment, with everything you could possibly need to create stage-set displays for merchandise. Antique beds and étagères are dressed in the finest sheets and duvets, layered with soft open-weave blankets and throws, and piled high with luxurious pillows in fine cottons, silks, and linens. Curtain sheers in rich colors drape from the ceiling, and entire displays are crowned with "Miss Havisham" style crystal chandeliers straight out of *Great Expectations*. ABC's philosophy? Everything is for sale; *the furniture becomes the fixture*. (See Figure 7.12.)

Fish's Eddy—another must-see store in New York City—uses "found objects" like well-worn tables and wooden packing crates and bins as fixtures. Perfect for this store's retro, open marketplace presentation, its presentation style places merchandise center stage throughout the store. (See Figure 7.13.)

Wall Fixtures

Discount stores and moderately priced stores use gondolas as freestanding capacity fixtures and also utilize them as interior walls in their home fashion departments. Strategic

Figure 7.12 ABC Carpet and Home is a multilevel home store in New York City with displays that seem to come out of fairy tales.

use of upper-wall graphics and displays become critical to draw customers to back walls through deep valleys of gondolas. In *Why We Buy,* Paco Underhill describes what he calls the *boomerang rate* as a measure of how many times shoppers fail to walk completely through an aisle, from one end to the other. "It [the boomerang rate] looks at how many times a shopper starts down an aisle, selects something, and then, instead of proceeding, turns around and retraces her or his steps."

Among the strategies Underhill recommends is one borrowed from Blockbuster Video where the newest movie releases are always positioned on the back wall and regular customers have been trained to go there first. Attractive graphics, dynamically merchandised back walls, and top-shelf displays can combat boomerang tendencies.

Bookcase units and *shelving* are two types of wall fixtures most often found in specialty and department stores. Pottery Barn uses a more upscale bookcase effect with a decora-

Figure 7.13 Fish's Eddy in New York City is filled with found objects that are used as fixtures.

tive cornice, giving the store a strong, residential feel, while Crate&Barrel works with the simplest white or natural wood-grained open-ended shelving. Both fixture strategies are very appropriate for the brand identity of each store, reinforcing other aspects of their interior design.

Merchandise Presentation

You would sort home fashion products for fixture presentations in exactly the same way you'd prepare to merchandise fashion apparel in a department—by end use, fabrication, style, and color. Let's assume that you're working out a floor and fixture planogram for an imaginary tabletop department where place settings and serving pieces of china, pottery, and plastic tableware are sold.

Step by step, here is the process for sorting merchandise for fixture assignment:

- *Categorize by end use:* fine dining, casual dining, and outdoor dining (or picnic).

- *Divide each category by fabrication:* for example, separate picnic ware into plastic and metal.

- *Sort the items by style:* If plastic plates are available in both square and round styles, for example, you'll have to separate the two styles.

- *Separate the styles by color.* Select just one color group for each presentation. Remember that the color rules from the apparel chapters apply to home fashions as well. For instance, if you are featuring a display of *bright* picnic ware, you could tuck a bouquet of *bright* flowers into a picnic basket prop. At the same time, a dinnerware pattern featuring a wreath of delicate pastel flowers would call for flowers in pastels to complement the display presentation. Always use brights with other brights, pastels with pastels, and so on, with all the color groups. Neutrals may be used alone or combined with any of the other groups.

- *Label and enter the resulting fixture layout on a merchandising planogram.*

Successful Presentation Strategies for Walls

Refer to Figures 7.14 through 7.17 to see examples of the following seven successful wall-merchandising strategies used by Woolworth's Homeware departments:

1. Use large graphics and simple displays to create dramatic focal points.

2. Present bedding in wall units in "library style" with some folded sheets faced front-out, some faced side-out.

3. Utilize all shelf space to accommodate products. Limit wasted space between shelves by filling shelves completely or moving them closer together.

4. Arrange pegged items so that the tops of each product are in a *straight row.*

5. Position pegged products over shelved products.

6. Rank shelves with smaller items on top, medium-sized items on middle shelves, and larger items on bottom shelves.

Figure 7.14 An effective wall presentation in the living room department at Woolworth, South Africa.

Figure 7.15 A display in Woolworth's kitchen department.

Figure 7.16 A display in Woolworth's bath department.

Figure 7.17 A display in Woolworth's bedding department.

Figure 7.18 A 12-foot wall planogram presenting dinnerware and serveware.

7. Strengthen presentations on eye-level and top-shelf displays by use of art principles like repetition, and so on. Another art-related strategy—one-color grouping per wall section—isn't visible in the black and white photos but is an important presentation tool for any retail store.

Basic Wall Planograms

Even if you aren't currently working in a home fashion store, you can train your eye to critically evaluate what you see when you visit home stores in your community. The only requirement is a sense of the basic elements that are illustrated by the five basic wall planograms shown in Figures 7.18 through 7.22. If you follow the simple directives they provide and duplicate any one of them in a store today, your presentation will be up to current

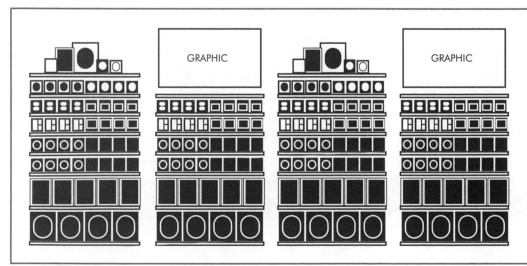

Figure 7.19 A 16-foot wall planogram presenting picture frames.

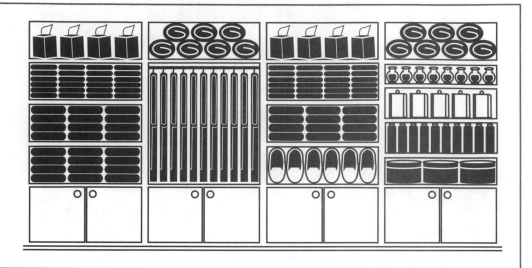

Figure 7.20 A 16-foot planogram presenting towels and bath products.

industry standards. You can start practicing right now. How many of the key wall presentation strategies listed previously can you find at work in the planograms that follow?

The planograms in this chapter represent a sampling of current best practices from leaders in home fashions. You will find them useful if a company doesn't already prescribe how it wants you to merchandise and display its walls. Many leading companies have created

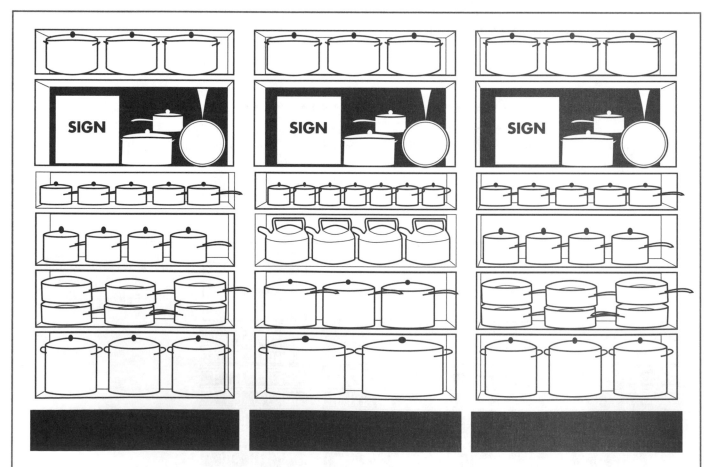

Figure 7.21 A 12-foot planogram presenting cookware.

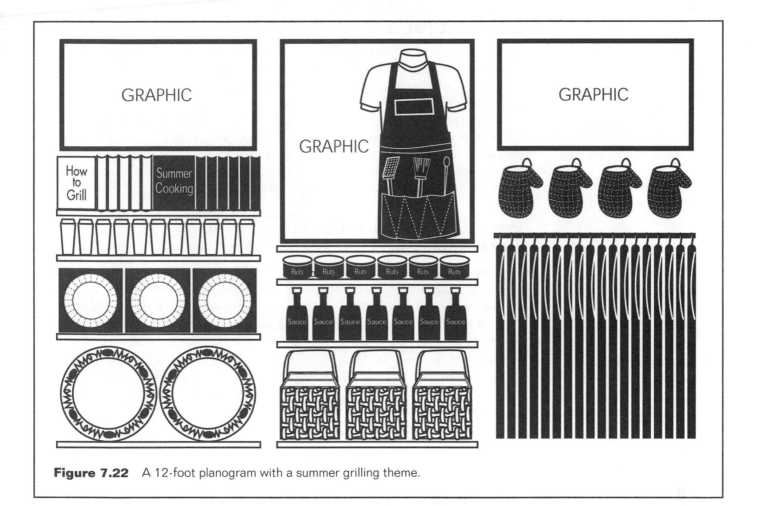

Figure 7.22 A 12-foot planogram with a summer grilling theme.

"signature" styling for wall fixture presentations, and they often provide stylebooks containing specific guidelines for employees to follow as they merchandise the stores. If you work for a company like this, its guidelines are the ones to follow. You must also respect the fact that it is a "proprietary" publication—meaning that it is the property of the company and not meant to be shared with competing stores.

Home Fashion Display Techniques

Self-Selection Displays

Home fashion items like small appliances, cookware, dinnerware, glassware, lamps, picture frames, vases, table linens, and candles may be presented using traditional build-up techniques and basic design principles. In keeping with the philosophy that shoppers like to handle and inspect things for sale, many of these displays are *self-selection displays* (self-service) where customers may choose items for purchase directly from the display. Here counters or tabletops combine displays with quantities of shoppable merchandise, some of it in boxes ready to go. Since shoppers are encouraged to handle products on these working displays, daily maintenance is a must. Visual merchandisers and sales associates must be alert to sell-down, dust, and fingerprints. None of these encourages sales.

167

Editorial Spaces

By teaming several large selling fixtures like étagères, tall shelf units, decorative tables, cubes (with and without shelving), dressers, desks, and chairs, you can create floor-standing in-store "windows" that tell shoppers merchandise stories about decorative and functional household coordinates they could have in their homes.

A major editorial presentation can be built on a platform to set it apart as a special focus area. A massive display with furniture or selling fixtures can be positioned on a large area rug to define its boundaries. In either case, signing and special lighting is appropriate. Where possible, these editorials should be displayed on both sides to present ideas and sell products to people both entering and leaving the area.

Basic Display Construction for Tabletops and Display Shelves

The basis for nearly all display staging in the home fashion area is the *triangle*. Building on it, you can create effective tabletops and shelf displays that have height variance, optical balance, and visual interest. When you're gathering things to feature, select products in odd numbers (threes and fives work best). The build-up is a step-by-step process demonstrated for you in Figure 7.23. Also refer to Colorplate 12 to see a dramatic tabletop presentation.

The first place to look for display props is the department you're working in and then any logical adjacencies. Home fashion products naturally lend themselves to use for both sale and props. Use rolling pins as props with marble pastry boards and cookbooks, and use picnic baskets with casual dinnerware.

Here are a dozen best practices governing home fashion display construction. Once you read them, you'll see the logic. Once you use them, you'll sell merchandise in profitable multiples.

Rules for Home Fashion Display

1. Don't use a prop if an item that is for sale will work just as well.

2. Use one manufacturer or brand per tabletop or display shelf, using all of the coordinates that have been designed for the specific style you've chosen. For example, use Mikasa dinnerware and accessorize with glassware and silverware from other makers only after exhausting all possibilities from Mikasa.

3. Use one theme. Example: Asian dining.

4. If there's an opening in a piece of merchandise, put another piece of merchandise in it or on it. For example, fill

   - Pitchers with long-handled serving utensils.
   - Glass canisters with cookie cutters and rolling pins.
   - Glasses with artfully folded or rolled napkins.
   - Vases with flowers or chopsticks or pinwheels.
   - Large bowls with nests of smaller bowls.
   - Pots with dish towels, pot holders, place mats, and so on.
   - Baskets with table linens, bath linens, soaps, candles, flowers, picture frames, books, stationery, potpourri, and so on.

5. Follow rule 4 with restraint. Don't fill everything. Two or three clever "fills" per tabletop are adequate. Use just one for shelf displays.

6. Remember that the back of the tabletop display for shoppers entering the area is the front of the display for shoppers leaving it. On a 4' × 4' tabletop, center your riser unit and display both sides in mirror image. Present merchandise that can be seen in both directions.

"A table is a portable stage."

10 Years of Peter Glen

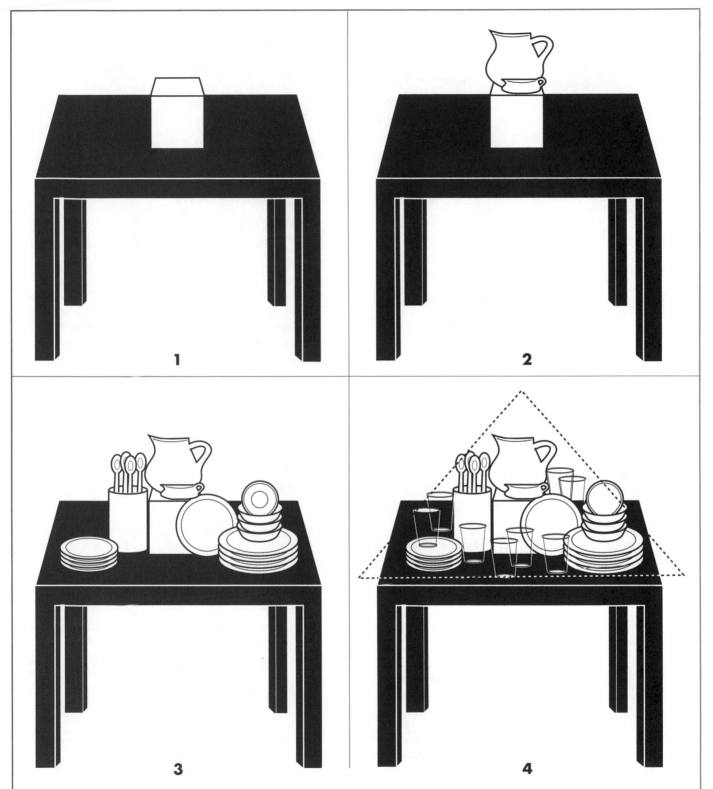

Figure 7.23 Build-ups with triangular composition add height, focus, and visual interest that will draw shoppers to home fashion products.

7. Masses of merchandise suggest opulence and largesse—the very feeling hosts and hostesses wants to present to guests visiting their homes. You want shoppers to purchase multiples. In this case, more is better.

8. Arrange multiples in rows from front to back on tables. Use the principle of repetition in your arrangement.

9. Present all products on small surfaces like pedestals and risers at the same angle. Shelved display products should face forward.

10. A *limited* amount of product overstocks and products in cartons (if they have attractive graphics) may be stored under nested tables. Cartons should be neatly stacked in parallel rows with identifying graphics facing forward. Small items may be placed in attractive baskets about the size of laundry baskets. Cartons and baskets should not obscure platform edges or table legs.

11. Don't put any products beneath a table that are not well-represented on the table top.

12. Watch closely for sell-down and replenish or reconfigure. Shoppers usually pass by assortments on half-empty fixtures.

Floral Displays

Floral designs ranging from dried miniature accessory arrangements on shelves and table-tops to floor-standing urns of oversize proportions are often seen as the domain of the visual merchandising department. Visual merchandisers are the store's artists-in-residence, and flowers figure prominently in all aspects of decorative art from fine paintings to textile designs in home decor. Visual merchandisers are generally charged with creating a warm, friendly store environment, and nothing adds more ambiance than the sight and scent of a lavish arrangement of fresh cut flowers or vases of live spring blossoms.

Where do flowers "fit" in a store? There are a number of places and occasions where flowers (fresh or dried) are a natural:

- At the store's main entrance—as a welcoming gesture, mood-setter
- On main floor showcase tops—to announce seasonal changes
- On display platforms at escalator heads—to complement editorial apparel and home fashion statements
- As window props and stage props—to complement a theme
- As complements to home fashion accessories—to demonstrate how a vase or container will look with a floral arrangement in it
- In customer service areas, concierge desks, and offices—as a humanizing element to diffuse tension or possible conflict
- As home furnishing accessories, in model room vignettes to establish a more homelike mood
- As special event centerpieces on stage or dining tables—to build theme or add festivity to the affair.

Some retailers contract with florists to keep the store's principal entrances supplied with large floral arrangements at key times of the year. Others purchase ready-made dried and silk arrangements from custom display firms that specialize in large-scale seasonal floral décor. Finally, members of the visual merchandising department may create wonderful floral arrangements—large and small—by practicing the art until it becomes second nature.

You can construct basic floral design shapes in containers ranging from casual baskets to formal vases and jardinieres (ornamental stands). The most common arrangements are the fan, circle, complex triangle, vertical, simple triangle, crescent, S-curve, and horizontal. Figure 7.24 has a chart that describes the various arrangement styles listed here and how to create them.

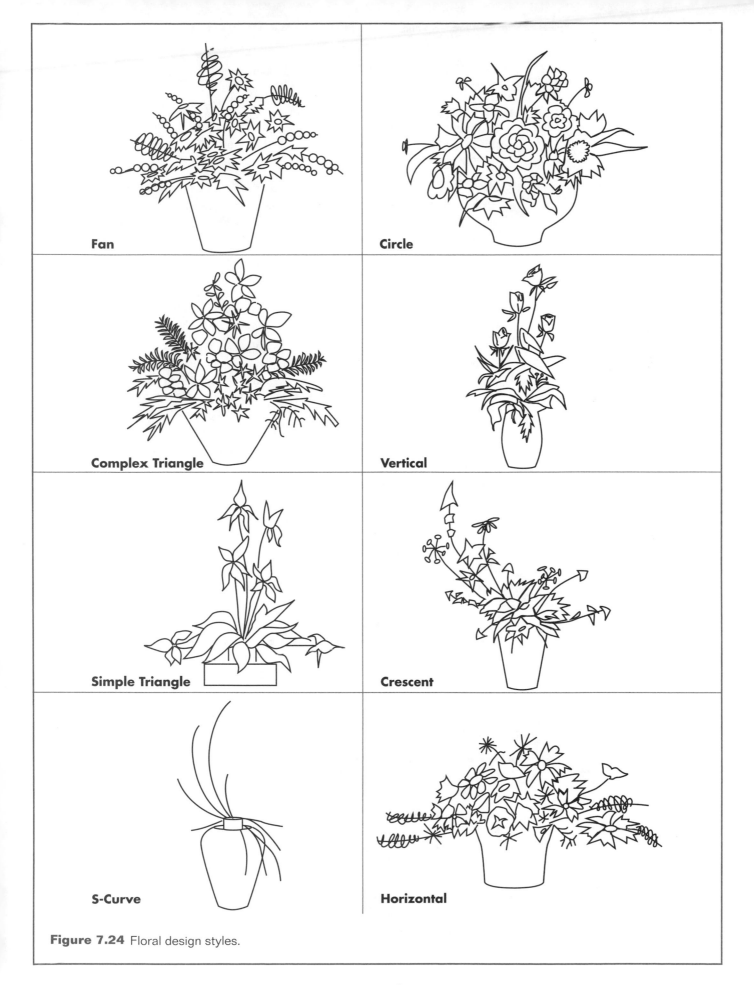

Figure 7.24 Floral design styles.

Fan

Circle

Complex Triangle

Vertical

Simple Triangle

Crescent

S-Curve

Horizontal

171

In addition to the basics of floral arrangement, here are some practical tips to get you started:

- Choose just one color group for each floral arrangement. For example, do not mix bright and pastel colors together. (See Colorplate 6.) As an alternative, you may opt to work with traditional color schemes like monochromatics for attractive arrangements.

- Work in odd numbers (1, 3, 5, 7), which are more pleasing to the eye.

- All sides of an arrangement are to be viewed "in the round." All views are as important as the front. Duplicate the elements used on the front of the arrangement on all sides.

- The theme of the area into which the arrangement will be used dictates its style and the container in which you place it. Theme will also tell you how formal or informal the structure of the arrangement should be. One current trend leans toward less formal arrangements that look as though they'd been freshly picked from a wildflower garden.

- The size and scale of the container dictates the size and scale of the arrangement, as does the space in which you plan to use the arrangement. A dining table centerpiece that will be used for a special dining event should not be so tall that it interferes with line of sight and therefore conversation across the table. However, if the dining table is set as an in-store display, an oversized arrangement can draw attention and emphasis to the table setting.

If you want to study floral arrangement from the masters, visit an art museum or the art department in the library. The Flemish and Dutch painters and the younger Impressionists really understood floral compositions, so you could start there. Look for literal, almost photographic paintings by Jan Brueghel the Elder (*Large Bouquet of Flowers in a Wooden Container*), Ambrosius Bosschaert (*Vase with Flowers*), Jan Van Huysum (*Flowers in a Vase*). Then study the looser, innovative floral presentations by Edgar Degas (*Woman with Chrysanthemums*) and Vincent Van Gogh (*Sunflowers, The Irises, Red and White Carnations*). There is a world of wonderful inspirations waiting to be discovered through the research of a lifelong learner.

Home Fashion Resources

The best way to expand your knowledge of home furnishing and accessory products beyond your own home is shopping every resource you can find regardless of budget category—yours or the store's. There is much to learn—even if it's what *not* to do. If you have Internet access, you can browse electronically in home fashion sites all over the world. Some are listed for you here:

- **www.homeportfolio.com.** Not only does this site have every possible home product and accessory, it has excellent color pictures and descriptions that can give your home fashion vocabulary a tune-up.

- **www.living.com.** This truly interactive site will let you design rooms, look at all kinds of furnishing and accessory choices in room settings, and zoom in or out and pan left and right to pick up photo details. Classic, mission-style, new country, and urban designs are all pulled together and accessorized correctly. The same site also features a magazine.

- **www.marthastewart.com.** Among the many home-related activities on these pages, you'll find flower arrangements, housekeeping hints and tools, entertaining ideas, and a way to keep in touch with lifestyle trends that affect merchandising.

Home Fashion Store Brand Analysis

Home fashion stores use many of the elements discussed in this chapter to create their own distinct brand images. (See Figure 7.25.) Cover the figure caption, and see if you can identify the four stores pictured. A store's brand image should be clear enough to make identification easy.

All of the stores use repetition in their shelved presentations. Which do you think uses it most effectively? Which wall area would best catch your eye at a distance and draw you through the store to reach it? How would you innovate and improve the weakest presentation?

Notice how most shelves are positioned according to product height in each presentation, resulting in a balanced look that is appealing to the eye. Where could Eddie Bauer have placed an additional shelf? The fourth shelf of Pottery Barn's wall does not hold products of all the same height, but it positions items from small to large, and the repetition of this pattern in each adjacent section makes it work.

The tabletop presentation leading into the wall at Eddie Bauer is a good example of using a pyramid to build a display. A lamp is at the peak of the pyramid but it is positioned a little to the right in asymmetrical fashion. Dried wheat sheaves add softness and texture to the hard-edged picture frames.

The tabletop presentation in Pottery Barn is a traditional setting with a chair used for rolls of table runners. The vase of orchids featured on the table is repeated in the back wall, and that, in addition to a common color story, ties the two presentations together as one unit.

You can use this type of analysis to compare other store presentations and begin to identify those that are most effective. It may be helpful to work through all of the design principles and elements as you analyze. You can refer to Chapter Three to review the core design strategies and compose questions for your analysis. For example: Does the presentation tell a color story? Is there a use of rhythm or movement? What kinds of lines do you see: curves, horizontal, vertical or diagonal? Is there an element of surprise in the presentation? Questions like these will make your analysis easier and will help to ultimately create your own dramatic presentations. Not every principle or element will be used in every presentation. For example, you would not want an element of surprise in every display you setup. But as you begin, it is useful to review all of the options available in your design tool kit.

Figure 7.25 Home fashion stores:
A. Crate&Barrel, B. Pottery Barn,
C. Eddie Bauer Home, D. Pottery Barn Kids.

A

B

C

D

175

Shoptalk ●●●●●●●●●●●●●●●●●●●●●●

Home Fashion Store Design
By Denny Gerdeman, principal, Chute Gerdeman Design

In late 1999, we began to develop a new concept for Eddie Bauer Home. After looking at what other home fashions retailers were doing in both specialty and department stores, we decided that we needed to create some romance around the Eddie Bauer brand and the home store product, and that the best way to accomplish this was through telling the consumer visual "stories." The challenge would be to create more "intimate" areas within the store, yet still keep sight lines fairly open. These areas would be stages for stories and give the customers a sense of discovery as they moved through the store.

In a home fashions store, it seemed only natural that we would create the feeling of rooms. To accomplish this, we designed two mobile, custom merchandising fixtures. One is a free-standing translucent wall, which allows sight lines to continue. The other is a tall fixture, substantial enough to capture the customer's eye. Both fixtures serve as backdrops to tell a visual merchandising story in vignette, while the other side holds quantities of the merchandise presented in the story. We also used pieces of large furniture, such as a bed and an armoire, as merchandising fixtures.

The trick in designing any retail space is in creating the right balance—between intimate versus open; feature versus mass; branding elements versus operational effectiveness; customer versus retailer. It's our job to find creative ways to achieve this balance. If you do it right, you've told the consumers the stories they need to help them make their purchase decisions, *and* increased sales. When it works, it's magic.

Out-of-the-Box Challenge ●●●●●●●●●●●●●●●●●●●●●●

1 Comparing Store Entrances

Look

Visit a shopping mall that has at least three home fashion stores. This may include department stores with housewares departments. Answer the following questions about the type of entrance each store is utilizing:

1. Does the store have a center aisle or is there a fixture positioned in the center front of the entrance?

2. If there is a center aisle, where does the aisle lead? To a fixture or to the back wall?

3. If there is no aisle, how many feet is the first fixture from the store entrance? Do you consider it to be a signature fixture? Is it featuring a trend or special pricing?

Compare

Compare the presentations by reviewing your notes. Which was your favorite? Why?

Innovate

How would you use innovation in all of the presentations?

Out of-the-Box Challenge ●●●●●●●●●●●●●●●●●●●●●●

2 Comparing Store Layouts

Look

Visit three home stores or departments and make notes about their layouts. What type of layout is each store utilizing? Is it a grid, a free flow, or a combination of both?

Compare

Compare the three layouts. Which do you prefer? Why?

Innovate

How would you use innovation to improve the three layouts?

Out of-the-Box Challenge ●●●●●●●●●●●●●●●●●●●●●●

3 Comparing Store Fixtures

Look

Visit at least two home stores, preferably a Crate&Barrel store and a Pottery Barn or Williams-Sonoma. Answer the following questions about each store:

1. What styles of wall fixtures are used? What colors are the fixtures? What are they made of?

2. What styles of floor fixtures are used? What colors are they? What are they made of?

3. If there are tables, how many different styles are used throughout the store? Do the table styles change from area to area? What do you think is the reason if they do change?

4. Does the style of wall and floor fixtures fit the store's brand identity?

Compare

Compare the wall and floor fixtures in the two stores. Which do you prefer? Why?

Innovate

How would you improve the choice of fixtures?

Critical Thinking

Assignment 1

In Figures 7.26A and 7.26B, you'll find a sketch of an empty tabletop plus drawings of a variety of home fashion merchandise and accessories. Create a tabletop that supports the dinnerware supplied for you. Use a combination of risers and baskets to design a display planogram highlighting some of the major pieces and merchandise the rest so that the tabletop space is used effectively. Trace any items that you think you need more of; eliminate any items you don't need.

1. Use props from Figure 7.26A only.

2. Merchandise the rest of the tabletop with self-selection merchandise provided for you on the page.

3. The floral colors on the plates should be one of the current color trends. Choose any colors you like as accents.

4. Be prepared to explain or justify your choices in a group presentation or one-on-one critique with your instructor.

Assignment 2

In Figures 7.27A and 7.27B, you'll find a sketch of an empty 8-foot wall section plus drawings of a variety of folded merchandise and accessories for a display on a specialty store's back wall. Present the items as stipulated below. Trace any items that you need more of; eliminate any items you do not need.

1. Do a Roy G. Bv vertical colorization of this wall section.

2. Color the folded items on the shelves.

3. Space the shelves appropriately.

4. Use the principle of repetition where appropriate.

5. Create two displays on the shelves that highlight possible uses of the merchandise.

6. Be prepared to explain or justify your choices in a group presentation or one-on-one critique with your instructor.

Case Study

The End-of-Season Mystery Display

This case presents a problem that visual merchandisers encounter frequently. When there is strong sell-through on merchandise, a department can take on a sparse, sold-down look. That's when you must come up with an interim editorial statement that communicates a fashion message while you wait for new goods.

The Situation

As a team, prepare a new tabletop display for the *casual dining area*. Assume that this is a short-term project and that the display will be up for only one week. Then the fixture will be used to introduce a new line of dinnerware, glassware, and flatware that has been delayed at the factory. The current selling season is summer. Your instructor plays the role of the department manager and will assign the color and overall merchandising theme. You will want to make this temporary tabletop exciting and inviting because this prime display space must always generate high-volume sales.

The Strategy

Each person in the class will bring one item from their home "stockroom" to fit into the merchandise and color themes which your instructor will announce. If the class is small, some people may have to bring more than one item. Do not discuss what you are bringing with others in the class. Your challenge as a group—and what makes this a realistic simulation—is creating an attractive display out of the merchandise at hand no matter what it happens to be. We encourage you to think outside-of-the-box and be as creative as you can be.

Working as a team, assign each person to bring one of the following elements:

- A table covering (a tablecloth, a table runner, or four place mats—even a small rug or a beach towel could be appropriate depending on the theme)
- Four napkins (or napkin alternatives—colorful bandanas, etc.)
- Four dinner plates
- Four salad bowls
- Four glasses
- Four place settings of silverware
- A serving container or large bowl
- A serving basket
- A serving platter or large plate
- Materials for a centerpiece—artificial flowers, plants, statues, toys—to fit the theme
- Container for a centerpiece
- A coffee carafe or a pitcher
- Riser units of some kind

Directions

Bring all the materials to the classroom and assemble a tabletop display that will show shoppers how they might pull together an eclectic and attractive table of mix and match elements in an eye-pleasing presentation.

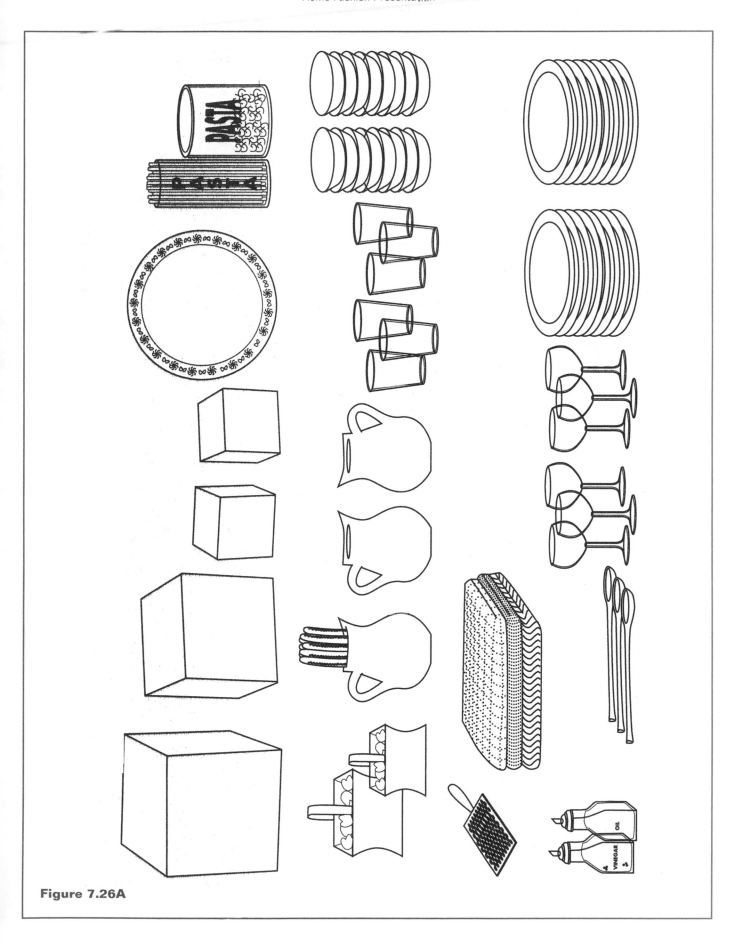

Figure 7.26A

Figure 7.26B

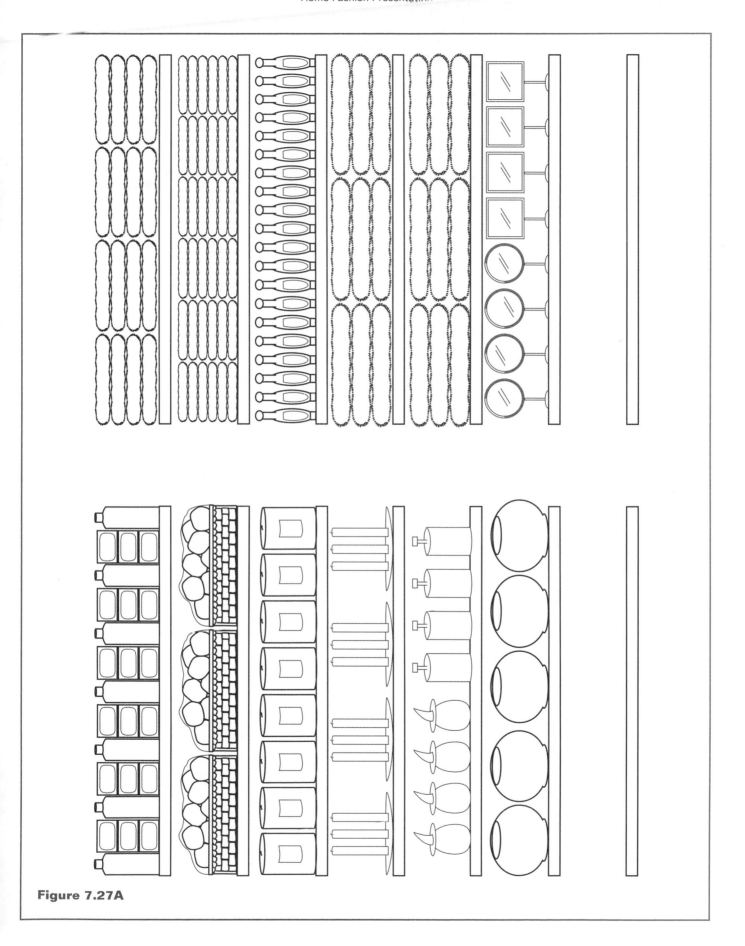

Figure 7.27A

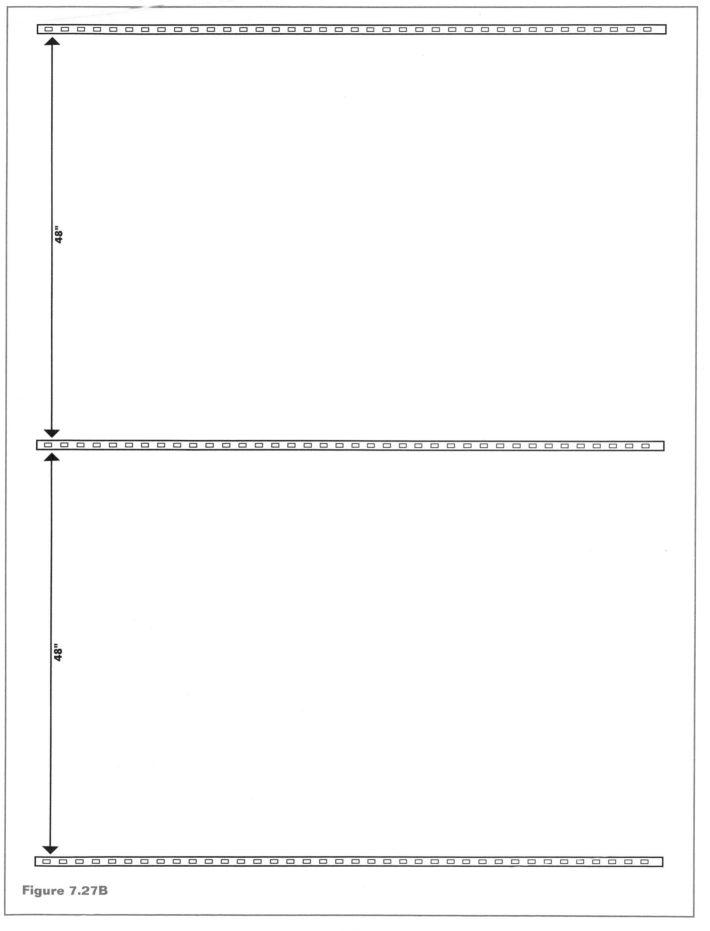

48"

48"

Figure 7.27B

Part Three

COMMUNICATING RETAIL ATMOSPHERICS

Chapter 8

SIGNING

After completing this chapter, you should be able to

Identify various signing functions

Compare the expanding variety of signing media

Decide when to sign merchandise

Explain the guidelines for setting up signs in the store environment

Write sign copy using a variety of techniques

Design your own sign layout

"As the decade unfolds, competition for your customer's attention is only going to get more intense. The impact of store environments will depend on careful execution and well thought out strategies to capture and hold attention. Look at the big picture—the overall look and approach— before you put ink to paper."
Ken Sinclair, Rainbow Signs, Minneapolis

Figure 8.1 C.V. Wrappers of Columbus, Ohio, communicates a clear message of what customers will find inside.

Communication through Signing

Retail stores begin to communicate with potential shoppers before the shoppers ever enter the store. From the minute shoppers read the store's name or see its logo on the storefront, they are getting a message. An effective sign attracts attention and conveys brand identity, giving shoppers their first impression of what they will find inside the store. The C.V. Wrappers food service pictured in Figure 8.1, is an excellent example. One glance at the storefront sign and the message is clear: C.V. Wrappers sells sandwiches—fast—and with a promise of fun.

Communicating Brand Image

A retail store's brand image should be carried through on every sign in the entire store environment, from **operational** signs to merchandise signs. The most successful signs have an identity that is so clear that even if they were taken out of the store environment, the name of the store would be evident. (See Figure 8.2.) The interior photograph of C.V. Wrappers features a full-figure cutout of a pilot. In this case, the "sign" has only one task; to carry the "flight and fun" theme from the storefront into the store.

Communicating through Operational Signing

Operational signs relate to the day-to-day business of a store—listing store hours, return policies, emergency exits, locations of help phones, department locations, and fitting room policies.

Operational signing information containing the location of departments, checkouts, and restrooms can be communicated in a variety of ways. One-level stores often use ceiling or wall-mounted signs, while multilevel stores post department and restroom locations near elevators and escalators. Some stores have interactive monitors that allow you to enter the particular item you're looking for and have the exact location pinpointed for you on a map.

Woodwinds and Brass, the music store pictured in Figure 8.3, calls out its information center with dramatic signing straight from a stage set. In Figure 8.4, Blazing Saddles employs a retro or nostalgic style to boldly call out operational messages that help bicycle renters to make purchase decisions.

Ruby's, a small café in the Loring Park area of Minneapolis, posts its operational signing on a sandwich board on the sidewalk that reads:

Figure 8.2 Notice the full-size cutout figure of a pilot in C.V. Wrappers, Columbus, Ohio.

eat late @ Ruby's Café!

10 PM to 2 AM

Thursday/Friday/Saturday

- Fresh New Menu
- Huge Pancakes
- Take Out
- Loud Music
- Groovy Lighting
- Tons of Fun!

Who says you have to go home alone?

As you can see, operational signing can enhance both store environment and brand identity—and never seem as mundane as the term *operational* implies!

Communicating through Signing Media

A store's ability to communicate is enhanced by the use of the following graphic elements.

- *Dimensional letters* may be layered over other messages to create a strong focal point, as in Figure 8.5. Letters like these are available in colored acrylics, woods, and metals. Foam letters in many fonts and sizes may be covered with metallic papers to create upscale looks at a modest price.

191

Figure 8.3 The information center in Woodwinds and Brass of South Bend, Indiana, employs a stage-set design theme.

Figure 8.4 Operational messages are clearly called out in Blazing Saddles, Seattle, Washington.

Figure 8.5 Fedco of Cerritos, California, uses dimensional letters to call out the fresh market department.

Figure 8.6 Floor graphics add drama to Hockeytown Authentics in Troy, Michigan.

- *Static cling decals* may be applied to glass doors or windows for an artful, hand-painted look. They are easily removed and may be reused if carefully stored.

- *Fabric scrims* (hanging panels) made of sheer fabrics like silk and polyester may be printed with images or sign copy.

- *Floor graphics* add unexpected emphasis, as you can see in the checkout area in Figure 8.6. Floor graphics may be permanently cut into the floor tile or applied in a nonpermanent version that adheres to the floor. A manufacturer-sponsored hopscotch game on the floor of a grocer's cereal aisle practically guarantees that a shopping parent and child will spend 15 to 20 extra seconds in front of that specific brand.

- *Light source signing systems* include neon, fiber optics, projected images, and lightboxes that hold Duratran images. In Figure 8.7, showing Gridiron Square at the Cleveland Browns' stadium, images of inspirational slogans are projected onto canvas. A simple lighted signing system is shown together with dimensional cutout signing in Figure 8.8.

Communicating Tone

Have you ever thought about a sign's "tone of voice"? Look at the difference between, "TAKE A NUMBER BEFORE ENTERING FITTING ROOM!" and "Please take a number

194

Figure 8.7   Images are projected onto canvas at Gridiron Square in the Cleveland Browns' Stadium.

before entering fitting room." Subtle details like type font, case, and copy style make a dramatic difference in communication tone. A sign in uppercase type "shouts," while lowercase copy is friendlier and easier to read. In some London stores, signs are very polite, and you might find one that says: "We would appreciate it if you would take a number on your way into the fitting room."

Signs rarely have a playful tone. The best of them are found in one-of-a-kind boutiques and some home fashion stores. In one New York shop, colorful cartoon-style signs in fitting

Figure 8.8   Dimensional cutout signs are combined with lighting for a carnival effect in the Best Fest Food Court in Concord Mills, North Carolina.

Figure 8.9 Cartoon style signing in the Emporium/ Photo Funnies, Universal Studios.

rooms read: "We call cops on robbers." A Chicago boutique painted "You look beautiful!" over its fitting room mirrors. Imagine what the rest of the store might look like from the tone of that single sign. A sign that underlines how pleasant it is to shop adds to the feeling or tone of the store and strengthens brand identity for that retailer. Figure 8.9 shows the Emporium/Photo Funnies at Universal Studios. The store design team's goal was to bring the Sunday Funnies to life. Do you think they achieved their goal?

Signing Merchandise

Merchandise may be signed with price points or copy to communicate that it is

- Advertised with sale pricing
- An unadvertised in-store promotion with sale pricing
- Value-priced merchandise
- Brand-name merchandise
- Trend merchandise
- A new product with special features
- Clearance merchandise

Clearly, these are all excellent reasons to sign a fixture. However, you need to take your store's routine pricing strategy into consideration as you decide how many fixtures will be signed. Retail stores with moderate or discount pricing often sign every fixture in the store, which sends a strong "savings" message to bargain shoppers. Shoppers expect to see signs announcing great values every time they visit the store. Some truly committed bargain hunters won't even look at merchandise unless there is a sale sign on the fixture.

When a store employing a strong regular-price strategy has limited sales events, it has to be more selective about signing its fixtures. If every fixture in the store were signed routinely, it would be difficult to emphasize particular items because they would not stand out. A major sale might lose impact because shoppers wouldn't notice much visual contrast between special sale days and business as usual.

Too many price point signs can have a negative effect on a store's brand identity. Imagine a high-end Madison Avenue fashion store filled with pricing signs. Incongruous? Bargain store strategies simply don't fit an exclusive store's image. In this strategy, price points are never used at all, unless merchandise is marked down.

Retail consultant Peter Glen once wrote that the proliferation of signs in retail stores was management's apology for not having enough salespeople on the floor. Somewhere between too many and none at all is the right number of signs for a store's image. Too many cause shoppers to ignore them all; too many words and shoppers won't read any; too few and customers won't get enough information.

Merchandise may also be signed with *lifestyle graphics*—signs that show apparel or home fashions in use—alone or in combination with price points. Some lifestyle graphics show only a portion of the actual product and focus more on models' faces. That's a soft-sell strategy. It tells shoppers that the retailer cares as much about the enjoyment of their product as it cares about making a sale. Photos that show expression or set moods that shoppers can relate to communicate brand image successfully. They are another version of window theater.

That theory may explain why recent fashion photography models aren't always flawless beauties. The trend has shifted, portraying more everyday people for lifestyle photography. French Connection—a New York and European junior and young men's fashion store—featured large closeup images of young women wearing glasses, even though they do not sell eyewear. Club Monaco featured billboard-sized graphics of a baby boomer with bushy gray hair and a full beard. Eileen Fisher stores used images of Eileen and her staff members as models. These new graphic images grab shopper attention because they are so unusual—and so recognizable. Real people, like you, doing real things, wearing real clothes, and using real products—that is the trend today. (See Figures 8.10 and 8.11.) As a visual merchandiser you must always be on the lookout for the next fresh image that captures shopper interest.

Signing Presentation

Accuracy, clarity, and a sign's appearance all communicate something about a store's brand image. Inaccurate or unclear signs setup negative reactions because shoppers resent the time it takes to locate sales associates for correct prices or other information. If signs are damaged, torn, or curled, shoppers may feel the store does not care about its customers or its image. Shoppers may respond by becoming careless about rehanging garments or about refolding merchandise properly after they have handled it. Another type of response may come in the form of shoplifting.

Here are five guidelines for effective signing presentation:

1. Be certain that a sign is necessary.
2. Display every sign in a holder. Signs are never tacked to walls or taped to fixtures.

197

Figure 8.10 Billboard-size lifestyle graphics in Larry's Shoes, Katy, Texas.

Figure 8.11 Billboard-size lifestyle graphics in The Athlete's Foot, the Avenue's Mall, Marietta, Georgia.

3. Do not write on preprinted signs. Do not cross out old prices or tape new prices on top of the old. If a price changes, the sign must be replaced.

4. Do not mix the type of signs used. If your store uses commercially printed signs, extra handmade signs are not appropriate.

5. Replace any signs that become soiled or damaged.

Handmade Signs

Signs that are handwritten with markers or calligraphy pens are rarely seen in today's shopping malls. One-of-a-kind stores, however, like the interesting shops in San Francisco's Castro Street area and in New York's Greenwich Village, use handmade, even quirky signs with great success. In these instances, the handmade signs invite shoppers to enjoy the stores' casual atmosphere, and, since many of them feature wearable art and artisan-made products, the informal signing complements the merchandise.

Stores like Fish's Eddy in New York communicate tone via handwritten paper signs that correspond to their retail image. These are charming additions, purposely designed components of the unique décor. In a world where it sometimes seems that everything has to be perfect, there is something spontaneous about handcrafted signs. That said, you must also know that these stores are an exception.

If a retailer is committed to hand lettering, it would be wise to hire a calligrapher whose work is uniform, immaculately rendered, and in line with its image. *Calligraphy* is a Greek word which means beautiful writing. An elegant designer store could use this special effect to communicate a tone of exclusivity to clients who are accustomed to receiving invitations crafted by skilled calligraphers and dining at tables with hand-inscribed place cards.

Sign Design

In most corporate organizations, store buyers will initiate requests for signs for their products by filling out forms listing the item and any other information they want to communicate about it. Estimated delivery dates and tentative ad dates are also indicated. They may request illustrations or photographs and indicate preferences—product-only shots or lifestyle photos, for instance. In some cases, manufacturers provide camera-ready artwork and/or co-op advertising dollars. The request is then routed to the in-store marketing (ISM) department (also called visual merchandising in some companies).

In-store marketing managers review and edit sign requests for accuracy—spelling, dates, and prices plus appropriateness to store image and brand identity. Naturally, buyers want unique department signs. However, if every sign were printed in a different style, the store would lose brand continuity, consistency in appearance, and points of emphasis.

A garment constructed of a new fabric or an electronic product featuring new technology *might* merit extraordinary treatment. There is a simple technique to focus extra attention on a sign—adding a sign "topper." This is an extra sign inserted at the top of a sign holder. These may be die-cut into any shape, and they may feature a store logo or advertising theme phrase. Alternatively, a "sider" can be added to the side of the sign, if the sign holder permits.

After approval of the ISM department, the request is passed on to designers and copywriters who produce basic signs following an established style—listing a few bullet points and a price, for example. Signing for a larger collection or a company wide seasonal theme may be done in-house, or it may be "outsourced" to a creative agency for a multimedia advertising campaign that includes signing. Corporate visual merchandisers or ISM departments often hire the agency and manage these projects. Concepts come back to them for approval. Managers must maintain the brand identity of their company, yet allow designers a certain amount of creative latitude.

A Retail Reality:
The homespun approach to signing is not effective in most retail operations, where hand lettering contradicts a store's mood, image, and décor strategy. There, handmade signs make the entire operation look unprofessional. This is especially true when employees who don't know how to spell, punctuate, or proofread are in charge of the marking pens.

"Hire brilliant people, get out their way, and clear the path for them to do great work."
Bob Thacker, president and CEO of BBDO Design, Minneapolis

In order to provide effective guidance, visual merchandisers must understand basic layout principles and copy writing. Whether they are part of a multiunit organization or a one-of-a kind store, the process for sign production requires that they develop an "eye" for excellent design.

Sign Layout

Most visual merchandisers are asked to design and produce store signs at some point in their careers. You will most likely do your work on a computer, but it's a good idea to practice designing some signs by hand as you build and sharpen your composition skills.

In preparing a sign, you literally lay out the elements on a sheet of signboard, hence the term layout. The elements of a sign are

- Sign copy—the facts about the product
- Artwork—drawings or photographs
- White space—the parts of the sign not taken up with copy or artwork

All three elements are equally important, and all three are subject to the art and design principles you learned in earlier chapters. For example, you may decide to use a perfectly symmetrical and formal layout with mirror image elements divided by an imaginary vertical line through the center of the sign. Or, you may use an informal, asymmetrical format and trust your eye to achieve an agreeable arrangement of the elements. In any case, your goal is to attract attention to the merchandise by designing a sign that will create desire and prompt action. To accomplish that, you must compose signing that draws shoppers' eyes through the lines of the message, encouraging them to buy the product.

Sign Copywriting

Creative copy for signing strengthens a store's brand identity. Crate&Barrel's unique sign writing style employs short paragraphs with product information that "speaks" directly to shoppers in conversational tones:

Our selection of pepper mills and salt mills is nothing to sneeze at! Choose from clear acrylic individuals or sets in a wide range of materials and sizes. Ah . . . Ah . . . Ah-Choo!

One of Restoration Hardware's copywriting strategies tells shoppers that it has searched the world to find the best product available. It also uses conversational techniques plus liberal doses of insider humor:

Classic American Mustard & Ketchup Bottles—Maybe you first encountered these babies at Nitzis or Toot an' Tell Em (I did). Or perhaps these were a great Greek diner type accouterment for you. Needless where, no matter when . . . we all used and use these trusty plastic dudes. American burger and fry icons for your home. No finer squeezers made. 12 oz. Capacity and, of course, American made. Bring a pair home right the heck now. $1.95.

Williams-Sonoma creates add-on sales by suggesting related products in its conversational sign copy:

Cinnamon Maple Syrup—Natural Vermont Maple syrup is infused with Chinese cinnamon for outstanding flavor. It transforms waffles and pancakes. It's great in coffee. And it's sensational over vanilla ice cream studded with *Williams-Sonoma's crystallized ginger*. A Williams-Sonoma exclusive. $12.75.

Conversational signs assume that shoppers will stand still long enough to read them. If the signs are exceptionally well written, are fun to read, and are used by a store whose image encourages browsing, shoppers really enjoy these "silent salespeople." However, most shoppers do not have the time to read lengthy copy. If conversational signs don't fit your store's image, you can also communicate product information by listing bullet points with concise descriptive phrases. Limit bullet points to three or four. Too much information may discourage the shopper from reading any of it.

Simple phrases make the best themes for seasonal concepts, where they are repeated, campaign-style, throughout a store on banners or other types of signing. Avoid overused, trite phrases—unless you can put a clever twist on them. Ideally, your store will hire a professional copywriter who can bring a fresh approach to a storewide advertising blitz. Skilled copywriters work so quickly that the cost is often lower than you might imagine. If outsourcing is not an option and you're elected to do the job, look for ideas in magazines and catalogs. A thesaurus and a rhyming dictionary are a good investment for your professional library.

Creative copywriting includes the following literary techniques:

- *Alliteration*—Use of two or more words with the same first letter: Relax, Refresh, Rejuvenate.

- *Familiar phrases*—Seeing Red!

- *Puns*—Plays on familiar phrases by substituting similar sounding words: Fit to Be Tried.

- *Quotes*—"I base my fashion taste on what doesn't itch," Gilda Radner.

- *Rhyming words*—Lace Embrace.

- *Themed Adjectives:* Pamper, Nurture, Indulge.

Designing Your First Sign

The following directions tell how you'd prepare a rough sketch for a printer if you were placing a sign order. The sketch gives you and the printer something tangible to refer to as you discuss the sign either in person or over the phone.

Assume that your sign will be laid out in a portrait (vertical) format on a sheet of 11 x 14 paper. You'll need a ruler and a pencil to rough out the spacing for this sign. The first thing you'll do is draw diagonal lines from the top of each corner to the opposite bottom corners on the sheet. The point where the lines intersect is the exact center of the page.

The *optical center* of the sign—a point where the eye naturally comes to rest—is just above the center point (roughly a third of the way from the sign's top edge). This becomes the focal point of your sign. Mark it with a small *x*. The sign's headline will be positioned in this vicinity.

Margins, or borders, for this sign will be 1 inch on the top and sides of the sign. The bottom margin will be wider—about 1¾ inches, which follows the general rule for matting and framing art prints. Draw the margins on the sign. Their lines should intersect at the diagonals you've already drawn. Now you can see the "frame" or boundaries for your sign's composition. The border provided by the margins guarantees that your sign will fit into a sign holder with enough surrounding white space to frame the sign's artwork and copy. These proportional margins are customary for sign making. (See Figure 8.12.)

Common sign sizes are 5½ x 7, 7 x 11, and 11 x 14. These sizes are primarily used for fixture signing. Full (22 x 28) and half (14 x 22) sheets are made to fit floor-standing sign holders and poster frames (on escalator walls, for example). Fixture companies carry sign holders in many styles and fabrications for all these standard dimensions.

With margins and optical center established, the center of the sign must be filled with copy. Imagine you are selling alarm clocks. The Signing Request Form (see box) describes plans for an alarm clock promotion. Figures 8.13 through 8.15 show how the copy translates into fixture signing in three styles: conversational, bullet points, and item/price.

A Retail Reality:
It is no accident that two half sheets are equal to a single full sheet. Historically, the six-ply cardstock used by sign printers always came in full sheets that were 22 by 28 inches. Smaller signs were created by cutting the full sheet in half (14 x 22) and then in half again (7 x 11) and again (5½ x 7). This was an economical way to utilize the entire sheet.

Figure 8.12 Note the exact center, optical center, diagonals, and margins (borders) marked on this blank signboard.

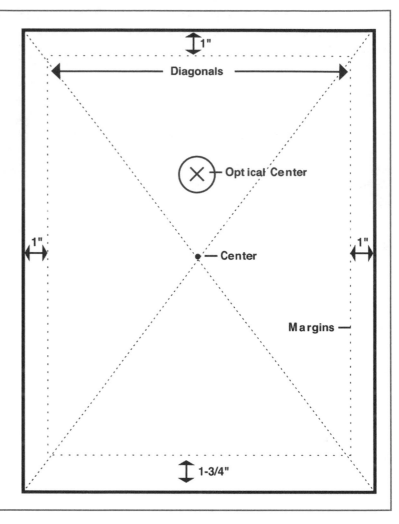

Signing Request Form

Department: Housewares—Bed & Bath

Buyer: Jack Smith

Product: Tymepeace(TM) chiming alarm clock

Special features: Gentle chime alarm with adjustable volume

Colors: Stainless, brass, white, black

Other: Trade in any working alarm clock and replace it with a new Tymepeace. Trade-ins will go to the Job-Seekers Project.

Price: $29.95 with trade-in; regular $39.95

Product in-store date: 8/15/2005

Advertising date: 8/21/2005

Signing Production

Professional sign production is a necessary expense of doing business. It is going to be more expensive than hand lettering a sign with marking pens, but regardless of cost, you

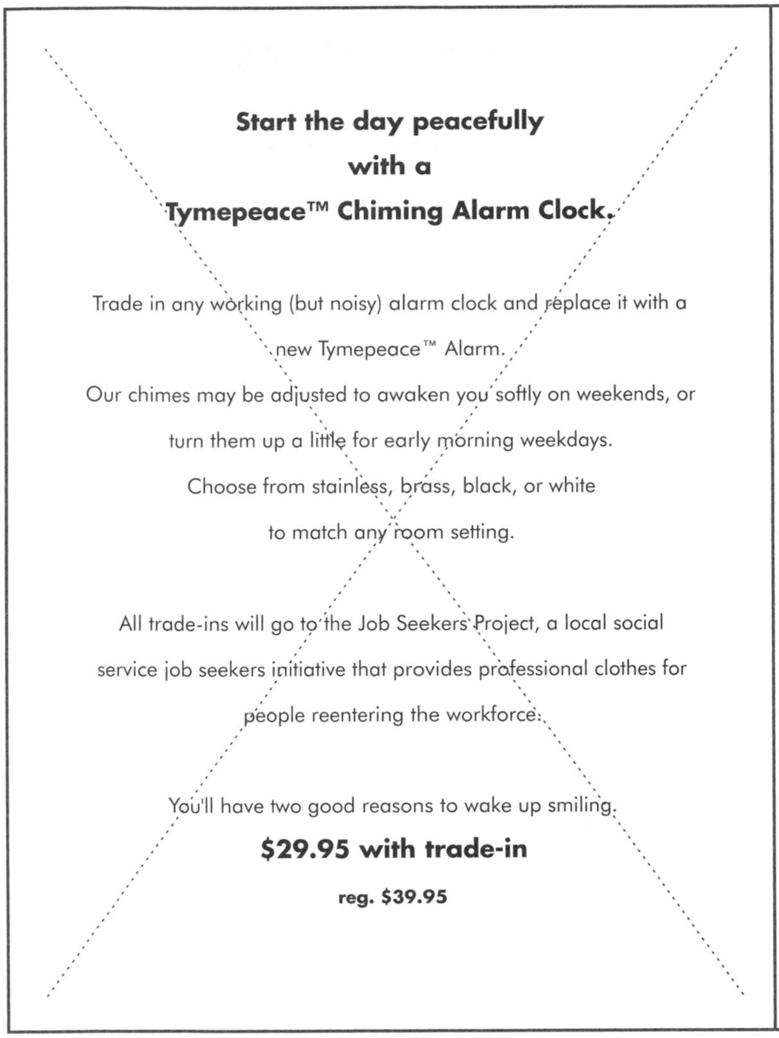

Start the day peacefully

with a

Tymepeace™ Chiming Alarm Clock.

Trade in any working (but noisy) alarm clock and replace it with a

new Tymepeace™ Alarm.

Our chimes may be adjusted to awaken you softly on weekends, or

turn them up a little for early morning weekdays.

Choose from stainless, brass, black, or white

to match any room setting.

All trade-ins will go to the Job Seekers Project, a local social

service job seekers initiative that provides professional clothes for

people reentering the workforce.

You'll have two good reasons to wake up smiling.

$29.95 with trade-in

reg. $39.95

Figure 8.13   Here conversational copy has been rendered in a formally balanced layout.

need to weigh what *not* having a quality signing program will cost your store in terms of image and effective communication with shoppers.

Chris Bailey from As Soon As Possible, Inc. (ASAP), a printing firm that serves Midwest retailers, says that signing style is all about image and target audience. "Look to whom you're speaking," he advises. "When you want a custom design for your store's signature, you ought to work with a graphic designer, either your own or the printer's." Bailey points out that larger signs necessarily belong in the professional printer's domain simply because of the limits of noncommercial printers. "After the 7 × 11 sign, you've run out of options." He adds that conventional word processing programs are not usually PostScript-compatible, which means that graphic design and copy writing done in a small store's backroom will not translate effectively to the professional printer's shop for large sign production.

Bailey says that small signs can be printed on regular printers if the cardstock is very thin, and he names Quark Express, Adobe PageMaker, Adobe Illustrator (Mac formats), and Corel Draw for the PC as professional software packages with good graphic capabilities for do-it-yourself signing done on a small scale.

Bailey says, "Good-looking custom-made signs aren't really expensive when you consider what they accomplish. Our industry's trends are bringing technologies that improve our speed and our quality. Faster, better, and cheaper—those are our goals."

Figure 8.14 This is bullet-point copy in an informally balanced layout.

Tymepeace™ Chiming Alarm Clock

- Gentle chimes with adjustable settings

- Stainless, brass, white, black

$29.95
with trade-in
(reg. $39.95)

Figure 8.15 Product and price copy rendered in an informally balanced layout.

Tymepeace™ Chiming Alarm Clock

$29.95 with trade-in
($39.95 value)

Trade-ins go to the Job-Seekers Project

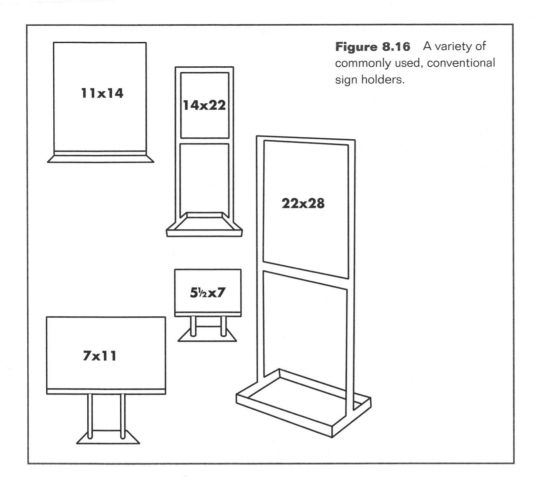

Figure 8.16 A variety of commonly used, conventional sign holders.

Sign Holders

You'll find every possible configuration of conventional sign holders in fixture manufacturers' catalogs. (See Figure 8.16.) Fabricated in metal, wood, and acrylic, or combinations of materials, all versions have advantages and disadvantages. Metal sign holders are sturdy and have no light reflection problems since the sign has no plastic covering. The advantage of acrylic is that the holder becomes more or less invisible, allowing the sign to "pop" (seem more prominent). Either version is acceptable. To promote visual continuity storewide, good retailers use just one type of sign holder.

Many retailers develop their own custom sign holders to further differentiate themselves from competitors. Speaking of competition, it exists in the sign holder industry, too. Sign holders in today's fixture market now include interesting curves and dimensional effects in response to retailers' demands for new fixtures and as a result of new capabilities in the printing industry. Dimensional paper sizing is no longer a limitation, which paves the way for tremendous signing creativity.

Signing Resources

A great place to begin to look for signing ideas is *Point of Purchase* magazine and its Website: **www.popmag.com** where a virtual trade show features in-store signing ideas from many manufacturers. You can visit "booths" featuring every product you could possibly use for in-store signing. Another informative site is the National Signs of the Times Museum (**www.signmuseum.com**). This project is an offshoot of *Signs of the Times* magazine;

a trade publication devoted to signing in all its forms. According to the museum's home page, "The purpose of the National Signs of the Times Museum is to preserve, archive and display a historical collection of signs in their many types and forms." In addition, the museum pages link to other sign-related Websites.

Visual merchandisers will also find it useful to peruse the magazine stand on a regular basis. Magazines like *Wallpaper* and *Real Simple* are amazing resources for cutting-edge sign copy writing, layout, and type style. Both of these magazines are relatively new in the marketplace, and they have taken an artfully designed, fresh approach to the subject.

Catalogs are another great resource, especially for conversational copy, lifestyle photography, and current color names. Crate&Barrel, Pottery Barn, Pottery Barn Kids, and Room (with stores in New York City and Miami) are all excellent resources for home fashions. J.Crew, J. Jill, Boston Proper, Fitigues, Banana Republic, and Gap are great for fashion apparel.

The best place to go for inspiration is your favorite shopping center. Visit a variety of stores to see first hand how messages are communicated. Look at the signs in Figure 8.17. Cover the figure caption and see how many stores you can identify. How well do the signing styles fit the company brand image? Which are easiest to read? Which style would most shoppers prefer, conversational or bullet points? Which signs give the most information? Which signs would most influence buying decisions?

Figure 8.17 Signing in home stores:
A. Crate&Barrel, B. Restoration Hardware,
C. Pottery Barn, D. Eddie Bauer Home,
E. Sharper image, F. Williams-Sonoma.

A

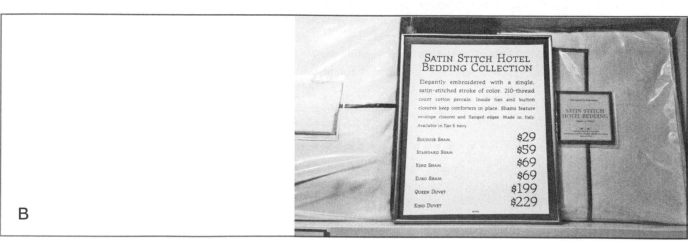

B

GRAND
TELEPHONE

- Shape and substance define a classic telephone.
- Available as freestanding phone or wall phone.
- Like the original, it features an authentic bell ring.

black, red or ivory	metal finish
59.00	79.00

C

HARVEST
CORDED AND DOBBY-STRIPE
TOWELS

BATH	$19
HAND	$12
FINGERTIP	$7
WASHCLOTH	$6

Eddie Bauer
HOME

D

Low-profile CD stereo
fits beautifully into
any home or office.

- Handsome stereo system delivers excellent sound through distinctive satellite speakers.
- Features clear motorized top, CD player and easy one-touch tilt volume control.
- Digital AM/FM tuner stores 20 stations (10 AM, 10 FM) in its memory.
- Plugs into wall outlet. Remote runs on 2 AA batteries (purchase separately).

**Digital Bookshelf Stereo 2.0
with AM/FM Digital Tuner & Remote**
$199⁹⁵ GM400

Powered Subwoofer
$99⁹⁵ SA251

90-day warranty.
Ask about our Replacement Guarantee.

Special Offer:
Subwoofer
only $69⁹⁵
if purchased with
this stereo. Save $30!

SHARPER IMAGE

E

WILLIAMS SONOMA

Soaps & Lotions with
Essential Oils

Aromatherapy for the cook!

Scented with essential oils of citrus fruits and various herbs, our soaps and lotions contain the natural cleansing properties of those oils. Their aromas will complement food preparation, not compete with it, and they are eco-friendly.

Developed exclusively for Williams-Sonoma, the liquid soap is enriched with olive oil; the hand lotion, with soothing aloe. The long-burning kitchen candle sheds a soft glow while masking cooking odors. The fragrant, concentrated dish soap contains nature's degreaser, soap-bark extract, so washing dishes is a positive pleasure.

F

Shoptalk
● ●

By Ken Sinclair
Rainbow Signs, Minneapolis

I'm a believer in professional sign production for retail stores that consider effective communication with customers as part of their mission. And I don't say that just because I am employed by a graphics and signing company, either. A full-service company with seasoned consultative salespeople and an in-house creative staff can support everything that you want to accomplish in your outreach to shoppers in a certain market—things you probably could never do in most stores using less than state-of-the-art printing equipment.

By interpreting what your company wants to say to its customers and turning that into the creative sign toppers, banners, full-sheet posters, and full-sized graphics that grab and hold your customers' attention, the professional sign maker reinforces your communications and builds brand equity for you. How could you do all of that without some help from experts?

A professional sign and graphics company is going to have more and newer equipment, better creative resources (often in-house), and the capability to produce higher-quality and more innovative printing than most signing you could create on your own—saving time and money in the long run. Your company wouldn't have to own the equipment or update it, staff the signing system, buy supplies, maintain equipment, print sufficient quantities to justify those costs, warehouse, or distribute the signs once completed. Qualified printing companies even employ their own "apostrophe police"—prepress staff who are trained to catch grammatical or syntax errors on finished art. It's hard to put a name on that kind of service—other than commitment to detail, pride in the work, and concern for customers. Always remember the age-old wisdom that "form follows function." Your most brilliant visual merchandising ideas can easily become too expensive, impossible to produce, or too cumbersome if you don't consider *how* they are to be made. Beginning designers need to get to know their sign makers' capabilities and then work closely with them during the design process. That way, designs *that work* can be created economically and efficiently. We're very proud of what we do as an industry. Hopefully, some day, we'll be able to do it for you!

Out-of-the-Box Challenge
● ●

1 Sign Layout

Look

Visit a local store that features signing as part of its merchandise presentation on the selling floor. Look for a sign listing only product and price, a sign that uses conversational copy, and one that employs bulleted copy. Sketch the copy and layout for each example.

Compare

Compare them to the sign layout guidelines and examples in this chapter.

Innovate

At home or at school, using any word processing or sign making software available, design an improved version of the store's signs.

● Use an appropriate font and type size for the sign's function and amount of copy.

● Draw the margins correctly.

● Identify the optical center of the sign.

● Think about balance, interesting lines that lead the eye through the components, appropriate use of white space, proportion (the relationship of the parts to each other), and effective communication.

Present your signs in class or to your instructor and explain your choices for font, size, layout, and copy.

2 Specialty Grocery Product Sign Layout

Directions

Use the following information to create copy and layouts for a 7 × 11 bulleted sign and a 7 × 11 conversational sign for the specialty product described here.

Look

Read the following product description. Identify the information to be featured in each sign. Product: PICNI-KIT®.

A wicker picnic basket that is prepacked with safe, convenient, ready-to-eat deli-style foods sealed in packages that can be reheated on a grill. Picni-kit® comes in three sizes with enough food and place settings to serve 2, 6, or 10. Prices range from $30 to $150. Contains appetizers, bread, meats, cheeses, dried fruits, and desserts.

Prepare at least two sketches each for your bulleted and conversational signs. For each sketch, do the following:

● Draw the correct margins.

● Identify the optical center of the sign.

● Consider balance, white space, proportion (the relationship of the parts to each other), and effective communication. Choose appropriate type fonts.

Compare

Select the best sketch for your conversational and bulleted signs. Be prepared to explain your selections in class and exchange reactions with your classmates.

Colorplate 1

Three window displays that exemplify out-of-the-box thinking.

"Who would expect vegetables and technology to go together?" asks Christine Belich, Sony's executive creative director, referring to Sony's "Couch Potato" window (A).

A

A window designed by Tom Beebe when he was creative director for Paul Stewart, the men's wear retailer (B), illustrates his philosophy: "The basis of a Paul Stewart window is to stop people in their tracks and get them to look at the window."

B

Simon Doonan brings attention to Barney's windows (C) with his unique, eye-catching use of mannequins. "Mannequins are the high-octane gasoline that fuels the throbbing of my window dressing Lincoln Continental," he says.

C

A

B

C

D

Colorplate 2
Miss Sixty stores have abandoned the "cookie-cutter" theory and are designing new stores for each location. (A) Miss Sixty, Nolita, New York City. (B) Miss Sixty and Energie, San Francisco. (C) Miss Sixty, Soho, New York City. (D) Miss Sixty, Costa Mesa, CA.

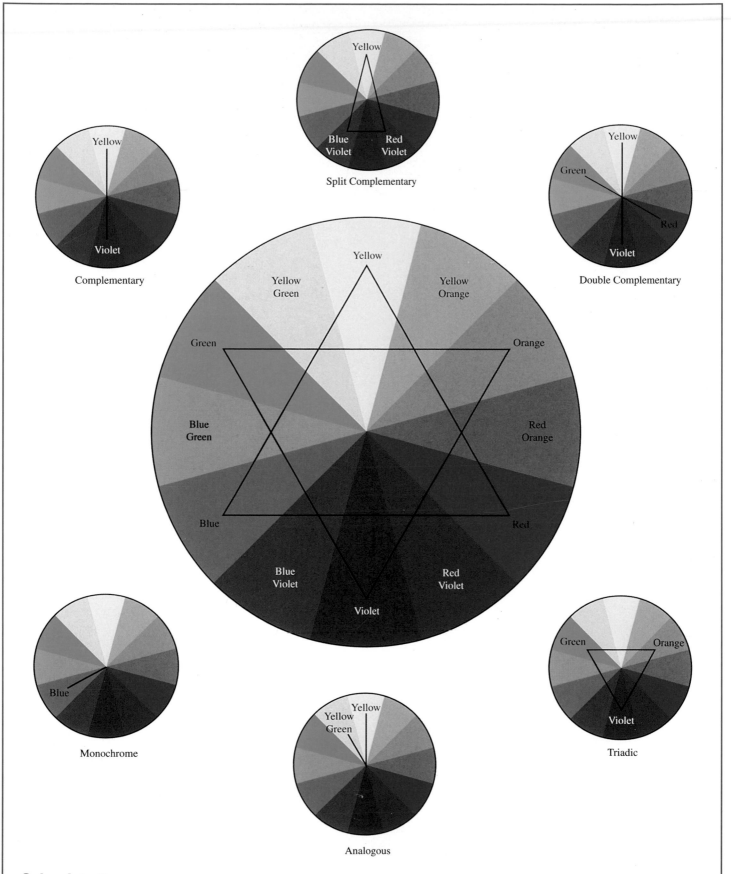

Yellow

Blue
Violet　　Red
Violet

Split Complementary

Yellow

Yellow
Green

Yellow
Orange

Green

Orange

Blue
Green

Red
Orange

Blue

Red

Blue
Violet

Red
Violet

Violet

Yellow

Green

Red

Violet

Double Complementary

Yellow

Violet

Complementary

Blue

Monochrome

Yellow
Yellow　Green
Green

Analogous

Green　　Orange

Violet

Triadic

Colorplate 3

The standard color wheel is a convenient reference for planning color schemes. The large wheel in the center shows that the primary hues—yellow, red, and blue—are equidistant from each other. Opposite each primary hue is the secondary hue that is its complement. The secondary hues are also equidistant from each other on the color wheel. Various color schemes are shown on the smaller color wheels.

A

B

Colorplate 4
Bright jackets are grouped together for a dramatic color statement in Macysport, at Macy's Herald Square, New York City **(A)**, Gerdeman design group. **(B)** At Crate&Barrel, brightly colored housewares are presented together. Notice the towels are arranged by color according to Roy G. Bv.

SEVEN COLOR GROUPS

R   O   Y   G   B   V

BRIGHTS →

PASTELS →

MIDTONES →

JEWELTONES →

MUTED/DUSTY →

EARTHTONES →

NEUTRALS →

Neutral colors may be combined with any color group.

Colorplate 5

You can remember the color order of the rainbow by using the mnemonic device: Roy G. Bv. Notice how each color in rows 2 through 5 corresponds to the color above it. For example, pink, in the pastels, corresponds to bright red in the top row, peach to bright orange, and so on.

A

B

Colorplate 6

A floral arrangement with harmonious color **(A)** is achieved by combining colors from just one color group, brights. In the incorrect example **(B)** the combination of brightly colored flowers combined with pastel pink is not pleasing to the eye.

Colorplate 7

The TO2 shop (Todd Oldham Jeans) at Macy's Herald Square in New York City displays a brilliant sense of rhythm and energy by varying fixture heights and using the TO2 ad campaign on columns. Custom fixtures of pink/orange fluorescent acrylic, a custom blue vinyl floor and lighting with a "star-in-the-sky" effect combine with the merchandise to become one unique, playful environment.

Colorplate 8

This is a sample of a student's color wheel collage. She put her hand-colored palette from another Chapter 3 assignment in its center as a reference point.

A

B

Colorplate 9
The wooden feature fixture in this correct example presents products from just one color group, jewel tones, for a harmonious color arrangement. Combined with the wall, which is also merchandised in jewel tones, a color coordinated shop is created (A). In this incorrect example, a pastel is combined with the jewel tones on the wooden feature fixture. When jewel tones and pastels are mixed in this way, the result is not pleasing (B).

A **correct**

B **incorrect**

Colorplate 10

The wall presentation in the correct example (A) features colors from just one color group, brights, combined with neutrals for a harmonious color arrangement. Refer to Colorplate 4. In the incorrect example (B), the wall presentation features colors from two color groups, brights and pastels, which do not blend together in a harmonious way.

Colorplate 11

(A) It is easy to color coordinate an outfit by repeating the colors in a patterned pivot piece. The repetition of colors creates rhythm as the eye moves around the garment pieces and accessories. (B) An outfit combining both brights and pastel colors. Repetition of colors in both groups is the key to creating a pleasing look. (C) A monochromatic outfit.

Colorplate 12
A dramatic dinnerware display using just one color and a "pyramid" model.

Colorplate 13
The lighting scheme for Benelava of Columbus, Ohio, combines several fixture types, from alabaster bowls to tiny halogen pendants.

Colorplate 14
The Chute Gerdeman design group chose lighting for Larry's Shoes that is both functional and atmospheric.

Colorplate 15
Three scenes from Marshall Field's "Glamorama" fashion event in Minneapolis.

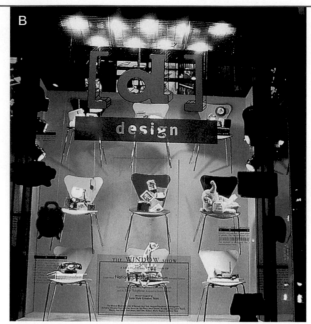

Colorplate 16
(A) Macy's institutional window, a salute to the "Window Wizard" Gene Moore during the Cooper-Hewitt's Window Show. Design: Sam Joseph. **(B)** Sony Style: The windows featured a Noguchi "radio nurse" (baby monitor) and a Sony baby monitor. Design: Christine Belich and Team. **(C)** Saks Fifth Avenue: A distinctly modern use of space set the stage for a salute to Charles and Ray Eames. Design: Randall Yaw. **(D)** Lord & Taylor: Both the gowns and the rug are made of wallpaper based on Cooper-Hewitt's wall coverings collection. Design: Manoel Renha Rezende. **(E)** Paul Stewart: Shooting over 100 rolls of Polaroid film with the Polaroid Swinger and the SX-70 camera paved the way to a veritable fantasia of beaded curtains and photographs. Design: Tom Beebe and Team. **(F)** Sherle Wagner: Based on actual paper dolls in the museum's collection. Design: Ann Kong.

Innovate

Refine your sketches, taking into account the advice of your classmates.

Critical Thinking

Play 20 Questions

1. How does your favorite retail store communicate with you outside its doors? What makes you want to go inside to shop?

2. Where have you encountered floor graphics in a store? Describe them and your reaction to them.

3. Describe your impressions of a store where you've encountered handwritten signs. Positive? Negative? Why?

4. The text listed seven reasons for signing merchandise (see page 196). Can you think of at least one additional reason for signing?

5. What are the dangers of "oversigning" a store?

6. Why would an in-store marketer be concerned with the appropriateness of a sign request from a department buyer?

7. Define the term *outsourcing*.

8. Describe three or four products for which it would be appropriate to use a formally balanced layout. Explain why you think so.

9. Describe three or four items for which it would be appropriate to use an asymmetrical layout. Explain why you think so.

10. Write a paragraph of conversational copy to sell the shoes you are wearing today.

11. Write three points of bullet-point copy to sell the shoes you are wearing today.

12. Write conversational sign copy including an add-on tie-in for a food you had at breakfast or lunch today.

13. Write alliterative sign copy for the toothpaste or skin care product you used today.

14. Write sign copy based on a familiar phrase for an accessory item that you or one of your classmates wore today.

15. Write a line of sign copy based on a pun for this textbook.

16. Write a line of sign copy for the type of transportation that brought you to school today based on a quotation from a celebrity, recent movie, or television program.

17. Use rhyming words to compose sign copy for your next vacation destination.

18. Choose four themed adjectives (words that modify nouns) to write sign copy advertising yourself as a job seeker.

19. Go to and explore **www.popmag.com.** Then describe the most interesting booth you visited. Describe the best product you saw and tell how it relates to communication with shoppers.

20. Bring a magazine or newspaper to class to show your classmates an advertisement (for any product or service) that you would nominate as "Best of Show." Be prepared to defend its effectiveness in communicating with a targeted audience.

Case Study

What's Your Sign?

The Situation: Phase One

You are the new visual department manager for a store that has what you consider a poor and confusing signing program. It combines all-purpose machine-made signs purchased from a store fixture catalog with hand-lettered signs that reflect last-minute merchandising decisions and price changes. Your store's owner asks you to create new signing standards for the company's two stores on opposite ends of the city. The only instructions you receive are "Make the signs uniform so that we can produce them for both stores at one time," and "Be budget-conscious, please."

The store, which is called "It's All in the Game," sells the following types of games:

- Board games for children and adults ranging from Monopoly and Scrabble to Chutes and Ladders

- Popular computer games from nearly every software company

- Miniaturized handheld games like golf and target shooting

- Classic games like checkers and chess

- Role-playing games

- Lawn games like croquet and boccie ball

- Educational games related to math, language, and science

All of the merchandise is boxed and shelved. Displays are confined to facing out the top box on the highest shelf so that shoppers walking up the aisles toward the natural birch shelving can easily review it. There is no back stock; everything is out on shelves. Part of the stock is locked into security cases because it is expensive or poses a security risk because of its small size. Currently, signs are taped to the front lip of each shelf below the stacked merchandise. The only information on them is the name of the item, an SKU number, and a price. Clearance merchandise and markdowns are marked with colored dots, and there is a chart explaining the pricing scheme on the wall behind the checkout counter.

The store's communication goal is to reinforce the store's playful game theme. That hasn't happened yet. Shoppers need more and better information than they are currently getting from store signs. Games are grouped on shelves alphabetically rather than by type or age group. The only table display is the clearance table just inside the front door.

Your Challenge

1. Describe the "tone" or mood you would communicate through your new signing program.

2. Select a type style or font that you think would help you accomplish this communication goal. Examine the various fonts included with your word processing program to get started.

3. Using the tone and the type style you've adopted, create an 11″ × 14″ sign that welcomes shoppers into the store.

4. Assume that you're going to retain the current clearance/markdown dot system. Write sign copy that will explain it to shoppers. You may supply any additional details you need. Describe where you would locate the "dot" information (end cap signing or floor-standing full-sheet posters, for example) and explain your reasoning.

5. Describe the merchandising shortcomings of alphabetizing the merchandise on shelves and devise another method for organizing the store's merchandise.

Then describe how new signing could make it work more efficiently for shoppers than the arrangement currently in use.

6. Explain why lifestyle graphics might be (or not be) appropriate tools for your new signing program.

7. Describe a sign "topper" or "sider" that might help you add some visual consistency to your two-store signing program.

The Situation: Phase Two

In addition to revamping the store's signing, another innovation to implement is an open computer game library so that shoppers can actually "test drive" games in stock before purchase. Someone on staff has proposed an area with tables and chairs plus two computer stations to facilitate this concept. This area is going to be a busy place and will need informational signing so shoppers know how to use it without necessarily having to get extensive directions from sales associates.

Your Challenge

1. Write the sign copy. Visualize the setting and write sign copy that welcomes your customers to the area and explains the process for testing the games and using your facility. For example, "Games are filed alphabetically in boxes at each computer station," and "Please return game in appropriate slot when you've finished."

2. Explain what you hope to accomplish with the language and tone you choose for this communication.

3. Describe where you would locate this informational sign and how large it would have to be in order to be readable.

Chapter 9

LIGHTING

After completing this chapter, you should be able to

Describe how lighting helps to define store brand identity

Explain why a lighting expert must always be consulted when a lighting system is purchased

Identify the three functions of lighting

Recognize three lighting systems

Establish lighting priorities

Discuss current best practices for lighting

"Lighting is a playful and creative
field as well as a highly
technical discipline."
Gareth Fenley, senior editor,
Display & Design Ideas **magazine**

Lighting Defines Store Brand Image

Lighting plays a major role in defining and strengthening a store's brand identity. It contributes to the overall atmosphere and feel of the environment. Think about the lighting in a Victoria's Secret store. It may remind you of the lighting in your own home, soft and warm with highlights and shadows. Compare that mental image to the lighting in a Wal-Mart— bright, cool, and shadow-free. Now imagine Victoria's Secret with Wal-Mart's lighting and vice versa. Aside from the fact that it is highly unlikely, think about what this kind of change would do to either store's brand identity. Victoria's Secret's environment would be entirely altered. Wal-Mart's value message would not be clear if it were lighted like a residence. It is easy to understand the degree to which lighting affects a store's brand identity.

Ed Pettersen, vice president of design and construction at The Wiz, says, "Lighting has become far more than the utilitarian device that it once was. It should be used to set an overall tone for the space, while accentuating specific product. Through various ranges of color and temperature, lighting can either illuminate the space in a generalized way, or it may be distinctly focused so as to elevate the perceived value of a particular product, particularly where soft goods are concerned."

Light fixture styling contributes to brand identity, too, as you see when you look at Colorplate 13. Benelava means "good bathing," and this store's subdued yet sumptuous environment was developed around a Roman bathhouse theme. Benelava's lighting scheme mixes several fixture types, each with a unique function. Large alabaster (translucent white) bowls filter lighting from their incandescent lamps. Tiny halogen pendants on tracks accent the products displayed on gray, claylike countertops. (These lighting systems are discussed in detail later in this chapter.) Handblown glass fixtures (not visible in colorplate) used over the cash–wrap are another unique element that adds ambience to this luxury bath shop. The unusually dramatic lighting fixture at The Wiz, shown in Figure 9.1, creates intimacy in this open grid ceiling store. Lighting is used to create appropriate levels and degrees of drama for a unique entertainment experience. Refer to Colorplates 7, Todd Oldham, and 14, Larry's Shoes, to see two other styles of lighting fixtures.

All four photographs demonstrate that lighting fixtures are more than functional. They add interesting atmospheric dimensions to store designs, helping to draw shoppers through the entire environemnt.

Lighting Technology

Lighting technology changes constantly. This presents a special challenge to store designers and visual merchandisers since lighting fixtures and systems are big-ticket items. Intense research in the preliminary stage is the only way to ensure that the system store planners select satisfies lighting requirements for the long term. Fortunately, retailers can consult lighting specialists familiar with retail environments to help with lighting strategies that provide atmosphere, safety, and security at the lowest cost possible.

Lighting manufacturers may have experts who can put together comprehensive, one-stop, lighting programs for retailers. They begin their task by asking questions about the store, its brand identity, its products, and its clientele. Once they understand the retailer's business, they make recommendations for specific lighting systems and offer advice on how to manage them. Maximum lighting effectiveness and minimal energy expenses are the goals. Since operational costs can easily outstrip the initial price of lighting systems, they also review hidden costs like energy and maintenance requirements, plus freight, handling, and processing for shipment. Independent designers, many of them members of the International Association of Lighting Designers (IALD), are also available.

At some point, you may get involved in a lighting system update for an existing store. One of the first things you'll look for is new **lamp** styles that are compatible with current

A Retail Reality:
Lighting systems also produce heat, accounting for 15 to 20 percent of a building's cooling load, which affects the expense of installing and operating air-conditioning equipment.

The word **lamp** has at least two distinct meanings. In the lighting industry, lamp is another word for lightbulb. In layman's terms, it applies to a lighting fixture complete with a bulb, a power source, a base, and a "shade" that is either decorative or purely functional.

212

Figure 9.1 The Wiz employs a dramatic lighting fixture in this New York City store.

systems. Replacing old lamps with efficient ones can dramatically decrease electrical costs for a store. However, updating the system to accept different lamps or light tracks may involve another set of expenses, which is sometimes higher than those for new construction. This is where lighting consultants are invaluable. They can wade through the pros and cons and help you find the best balance between up-front expenses versus long-term savings.

Don't lose sight of the major reason for changing an existing lighting system—the opportunity to show your wares in the best possible light. It's tempting to worry about dollars leaving the store rather than thinking about dollars coming in. Compare costs incurred to advantages gained. In addition to operational savings, new lamps may improve color clarity for displayed merchandise. Stores that take advantage of new technology in lighting systems do so to enhance the appearance of merchandise colors and to provide customers with optimal conditions for making purchase decisions.

Baro, a European lighting firm that specializes in grocery lighting, offers a specialized limited spectrum system that enhances the colors in food products. According to Baro, effective lighting for bananas could be quite different from lighting for strawberries. That degree of specialization ought to tell you how intense competition for shopper attention has become and the part that lighting plays in it. If grocers compete to show redder and riper strawberries, or shinier avocados, can fashion be far behind?

Lighting Functions

Lighting systems actually perform three functions in a store environment: ambient, accent, and task lighting. **Ambient lighting** is general, overall lighting that determines color

Ambient lighting describes general, overall lighting.

213

Color rendition is the degree to which lighting allows colors to be viewed under conditions that are closest to those offered by natural light. The lighting industry uses the term *Color Rendering Index* (CRI) when listing specifications on each lamp.

Accent lighting describes lighting effects designed to emphasize certain wall areas, merchandise displays, or architectural features in a retail setting.

rendition. If you've ever had to ask a salesperson to take two garments out of the store into daylight to compare or match colors, you were shopping in a store environment that didn't provide adequate lighting. In view of recent developments in the lighting industry, that is unacceptable. Lighting that gives merchandise the best **color rendition** possible is never an option; it's a necessity.

Just as colors appear brighter on a sunny day and duller under cloudy conditions, merchandise colors appear to change under different lamps within a store. Color rendition will vary from one store to the next, just as lamps vary from store to store. Even if two stores used identical lighting systems, other factors like ceiling, wall, and floor coverings all influence the lighting levels in any environment. Dark colored carpeting, for example, will absorb more light than a light carpet, resulting in a lower level of ambient lighting in a store.

Accent lighting is a supplemental light fixture that adds "sparkle" or "punch" to displays and creates special focal points in areas that already have general light sources. Accent lighting also adds atmosphere to a store environment. A case in point is Illuminations, a national specialty retailer selling candles of all kinds, shapes, and sizes. At Illuminations in New York City, accent lighting is a dramatic atmospheric element, giving shoppers the impression that the entire store is lit by candlelight, even though only a few candles are actually burning in the store. Under its spell, time seems to lose all importance for shoppers moving from one focal area to the next, savoring the mood of the store.

Task lighting is implemented in work areas—checkouts, alteration rooms, fitting rooms, stockrooms, restrooms, and offices. Lighting professionals pay special attention to task lighting in apparel fitting rooms and above full-length mirrors on the selling floor. Here, the task is trying on clothes. Designers understand that shoppers need to do this in a setting with lighting that enhances both skin tones and fashion colors.

Ideally, fitting room lighting levels will be closest to those used in homes, enabling shoppers to see themselves under conditions that match residential lighting where the garments will be worn. Here's something to keep in mind when fixturing fitting rooms: Overhead light, particularly if it's fluorescent, must be counterbalanced with incandescent lighting over the mirror area. General lighting—or anything that resembles "down lighting"—casts unflattering shadows. Investment here will reflect more favorably on the shopper and the garments. A fitting room is an intimate space. Light should amplify the sense of privacy and flatter the viewer and the garments. Investigate the sort of lighting used by cosmetic makeup artists—soft and flattering to the face.

Lighting Systems

There are three systems of lighting available to achieve the various lighting needs: fluorescent, incandescent, and halogen.

Fluorescent lamps provide the best ambient lighting. They are also the least expensive to operate because they use only one-fifth as much electricity as incandescent lamps to produce the same amount of light. Commonly used as the only light sources in discount and warehouse retail stores, fluorescent lamps have a long life and offer a high degree of lumens per watt. A *lumen* is a measure of light coming from any source compared to the amount of light produced by a burning candle.

A **fluorescent** lamp is a sealed glass tube filled with mercury vapor. Its inner surface is coated with a mixture of phosphor powder. When electricity arcs through the gases in the lamp, it produces ultraviolet energy that is absorbed by the coating and causes the powder to become fluorescent, emitting visible light.

Fluorescents produce only one-fifth as much heat—which may explain why they are sometimes called "cool" lights. Fluorescent lighting is commonly combined with other lighting systems in department store and specialty retail stores. Although fluorescent lamps provide inexpensive general lighting in the store environment, they cannot effectively accent merchandise or displays—a requirement in most retail stores.

Fluorescent lamps are nonshadowing. This makes merchandise appear flat or nondimensional. The effect is due partly to the plastic glare-diffusers employed in most recessed fluorescent ceiling fixtures. The problem with diffusers is reduction in light levels that actually reach the merchandise. Egg-crating or some other form of openwork fixture covering may take care of this to a certain extent. Retailers have requested general improvements in fluorescent systems, and in response, several lamp manufacturers have worked together to produce a line of high light-output and color-performance bulbs that complement merchandise and skin tones.

Incandescent lighting is the best method to use for accent and task lighting. Incandescent lamps give off a defined area of light rather than the overall light produced by a fluorescent system. The type of lamp used determines the scope of the defined area. Flood lamps light a wide area; spot lamps cover a narrower area. Spot lamps are made in a variety of sizes and intensities. They can effectively cover a range from 1 inch to 6 feet. Once you understand the range and capabilities of individual spots and flood lamps, it's simply a matter of choosing the correct one for the task and fitting it into an adjustable can on a track system.

Incandescent light systems offer excellent color rendition, but they have a shorter lamp life and produce lower degrees of lumens per watt at a greater cost than the fluorescent system does. Incandescent lighting enhances reds, oranges, and yellows, but blues are dulled. They are available in nonreflectorized versions, or reflectorized versions, for more "punch."

To observe the different lighting effects of incandescent and fluorescent lamps, place your hand first under a fluorescent lamp and then under an incandescent lamp. Which lamp gives your skin the warmer tone? Which lamp creates shadows?

Halogen is another type of incandescent lighting. It provides the color rendition closest to daylight. It offers longer lamp life and the highest lumen efficiency of any system. In fact, halogen is more efficient than standard incandescent lamps by 10 to 20 percent, which translates to considerable savings over time. Installing dimmer switches and turning down light levels where appropriate may extend the life of a halogen lamp up to four times. If dimmers are used, however, manufacturers recommend turning lamps up to full capacity for 15 minutes each week to ensure even greater efficiency.

Halogen lighting is commonly used for accent and task lighting, and it is growing in popularity as an ambient lighting source. The cost for a halogen system is high initially, but its efficiency makes it cost-effective over time. It is important to know that you should not handle halogen lamps with bare hands; oil from hands will cause the lamp to burn out more quickly. Keep in mind that the person responsible for changing lamps will need special training.

Safety Concern!

Halogen lamps give off intense heat. Using them in selling areas requires extra caution so that the lamp never comes in direct contact with merchandise or atmospheric drapings. Fixtures with halogen lamps should not be placed where they might be touched accidentally. Be especially aware of torchères (floorlamps with exposed halogen bulbs) that might tip toward hanging merchandise if bumped by shoppers.

Combined Lighting Systems

Today, most retailers use combinations of available lighting systems to accomplish all three lighting functions in their stores: ambient, accent, and task lighting. Figure 9.2 illustrates how fluorescent and halogen systems may be used together in a store layout.

An **incandescent** lamp is a glass bulb with an interior tungsten filament that is heated by electric current, producing light. You know it as the common lightbulb.

A **halogen** lamp contains highly pressurized halogen gas that, combined with evaporated tungsten, cycles the gas back to the filament which, in turn, cleans the glass while maintaining lumen output throughout the lifetime of the lamp.

"The color-rendering index of halogen lamps is at a higher temperature range, producing crisp, white color. Creating precise light beams is another of halogen's major benefits. Halogen lighting emphasizes texture and form, creating dramatic visual impact."

Deb Schlingmann, certified lighting specialist and member of The American Lighting Association

Figure 9.2 A lighting plan combining fluorescent fixtures for ambient lighting with halogen fixtures for accent and task lighting functions.

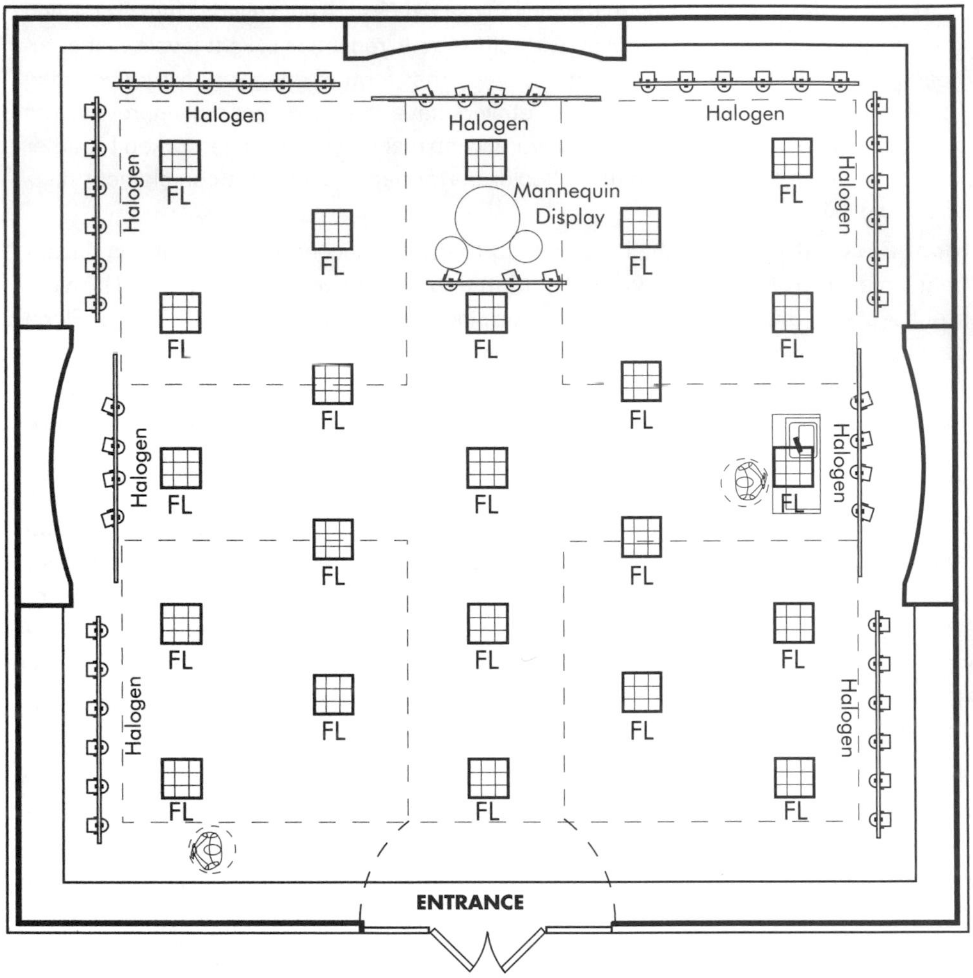

Lighting Windows and Editorial Displays

Lighting merchandise in windows and in editorial displays is a trial-and-error process as you learn your craft. The last thing you want to do is distort a product's true color. If possible, you want to enhance the item or achieve dramatic effects with a hint of additional color or emphasizing the product to make it stand out in the presentation. Lighting a display window may require adding colored lighting to correct color distortion that results from the sun shining onto merchandise or to heighten color contrasts for noon-hour window shopping.

In *Visual Merchandising & Display,* Martin Pegler coaches visual merchandisers through the often difficult process of selecting colored lamps to enhance product colors in windows and editorial displays. In closed windows, you'll be working with display-specific light sources rather than ambient lighting and will have more control over your lighting effects. With open-backed windows and on the selling floor, you may have to override ambient lighting to create a special impact. You may also want to create a uniquely colored lighting scheme for a certain department's atmospherics. That's when you need to know the techniques that Pegler teaches so well. For instance, he says that red light on red paint or textiles will "pop" the red, adding brilliance to the basic color. The same red lamp shining down on a blue garment will make it look brown-purple. Red light on a green garment will make it seem dark gray. On orange, red will make objects look quite pale. On yellow, a red light will leach the color, leaving it nearly white in appearance. This means that you must use caution and good judgment when you add colored lighting effects to display presentations. A light that adds atmosphere to your propping and general presentation may communicate a distorted picture of the merchandise to shoppers.

Blue light on red merchandise will turn the item violet, while blue on blue adds that brilliant "punch" you may be after. Blue on yellow creates green hues, and blue on green will yield turquoise. On violet, a blue light will create blue-violet, perhaps adding depth and richness to draped fabric, and that may be an admirable goal. Always use your best judgment.

Green light on red turns the object brown. Green on yellow takes the color in chartreuse directions, and green on green gives you a more brilliant green. On orange, a green light will burnish it to the color of old gold. Green on violet will give you a dark gray-green.

If you want to emphasize orange, use an amber light for a brighter, truer orange. Magenta on orange will give you a bright red-orange; on red you'll have cerise. Magenta on blue brings up ultramarine blue, and on yellow you'll see orange. To get a hint of these lighting effects, you can experiment with colored pencils by layering the lamp color over the colors you lay down on a sheet of paper.

Priority Lighting Checklist

Visual merchandising managers and store planners who are researching lighting updates for existing systems wisely use a checklist approach to avoid overlooking critical items. A list serves as a planning tool, helps prioritize key areas where improved lighting will make a difference to store image and sales, and helps assess maintenance requirements once the improvements are installed. The items on this checklist will show what areas are really important in terms of lighting and store image:

- Spotlights at the store entrance
- Fixtures on the store leaseline or department leaseline
- Priority walls on either side of the store or department entrance
- Back wall of the store
- Editorial spaces, niches, and coves
- Selling floor display areas; display windows
- Task areas: checkouts and fitting rooms

You may think that all of this updating and retrofitting is a managerial activity and not something for an entry-level merchandiser to be concerned about. To a certain degree, that's true. You probably won't be selecting the systems or placing the orders. However, you do need to be interested and concerned because as a practitioner you will be checking the lighting on the checklist daily. You may also be asked to train the selling staff to do the same. Later in your career, you may be one of the decision makers participating in the research and planning.

General Guidelines for Lighting

1. Focus any adjustable light *on* merchandise. If you move a fixture, check if a light fixture needs to be adjusted. Lights focused on blank walls or blank floor areas serve no purpose. (See Figures 9.3 and 9.4.)
2. Set adjustable lights at an angle rather than straight on to maximize the area that is lighted. (See Figure 9.5.)

Figure 9.3 Flood lighting in a fashion apparel wall presentation. In the correct example, light fixtures with flood lamps are focused on the merchandise. In the incorrect example, light fixtures are set on the blank wall rather than on merchandise.

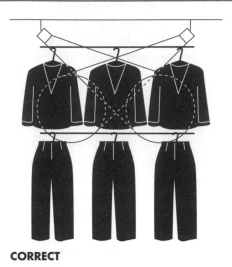

CORRECT

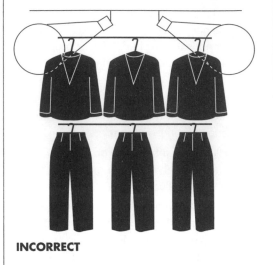

INCORRECT

3. Combine spots and floods in a display area for a more dramatic look, as shown in Figure 9.6.

4. Setup accent lighting for displays with three to five times more intensity than the ambient lighting levels in the store.

5. Adjust lights in areas with glass countertops or in wall areas with mirrors so that there is no glare in shoppers' eyes. (See Figure 9.7.)

6. Replace burned out lamps *only* with the same style of lamp. Spots should be replaced with spots; floods replaced with floods.

Figure 9.4 Lighting in a fashion apparel floor presentation. In the correct example, a light fixture with a flood or spot lamp is focused on merchandise on the floor fixture. In the incorrect example, the lighting fixture is focused on the floor.

CORRECT

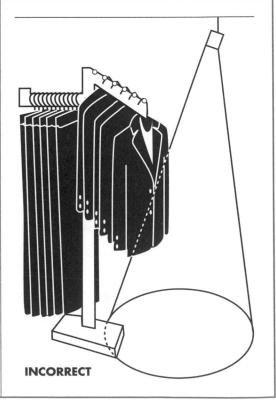

INCORRECT

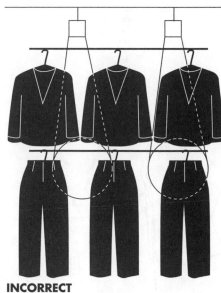
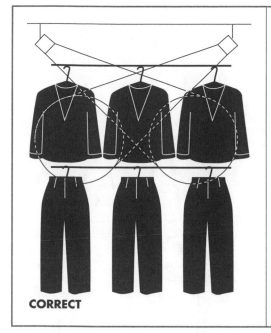

Figure 9.5 Flood lighting in a fashion apparel wall presentation. In the correct example, fixtures with flood lamps are crossed over the merchandise to maximize lighting. In the incorrect example, fixtures are not crossed. Notice how the range of lighting is minimized.

CORRECT

INCORRECT

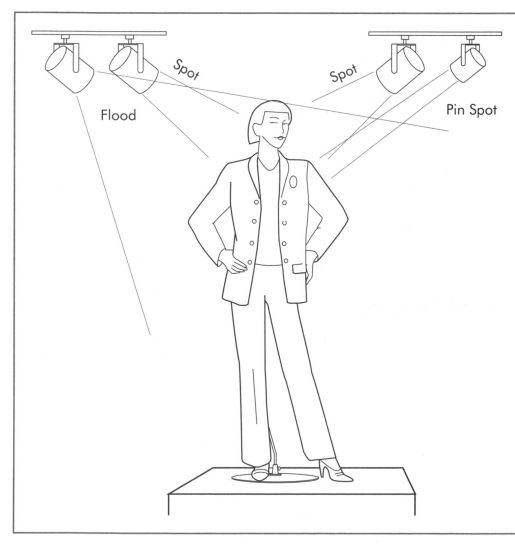

Figure 9.6 Lighting fixtures with flood lamps, spot lamps, and pin spot lamps are combined to create impact for this outpost mannequin display.

Spot

Spot

Flood

Pin Spot

Figure 9.7 Showcase lighting. In the correct example, the position of the light fixture is angled so that the light does not create glare. In the incorrect example, the position of the light creates glare, which may irritate the shopper.

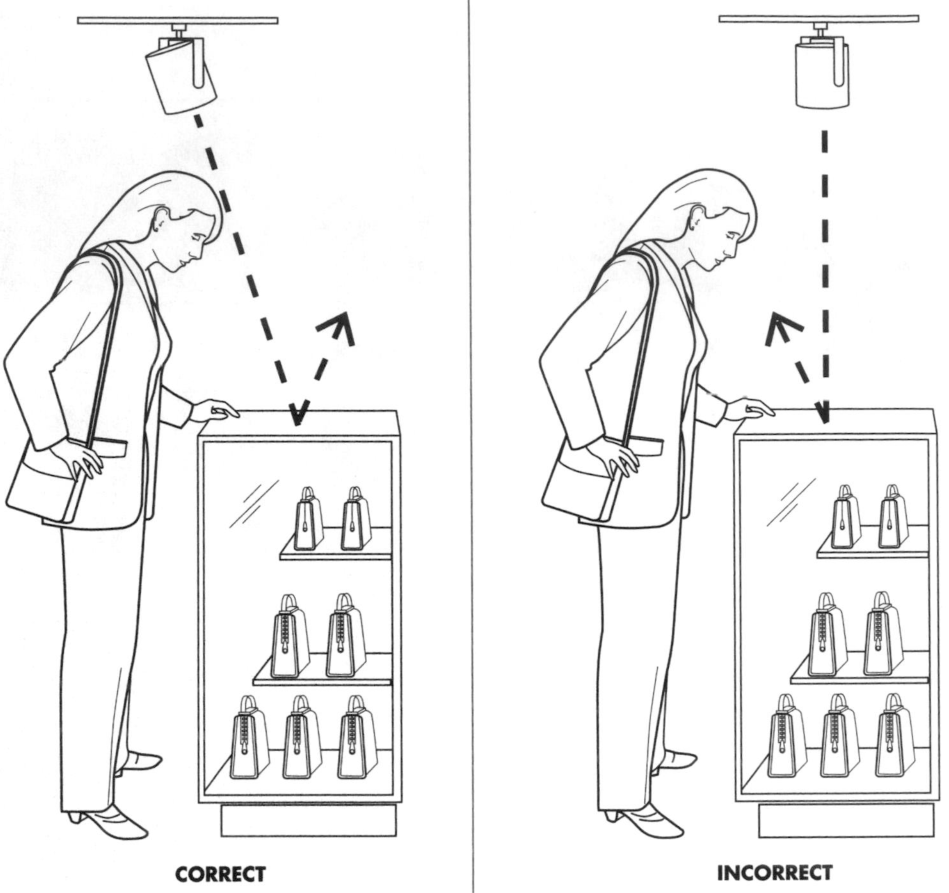

CORRECT   INCORRECT

7. Keep fixtures and bulbs clean. Dusty lamps may drastically reduce lighting output. Clean the interior of the fixture, too, because the surface serves as a reflector for the lighting.

8. Schedule regular cleaning or painting of store walls and ceilings. Dust and dirt on these surfaces decrease light reflection.

9. Dark floors and carpets absorb light, so light, neutral colors are better flooring choices.

Trend Awareness

You've read about several recent technological developments in the lighting industry, and you know that there will be more changes every day. In a trend-driven industry like retailing, there are other factors that will affect how you'll do your lighting tasks over the next decade. Here are at least two important trends to watch:

Color Marketing Group (CMG), a professional organization that forecasts color directions for manufacturers, sees a trend influencing how shoppers will respond to color. CMG predicts that they will become disenchanted with the "fast-paced digital age" and look for more soothing and spiritual elements in their surroundings.

Water—a symbol of tranquility—and all the ways light reflects various colors on water will strongly influence design palettes. CMG predicts that neutrals and soft pales are going to be very important, led by aqua and what CMG calls "a true lavender." Earthy reds, oranges, and browns will provide contrast.

Visual merchandisers may need lighting expertise to bring out the best in these colors because, once they surface in apparel, they will be reflected in home furnishings, automobile market, and so on.

In-store lighting that creates a less hectic, less stressful shopping environment has the potential to attract more customers and capture more business for stores. If retailers use high-tech lighting tools to promote satisfying high-touch shopping experiences, they will balance important philosophical and environmental trends.

Research by Envirosell predicts that baby boomers will soon have trouble seeing gradations in color. This is simply a result of growing older. Distortions in color perception among this age group has implications for visual merchandisers because of the large number of people in this demographic group. According to Envirosell director Paco Underhill, "The difference between blues and greens will become more difficult for many [older] shoppers to perceive, and yellow will become much trickier for designers to use—everything will look a little yellow."

Our eyes work like cameras because light must pass through an opening (aperture) and optics where pictures are formed. Aging clouds and yellows the eye's optics and shrinks the pupil. As an entire generation's corneas yellow with age, visual merchandisers will have to find ways to compensate with lighting techniques that render store and display colors as truly as possible.

About the amount of light needed for shopping, Underhill says, "The typical 50-year-old's retinas receive about one-quarter less light than the average 20-year-old's. That means lots of stores, restaurants, and banks should be brighter than they are now. There can't be pockets of dim light, not if shoppers are going to see what they're shopping for or even where they're walking. Illumination must be bright, especially during the time of day when older shoppers tend to arrive."

As clear distinctions between steps and risers disappear, stairs will have to be better lit. Lighting aimed at directional signing will have to be fairly intense because aging also reduces the ability to see contrasts—edges and borders, for instance. Words and numbers will have to be larger. Needless to say, any signing—especially conversational signing—will require easy-to-read type and also better lighting levels than those currently used in some retail stores.

In July of 1999, *Display and Design Ideas* (DDI) magazine published an article called "Designing Displays for the Aging Population," which offers several effective lighting practices that will prepare retailers to make older shoppers happier with the shopping environment. Glare isn't much of a problem for young eyes, but it can be a huge discomfort for older ones.

Bright overhead lighting combined with highly polished hardwood floors and glass display cases can cause great discomfort in the elderly. Writer Marc Green, Ph.D., coprincipal of Toronto-based Ergo/Gero Consulting and adjunct professor at the University of West Virginia's Medical Ophthalmology Department, suggests that retailers use many small light sources rather than a few very intense ones or recommends more indirect lighting. He also recommends applying matte finishes to floors and covering highly polished floors with light-absorbing rugs or mats.

Bringing the trend discussion full circle, Green points out, "The eye's yellowing optics also affect color perception by filtering out blue [CMG's color for the decade]. Blues become especially dark and often appear as black. (This probably explains why studies find that older people frequently dislike blue.) Moreover, colors look different; purples appear red and blue-green appears dark green."

Here's a lesson for you as a lifelong learner: CMG predicts that blues are going to be the next trend colors while Dr. Green is saying that most baby boomers—the generation with the most members and the most money to spend—can't see them properly. What you have here is a riddle. Research the facts and then weigh their implications for your work. Only you can decide what is correct.

Shoptalk

The Lighting Designer's Toy Shelf

By Gareth Fenley, senior editor, *Display and Design Ideas* magazine

When I step into the studio of a lighting designer, I look for the "toy shelf" brimming with fanciful and often colorful assemblies of glass, metal, and plastic, many energized with electrical wire. I'm seldom disappointed. Lighting is a playful and creative field as well as a highly technical discipline requiring a thorough comfort with the calculation of lumens, watts, and voltages.

The exciting news about lighting for visual merchandisers is that anyone with a flair for display can learn to use basic lighting techniques to improve sales. The daunting factor for you is that lighting is technology, and a highly evolved and fast-changing technology at that. Although incandescent lamps directly descended from Edison's bulb are still in use, today's retail stores are increasingly lit by energy-efficient sources such as ceramic metal halide with its flattering color rendering, produced by a capsule of highly pressurized glowing gas. One of the most advanced new technologies, LEDs (light-emitting diodes), actually incorporates a computer chip inside the lamp!

Efficiency is critical, and not only because governments have begun to impose energy consumption restrictions in many states. Electricity costs money, and lighting consumes 20 to 25 percent of the energy used in a typical building. Lighting systems also produce heat, accounting for 15 to 20 percent of a building's cooling load, which affects the expense of installing and operating air-conditioning equipment. Even more advanced integration of systems is involved when the retailer wants to install skylights and take advantage of daylighting, which was shown in one recent study to boost sales by 40 percent.

So it will serve you well to become familiar with basic electrical terminology and to explore with curiosity the magazine pages, trade show aisles, and showroom displays where advanced lighting technology is marketed. The more you learn about lighting products, the more your imagination will have fodder for creative new concepts.

But for a grounding in lighting design techniques, there is no better training ground than the theater. If you really want hands-on training in how lighting can sculpt form and alter mood, volunteer to join the lighting crew of a theatrical production. There you'll learn about beam spreads, color filters, gobos, and a hundred tricks of the trade. Attend concerts and plays lit by professional designers with an eye to observing how they get their effects.

Wherever you go inside buildings, look up to the ceiling and under shelves and ledges to discover light sources. Is that creamy glow from neon or fluorescent? Did the lamps in those sconces glare in your eyes as you descended the escalator? What kind of accessory is mounted on that PAR lamp to give that dappled effect on the mannequin? How would you change the equipment or mounting angles to make the lighting work better?

If lighting truly fascinates you—and you don't mind math—you may want to make a specialty out of lighting design, eventually aiming for the prestigious initials LC after your name, telling other designers you are Lighting Certified. But if lighting merely intrigues you as an element in the palette of visual merchandising, that's fine too. Keep your eyes open and when you see a shimmering gizmo you can't resist, start building your own toy shelf.

Out-of-the-Box Challenge

Lighting Evaluation

Look

Visit two fashion stores of your choice. Answer the following questions for both stores.

1. Are the fixtures on the store leaseline brightly lighted?
2. Look at all of the walls of the store, including the back wall. Are they well lighted? What types of lighting are used?
3. Are any lights focused on blank wall or floor areas?
4. Are displays more brightly lighted than other areas of the store?
5. Is the checkout lighted well enough for transactions to be easily handled?
6. What is your opinion of the lighting in the fitting rooms?

Compare

Compare the lighting in the two stores. Which store has the best overall lighting plan?

Innovate

How would you improve the lighting in both stores?

Critical Thinking

Discussion Questions

1. Visit the Internet site **www.fashionwindows.com.** Look at the site's Store Windows Gallery. Take about 10 minutes to view as many store window photos as you can. Based on your readings in this chapter, select the most outstanding example of effective window lighting and the example of the least effective lighting. Print each one. Bring your selections to class and report why you

thought the lighting was effective (or not). Even though all of these photos may not have been professionally shot, they will give you an idea of what the designer attempted to do.

2. Visit the Internet site **www.visualstore.com** and take a few minutes to examine the format of this excellent electronic trade magazine from the publishers of *VM+SD* magazine. Go to Resources and then choose Lighting. Visit at least five resources and report back to the class on the lighting products you discover on this virtual sourcing trip. If you can, print one picture from each link you visit.

3. Review the following statement from this text. CMG predicts that blues are going to be the next trend colors while Dr. Green is saying that most baby boomers—the generation with the most members and the most money to spend—can't see them properly. Do you think a retailer should make adaptive changes in a store serving baby boomers? What do you think a store should do if it appears that the necessary changes will also change the store's brand image?

4. The U.S. Census Bureau predicts that nearly 40 percent of the American population will be over 45 years old in the year 2015. What kinds of retail stores will exist at that time? Will retailers design, light, and lay out their stores differently from the way they do today?

Case Study
Let There Be Light

The Situation
Assume that you are a visual merchandiser consulting for three entrepreneurs who are about to enter retailing for the first time. They have several possible store concepts in mind. You are preparing to guide them as they weigh the possibilities. One of their concerns is the lighting of the store because they've discovered that fuel costs are rising again. Since they own their own building (which previously housed a hardware store) and will have to pay for the store remodel and monthly energy expenses, they are concerned about containing costs. "We want to operate efficiently enough to protect the bottom line on our balance sheet, but we don't want to cut back on the necessary atmospheric elements, either."

The entrepreneurs are looking at two types of retail options:

● A budget do-it-yourself picture framing "warehouse" that also sells inexpensive art prints and photography

● A high-end photography equipment/photo gallery business with custom framing

You're not a lighting expert by any means, but you do want to offer them some basic guidelines.

Your challenge
1. Suggest a lighting format for each type of store and explain why each type of lighting (or combination of lighting types) would be most effective for the situation. Start the planning by discussing the type of lighting needed to establish a strong brand identity or image for either retail concept. Address issues for ambient, accent, and task lighting.

2. Identify several sources where you might gather more information about current lighting technology for retail settings.

3. The building has traditional store display windows. Suggest how they could be used for each type of business. Discuss the impact that decision will have on interior lighting as well as on window lighting. For example, do you envision open windows or closed display windows for either store?

4. Draw a lighting layout for each store (referring to guidelines and illustrations found in this chapter).

5. Go to **www.visualstore.com** or any other store fixturing site and select some lighting fixtures that you believe will accomplish the tasks outlined in your criteria list for each store. Print the photographs or drawings and attach them to your case study before turning it in for evaluation.

Part Four

VISUAL PRACTICES FOR NONTRADITIONAL VENUES

Chapter 10

GROCERY AND FOOD SERVICE STORES

After completing this chapter, you should be able to

Recognize important trends and fashions that drive grocery retailing

Identify different types of grocery and food stores

Recognize common layouts and fixtures

Describe key locations for product displays

Utilize techniques to create mass displays and focal areas

Locate resources for creative inspiration

"Food is always at the height of fashion—whether it's the newest, most chic restaurant in New York City or a local farmers' market in your hometown. Visual presentation is a key ingredient for any food strategy. Color, texture, shape, and style all combine to create a visual harmony that will appeal to all of the senses."
Cindy McCracken, Director
Visual Merchandising, Big Lots

Food as Fashion ●●

Just as fashion has touched every item in the home from trend-colored vegetable brushes to Zen-style bamboo place mats, fashion has reached out to food. Minneapolis-based Byerly's said it best with its "You Are What You Eat" fashion show, which launched the opening of its Maple Grove, Minnesota, store in 1999. Byerly's unusual show featured fashion models dressed in outfits fabricated or trimmed in food products like cinnamon sticks, chocolate pieces, and Coca-Cola cans. (See Figure 10.1.)

Minneapolis *Star Tribune* staff writer Terry Collins reported as follows:

Denishia Simmonds had a case of the chills Thursday. No, the Minneapolis model wasn't nervous before taking the runway at a benefit fashion show at a soon-to-open upscale grocery store in Maple Grove. She had to spend three 2-minute intervals in a 36-degree freezer to keep her dress, made mostly of milk chocolate, from melting. Later, model Dawn King shook, rattled and rolled onstage in a dress made of aluminum Coca-Cola cans, much to the delight of the diverse audience.

Model Gina Koenen kept her balance with a straw hat featuring a seven-pound lobster, mussels and clams. And to top it off, she wore a cocktail dress with shrimp inside the neckline. "I felt like a crustacean," she said later.

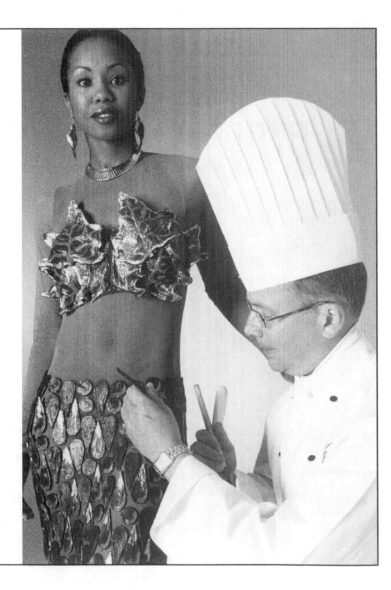

Figure 10.1 This model is wearing a dress trimmed in chocolate pieces for Byerly's "You Are What You Eat" fashion show in Maple Grove, Minnesota.

Taking the "food as fashion" promotional theme a step further, Byerly's put a smile on the face of every shopper by placing full-sheet posters in the store entrance featuring a woman wearing a red beret—feathered with a croissant! With this brilliant campaign, Byerly's proved not only that food can be fashion, but that food can be fun.

How is the "food as fashion" trend reflected inside today's grocery stores? From floor-to-ceiling—in store design, signing, packaging, and even the product inside the package. Good design and effective retail strategies are not limited to apparel retailing. They can bring new excitement to gourmet chocolates as well as to basic cans of green beans. And grocery stores, with their tremendously varied product assortments, have thousands of opportunities to be fashionable!

In 1968, Byerly's was billed as the first "premier" grocery store in the country. Reviewed like a theatrical debut in Twin City newspapers, the store opened with top-of-the-line gourmet and private-label products, an upscale deli, wide carpeted aisles in its dry grocery departments, an elegant gift shop with a crystal chandelier, and service shops located at the store entrance. More than 30 years later, it continues to build on its successes—adding culinary specialists to the staff in each of its stores. These experts provide customers with answers to questions about special diet needs, recipes, and party planning. Byerly's Website, (**www.byerlys.com**) features excerpts from *The Byerly Bag,* an in-store complimentary magazine, posts an on-line special event calendar, and handles on-line registration for classes at its School of Culinary Arts. Byerly's has pulled together a brand image campaign that any apparel retailer could envy.

Display and Ideas Magazine associate editor Michelle McLachlan calls Zagara's (a New Jersey-based specialty grocery company) an "art deco food paradise." She believes that the store will be memorable because the store's owner, John Zagara, and designer, Kevin Kelley, worked together to fashion a strong brand identity in a former department store building in Jenkintown, New Jersey. (See Figure 10.2.)

According to McLachlan, "What the Zagara's brand says to shoppers, as clearly as Victoria's Secret says 'sexy' or the Gap says 'casual fashion,' is that they've found a culinary haven where healthy nourishment need not cramp the hedonist's style. And that's exactly what the Zagara's customer, a busy, health-conscious but epicurean food adventurer, according to Kevin Kelley, Shook Design Group (Charlotte, N.C.) project principal, wants to hear.

"We equated food with fashion," says Kelley. "It's fashionable to learn about food and how to assemble it. And," he adds, "the excitement of reveling in food and its preparation can actually make the shopping experience a stress relieving one—a welcome change from the hectic environs of the typical grocery store during the after-work rush."

In another architectural revival, the neighborhood produce market that once prospered under the brick arches and structural iron of the Queensboro Bridge at 59th Street on Manhattan's East Side in the 1890s has found a second life as part of the landmark BridgeMarket plaza redevelopment. Here, Food Emporium, with more than 16,000 square feet in the restoration's cathedral-like selling halls, uses a great deal of daylight and architectural ambience to showcase fresh produce and flowers in a store environment with an open market feel consistent with the building's historical origins. There are separate gourmet shops under Food Emporium's 35-foot vaulted and tiled ceilings—a bakery, a fresh seafood market, and a butcher shop—much like the old public market stalls that flourished there a more than a hundred years ago. In addition, there are eight chefs in-house preparing dishes for a California grill, a clam bar and a sushi bar, plus an Eight O'Clock Coffee Shop named after a coffee brand made famous since 1859 by Food Emporium's parent company, A&P (The Great Atlantic & Pacific Tea Company, Inc.). (See Figure 10.3.) As with any fashion, the grocery merchandising cycle has repeated and has been updated for the new century.

Figure 10.2 Zagara's "art deco food paradise" in Jenkintown, New Jersey.

Figure 10.3 The Food Emporium uses daylight and the pre-existing architecture of the site in this New York City store.

A Brief Grocery History ●

American grocery stores in the early 1900s were strictly full-service affairs. You would hand the clerk your written order, and he (rarely she) would fill it for you. Since stores seldom carried more than one brand of an item and since they carried only dry goods, you were not a one-stop shopper. Baked goods came from a bakery, produce came from the greengrocer, meat came from the butcher, and dairy products came from a dairy store—or the milkman!

In 1916, the grocery shopping paradigm shifted on the East Coast when Memphis entrepreneur Clarence Saunders came up with a novel concept, a patented "Self-Serving Store" with a novel name—Piggly Wiggly. Asked by a reporter about the odd name, he replied that it had everyone asking "why." He was only too happy to respond, because answering gave him a chance to explain how his unique self-serving store operated.

On the West Coast, another entrepreneur was blazing a historic trail, seeking his fortune in the Gold Rush. On his way from Brooklyn, New York, 19-year-old Fred G. Meyer stopped long enough in Chicago to see a large store called The Fair, where everything imaginable was sold under one immense roof. The Gold Rush was pretty much over by the time Meyer got to Oregon, but he stayed on. He entered the retail field by selling from a horse cart, but soon upgraded his merchant status by renting a stall in one of Portland's open public markets where he sold tea and coffee beans by the pound. Before long he was managing the entire market for a percentage of sales and developed the "loss leader concept" in use today as a strategy for increasing his share of profits.

Pricing one item per week below cost, Meyer lured shoppers to the back stalls of the market where the item was stocked—a trip that incidentally carried them past other stalls that made good use of the increased traffic. His tactics were so successful that the market owners decided to renegotiate Meyer's share (downward). Motivated to strike out on his own again, Meyer sold retail groceries as "cash and carry"—a novelty in an age where most people charged their purchases and had them delivered.

Putting good managers in charge of individual stalls in the public market led to Meyer's next innovation—one-stop shopping. He, his wife, and his brother invested in their venture—Mybros (Meyer Brothers) Public Market—where all bulk goods were prepackaged (another innovation). This was a far cry from the day when clerks measured out and packaged flour, sugar, corn meal, and so on from bulk containers for customer orders. In later years, Meyer would give public libraries credit for inventing self-service, saying that he had merely found a good use for their system, but it was really the automobile that made one-stop shopping work for Meyer. Shoppers no longer had to carry their purchases home on foot or haul bulky parcels on trolley cars; therefore, they could buy more on a single shopping trip.

At the turn of this century, Fred Meyer Stores (now a subsidiary of The Kroger Co.) still operated multiple businesses under a single roof. Most stores boasted a supermarket, a department store, a drugstore, a home improvement center, a garden center, a home electronics store, and a fine jeweler.

While many retail strategies you see in grocery store operations today are the result of the innovations of pioneers like Saunders and Meyer, what's truly remarkable is the fact that so many of their ideas seem as fresh now as they were 100 years ago. In fact, as you read about other trendsetters in this chapter, you may get the idea that the grocery business is headed back in that direction—but this time around, you'll see many twenty-first century twists.

Consumer-Driven Changes ●

In an age of lighting-speed technology, the average consumer's waking day is increasingly busier and longer. Evening meals, and their preparation, sometimes feel like unaffordable

A Retail Reality:
You can still see the inside of the original Piggly Wiggly store if you visit the Pink Palace Museum in Memphis, where a replica of the original store is housed.

luxuries. Food marketers have responded by developing *ready-to-eat* offerings. Customers can choose from a wide variety of meals to please every member of their family. A quick warm-up in a microwave or the oven, and a meal close to "home-cooked" is served.

Home Meal Replacement

In his article "Tracking Eating Trends," John Lofstock writes about what the industry is doing to take advantage of the opportunities that open up as consumers' lifestyles change:

> The supermarket industry is changing to provide quicker service to attract a big chunk of the **home-meal-replacement** business. The average visit to the supermarket from the time the person leaves the car to the time they get back in their car is 21 minutes, down 20% from five years ago. During that time period customers will shop only 22% of the store. As consumer demand has changed, more supermarkets have redesigned their format to accommodate the time-pressed consumer. (*CSP* magazine, March 2000)

Grocery retailing is truly consumer-driven. Today's grocery consumers want to shop where, when, and how they want to. For the most part that would be near home, any time of day or night, and quickly. They want grocers to provide pleasant ambience, easy to understand floor plans and shelf layouts, accurate and informative pricing and signing, along with innovative and value-added products or services (ethnic variety, health-promoting foods, and enhanced functionality, for example).

Many neighborhood grocery stores have addressed these consumer demands. Some have positioned an actual convenience food department near their front doors. These "specialty shops" feature home meal replacements, ready to warm up in the microwave, in addition to soups, salads, wine, breads, and desserts. Checkouts are often just a few steps away, or right at the deli counter, with quick in-and-out service for time-starved shoppers.

Even in supersized grocery stores, fresh produce, bakery goods, meats, dairy products, and deli sections are looped near the store entrance for one-stop shoppers looking for convenient HMR foods on the way home from work. In a way, this floor plan creates a food boutique featuring higher-end, higher-margin (profit) convenience food and deserves this prime location on the larger store's floorplan. In terms of atmospherics, this approach immediately displays the megastore's most attractive sights (garden fresh produce) and scents (freshly baked breads and roasted chickens) to shoppers entering the building—presenting atmospheric elements that promise a pleasant shopping experience.

Impulse Shopping

Consumers' "time crunch" has undoubtedly led to more impulse shopping. Michael Wahl, in his book, *In-Store Marketing,* states,

> The typical consumer comes into a store with 20,000 choices, five of which are new every day. She scans more than 300 items per minute looking for items she knows she needs and looking for suggestions as to items she wants.
>
> The consumer enters this marketplace virtually unarmed. Over two-thirds have no shopping list at all. Nine out of ten do not bother to check the store's circular for specials when they arrive. Eight out of ten bring no coupons.
>
> With the exception of a few specific items which triggered the trip to the store and staples purchased virtually every trip, *the majority of items are purchased on impulse.*

Internet Convenience Shopping

You can go to **www.egrocer.com** to see how traditional grocers without Websites can participate in electronic grocery shopping. There, grocers can subscribe to the service and have their entire inventory listed on-line. Shoppers bring up e-grocer on-screen, pick the

Home meal replacement (HMR) foods are complete ready-to-eat meals (portioned out in microwave-safe covered serving plates) or prepared entrees like meat loaf or roasted chickens.

nearest store, choose the products they want, and later stop off at the store where their favorite products have been selected for them, bagged, and rung up.

Organically Grown Foods

An important change in American eating habits is reflected in the consumer movement toward healthier foods—including a strong trend toward "organic" foods. *American Demographics* reported in October 2002, that 6.3 billion dollars were being spent yearly on organic foods, up from 1.8 billion five years ago. In an article titled, "Growing Naturally," St. Paul Pioneer Press writer Lee Egerstrom writes, "Some confusion continues to exist over definitions, but consumers generally know what they're getting. Healthier foods, such as low-fat items and special dietary foods, sell into these same markets, although they may not be considered organic or 'natural' foods."

The U.S. Department of Agriculture (USDA) has developed a system for certifying producers and manufacturers in order to assure consumers that food items on store shelves labeled as organic are produced according to acceptable organic standards. As part of that system, USDA has provided guidelines for food companies that are marketing their organic products as organic or natural.

Taking organics a step further, two private companies in California have developed a Seal of Approval. In a *New York Times* article, "Natural Food Stores Pursue Organic Seals of Approval," writer Dennis Blank reported that the seals are available for $1,000 to $2,000 per store and they are offered only to companies that separate organic and nonorganic foods when processing, shipping, storing, and selling. Whole Foods (**www.wholefoods.com**) became the first major grocery chain in the United States to receive independent organic certification for all 140 stores in 2003.

Visual merchandisers who are involved with signing and presenting organic foods with or without seals of approval along with foods labeled "natural," need to pay close attention to definitions. Natural products are usually not organic, and those labeled organic may also have the seal of approval—like Whole Foods products, affecting presentation adjacencies.

Genetically Modified Organism Products

Another category of food products that many consumers want to be informed about are GMOs (genetically modified organisms). The Institute for Agriculture and Trade Policy in Minneapolis explains the development of *genetically modified organisms* as "artificially transferring genes from one species to another. For example, animal genes could be inserted into fruits and vegetables. This process creates organisms that have new combinations of genes, and therefore new combinations of traits that are not found in nature."

Organic and Natural Food Markets

Conventional grocery stores are going head to head in competition with a new breed of specialty stores that is moving into their neighborhoods, like Whole Foods and Wild Oats markets, both chains with more than 100 stores. To do so, some grocers are positioning organic dry goods and refrigerated product sections adjacent to their fresh produce sections, creating a department identity for this growing retail category. Others are integrating organic products with nonorganics, but calling them out with special signing. In terms of stock-keeping units (SKUs), stores committed to the concept carry between 400 and 1200 items in their organic food departments, many of them private-label offerings.

The Mississippi Market natural foods co-op, St. Paul, Minnesota, is a good example of a marketing response to consumer demand for fresh food in an ethnically diverse neighborhood. Opened in 1999, the nearly 12,000-square-foot store has streetside windows in its deli preparation area—an idea that adds a theatrical ambience and welcomes passersby to enter and taste its products. Ample daylight underscores the store's natural theme as much as its down-home deli menu that offers fare like turkey meatloaf and various combinations of greens, rice, and beans aimed at the Market's health conscious as well as ethnic food fans. Add to that a juice bar near one entrance where shoppers can socialize, and you have a neighborhood store that becomes a destination.

The Wedge Community Co-op (**www.wedgecoop.com**) in Minneapolis, Minnesota, is another natural/organic grocery operation owing its name to the geography of the neighborhood where it started out in the 1970s. Cooperative stores don't really have typical square-footage descriptions because they often sprout up in rented space in shops and stores once inhabited by other businesses—from convenience stores to former gas stations. They are often found in older parts of cities, near colleges, and on public transportation routes.

Elizabeth Archerd, member services director for "The Wedge," says that it is owned, used, and controlled by its members for the mutual benefit of all. It operates as a member-owned business, reinvesting its profits in the business and returning a share of profits to members based on their purchases during the year when the health of the business allows it.

"The historic principles guiding the cooperative are very much the same as they were in 1844 when the movement began in England," says Archerd. "The seven Co-op principles are: open and voluntary membership; member economic participation; democratic member control; autonomy and independence; and special practices like member education, training and information; a demonstrated concern for the community; and cooperation with other cooperatives."

To find out more about the growing interest in organic and natural food co-ops, check out the International Co-operative Alliance (ICA) Website at **www.coop.org** or The Common Ground Food Co-op through **www.prairienet.org** (a Website of the University of Illinois).

Wild Oats is a natural foods business that started out near the University of Colorado campus in Boulder in 1987 and grew to more than a hundred stores in 22 states and British Columbia by the turn of the century. Much of the growth has come through acquisitions of already established natural food stores that have, for the most part, maintained their original store names. The company's managers astutely realized that many of their loyal customers would not be fond of large store chains, so they left stores with good reputations and strong customer goodwill with their unique brand images intact. Apparently the name of a store isn't important to Wild Oats's ownership as long as it can benefit from the economies of massed buying power and efficient operations that can be accomplished behind the scenes at the corporate level. This is an example of working with your target customer's demographics and psychographics to create a brand that works.

Ethnic and Exotic Foods

As American consumers travel more frequently and experience different cultural cuisines, they develop preferences for exotic foods; and as more and more diverse ethnic groups migrate to American cities, demand for foods from their native cultures grows. Grocers wisely respond to these new preferences and demands. Whether these newcomers are feeding their own families or feeding other consumers by opening ethnic specialty restaurants, their "foreign" cuisines are the new "staples" in the average American consumer's diet. Nonethnic shoppers now purchase these once hard-to-find foodstuffs in local grocery stores, and they also request recipes or seek out ethnic cooking classes to help with preparation.

Future Trends

Grocery industry expert Gary Lind, principal of Lind Design in College Point, New York, predicts that:

In 2010, baby boomers will be thinking about retirement. Older people don't want to walk around a 150,000-square-foot store to shop, and the average supermarket could shrink [by] 20,000 to 30,000 square feet.

As the population gets older, supermarkets are going to have to offer rest areas up front. The supermarket could become a retail main street—a little town center for banking, shoe repair and dry cleaning services, as well as a second level with offices for doctors, dentists, and opticians.

Good graphics, lighting, colors, and layout are what make a store exciting. What's needed is a sense of discovery. When a shopper turns a corner, the response should be, "Look what I found."

What excitement can do for a store is proved by sales results at a Solomon's warehouse club store in the Bahamas that was designed by Lind's company.

We went totally crazy and created tents, awnings, 32-foot circles, 3-D fruits and vegetables. We changed the lighting, repainted, and put in a wharf-like floor in the produce area. The store was doing $30,000 a week in produce. When we were finished, it was doing $20,000 a day. (*Progressive Grocer,* November 1999)

A *Wall Street Journal* article, "Price War in Aisle Three" by Callahan Zimmerman draws attention to the growth of Wal-Mart Superstores and their effect on other grocers. "If Wal-Mart's supercenters continue to expand at their current pace, within this decade, more than three-quarters of the nation's Krogers and Albertsons Inc. stores, and more than half the Safeway Inc. outlets could be within ten miles of a Wal-Mart supercenter. . . .

Traditional grocers are reinventing themselves as a result, competing with Wal-Mart on price, private label products, and presentation. The article continues: "Wal-Mart still has problems to solve. With 100,000 people visiting an average supercenter each week, the stores' displays get messy and dirty quickly; aisles are jammed with new stock waiting to be shelved. Neatness is one quality in which Kroger and other competitors aim to outdo Wal-Mart."

The grocery industry offers a multitude of opportunities to creative visual merchandisers. Little has been done in this arena to showcase food in a new way, or to create a unique in-store experience for shoppers. The door is open to reinvention in presentation of food products, in order to differentiate the various food retailers.

Types of Grocery and Food Service Stores

There are nine types of stores in this category: traditional or conventional grocery stores, specialty food stores, hypermarket/superstores, warehouse stores, wholesale clubs, public markets, pharmacy/food, convenience stores, and co-ops.

Traditional/Conventional Supermarkets

The traditional or conventional supermarket is a full-line, self-service grocery store with annual sales of $2 million or more. These stores are generally less than 30,000 square feet and carry all food categories plus a variety of household gadgets, paper products, health and beauty aids, and sometimes greeting cards. They may even provide one-stop-shopping amenities like pharmacy, banking, post office, videos, coffee shops, and other services. Some focus on specialty foods like organic/natural and international products. American examples include Wegman's, Byerly's, Albertson's, Harris Teeter, Kroger, Meier's, Ukrops, Publix, Topps and Topps International. Tesco, and Sainsbury. Marks and Spenser in London and Obs! and B & W in Stockholm are among Europe's better-known supermarkets.

235

Specialty Grocers

Much smaller than conventional supermarkets, specialty grocers range from about 1,000 to 15,000 square feet and focus on a particular grocery category. An example would be Pete's Frootique, known as "Canada's greengrocer." Eatsies, in the United States, features fresh produce, gourmet foods and desserts, freshly baked breads, and hot meal delis. Whole Foods and Wild Oats Markets focus on unprocessed "natural" and organically grown foods. Other notable specialty stores in the United States include: Zabars, Balducci's, Eli's, and Dean and Delucca. European specialty stores include the beautiful, upscale Fauchon stores and the famous food halls of Bon Marché in Paris, and Harrod's in London.

Hypermarkets/Superstores

Stores of over 150,000 square feet that carry both groceries and fashion apparel, home fashions, and other hardline categories (generally 40 percent or more of the total space) are considered hypermarkets or superstores. The two "stores" are side by side with only a traffic aisle to separate them. Also known as combination stores, they may have separate entrances but frequently share a common checkout, with service shops along the entire front of the store. Examples are superstore versions of Fred Meyer Stores, Wal-Mart, and Target in the United States and Carrefour in France.

Warehouse Stores

Warehouse stores like Cub Foods are around 40,000 square feet and feature value-priced products for the budget-conscious consumer. They carry more than 1500 items, primarily packaged dry grocery products, and they usually carry complete assortments of perishables like fresh produce, meats, and bakery products. Dry goods sometimes remain in their cardboard shipping boxes on store shelves. A *hybrid warehouse store* has the same characteristics but includes over 7500 items, mostly perishables, and possibly some specialized service departments like a deli, a garden shop, or a tire center.

Membership/Wholesale Clubs

Membership or wholesale clubs like Sam's Club and Costco are retail/wholesale hybrids that are frequently over 90,000 square feet in size. They tend to eliminate frills, concentrating instead on price appeal in a warehouse type of atmosphere. They carry 60 to 70 percent general merchandise and health and beauty care products as well as a grocery line dedicated to bulk sales and items in case lots, large packages, and multiple packs. Sam's Club stores also carry fresh and frozen perishables, many of which are in bulk packaging.

Public Markets

Public markets represent a century-old selling concept, wherein a variety of food vendors and small farmers join together under one roof. One example is the Portland Public Market in Portland, Maine. This 33,000-square-foot space also includes a café and demonstration kitchen and community rooms on its mezzanine level.

Pharmacy/Food Stores

Stores such as Walgreen's carry a limited amount of convenience dry grocery items, dairy products, frozen entrees, and ice cream, in addition to a full-service pharmacy, nonprescription products, and toiletries.

Convenience Stores

Convenience stores are generally around 2000 square feet and carry a variety of the best-selling basic items often paired with a vending area and gas station.

Co-ops

Cooperatives are businesses jointly owned by the people who use them to provide themselves with goods and services that might otherwise have to be purchased elsewhere. Co-ops are formal organizations founded by their member-investors to meet their common economic, social, and cultural needs and aspirations through a democratically controlled enterprise.

Store Layout and Fixtures

Most grocery stores today use a simple grid layout because of the sheer size of the stores and quantity of gondola fixtures required to house thousands of inventory items. Retailers who utilize special feature fixtures for produce and bakery items may elect to use combination grid and free-flow layouts. As store architects and designers push the envelope to create new ways for stores to differentiate themselves, other layouts are being tested. Look at the circular floor layout in Figure 10.4, where the design firm Chute Gerdeman positioned the important produce category in the center of the Woolworth's store, surrounded by radiating gondola runs.

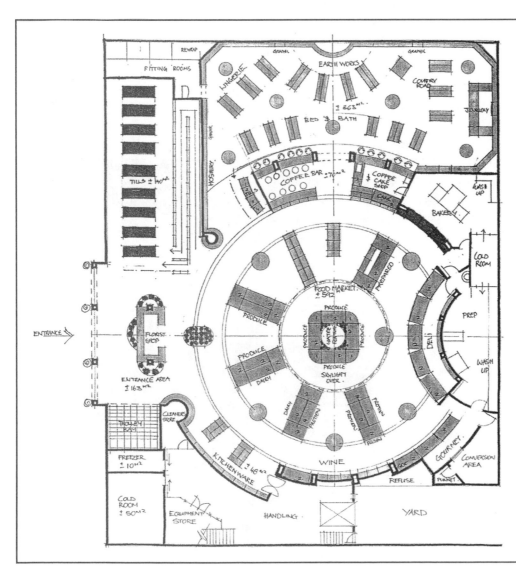

Figure 10.4 Woolworth's circular floor layout in South Africa.

Chute Gerdeman's circular layout can also be described as an *integrated layout*, where fresh and packaged/dry goods are not separated into rigidly gridded aisles as they are in many conventional grocery stores. Idaho-based Albertson's "station store" prototype fills the middle of the store's floor plan with several center-of-the-store departments, breaking them out of the grocery aisles. Either way, there is more potential for the cross-merchandising strategies that build new product partnerships when forward-looking plans like these are implemented.

Gondola Fixtures

Gondolas are the basic capacity fixtures of grocery stores. They often seem long and monotonous to a critical eye, but they may be updated with new finishes and materials. In Figure 10.5, Sentry Foods has used custom wood finishes and a grid fixture that supports graphics. It extends over the row of gondolas to create a "wine shop" identity. Intriguing flooring patterns draw even greater attention to the store's specialty area. Gondolas may also be enhanced by adding cost-effective and flexible signing with interesting graphic designs along the entire run or by spacing signs at intervals to create in-line focal points.

Custom-Made Fixtures

Custom-made fixtures are becoming more common in grocery and food store "furnishings." Fixture designers used black granite ledges around all table fixtures to accentuate the colors of produce and packaged goods for Lotte Chamsil (Figure 10.6) in Seoul, Korea. Decorative stainless steel rails replace standard fixture bumper guards, that are normally used to protect fixtures from damage by shopping carts.

In Candy and Spice (Figure 10.7) an interesting collection of specialty floor fixtures with a **high-craft look** and the simple carpentry of floor-to-ceiling wall fixtures define a "gen-

A **high-craft look** describes fixtures that appear to have been made by a cabinetmaker rather than mass-produced in a factory.

Figure 10.5 Sentry Foods of Walworth, Wisconsin, uses custom wood finishes and a grid fixture that supports graphics to enhance its basic gondolas and create a "wine shop."

Figure 10.6 Custom fixtures at Lotte Chamsil in Seoul, Korea.

eral store" theme. The Orlando, Florida, store wanted a look promoting the sampling of edibles (with hopes of purchases to follow) reminiscent of a bygone era when stores had taster-accessible cracker and pickle barrels.

Walls

In Hawaii's Foodland, shown in Figure 10.8, walls are treated almost like a stage set. Store owners sought to create a "fun-filled family marketplace" in response to their market's changing needs. Designers understood that shoppers were looking for quaint, individual

Figure 10.7 Notice the high-craft fixtures in Candy and Spice, Orlando, Florida.

Figure 10.8 The bakery at Foodland, Ewa Beach, Hawaii.

boutiques to enhance their shopping experiences, and so they created an exciting environment. A series of small, interconnected shops—a bakery, a butcher shop, a produce shop, and others—lead shoppers through what appears to be a dramatic streetside market. Look more closely at the bakery in Figure 10.8. Displays are designed to give the area and its products a "fresh-baked from scratch" look. The breads and other bakery items are arranged on several levels in an assortment of "country style" woven reed baskets, accented with rustic napkins.

Store Furnishings

Store furnishings can go a long way toward establishing theme and setting mood. A highly theatrical environment was created in Celestial Seasonings' store (Figure 10.9). The store has a decidedly residential feel and invites shoppers to linger, relax, and enjoy a cup of tea by the fire. Trading traditional store shelving for homelike furnishings, hutches are integrated with custom wall fixtures. Lavish cream-colored draping breaks the long, narrow store layout into more manageable zones. Teas are cross-merchandised with other products that reinforce the themes or special characteristics. Wellness items such as soothing bath oils and atmosphere-enhancing candles are presented with healing herbal teas like Echinacea or calming Tension Tamer.

Amazing changes are taking place in liquor store and department design. Look at the focal fixture featuring wine at Woolworth's in Figure 10.10. This floor-to-ceiling, library-style fixture offers the ultimate in visual impact. Now look at Figure 10.11, which is the result of Ontario's Liquor Control Board (LCB) setting out to become "the source for entertaining ideas" for its store's customers. The theme and materials used in the design of this flagship store emphasize the romantic and natural origins of the store's products.

Planners for LCB created an oval floor plan to subdivide the space into distinct shopping areas and designed 20 new fixtures to support innovative merchandising concepts. For example, they combined square interlocking units with a round tiered table to present an appealing martini presentation, with liquors, shakers, olives, glasses, and recipes. Nesting tables feature food and drink accessories. Circular, tiered, metal-rimmed floor fixtures with satin nickel rail details encase bottled white wines.

Figure 10.9 The residential design of Celestial Seasonings in Cherry Creek Mall, Denver, Colorado, features soft draping, which breaks up long walls and provides atmosphere.

Figure 10.10 A unique, library-style fixture features wine at Woolworth, South Africa.

Figure 10.11 Ontario's LCBO (Liquor Control Board of Ontario), the "Source for Entertaining Ideas."

Graphics

Graphics are an important element in any fixture design, and an excellent example is the beverage center at Mac's Langford Market, a convenience store in British Columbia. (See Figure 10.12.) Try to imagine the pictured area without graphics. You'd be looking at a store wall that is only one-third utilized, leaving a great deal of blank (and wasted) retail space. Instead, the design team wisely added bright floor-to-ceiling graphics to enhance the store atmosphere for customers while they serve themselves beverages.

Figure 10.12 Floor-to-ceiling graphics enhance the atmosphere at Mac's Langford Market in Langford, British Columbia, Canada.

The Visual Merchandiser's Role

Professional Development

Continuing professional development should be at the top of your to-do list, no matter what aspect of the retail industry you work in—fashion, food, hardware, or home store. There are three strategies—looking, comparing, and innovating—which will always help you grow professionally. You can use them in virtually any segment of the retail industry. Moreover, you can apply them in this chapter to discover and even forecast grocery retailing trends by

- Reading trade magazines specializing in foods and learning from valuable statistics on consumers' eating and shopping habits
- Visiting Websites devoted to food preparation, home entertaining, and fine dining
- Watching activity in the restaurant industry and exploring cultural food trends
- Reviewing the latest cookbooks and lifestyle magazines and discovering popular food-related trends in home entertaining
- Shopping a variety of grocery stores and making note of the items that are being featured and the ways they are displayed
- Visit specialty stores like Williams-Sonoma that carry food items and study the tabletop displays.

After you have looked and compared, you can embrace the trends and use them to improve your work—highlighting products and creating focal points that will stimulate more

"In this kind of business it's almost obligatory that you become part of the community and you're conscious of the environment. So we have a few more obligations than the conventional [supermarkets] do. We're not totally a bottom-line-driven business, [shoppers] have to feel warm and fuzzy about us.**"**

Wild Oats' founder Michael Gilliland, **www.storequip.com** feature story, David Litwak, May 30, 2000.

"I look at our presentation as if I am a customer. If it's not clean, colorful, and fresh, I won't buy it.**"**

Dan Blackburn, store team leader, Whole Foods Market, Minneapolis, Minnesota

impulse shopping in the grocery (or any other type) store environment. As supermarket pioneer Fred Meyer always advised his associates, "Adapt others' ideas, don't adopt. What works for others may not work for us. Find and keep the best parts, disregard the rest."

Remember that the store's brand identity is always tied into every single retail element —signing, fixtures, and presentation. Also keep in mind that "food is fashion."

Grocery and Food Product Presentation

In this chapter, you have had a look at several outstanding grocery and food store prototypes, with some of the latest innovations in the industry. You can see how stage-set environments and custom fixtures help attract shoppers into a store. But once inside, they have basic expectations about things you'll do to enable them to have easy, pleasant shopping experiences.

Michael Wahl's *In Store Marketing* lists the ten most important consumer criteria in choice of a grocery or food store:

1. Cleanliness
2. All prices labeled
3. Good produce department
4. Accurate, pleasant staff
5. Low prices
6. Freshness date marked on products
7. Good meat department
8. Shelves usually kept well stocked
9. Unit pricing signs on shelves
10. Convenient store locations

Wahl says, "Virtually every successful store operator measures up to these standards, yet we know that some stores are hugely successful because they have something extra. There are two factors that make some stores special. The first is that they manage to instill a sense of ownership in the store customers . . . 'It's my store' or 'it's like I designed the store.' The other factor is the ability to instill a sense of familiarity in the customer that leads to a feeling of speed and efficiency in shopping—a sense of being in command or in control. 'I just feel comfortable there,' . . . 'Everything is so easy for me to find.'"

Grocery Shelves and Endcaps

Visual merchandisers can provide many of the links that make a store special. They can develop guidelines that teach their store's general staff the basics of grocery presentation and then support implementation as part of the daily store routine. They can also see that the store's overall presentation is enhanced by effective use of design principles. Dan Blackburn, store team leader of the Whole Foods Market in Minneapolis, shared some of the guidelines he uses—what he calls "The Three C's":

- Cleanliness
- Common sense
- Color breaks

Advice about keeping a store clean and using common sense is easy to understand, but what about color breaks? Blackburn uses fruit juices to illustrate his color strategy: To avoid confusion for shoppers looking for particular juice products among many arrayed on store shelves, Blackburn reasons that cranberry juice should not be positioned next to strawberry juice on the store shelf because the colors are so similar. He advises alternating juice colors: cranberry (deep red), peach (yellow-gold), strawberry (medium red), pear (neutral), cranberry-raspberry (deep red) so that shoppers can differentiate flavors more easily.

Blackburn also recommends guidelines for positioning dry grocery items on shelves:

1. Products should always be *fronted*—meaning that stock is pulled forward to the front edge of the shelf. This makes the shelf seem full, even when it needs restocking.

2. Products should always be *centered*. Labels on all stock should face the front—even the stock behind the first row, so that as products sell down, the front of the next package is clearly visible to shoppers.

3. Products should always be *aligned*. Line up items from front to back, military style.

Blackburn prefers *vertical presentations*—ranking brand selections in sections from top shelf to bottom shelf. For instance, a conventional grocer's pasta section might contain side-by-side brands—Creamette products ranked on the top, middle, and bottom shelves next to the Vigo brand's three-shelf, top-to-bottom array, followed by a similar arrangement of private-label pastas.

He also advises that no more than two to three separate types of grocery items should be stocked per endcap. If all canned soda pop is on sale, for example, Blackburn suggests that you choose only the three best sellers (often from a single beverage bottler) for an endcap presentation, effectively narrowing the assortment for shoppers and directing their choices to your highest-profit items. He adds that using multiples of one brand, color, or package design creates a much stronger brand identity and has a more colorful visual impact that will draw shoppers from a distance.

Endcap display units are one of the most effective ways to make customers notice center store merchandise, according to a *Supermarket News* consumer poll. Of 1000 consumers surveyed by telephone, 42 percent said endcaps would draw their attention to a particular product, compared to in-aisle displays, 30 percent; shelf signs, 25 percent; or packaging, 3 percent. The survey was conducted for *Supermarket News* by America's Research Group, Charleston, South Carolina. The poll also revealed the following:

Of shoppers who feel that sale items aren't adequately marked, 19% said the product should be moved to an endcap. Similarly, 71% said they occasionally make an unplanned purchase from an in-store sale display, such as an endcap. Of the rest, 25% said they make an unplanned purchase from a display very often, while just 4% said never." (*Supermarket News*, February 3, 1997)

In many conventional grocery stores, shelves and endcaps are checked, restocked, and straightened several times during business hours. Major replenishment shipments or planogram changes are generally scheduled to be done overnight or at least during slower traffic periods. With this strategy, shelves always appear to be full and appealingly arrayed. At Whole Foods, shelves are restocked continually during business hours, so that staff members are able to interact with shoppers while they work.

The Whole Foods Markets have a variety of special features that make shoppers comfortable, enjoy every shopping experience, and feel as if they "own" the store. Produce is presented with a marketplace approach; using large clay bowls for items like red, green, and yellow peppers. (See Figure 10.13.) Colorful signs inform Whole Foods customers about new or unusual products. They even make shoppers smile with fun-to-read signs: "Our organic tomatoes in glass are uncanny!"

Large graphics over wall areas tell stories about the people who produce food for Whole Foods Markets. Featured products are displayed on tables throughout the store. A dining room with natural light provides a pleasant place for customers to meet friends, relax, and enjoy the store's assorted deli and hot food offerings. You can learn more about Whole Foods Markets at **www.wholefoods.com.**

A Retail Reality:
Cross-merchandising influences many grocery shopping decisions. Shoppers are pleased when salad fixings like croutons and dressings are conveniently merchandised with main salad ingredients in the produce department. Smart grocers were selling one-stop salad "kits" long before suppliers started packaging them in plastic bags.

Figure 10.13 Whole Foods Markets in Minneapolis, Minnesota uses an open market approach with large clay bowls to hold produce.

Cross-Merchandising Tabletop Displays

Tabletops provide an opportunity for visual merchandisers to reinforce the idea of food as fashion. Tables are portable stages, giving grocers great flexibility to stimulate appetites for store products. A simple tabletop displayed with a basket of lemons, a pitcher, glasses, a stirrer, and a bag of sugar for making lemonade could sell crates of lemons in a produce section by the power of suggestion alone. And if that display were to include a tablecloth, napkins, and a serving basket filled with lemon-iced cookies, an attractive platter with a lemon-frosted cake, or a lemon meringue pie in addition to the lemons, you would have devised a cross-merchandising opportunity for multiple sales.

You can apply all of the principles you've learned from other chapters to build displays like the hypothetical lemon-themed tabletop. In fact, the list of considerations for a fashion apparel display is exactly the same as the one used to merchandise grocery displays. If you were setting up a planogram for a grocery chain, you'd probably devise a form that would resemble a list of considerations for a fashion apparel display.

Today, food really is fashion—or at least one aspect of it. How we view food and other elements related to our home lives is our expression of the things we value, how and with whom we spend our leisure time, and where we live our lives away from work.

Living well means living with a certain style. Speaking about the importance of a design aesthetic for housewares that would appeal to high-income consumers, Wendy Liebmann, founder and president of WSL Strategic Retail, says:

> Just because I have less time to cook from scratch, doesn't mean I don't want to have a home-cooked meal or entertain. Presentation has become important. The thinking is, when I do eat at home, I want it to be a great experience. (*HFN The Weekly Newspaper for the Home Furnishings Network,* May 1, 2000)

Liebmann and her counterparts are the consumers to visualize with every tabletop you build and with every cross-merchandising strategy you display—the person who is time-poor and resource-rich. When life gives them lemons, suggest that they slow down long enough to enjoy a sweet, refreshing, restorative glass of lemonade. Then sell them the glasses, the napkins, and the cookies, too.

Resources
● ●
Fixture Trade Shows

A variety of feature and capacity fixtures for floor and walls are available from grocery fixture manufacturers. The FMI (Food Marketing Institute) show held each spring in Chicago showcases the latest fixtures and food products, in addition to hosting an array of seminar speakers covering topics from electronic commerce to the store of the future. The FMI is a nonprofit association conducting programs in research, education, industry relations, and public affairs on behalf of its members and their subsidiaries—food retailers and wholesalers and their customers in the United States and around the world. You can learn more about them at **www.fmi.org.**

Another excellent trade show, Euroshop, is held in Düsseldorf, Germany, every three years. Its Website describes Euroshop as the "very first trade fair to cater for the entire needs of the shopfitting industry." This international show features more than a dozen warehouses filled with exhibits from hundreds of international manufacturers with every type of fixture needed in any retail store. Products relating to grocery and food stores include: checkouts, shopping carts, deli and meat showcases, dairy cases, and specialty bakery fixtures. Manufacturers that specialize in lighting for food products also exhibit at the show.

Websites

You may enjoy a visit to the Store Equipment and Design Website at **www.storequip .com,** where you can shop for grocery retailing equipment, store décor systems, custom fixtures, grocery store design companies, and news of industry trends and events. There is another excellent site, **www.ideabeat.com,** launched in 1998 by grocery publication veterans with excellent connections to the industry. IdeaBeat offers retailing and marketing ideas in the form of news reports and contemporary issue articles from industry experts writing about specific subjects for the retail food field. It was recently rated as an "About.com Best of Net site" for the retail industry. Two other Websites worth a look include **www.epicurious.com** and **www.greatfood.com.**

Magazines, Books, and Television

Browse the book and magazine stands regularly because new publications with food trends are arriving every day. Some of the current best include: *Real Simple, Bon Appetit, Food & Wine,* and *Better Homes and Gardens.* The Food Network cable channel is another great resource for the newest food trends and recipe books.

Shoptalk
● ●
By Greg Duppler
senior vice-president, general merchandise manager, SuperTarget

Creativity and innovation are essential elements in the success of any retailer in today's ultracompetitive world. There is an overabundance of "sameness" as you walk through shopping centers and malls. People who take risks, break the molds, and innovate will have the most fun *and* become the most successful.

Before coming to the grocery industry, I was in the toy business, which is as exhilarating as work can be. Creativity, trend, and innovation are ways to bring life to toys. Meanwhile, food was viewed as a mundane category. However, in the past couple of years, there have been quantum-leap improvements in merchandising, packaging, and visual presentation of food.

Today's business world is a sprint. If you stand still, you'll be passed! Great ideas are quickly copied so you need to relentlessly pursue differentiation. You always need to listen, look, be open-minded—*really* open-minded—to generate new ideas and then implement them quickly to stay ahead of the competition.

The bottom line is . . . have fun, think outside the box, and make things happen—fast!

Out-of-the-Box Challenge
Give Them Something "Extra"

Look

Visit three grocery stores and observe how they are presenting the newest food trends.

Compare

Take notes on each presentation and compare them.

Innovate

Which presentation do you think is the best? Why? How would you improve all of the presentations? Present your ideas to the class.

Critical Thinking

1. Visit a grocery store and make a cross-merchandising "shopping list" of products to include:

   - Fall apple display featuring apple cider, caramel apples, and everything you need to bake an apple pie (Figure 10.14A)
   - Gingerbread cookie baking display (Figure 10.14B)

2. Sketch a maximum of three appropriate prop elements per display.

3. Incorporate a sign and sign copy into your design for each display.

4. Draw a planogram (using Figures 10.14A and 10.14B at the back of this chapter) for each of the two assigned display projects. Include merchandise, sign, and props in your drawing.

5. Present and justify your choices in a class discussion.

Case Study
Demographic-Related Design

The Situation

You are opening a small but complete grocery store for a "shopping/service village" in a senior citizen housing development which contains one-level homes, multistoried (but totally accessible) apartment units, and a nursing home complex. Among the other stores in the village are a barber and beauty salon, a pharmacy, an adaptive gadget store, an optician, a medical-dental office, a post office, a men's clothing shop, a women's clothing shop, and a travel service.

Your store will carry fresh meats, produce, a bakery, and dairy products as well as frozen foods and canned goods in smaller-sized packaging.

Your Challenge

Based on what you've read in the text, your own personal knowledge, and additional research, write a paper describing the features you'd ask a designer to include in a store layout that would accommodate grocery shoppers in your location. Think about aisle width, signing, seating, and so on.

- Include a section about services in your shopping environment that shoppers in this demographic group would value.

- Include a bibliography of resources you consulted in order to complete the paper.

Getting Started

You may find the site for The Center for Universal Design at North Carolina State University (**www.design.ncsu.edu/cud/univ_design/princ_overview.htm**) to be the most informative site for this project. To discover specific legal requirements for equal access to public spaces, you may also want to visit the Americans with Disabilities Act (ADA) Accessibility Guidelines for Buildings and Facilities Website at **www.access-board.gov/adaag/html/adaag.htm** to find a useful glossary of terms as well as the language of the law itself.

Figure 10.14A

Figure 10.14B

Chapter 11

NONTRADITIONAL RETAILING

After completing this chapter, you should be able to

Identify the various types of retail kiosks

Discuss the visual merchandiser's role with interactive kiosks

Present merchandise on a cart

Explore the career potential for visual merchandisers on the Internet

Evaluate the visual merchandiser's role in fashion show and special event production

Develop a special event or fashion show concept

"From high-tech interactive kiosks to electronic commerce Web sites to mall pushcarts, non-traditional retailing is exploding on all fronts. It offers unlimited opportunity for growth—and cries out for talented visual merchandisers who can help these non-conventional selling environments come alive to shoppers."
Marianne Wilson, senior editor, *Chain Store Age*

Specialized Marketing

Changing shopping preferences and emerging technology have encouraged retailers to alter some of their customary methods of communicating about their stores and the products they sell. These new retailing strategies may affect your career path because they are opening up new opportunities for visual merchandisers. Some of the strategies are an update of old concepts, some are as new as this century. You'll never be able to say that visual merchandising is static. There are several developing trends discussed in this chapter that will influence the work you'll do—and where you'll do it.

Kiosks

Retailing always moves forward with experimental spirit, yet some of its newest discoveries look vaguely familiar—like the proliferation of "pushcarts," kiosks, and booths in the walkways of shopping malls all over the country. At one time, pushcarts transported the goods of street vendors from block to block in crowded cities. Kiosks sheltered outdoor newspaper sellers and food vendors. Small booths were used to hawk tickets or hot dogs on city sidewalks.

Today, updated versions still sell food and drink, along with small fashion goods and household gadgets. Some kiosks sell products that are too large to be stocked in retail stores but may be delivered directly to customer's homes. Others provide bridal and newborn gift registries, and entertainment kiosks sell tickets for events. Traditional kiosks may still stand on the sidewalk, but modern kiosks are located in shopping malls and even inside some retail stores.

Kiosks are freestanding selling units, open on one or all sides.

All three—pushcarts, booths, and kiosks—are now generally defined as **kiosks** even when they are wheeled carts. Today's kiosks may require one or more salesperson, depending on the merchandise sold and size of the unit. In smaller kiosks, without an open central core, salespeople are stationed adjacent to the unit. Some recent models are built into walls or partitions along mall corridors, maximizing selling space while accommodating dense foot traffic.

One of the most exciting present-day uses of the kiosk is that of "incubating" a new retail business in a shopping mall—testing to determine if a start-up merchant has a merchandising concept with enough potential to warrant investment in a full-sized store space. Many small incubator businesses have grown to brick-and-mortar status after successful gestation as a kiosk or pushcart tryout. Often new kiosk businesses are even copyright protected in an attempt to assure their originators that they will not quickly be knocked off, or imitated, by competitors.

To a retailer, **niche marketing** means identifying a very specific market segment and offering a product or assortment of products that research shows the segment wants or needs and can afford to buy.

Because they can be rather small in terms of square footage, kiosks facilitate **niche-marketing** strategies—reaching out to very specific groups of potential customers with highly specialized or seasonal product offerings. For instance, a kiosk selling fitness food products in a shopping mall court with an established fitness apparel store nearby might be a perfect place for a start-up retailer to sell protein powders and energy bars to health enthusiasts. In this way, the small business can test the market without having to lease, fixture, decorate, or stock a store for an entire year. That's a sensible adjacency (for both businesses) and a way to target a very specialized customer.

Kiosk Fixture Design

Just a few years ago, kiosks were simple, freestanding units built in a few different shapes and sizes. Mini service kiosks housing automated teller machines (ATMs) and retail store gift registries began as vertical boxes often covered in bland almond-colored laminate. No-frills functionality seemed to be the design criterion. Today, the kiosk design industry has

Figure 11.1 Child-size interactive kiosk, The Disney Stores, Inc.

exploded to include interactive models ranging from a child-sized Mickey Mouse figurine (Figure 11.1) to the futuristic, sleekly curved units in Playstation (Figure 11.2).

Kiosks may be custom designed to coordinate with store or shopping mall architecture and image. Fabricated in materials from cardboard and plywood to space age plastics and laminates, kiosk designs can range from basic counters with overhead canopies to elaborately themed miniature stores. Brand manufacturers frequently design their kiosks to build brand identity inside department stores or as stand alone mini-stores in mall settings.

One major advantage to using in-store kiosks is the retailer's ability to build in a profit center that takes up very little floor space. For example, a discount store photo-finishing kiosk can take up less than 24 square feet yet produce very high dollar volume. Demonstration kiosks that spur sales in a department store housewares department can be equally lucrative in terms of sales per square foot.

Kiosk Types

There are five basic types of kiosks:

- Freestanding permanent units located in high traffic areas in shopping malls
- Freestanding permanent units located in stores

A Retail Reality:
The overuse of kiosks within a space may lead to visual clutter and loss of continuity. Open traffic spaces are as valuable to floor layout as white space is to signing. Open space helps shoppers to "read" a store's layout and get a sense of the store as a whole, and it assists them to move through the store. When too many manufacturers' brand kiosks fill open spaces, the shopping environment (mall or store) can lose its own brand identity.

Figure 11.2 Interactive kiosks at Playstation, San Francisco, California.

- Carts—nonpermanent, mobile units located in high traffic areas in shopping malls (also referred to as RMUs, retail mobile units)
- Mini-kiosks—permanent units like ATMs or gift registries located in malls or in stores
- Newsstand or refreshment kiosks, which may be permanent or mobile units, located in malls or on city streets

Depending on their sizes and projected life spans, kiosks may be basic or as elaborate as Screenzone's giant kiosk, shown in Figure 11.3, with multiple interactive stations where mall patrons can visit entertainment sites, view movie schedules and previews, and reserve tickets.

The dramatic Fossil watch kiosk in Figure 11.4 becomes the focal point inside a Fossil store; but it is easy to imagine it as a stand-alone kiosk in a mall setting as well. Beautifully lighted from the top of the fixture to the columns down to the showcases, it is an example of design excellence and truly a signature fixture.

Miniature Interactive Kiosks

A Retail Reality:
The philosophy behind making fast food restaurants into destinations—places to eat *and* play—makes merchandising sense. Entire families can enjoy relatively inexpensive (and value-added) visits to eateries where youngsters can have food they like and then engage in safe, supervised, age-appropriate physical and educational activities. Restaurants build brand image plus goodwill with these unique kiosks.

Miniature kiosks with interactive monitors offer retailers some of the most outstanding innovations and technology. Even though visual merchandisers may not personally design the kiosk fixture or the programming viewed on the monitor, they may be asked to comment on how well the proposed design of the units fits their stores' brand identities or be consulted about colors and artwork to be used on-screen. Placement of these new selling tools is critical, too. Visual merchandisers know their store layouts and will be able to identify locations that will draw shoppers into the store and keep them in the store once they have arrived. They will also know where glare from natural sunlight or atmospheric lighting could affect interactive screen viewing and where sound from the kiosk might conflict with other programmed sounds in the store.

256

Figure 11.3 Screenzone's super-sized kiosk consists of two large screens that are mounted at a height of 15 feet. Each of six interactive stations has two headsets to encourage shoppers to use the equipment with a friend. Natick Mall, Boston, Massachusetts.

Strategically located kiosks can become focal points for selling activities in a department. The REI (Recreational Equipment Inc.) kiosk in Figure 11.5 is a design that provides a definite point of emphasis and becomes a destination in the store. The fixture is fabricated to fit in with the atmosphere of the store environment, where most materials used are raw, in their natural state, or of a highly recycled content. REI's entire design responds to its customers sensitivity to the environment in general.

Figure 11.4 The Fossil store at Universal City Walk is anchored at the center by a signature kiosk, which showcases watches and nostalgic custom cases.

Figure 11.5 REI's (Recreational Equipment Inc.) kiosk became a destination in this Reno, Nevada, store.

Miniature interactive kiosks can sell products, support brands, give information, or simply entertain. Not satisfied with tray liner crayon games and small promotional toys, Burger King joined forces with Frank Mayer & Associates, Inc., a full-service merchandising company, to create interactive Virtual Fun Centers for placement in Burger King's stores around the world. Aimed at children ages 4 to 10, colorful kiosks feature interactive touch screens with software offering more than a dozen entertaining educational games. A built-in camera allows children to pose for a picture and place their own image into different "postcards" on the screen or add funny disguises to their faces. The kiosk also enables children to manipulate puzzle pieces, paint pictures, and answer trivia questions.

In addition to the obvious entertainment capabilities of minikiosks, stores are using them to expand their selling capabilities by offering shoppers the opportunity to purchase products for home delivery that are not available in the store through intranet (an internal network maintained by the store) or Internet links to store catalogs. Kmart does this with its Kmart Solutions interactive program and so does Lands' End Inlets. Company wide intranet bridal and baby gift registries are practically a given in today's retailing environment and many Websites, such as Pier 1 and Bloomingdale's, offer registries that are available nationally and internationally.

Kiosk Fixture Resources

Today's "designer" kiosks really had their origins in the point-of-purchase (POP) industry. Brand manufacturers created their own merchandise display fixtures and offered them to retailers at little or no cost. Strategically, they hoped to provide greater in-store visibility for their products, to secure floor space in tightly merchandised stores, to maximize brand awareness, and to drive impulse purchases.

Most of the earliest POP displayers were temporary structures with limited life spans—often built to last only the length of time of a special promotion. Later, many vendors offered more permanent racks and fixtures designed to hold their products exclusively. Stores with limited budgets for fixtures welcomed them. The only drawback was that POP fixtures didn't always fit into store décor schemes, diluting the store's brand identity. As unified store design became more important to retailers, vendor POP fixtures became less popular.

From early POP spin racks filled with packages of pantyhose and disposable razors near checkout counters to countertop free trial sample units, they've come a long way from their throwaway roots. Today, competitive organizations specializing in kiosks provide complete design and prototyping services, extensive warehousing and distribution facilities, and state-of-the-art-manufacturing resources, even though they still continue to design the shorter-lived POP displays. Kiosk merchandising promises to be one of the most highly creative segments of the retail design industry.

Point of Purchase magazine is an excellent resource for the latest information, technology, and photographs of kiosks and other point-of-purchase materials. Check out the magazine's Website at **www.popmag.com** for information on its market show dates. Visit its ongoing Virtual Trade Show on-line to learn about dozens of companies specializing in kiosk design, manufacturing, installation, and merchandising.

Presenting Merchandise in Kiosks

Carts as Retail Mobile Units

Larry Gerow, president of Area Code 212 Display and Design, is responsible for the design, implementation, and merchandising of Minneapolis's Mall of America's 80 carts. Offspring of original vendor pushcarts, these updated versions were designed to fit into the style of the mall's architecture. They are leased by individual tenants. (See Figure 11.6.)

Gerow says: "The carts are really just the same as stores—every square inch of space is utilized, and the goal is to find a 'hook' that will catch shoppers' attention. Even though there isn't a physical entrance to a cart as there is with a store, the side of the cart gets the highest traffic functions as a store entrance."

In devising a merchandising design for a cart, Gerow says that you must be aware of mall regulations, including the position of signage and how far signs or displays can extend out from the cart. Safety concerns develop as props are attached to cart roofs, and elsewhere, so all prop items must be carefully secured. Every mall has different guidelines, and today, every mall has carts—usually from 10 to 30.

Cart Design Strategies

Area Code 212's Gerow says that cart merchandising and design strategy involves eight steps:

1. Discover the tenants' needs. Learn as much as you can about their products—and their personal taste, even their favorite colors. Gerow says that these people are "close" to these carts; they have to live with them, and so it is important that they are comfortable with them.

2. Know the mall regulations for cart design and signing.

3. Render a design that meets both the tenants' needs and the mall's regulations.

Figure 11.6 A cart in Mall of America.

4. Prepare a budget for fixtures, props, signs, and any special lighting.

5. Get design and budget approval.

6. Gather props and other materials and set the cart.

7. Do a safety check to ensure that there are no unanswered concerns.

8. Do a security check for blind spots. Mirrors may be attached to the cart to provide better visibility from all vantage points. Carts usually have pull-down doors or canvas wraps for after-hours security.

Internet Retailing (E-tailing)

As Internet retailing competition heated up at the turn of this century, store retailers worried about e-commerce, viewing it as a threat to their businesses. Some took a wait-and-see stance, but others jumped right in only to find themselves swimming in red ink. Many new on-line businesses have yet to make a profit, and many more have pulled the plug on their e-shops as a result.

As the shakeout progresses, expect the survivors to be companies that deliver in two major ways: first, with dependable, attractive, easily navigable Websites; and second, with accurate, quick, and inexpensive product delivery. E-tailers have learned that it is not enough to have a great-looking shopping site; they have to deliver on their visual/virtual promises. Customers who become frustrated by delays on Websites, who have trouble placing orders, or who do not get on-time gift deliveries simply "click away" (the virtual equivalent of walking out of a store that fails to deliver satisfactory customer service) and return to brick-and-mortar stores rather than risk disappointment again.

Which retail Websites are the best? You can find a wide selection at **www.forbes best.com.** Go to Forbes Favorites and click on "Luxe Shopping." A brief description of each Websites is included with positive and negative comments, plus a direct link to each site. Here are ten of their picks, from the Websites in January 2005. Some are a blend of "bricks and clicks," where established retailers like Sears expand their shopping hours by adding around-the-clock internet convenience. (See Figure 11.7.)

Forbes Favorite Websites—Luxe Shopping
- Baby Gear < **www.store.babycenter.com** >
- Books < **www.powells.com** >
- Casual Apparel < **www.landsend.com** >
- Gifts < **www.surprise.com** >
- Home Furnishings < **www.potterybarn.com** >
- Jewelry < **www.bluenile.com** >
- Online Shopping < **www.sears.com** >
- Outdoor Gear < **www.rei.com** >
- Toys < **www.etoys.com** >
- Well Dressed < **www.neimanmarcus.com** >

Does all of this have career implications for you? James Mansour, founder of Mansour Design in New York City, sees it this way: "The Internet is creating new opportunities for us to apply our skill sets online. . . . We can be at the forefront, integrating the shopping experience into cyberspace, utilizing our understanding of current land-based visual merchandising and customer shopping patterns." Mansour, who says his design job is to "craft consumer experiences," predicts that entertainment, e-tailing, and interactive technologies will come together in ways that have previously only been imagined.

E-tailing is risky business without a well-built infrastructure and good business practices firmly in place. For those who have survived, hope is on the horizon. In a *New York Times* article from October 2003, writer Bob Tedeschi reported that E-tailers are starting to feel welcome on Wall Street again: "After a three-and-a-half-year span in which only one online retailer, Overstock.com, went public, RedEnvelope, the online and catalogue gifts retailer, raised roughly $31 million in its initial public offering of shares. Provide Commerce, the parent company of the online florist proFlowers.com also registered to go public . . . with plans to expand into other online gift areas. Executives at privately held Internet retail companies say these public offerings show that investors are beginning to pay attention again to this sector."

Presenting Images for the Camera

Every product image you see on a Website was passed through a camera's lens at some point and was translated into digital format for your monitor. Getting products ready for those shots is very similar to building displays or dressing mannequins, but the e-tailing visual merchandiser often has a different title—that of photo stylist. Rather than being employed in-store, this visual professional works in a photo studio creating and propping merchandise setups for cameras.

261

Figure 11.7 Neiman Marcus' Website features its famous Christmas catalogue.

Minneapolis independent stylist Lisa Evidon got her start after 3 years in retail visual merchandising and has since spent 15 years as a photo stylist. Her specialties are fashion and tabletop setups. Additional visual skills—working with lighting, for instance—make a photo stylist even more valuable in the studio. Many of these skills come strictly from hands-on experience, says Evidon, and are learned while stylists are assisting more experienced stylists. Being able to manipulate merchandise effectively for the camera is a plus—larger garments might require special draping techniques to make them seem less bulky, for instance—something a visual merchandiser already knows how to do.

Repeated items that have to be specially folded or stacked to show an entire color range in a very limited space are nothing new to a visual merchandiser either. Food and grocery products might require special treatment to make them glisten in the light or hold up under the extreme heat generated by studio lighting. Those complex tasks may be easier for visual merchandisers to learn because they already know how to improvise for the sake of appearance and to arrange products attractively. With enough practical experience, many stylists develop specialties in specific areas of photography like food presentation.

"On set" in a photo studio, whether the "shoot" is intended for print advertising or for electronic retailing, Evidon describes her role as being the interpreter for the art director's vision. "The art direction helps me make decisions as I compose the elements of the shot for the camera," she says. "For instance, I'll know how busy or how clean the shot needs to be. Or I'll know whether we're setting up for a vertical or horizontal format." Evidon says that her visual merchandising skills have "transferred completely" and that preparing for a shoot—including searching out and securing exactly the right props and visual elements like antiques or flowers and greenery—is a large part of her work. "Then it's all composition from that point to the end of the shoot."

For Evidon, a day's work means anything from preparing a steamed, wrinkle-free garment and procuring trend-right accessories for a fashion model to building a beautifully composed tabletop presentation for a home fashion publication. She says that what happens to the image after the shoot is the art director's or photographer's concern, not hers, and that she doesn't have to do anything out of the ordinary to prepare for a photograph that's slated for a Website. "I always pay close attention to the colors, patterns, and other visual elements of the composition, no matter where the shot will be used," she says and then adds, "I like the little challenges that I get with each shoot."

Presenting Images On-Screen

Showing true and compatible colors for Web page catalog presentations is another e-tailing challenge. At this stage of its development, on-screen color registry is not perfect. Because colors are difficult to reproduce accurately, it's going to be Website technicians, software developers, and computer manufacturers who rule the appearance of products shown in on-line retailing rather than retailers. For now, many Web retailers simply print disclaimers saying that what you see (in terms of merchandise color) may not be what you get.

Software vendors are aware of the need for accurate color graphic representation as well as the need for higher resolution to produce crisper, clearer product images. Products like PhotoShop already allow photographers to shoot and store multipurpose images simultaneously—lower-resolution shots for Websites and much higher-resolution shots suitable for print media. They know that shoppers on-line or off want to be sure that what they see displayed on-screen matches what they get when the delivery truck or mail carrier arrives at their home bearing packages. They also know, according to Shawn Kringstad of Tele Edit, a postproduction company in Minneapolis, that the major limitation for on-line accuracy is the end-user's in-home color monitor. "The monitor is like an electronic filter that tells viewers, 'This is how I was calibrated, so these are the colors that you're going to see.' People may not have the technological capability to view everything that we shoot their way, so we have to prepare our images for what we believe the average on-line shopper is able to receive. Today, that's usually 25 colors rather than the millions we could use." Postproduction companies like Tele Edit translate the subject matter photographers have captured on film or in digital format into usable images for video production. Other companies can take those same images and prepare them for print media.

David White, executive producer for landsend.com says that his company's e-store site does not color-correct for individual Internet shoppers. Because of the variety of computers and monitors available on the market, "End-users do control many aspects of how they will view our product presentation." And he adds, "There is a wide variety of compatibility issues. We have chosen a lowest common denominator approach to our site that allows most people to have a good experience. We do not require any browser plug-ins to use our site. We are constantly exploring ways to make the presentation of our product better. As new technologies evolve and mature, we will use the ones that make sense for our business."

Special Events

Special events bring potential customers into the store. Under the special event umbrella, fashion shows, institutional shows, cultural exhibits, product demonstrations, workshops, and book signings are invitations to come into the store or to visit store promotions off-site. They are image-enhancing goodwill gestures to the community—"doing well by doing good." Special events are used to

- Make stores into destinations for entertainment and education as well as goods and services. In fact, one of the buzzwords for the decade is "retailtainment." It suggests that the store's function as a source of entertainment is becoming more and more important to shoppers who can get merchandise virtually anywhere on earth.

- Promote brand image by bringing fashion designers and product-related experts or celebrities into the store.
- Enhance retailers' positions as community leaders by sponsoring and participating in local events.
- Teach shoppers how to use products that might otherwise seem too complex or technical to purchase.

Historically, special events have been the domain of the large department store (with the correspondingly large promotional budget). However, as smaller retailers watched the "bigger ones" reap the benefits of special events—increased store traffic, enhanced leadership image, event-related revenues—many have decided to enter the event arena. And they're doing so creatively, inexpensively, and effectively. Fashion Bug, a national chain of budget fashion stores, invites women who are regular customers to model informally for in-store fashion shows. It offers attractive incentive discounts to participants who frequently purchase the outfits they wear in shows, feature merchandise prize drawings, and, of course, invite the models to bring their "fan clubs" with them to see the shows and shop. Events like these generate handsome sales for the price of a few posters, phone calls, invitations to customers on local mailing lists, and the time it takes to do fittings for the models.

Garden, fabric, and home stores routinely offer in-store how-to workshops that teach shoppers how to make the best use of their latest products. Shoppers who stop by to learn about wallpapering or stencil-painting get hands-on demonstrations and go home with information plus products and accessories—confident enough to do the jobs themselves.

Visual merchandisers' roles in special events are as varied as the events themselves. They may be called on to create a store presence in off-site locations by erecting and decorating booths, tents, and stages at bridal fairs, career workshops, or investment seminars. They may be required to setup signing, tables, and product displays or establish traffic patterns with ropes and stanchions for book signings. They may setup demonstration platforms and tables for product demonstrations as well as collateral (supporting) displays for product outposts outside of normal department selling spaces. They may participate in the design and execution of flower shows, gala parties, holiday animations, fashion shows or special interest programming for targeted consumer groups (National Baby Week, back-to-school promotions, or a women's health expo).

The principal requirement for visual merchandisers involved with special events is the ability to anticipate what will be needed to make the event run smoothly. Checklists are invaluable. To simply skirt and sign a fashion show ticket table for a bank lobby ten blocks from your store, you'd need to preplan everything required—sign, signholder, table cover, prepleated skirting, bank pins (in case the skirt arrives without clips), and masking tape (in case the hem is too long).

Thinking like a visual merchandiser, you'd probably feel dissatisfied to let it go at that. You'd probably want to make the table into a vignette (story scene) of some kind—turning the off-site location into a better merchandising opportunity for your store. Again, any display work done to enhance the lobby ticket table would call for skills you've already learned. Perhaps some tall greenery near the signholder might create a better backdrop for the table. Perhaps a dressed and accessorized mannequin might reinforce the fashion show's theme. If you're a true visual merchandiser, you'll always think about what you can add for emphasis and interest. You'll always want to give something "extra."

Fashion Shows

Fashion shows range from models traversing improvised aisles on designer showroom floors to performance art—theatrical productions with lights, music, **catwalk** staging, and full stage-set constructions. In between, you'll find models "working the tables" in retail store restaurants, "still-modeling" in store windows, and strolling through department store aisles

A **catwalk** is a narrow walkway. In theatrical production, it's the bridge over the stage lights, up in the "fly" area that allows technicians to change and aim spotlights. In fashion, it's the narrow runway extending out from the stage that allows fashion show patrons unobstructed views of models and garments.

during informal shows. Retailers are always looking for new ways to involve customers with merchandise.

As a visual merchandiser, you may be asked to become involved with a store's fashion show productions. You may be working for a store, working for a manufacturer or designer, working for a production company, or freelancing for any of them. Your shows could be done in several venues (locations): on the retail site or in theaters, auditoriums, or hotel ballrooms.

The extent of your involvement in show production will depend on your skills, experience, and ability to work gracefully under extreme pressure. Fashion shows are frequently last-minute productions with as little as a day or two to produce a show away from the store because of rental expense and space availability. If you're presenting a show in-store, you may only have hours to execute your plans because disruptions that interfere with normal operations must be minimized.

Types of Shows and Venues

Even with all the constraints, fashion shows can be great fun. Fashion shows give visual merchandisers a chance to use skills they don't get to practice every day. (See Figure 11.8.) What follows is a cross-section of typical fashion show formats:

- *Haute couture shows,* season (semiannual) openings, and press previews that allow influential customers and fashion journalists to see original designs in especially festive atmospheres before the rest of the world sees them. These events can happen anywhere in a fashion city—designer showrooms, themed restaurants, trendy nightclubs, or hotel ballrooms—depending on the designer's budget and the size of the expected crowd.

- *Trunk shows* involve better, bridge, and designer name manufacturers' representatives showing distinctive and exclusive items from selected fashion lines to clientele in the specific department. In some cases, the items come literally out of a trunk on hangers. But in most cases, trunk shows use one or two models who try garments on for clients' approval and special ordering. Preparation for this type of show generally entails facilitation rather than production, creating comfortable salonlike seating areas, rearranging fixtures, adding furniture and accessories in the department, skirting refreshment tables, adding fresh-cut flower arrangements, and adding accent lighting to the trunk area.

A Retail Reality: A fashion show can feature nonapparel merchandise—a trade show in the window fashion industry featured leotard-clad dancers "modeling" swaths of elegant design and colorful drapery fabrics.

Figure 11.8 Notice the floor graphic at this Target fashion show, held in New York City.

- *Tearoom/restaurant shows* are mostly informal with models working a predetermined pattern through the dining area. This is generally done with appropriate music and no commentary. Formal runway shows require commentary, special lighting, and a stage treatment scaled to the stage and venue.

- *Informal department shows* are likely to involve models and clothes, but little else. If there is to be commentary by a sales representative or retail fashion director, things may become more formal. Perhaps a low stage will be erected, at which point you'll be required to create a small on-stage vignette or a simple backdrop and perhaps provide special accent lighting. Seating is generally provided if there is a stage.

- *Themed expositions* (a women's fitness expo, or a bridal fair, for example) take place in auditorium settings with retailers often participating in sponsoring roles. If your store hosts a fashion show, it's frequently done on a main stage at the venue. You might be required to supply a special stage setting for that show or as your store's contribution to the event overall. In addition, your store may have a large booth space to decorate—related to merchandise that fits the expo theme or to the corporate image and brand identity of the store.

- *Special event shows* in the community frequently team retailers with other businesses in co-sponsorship roles. For example, a major fashion store may partner with a newspaper or magazine to present a spring and a fall fashion show at a theater or concert hall, auditorium, arena, or other public venue. The events may be part of a downtown retailers' initiative to bring shoppers into the city or, with charitable tie-ins, be positioned as fund-raisers. These tend to be rather elaborate shows with large budgets and tremendous production value. They often have the excitement of a Broadway stage show and offer a challenging but satisfying medium for the visual merchandiser.

Production Basics

Location   Fashion shows take place in many types of **venues.** A show's location is important only if you're the one who must select the site and make the rest of the arrangements. Otherwise you and your visual team simply cope with whatever the venue offers in the way of staging challenges.

> **Venues** are locations where a special event or entertainment takes place. The word comes from the Latin verb *venire* meaning "to come."

Themes   All shows have themes, stated or implied. Sometimes they reflect the fashion seasons; sometimes they name or honor notable fashion designers; sometimes they link retailers with nonprofit causes, civic or social organizations; sometimes they tie in with major community events. Themes often dictate the mood and the pace of the production.

Themes also assist show planners in creating effective advertising and publicity campaigns necessary to bring a targeted audience to the fashion show. Retail sponsors often schedule and coordinate fashion windows to be part of the overall publicity and advertising campaign. Themes also give visual merchandisers their basic window and set design cues.

Equipment   Most of the places where you'll be asked to stage fashion shows won't have appropriate lighting or sound equipment for your purposes. That means specifying and renting equipment and arranging lighting and sound professionals to set the equipment up and run it during the show. Be aware that most nonretail venues have contractual requirements to provide union labor for any stage lighting or sound production required.

Store departments generally have adequate accent lighting for perimeter and aisle displays but haven't been fixtured for stage lighting. In-store sound systems don't have to be elaborate. Most stores use portable systems with cordless microphones. As is the case with lighting, off-site shows may require equipment rental if the venue does not have a built-in system. Naturally these are expense items. Major shows in-store or at a different venue will have planned production budgets to cover major equipment rentals. In-store, your production charges will probably be based on cost recovery for store-owned equipment and in-house staff.

Staging   Designing a fashion show set involves essentially the same elements used in enclosed window planning with one notable exception—the mannequins move and you don't have to dress them. However, the backdrop you provide must complement fashion and color trends, restate the program theme, and create a favorable mood for viewing fashions for sale. Like window backdrops, fashion show sets must never be more important or elaborate than the fashions shown.

An Exemplary Event

To see how all of this works, let's envision a large-scale fictional charity fashion show to launch a spring "pops concert" series in an orchestra hall. It will be a joint venture for several sponsors:

Theme   "Spring on the Seine."

Beneficiary   The USO—an organization with sites in major airports. The USO offers hospitality and assistance to traveling military personnel and their families. The nonprofit organization needs to upgrade its airport facility. All proceeds (after expenses) from this event will go to this project.

Specifics

- The orchestra plays as part of its spring concert series, donates the cost of added catwalk staging sections plus lighting and sound technicians. Since the event is planned for a scheduled concert, there is no hall rental fee.

- The airline donates round-trip tickets for two to Paris (or any destination on its normal routes) plus catered food and soft beverages for show attendees during the concert. The trip will be the event's major door prize.

- The florist donates fresh-cut spring blossoms for patron tables and set pieces. Table pieces will be arranged in vases; cart flowers will arrive in galvanized containers scaled to fit the carts.

- The newspaper donates three full-page ads, plus a feature story about the USO's good works, its current needs, and the benefit show. It guarantees advance publicity in prime space right up to show time. It also furnishes the event signing and programs.

- The retailer supplies all garments; arranges for a well-known fashion designer to do commentary; books and pays models for fitting rehearsal and show; pays the fashion coordinator's salary; furnishes a professional choreographer; and donates set design, execution, props, and services of the visual merchandising department.

- The USO handles ticket sales and all related expenses.

For this hypothetical show, set design will be influenced by structural changes made to the concert hall. Venue managers plan to install a false floor covering their normal main floor theater-style seating. Ranked in tiers that follow the floor's natural slope, the new decking will hold tables and chairs where patrons may eat and drink during the concert and fashion show. Table-high decorative white fencing and shrublike greenery provide safety and add to a parklike atmosphere.

The visual merchandising team sits down with the fashion coordinator and decides to

- Design their set pieces to tie in with the hall's existing parklike décor.

- Install two catwalks leading from the stage to the first deck aisles so that models can walk into the crowd and exit into the side halls leading backstage. As a safety measure, potted summer flowers will edge the catwalks.

- Build twelve white flower carts as stage set pieces and fill them with fresh-cut flowers. Models will gather flowers from one of the carts and present them to patrons at tables as they come off the catwalks.

- Project light-effect silhouettes of Parisian images on hanging screens in colors matching each segment's fashion statement.

Although the planning must take place months ahead of the event, this project will be executed in a very few hours, since the flower carts, platform riser unit, and catwalks will be completed well in advance of deadline and delivered to the hall by rehearsal time. The rest of the visual merchandisers' chores will depend of the arrival of the flowers and the amount of time needed to set them in place.

Some large-scale fashion events layer in many different "scenes" onto a basic stage set through the use of plasma screens, banners, and other visual devices. One set may feature a specific fashion designer, another may present a theme like evening formal wear, while another may provide a backdrop for an emerging trend. Many fashion shows also include segments with dance performances and musical acts ranging from choirs to rock bands. Each theme offers an opportunity to create theatrical sets far outside the realm of traditional fashion shows.

Marshall Field's annual fashion show, "Glamorama," is the major fashion event in the two cities of Chicago and Minneapolis. Proceeds from this event are donated to the Art Institute of Chicago and the Children's Cancer Foundation in Minneapolis. Jamie Becker, Creative Director of Visual Marketing for Marshall Field's and one of the events planners, said, "About twelve months of planning go into this remarkable event; and the process is critical because there are only a few days to set the show before the performance."

Look at Colorplate 15 to see examples of a few of the "scenes" which were layered on to a basic two-tiered stage set. The show, held in 2003, presented not only fashions, but was emceed by celebrity Tracey Ullman, included musical performances by Uncle Cracker, and the Bond Girls, a violin trio.

Shoptalk

Interactive Retail Experiences

**By James Mansour
founder, Mansour Design,
New York City**

The convergence of entertainment, information, and commerce is opening up ever-widening opportunities to create high-touch, relevant, and fun experiences for consumers. The best interactive interfaces and kiosks lead the consumer into a unique relationship with a brand that is both a virtual and a three-dimensional experience.

Today's exciting, innovative, seductive retail experiences have their roots in the 2000 years of human enterprise. I have accumulated a fascinating library of images of markets, bazaars, and stores through the centuries. It's amazing to discover how relevant they are to today's world. After all, we are still trying to entice the same women, men, and children just a few generations later. Shopping has become a part of our DNA! Here are a few inside tips I give my clients and associates:

Six Steps to Successful Visual Merchandising:

1. Visual merchandising is 3-D branding. Know your brand mission, support it, refine it, and evolve it.

2. Think and create from a strategic point of view. Do not work in creative isolation; try to understand how all areas of the business interconnect.

3. Set the highest standards for your work and compare your work to the best in the world.

4. Every time you find yourself shopping—at flea markets, in record stores, or in delis—study the process: apply what you learn to your own work.

5. Use visual merchandising to organize the customer's experience. Imagine that you are creating a theme park and the merchandise is a souvenir.

6. Be passionate!

Out-of-the-Box Challenge

Kiosk Design

Look

Visit a mall. Look for kiosks in the open (commons) areas.

- How many are there? Describe the kiosks you find by type and merchandise categories.

- Do they appear to be part of the mall's architecture and overall décor scheme?

Compare

1. Visit larger retail stores in the mall. Do you see kiosks employed inside any of the stores?

2. How large are these in-store kiosks? Describe their purposes.

3. Do the in-store kiosks harmonize with the overall store décor?

Innovate

1. Explain why you think the mall and/or store kiosks complement or detract from the overall décor.

2. Describe what you think should happen to bring each kiosk design you saw into better harmony with its surroundings.

Critical Thinking

Activity 1

Kiosks

1. Create an interactive kiosk concept for the following retailers:

   - A garden supply store
   - A florist shop
   - A gourmet grocery store
   - A women's shoe store
   - A male-oriented interactive kiosk for a men's fashion accessory department
   - A parent-oriented interactive kiosk to be placed in a children's clothing department

2. Give each kiosk a name or identify its theme.

3. Describe who would use it and what its purpose would be.

4. Make a rough sketch of each kiosk.

5. Include a brief specification list of the visual elements you'd use—colors, materials, sign style, and so on.

6. Be sure that your design allows room to display or present the merchandise. Identify merchandising spaces in your sketch.

7. Present your ideas in class discussion or use as a team brainstorming exercise.

Activity 2

Carts and Retail Mobile Units

1. Create a cart or mobile unit for the following start-up retailers:

   - Imported ethnic foods, groceries, and food-related products (choose a culture or country)
   - Pocket-sized toys for children of all ages
   - Luxury giftwrap
   - Fashion hats for women and girls
   - Travel accessories

2. Give each business a name.

3. Choose a theme for the cart's design.

4. Describe the range of products to be sold from the cart.

5. Make a rough sketch of each cart that incorporates name, theme, and product line into the design.

6. Be sure that your design allows room to display or present the merchandise. Identify merchandising spaces in your sketch.

7. Present your ideas in class discussion or use as a team brainstorming exercise.

Case Study 1

Designing a Food Fashion Show

The Situation

You work for a grocer who is known for innovative merchandising ideas. You have been asked to prepare a food-related fashion show for the store's anniversary party in mid-October.

Your Challenge

Using food products of all kinds:

- Develop a theme for an in-store fashion show to be held on the store's anniversary weekend.

- Think outside the box and describe as many food items as you can that could be used as a costume decoration. The food decorations may be applied to neutral or black garments like plain tops and skirts or T-shirts and trousers, or they may be fabricated from clear plastic shower curtain liners and sewn by a dressmaker. You may apply your food products to either type of garment, or you may specify other types of clothing. Hats, shoes, and belts may also be trimmed with food products. Assume that you will be able to hot glue or hand stitch any items you choose to the clear plastic garment (and, yes, think about refrigeration if you're using anything that melts easily).

- Design a woman's long formal gown, a child's shirt and pants set, a man's suit, and a chef's hat and apron. You may accessorize with food products, too. Attach your sketches to your project.

- Write fashion show commentary for the garments you've designed.

- Design a 6-foot diameter round platform stage that is 2-feet high and include two sets of steps—one for entering the stage and one for exiting. Include stage decoration that's appropriate to the theme.

- Design a full-sheet sign to announce the show to the public. You may assume that an 8 1/2 × 11 sheet of typing paper is the full sheet. Attach it to your completed project.

- Present your minifashion show to your classmates.

Case Study 2

An Ethnic Kiosk

The Situation: Phase One

Martin Ogabe and Suan Tepu have decided to open a small retail operation that will feature food items and other treasures from their native Kenya. Since their arrival in the city, they've been in touch with a number of immigrant families in the area who long for the sights, sounds, and scents of home. Many of them were not able to bring many artifacts with them when they left for America and have asked Martin and Suan (who both work for a major airline) to bring them certain things when they travel to Africa on business.

The city has a thriving international community near the State University, and Martin and Suan are investigating leasing store space in a building near that community. They have also contacted the managers of a large regional mall in the city's suburbs to see what opportunities they might have for a space there. Rents in the university area are fairly high, but they suspect that the regional mall's fees will be even higher.

The regional mall managers surprise them. "We want smaller start-up businesses in our tenant mix," they tell the two entrepreneurs. "And, we want to build more diversity in the retail mix." They add, "We'd like to offer you a larger kiosk at a reduced cost, and help you get started by not charging you for the first three months of your lease. This will enable you to invest in a custom design to establish your kiosk's 'look,' and bring in more merchandise. If you do well, you'll be third on the waiting list to move into a permanent space when one becomes available. We don't anticipate a long wait, as there are a couple of lease renewals due at the first of the year. We generally see some movement among stores at that time."

Martin and Suan are intrigued. There are currently two other ethnic businesses in the mall; one of them has moved into a store space and the other appears to be struggling in its kiosk. The drawback to the kiosk space may be its size—a third of that of the stand-alone storefront. They are also concerned about traffic. They wonder if they will attract enough customers if they are out of the university neighborhood and away from the concentration of international students and immigrants living there.

Your Challenge

1. Explain the advantages of each potential business site for this fledgling business.

2. Outline the disadvantages to each.

3. Create a list of critical demographic factors the partners should weigh carefully as they evaluate each business site.

The Situation: Phase Two

Martin and Suan plan to carry traditional artisan-beaded suedes, native textiles (khangas—printed fabric, and kikois—woven goods), jewelry, books, art objects, and certain nonperishable food items like spices and canned goods from Nairobi's City Market. To establish a brand identity for their space in the mall, Martin and Suan would like to be able to use some special ethnic design features to make the kiosk reflect its merchandise theme.

Your Challenge

1. Do you think there will be any constraints for kiosk design and operation that they must research prior to design of this kiosk?

2. What questions should Martin and Suan ask when they speak with the center's managers?

The Situation: Phase Three

If you are not familiar with African art, clothing, or food products, you may want to visit the college library for more information. Look in encyclopedias, the economics section, or the art history section. It is also quite possible that your college has an expert on campus. Don't overlook faculty and staff resources. Your own Internet search may find sites such as (**www.ainamoja.com/catalog/art/fabric.htm**).

Your Challenge

Think about the type of merchandise that will be sold and list the kinds of fixturing that should be included in the kiosk design: for example, wooden poles, masks, baskets, woven mats. Sketch the front elevation of an ethnic kiosk that Martin and Suan might use.

Part Five

TOOLS AND TECHNIQUES FOR MERCHANDISE DISPLAY

Chapter 12

THE MAGIC OF THE DISPLAY WINDOW

After completing this chapter, you should be able to

Recognize a variety of architectural window formats

Explain how windows function as vehicles for communication

Apply basic window display theory to meet retail goals

Plan effective window merchandising themes

Identify appropriate props and signs to carry out specific display themes

Adjust lighting for windows and editorial displays

"If you take any activity, any art,
any discipline, any skill, take it and push it
as far as it will go, push it beyond where it
has never been before, push it to the
wildest edge of edges, then you force it
into the realm of magic!"
Tom Robbins

Vignettes are a condensed version of a larger scene. For example, a home furnishings vignette might establish the mood and the scene of a larger room with only a few elements—a chair, an end table, and a lamp.

Store window displays have the potential to create magic. From an animated holiday scene to merchandise inventively displayed in lively **vignettes,** window displays can entertain, educate, and stimulate demand. This ability is known in the industry today as the "Wow! factor." Strategic window designs draw traffic into the store from the street and support sales.

Retail Theater

From a creative point of view, presenting merchandise in the confines of a traditional store display window is a tightly controlled exercise in retail theatrical production. Retail theater, like conventional theater, is a vehicle for communication. It has the potential to carry merchandising messages. The traditional enclosed window offers an advantage because nothing happening inside the store can distract attention from the window's presentation of fashionable, desirable merchandise.

Window designers can isolate and emphasize merchandise to create moods, project attitudes, teach lessons, make announcements, or present fashion statements. By controlling every element—lighting, props, color, texture, scale, mannequins, forms, signing, and theme—they control communication. Window designers believe that windows help shoppers project themselves into the displayed merchandise and prompt them to visit the store interior.

Window designers also believe that memorable windows are an integral part of both store image and reputation for fashion leadership—that windows *say* something tangible and important that differentiates the store and its products from competitors.

Over the last two decades, many retailers saw enclosed windows as barriers. Storefronts evolved from block-long banks of enclosed windows to plate glass sheets that allowed shoppers to see directly into the store. The theory behind this change was that people would buy more if they could see, touch, and try. Display windows in shopping malls followed that trend as well.

Today, enclosed windows are more the exception than the rule. However, some developers are beginning to specify that enclosed windows be built into new retail stores' architectural plans, even in big-box discount and specialty retailers. Windows are beginning to come back, making this a very important chapter for your professional development. One possible reason is the cyclical nature of fashion and all things related to it. Retail developers are looking for ways to differentiate their shopping centers, and windows have been open-backed for an entire generation. Perhaps it's time for something "new." That something may come in the form of enclosed display windows.

Architectural Window Styles

Window styles are as varied as the architectural styles of store buildings. A downtown department store may have flat, *straight front windows,* where the glass is flush to the exterior walls and runs parallel to the sidewalk. (See Figure 12.1.) Some older stores feature *arcade windows,* where store doors are set back several feet from the sidewalk and display windows line both sides of the recessed entryway. (See Figure 12.2.) Sometimes, *angled windows* start at a building's corners and slant toward set-back doors, forming a triangular recess beneath an overhang. (See Figure 12.3.) Occasionally you'll see a *corner window* with one solid wall and two glass sides—a triangular display space offering a clear view of all but a very small part of the presentation's "back side." There are also *bump-out windows,* which resemble bay or greenhouse windows. Many indoor mall stores are totally open at the front with no glass at all.

274

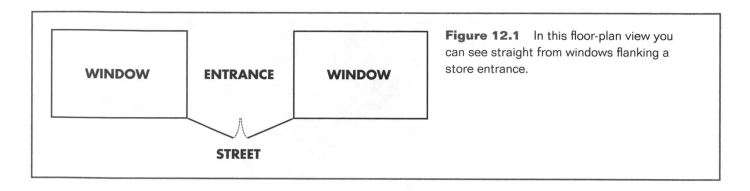

Figure 12.1 In this floor-plan view you can see straight from windows flanking a store entrance.

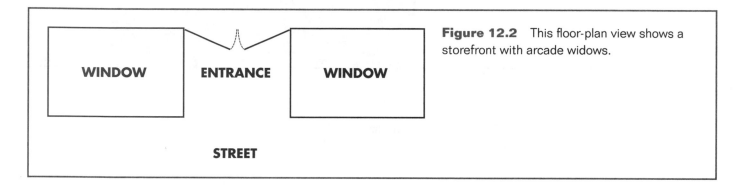

Figure 12.2 This floor-plan view shows a storefront with arcade widows.

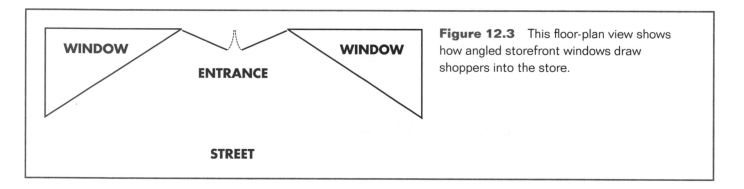

Figure 12.3 This floor-plan view shows how angled storefront windows draw shoppers into the store.

Enclosed Windows

A fully enclosed display window has a solid back wall, two side walls, and a glass front that faces the street (or indoor mall leaseline). It is essentially a box. Visual merchandisers generally enter these windows via hidden doors leading from stockrooms or fitting rooms. A bank of three or four windows may share a common access door.

Most enclosed windows borrow elements from theatrical production to create ambiance or conceal artifice—painted backdrops, scrims, masking and proscenium arches, and lighting grids. (See Figure 12.4.)

The famous Lord & Taylor *elevator windows* in New York City take theatrical techniques a step further and can actually be raised and lowered so that the entire window box can be "trimmed" in the store's basement and then be brought up to view at street level. An elevator window can also be positioned slightly below street level so that passersby can look down and into the display window if that view makes sense to a particular theme at the time.

Figure 12.4 A masked window presentation at Marshall Field's, Minneapolis.

Some stores—particularly jewelry stores—feature closed *shadow box windows* that are situated several feet above the sidewalk for eye-level viewing of smaller-scaled merchandise. In New York City, the display windows at Tiffany, Bulgari, and Cartier are elegant shadow boxes.

A few stores employ freestanding *island windows* (also described as *lobby windows*) or *kiosk displays* that have glass on all four sides, rendering them viewable from any direction. You might find this type of window as a unique feature of an older store with an arcade front or as a stand-alone display feature in a courtyard or indoor mall setting. These specialized windows are as difficult to display as corner windows in that the merchandise can be seen from all sides, making it hard to hide any artifice or "tricks of the trade" used to put the display together.

Open-Back Windows

Open-back windows usually have little formal display; the merchandise on the store fixtures becomes the display. However, many retailers place a display platform in front of the window glass and create a formal display there. The platform differentiates the display area from the selling floor, and the presentation is viewable from both inside and outside the store. People who are on the street will see not only the merchandise display, but also other merchandise and any activities taking place on the store's main floor. Open-back window displays must be simply propped and carefully focused or viewers will miss the fashion message in the competing visual clutter. For these reasons, it is important to develop strong focal points, color schemes, or merchandise themes for window displays and any feature fixtures in the window's immediate vicinity.

Occasionally, visual merchandisers will drop swags of fabric or no-seam paper panels from the store's ceiling to the floor behind the open-backed window displays. This strategy provides the impression of a backdrop for the display without limiting too much of the view to the store's interior. Another unusual open-backed window treatment might involve painting or applying colorful "seasonal scenery" or graphic messages directly onto the window glass.

Half-open windows use partitions or architectural dividers of some kind to separate the display space from the store proper. The divider must be compatible with the store's interior theme, yet plain enough to enhance the presentation. In a resort town shop selling casual weekend wear, one retailer uses split-rail fencing and artificial evergreens as an open window backdrop, suggesting a woodland theme that is very much in sync with the rustic wooden walls and fixturing used throughout the rest of the store. Some retailers use the plain backs of shelving units as the rear "wall" of the display area; others use pieces of antique furniture to define their window display space.

Window Display in Practice

Open or enclosed, windows play a critical role in a store's merchandising strategy. They are communication tools that reach out to current customers and potential customers. When store management commits advertising and promotional dollars to an item of merchandise, a chain of retail communication activities begins.

As soon as department store and specialty chain store buyers return from market trips where they have purchased goods, they communicate with the sales support departments about to launch promotional campaigns featuring some of the more important fashion items. This support group—composed of buyers, merchandise managers, the advertising team, and visual merchandisers—discusses ad timing, theme development, and relevant trends. Members decide what the intent of window display should be—promotional, institutional, fashion, or sale-oriented.

Merchandise managers make plans for receiving the merchandise and placing it on the selling floor. The advertising department prepares, schedules, and places ads in selected media. Visual merchandisers schedule display windows and plan in-store editorial displays and department presentations, selecting props and mannequins and ordering signs that tie directly to the ad copy or theme.

When the merchandise arrives in the store's receiving department, it is unpacked, hung, steamed, ticketed, and moved to the selling floor where it will be strategically placed on wall or feature fixtures. Visual merchandisers visit the selling department, select agreed-upon merchandise and accessories for windows, platforms, and displays in the selling department. Then they do their magic. The artfully presented merchandise sells out, and the cycle is repeated with new merchandise. If the store is a smaller mom-and-pop operation, there may be fewer specialists involved, but the process is essentially the same.

Window Merchandising Functions

Fashion apparel windows tout the store's fashion leadership position by presenting the store's newest trend merchandise. They also educate shoppers by showing mannequins that exemplify how current trend garments may be coordinated with accessories and shoes.

Home fashion windows may feature the latest dining trend, complete with the utensils needed to cook and serve a meal. They may also feature candles, dinnerware, and table linens that relate to the dinner theme, encouraging shoppers to create all of the ambience they might find in a restaurant in their own homes.

Promotional windows feature products that are part of an advertising strategy promoting an entire line of goods, a single item, or a special storewide event. Holidays like Mother's Day and Valentine's Day also provide opportunities to stage exciting window productions.

Sale windows announce the store's major sale events and may not feature any merchandise at all—implying that the store is stripped down and ready to sell out to the bare walls at low, low prices.

Drive-by windows are exterior store windows viewed by people driving on city streets or passing through shopping mall parking lots. As you might imagine, these window treatments must be larger in scale to be seen and understood from a distance. Large items—if they are repeated—can say a great deal about the store and its products. Visual impact can also be achieved by using masses of merchandise, larger-than-life graphics, backdrops, and intense, well-lit color schemes. Michigan Avenue's Crate&Barrel in Chicago capitalizes on large second- and third-story windows to repeat specific merchandise items like sofas, lamps, ceramics, and stoneware pots. In many cases, huge photographs carry themes and images that identify both the merchant and merchandise to passersby who see them from blocks away.

Live or *demo windows* are one of the more effective ways to capture shoppers' attention. Live models in windows have caused many shoppers to stop and notice when they suddenly waved or winked at an unsuspecting passerby. It never takes long for a crowd to gather in front of a window that has activity and movement.

Imagine a kitchen product shop with crisp white café curtains hung on a brass rod across the lower third of its display window. Inside, raised up on a black and white tiled platform stands a butcher-block demonstration table. The window's sign—a hand-chalked menu board—asks: "What's Cooking?" In smaller letters, you see the response: "Pasta Fagioli! At 3 P.M. and 5 P.M."

What will be on display in this window? According to the sign, one special item will be the store's resident chef—demonstrating how to use many of the kitchen utensils and equipment the store sells. During nondemonstration hours, there are dozens of display possibilities for the butcher-block table: stacks of cookbooks, small appliances, cooking pots and utensils, spice racks, kitchen linens, and packaged food products.

Retail theater with a live actor has the potential to draw curious crowds into the store any time there's something cooking. And, when there is no "show," the demonstration table and platform will be filled with related products. The final touch would be to send cooking aromas "wafting" out into the street through strategically located ventilation fans.

Interactive or *through-glass windows,* featured in a Stores of the Future exhibit at Globalshop 2000, were created by retail architect/designer David Kepron. The store windows in Kepron's "dot com" shop could literally communicate with shoppers day and night. Electronic components invited passersby to interact with window displays by touching sensitive panels on the exterior glass, which were connected to oversized screens set up in the window's interior. Viewers could virtually design their own window displays by calling up brands and images that interested them from a programmed menu.

According to Kepron, "The 'dot com' experience demonstrates that we no longer need to consider e-commerce and traditional bricks-and-mortar retailing as *separate* approaches to selling goods or services. Indeed, technology and retail design *can* exist together, where the root of retailing—the social experience—is enhanced, **leveraging** your brand to create lasting customers. Shoppers will be able to view many stores as Websites in much the same way they now view many Websites as stores."

Since one of the major challenges in successful Internet retailing is delivery of goods at profitable margins, this new development in technology is a real breakthrough. Experts are forecasting e-tail success for merchants who have both brick-and-mortar and click-and-mortar stores.

Kepron points to the practical opportunities that interactivity offers for retailers whose shopping mall stores close by 10 P.M. nightly. "Look at the number of malls whose tenants include entertainment [movies, restaurants, nightclubs] venues that operate beyond the mall's normal shopping hours. Why shouldn't retail stores continue to interact with shoppers after hours? Imagine the possibilities if shoppers could still look at and order merchandise when the store's doors closed for the evening."

An artist, retail architect, and store designer, David Kepron looks forward to the day when "technology leads the process for retailers rather than being added as a design afterthought." He adds, "Technology does not have to be an either/or proposition for a retailer. Stores of the future can blend real and virtual boundaries into truly three-dimensional catalogs that function twenty-four hours a day, seven days a week."

Leveraging, used as a verb, means gaining a mechanical advantage, or adding impact, power, or effectiveness. An example would be adding impact to a store's brand identity by using an interactive display window.

278

Nonmerchandising Window Functions

Window displays serve purposes other than showing tangible items of merchandise. Non-merchandising displays—devoted to intangible ideas and causes—are described as **institutional windows.**

Institutional display windows are often "donated" by civic-minded retailers to publicize and support special events that benefit nonprofit charitable organizations in their communities. Examples are the Special Olympics and The Easter Seal Society, civic groups like museum docents (guides), and supporters of orchestras and zoological gardens. These institutional windows can also be used to publicize social issues, such as raising public awareness for causes like AIDS.

Retail store windows respond to national and local news events, too. Cities with championship sports teams may do congratulatory windows. When famous people die, stores offer memorial windows honoring them and their contributions to our lives. Look at Colorplate 16A to see Macy's institutional window for a tribute to Gene Moore during the Cooper-Hewitt Museum's "Window Show."

During local, national, and international crises, there have been special windows showing support for the people and issues involved. It all revolves around retail management's desire to project an image of community involvement, humanitarian concern, or support for the topic.

Retailers do these special windows to enhance corporate image and build goodwill for their companies. In addition, they may choose to celebrate milestones in their stores' histories, publicize their own activities, or simply promote their own community leadership position in windows that exhibit no merchandise at all.

> Institutional windows are devoted to intangible ideas and causes and promote an image for the store as an institution rather than featuring merchandise.

Window Display Theory

Many retailers believe that exciting fashion displays in store windows are miniature theatrical productions that turn passersby into window shoppers. A display window's fashion image must be strong enough to stop traffic—foot traffic, that is. The fashion message must be strong enough to compel window-shoppers to enter the store and locate the item in the department. Effective fashion windows mark the first step in a planned progression that leads shoppers from viewing to purchasing.

Fantasy-to-Reality Theory

Window theatrics may be retail fantasies, romances, dramas, comedies, or adventure stories, but they are always designed to engage imagination and make shoppers think about what it would be like to own the merchandise on display. The fantasy-to-reality theory guides shoppers from their first look at merchandise in windows and editorial displays to the selling floor and into the fitting room in three steps:

Step One The window's larger-than-life version of fashion—merchandise that is propped or posed to amaze, amuse, and enthuse—draws window shoppers into the store. This is the fantasy stage.

Step Two The retailer presents the window merchandise inside the store and less theatrically, using editorial space in prime interior locations. These are stepped-down presentations. That is, they echo the theme of the window display, but are now presented in the context of the store. If the window display is fantasy, the platform presentation is more realistic. Merchandise here looks more "true to life" than it does in the window, and lighting and props (if any) seem less dramatic. Shoppers now have a chance to personally inspect

> **"**Windows entice people into our world and into our mindset. The basis of a Paul Stewart window is to stop people in their tracks and get them to look at the window. With fourteen windows, they can walk around the block and get an image of what the store's about.**"**
>
> Tom Beebe, former creative director, Paul Stewart, New York City.

279

the merchandise—touch the fabrics, examine garments and accessories, and look at price tags. Editorial signing directs them to appropriate selling departments.

Step Three   In the selling department—on feature fixtures or walls, shown on mannequins or not—the window merchandise is ready for purchase. Here is reality, where shoppers can actually handle the items they've admired or try them on. Departmental signing gives information about price or product use and care, or it may describe occasions where shoppers might wear the fashions or use the products appropriately.

Fantasy-to-Reality Theory

Step 1: Window display features fashion in a theatrical presentation.

Step 2: Interior platform features fashion in the context of the store.

Step 3: Department features fashion on hangers, to try and buy.

Window Display Themes

The prime source of thematic inspiration for window displays is always the merchandise itself. Visual merchandisers take their creative cues from the store's merchandise, looking at each product's end use, fabrication, style, and color as they begin to develop display themes. The window's *motif* (dominant theme idea) is only a supporting device. When theme choice is the visual department's responsibility, it seeks ways to support the selected merchandise with ideas that will bring focus and direction to the presentation. The store window is such a powerful communication tool that it is crucial that themes speak directly to targeted customers and focus attention on the merchandise. In this case, communicating requires a common language—*theme*—that the store's target audience will relate to and understand.

Sometimes window themes are set by the corporate advertisers. Merchandise drives theme there, too. When the advertising department composes a theme, the visual merchandiser's task is to find a creative way to reinforce the retail ad's message. Tying in with the ad can double the impact of the fashion message. Shoppers who see both forms of communication are more likely to make the connection and realize the retailer's commitment to the merchandise. They have been reminded twice that the retailer is a fashion leader.

Theme inspiration can come from

- Product's end use, fabrication, style, and color

- Current directions in fashion design—hem lengths, fashion silhouettes, popular designers

- Popular color palettes—seasonal traditions, designer, or market-driven color choices

- Recent, current, or upcoming events—global, national, or local happenings that involve or influence fashion

- Influential cultural directions—fads, merchandising and lifestyle trends, new books, magazines, recent films, plays, art, architecture, entertainment

- Historical perspectives—well-known symbols, recurring or retrospective fashion designs, significant anniversaries of events

- Retail image decisions—unique or "signature" architectural, decorative, or stylistic elements exclusively characteristic of the retailer's image or the store's design

- Holidays—Valentine's Day, Mother's Day, Father's Day

- Nostalgia—1950s, 1960s, 1970s, 1980s
- New developments in props or decorative items available from the display industry—innovative items like metal shopping bags and crystal-clear up-scaled ice cubes, unusual-looking mannequins and alternatives

Whether you determine the window theme or you are carrying out a theme chosen for you, the next step involves using your own ingenuity to search for ideas.

The Mechanics of Window Magic

The mechanics of creating window magic can be broken down into seven steps:

1. Select the merchandise category: for example, children's licensed Looney Tunes T-shirts.

2. Select the color story. If the license shirts come in both brights and pastels, choose just one color group for the window.

3. Select theme. The licensed children's T-shirts could tie in with the issue of a new postage stamp in the Looney Tunes series from the United States Postal Service. A promotion for the launch of the 2000 stamp featuring Wile E. Coyote and the Road Runner would be an example. Copy in vinyl lettering pressed onto the window glass: "Cotton Collectibles to Write Home About—Join STAMPERS [the USPS collecting club]." This strategy combines a fashion and an institutional window.

4. Select props. Each of the four current postage stamps in the series could be rendered as a 4 × 8 poster. There could be one per window. Mannequins would carry oversized lined tablets, colored pencils, and envelopes with smaller cartooned "postage." In addition to the stamp graphic, there could be two wooden cubes in stepped-up sizes (each size painted to match one color from the stamp backgrounds) per window. Window backdrops, floors, and returns could be painted flat black.

5. Select mannequins. Three to five mannequins per window will represent infant through preteen sizes, both genders, diverse ethnicity, and various active poses—climbing, sitting, and so on.

6. Select accessories. Colorful play clothes, footgear, hats, socks, hair accessories, eyeglasses, sunglasses, outerwear, toys, would all complement the licensed shirts.

7. Sketch proposed window presentation. Even a rough drawing with stick figures saves unnecessary mannequin and prop handling later. A sketch helps visual merchandising designers build focus, work out optical weights, and bring balance to all the elements that must work together. It allows presetting prop placement and preliminary lighting strategies. It also clarifies color schemes. Sketching ensures quality and consistency through an entire bank of windows—especially when more than one person is doing the work. (See Figure 12.5.)

Seven Mechanics of Window Magic

Step 1: Select merchandise category.

Step 2: Select color story.

Step 3: Select theme.

Step 4: Select props.

Step 5: Select mannequins.

Step 6: Select accessories.

Step 7: Sketch proposed window presentation.

"The window display is the first message you are sending to regular and potential customers. Therefore, you must carefully plan the merchandise and how it is presented. It's like how you get dressed each day. You carefully coordinate the clothes you want to wear and the manner in which you style your hair or apply makeup. Your storefront window displays should be given the same level of importance."

Greg Gorman, *The Visual Merchandising & Store Design Workbook.*

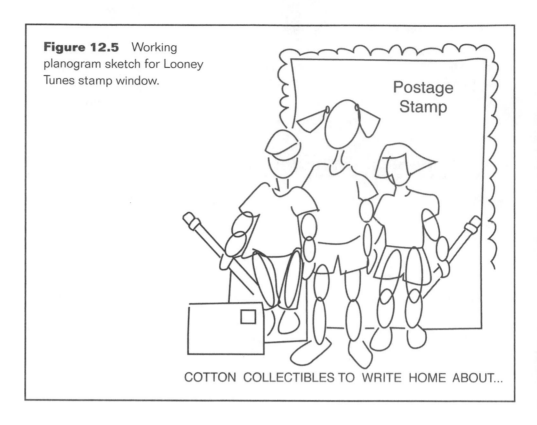

Figure 12.5 Working planogram sketch for Looney Tunes stamp window.

Postage Stamp

COTTON COLLECTIBLES TO WRITE HOME ABOUT...

Techniques for Positioning Mannequins in Windows

When you see window mannequins that seem to stand on their own, you're seeing an example of window magic. **Striking** a mannequin means removing it from its customary metal support rod and metal or glass base plate, then securing it to the window floor with wire so that it seems to be standing on its own in the display setting. Why not use the base plate? Many visual merchandisers think that the mannequin's base plate and rod detract from the drama they want to achieve in their windows. Some are not fond of the mannequin that has its support rod built into its foot, making it impossible to accessorize with real shoes without destroying them. Nor are they comfortable with mannequins with premolded "shoes." They reason that shoppers expect to see an entire outfit down to the last fashion accessory—including shoes.

In *Confessions of a Window Dresser,* author Simon Doonan says that mannequin wiring is one of the "few manually skilled activities in display." The process of striking a mannequin requires two people. There are several approaches to striking, and each method is useful in certain merchandising situations:

Option 1   Many visual merchandisers prefer to use a wiring technique that circles the mannequin's waistline with a tight loop of wire. This technique is very useful when a mannequin is dressed in pants, since the back seam of the garment does not have to be cut to accommodate a wire attached to the butt screw as it might be with Option 2.

1. Lift the mannequin from its base, and position it on the floor.

2. A second person will attach a single strand of wire around the waist and twist it tightly to complete a loop. Then the trailing end of the wire is extended to the floor where it is secured to a nail. The mannequin must tilt slightly against the wire to counterbalance without its base plate. Note: If the mannequin is "steady on its feet," a single wire may suffice.

Striking a mannequin means removing its support rod and base plate and securing it with wire so it seems to stand on its own in the display. This technique is used exclusively in closed window displays because of concern for the safety of both customers and mannequins.

282

3. If the mannequin does not seem stable, add a second wire to the waist loop and extend it to the floor for additional stability. See Figure 12.6.

4. If the wire develops a shine once the spotlights are set, apply a colored marker or paint along the wire to dull the reflection and camouflage the device. For example, a black marker will dull silver wire. The color you choose should match the color of the background. Take great care to protect the garment worn by the mannequin.

Option 2   This option works well when the mannequin wears a snug-fitting garment that must not have heavy gauge striking wire piercing its fabric or seams—a one-piece slip dress without a waistband, for example. Two-piece swimwear and other bare midriff looks challenge the waist loop option, too. In cases like these, striking wires may be attached to the thumbscrew that normally secures the mannequin to the support rod at its buttocks. Steps 3 and 4 the next two steps are the same as in Option 1.

Option 3   With this option, which ensures most stable stance of all, the mannequin remains on its supporting rod. The rod is then slipped into a normal base plate socket that has been removed from a glass or metal base and bolted permanently to the window floor. Once the mannequin and rod are in position, it is simply a matter of tightening the screw where the rod fits into the base plate's socket.

Striking mannequins is a style choice, not a rule. Barney's Simon Doonan observes that seeing mannequins with two strands of taut piano wire emerging from beneath their skirts "erodes fantasy" just as much as being able to see their base plates, so his strategy is to design and order better-looking base plates.

Safety Concern!

Striking mannequins is a technique to be used only in enclosed windows. You'd never strike a mannequin in an area where there was the slightest chance for a shopper to come in contact with a wire. It's not safe for shoppers or mannequins.

Mannequins with Trousers

If a mannequin is to wear trousers, the garment's back seam must be carefully slit open with a seam ripper to accommodate the striking wires for Option 2, or, with Option 3, the support rod. Garments with flat-felled seams and lined garments must be handled very carefully so that you do not damage the fabric. The opened seams must be repaired before garments are returned to the selling floor. If you have an in-store alterations department, repairs can be done there. If not, garments must be sent out for expert repair. This is a routine display expense. Customers should not be able to detect any repair work. For obvious reasons, Option 1 is the preferred technique for mannequins in trousers.

Hosiery and socks shown on mannequins cannot be returned to stock and are generally charged to the visual department or written out of stock by the fashion department manager.

Tips for Propping Windows

The following tips will help you maintain unity within a window or span of windows.

Tip 1   Select *one* major prop that you can support with strength throughout an entire span of windows. You may use a different single prop per window if it has equal thematic value: for example, a different leisure sport activity and related paraphernalia for each window in a Father's Day series—golf in one, tennis in another, biking or bowling in others. The unifying element is the leisure sport. Even so, the props should be consistent in scale from window to window—oversized tee, ball, and club, gigantic tennis racquet and net, huge bike chain and spoked wheel, 3-foot high bowling pins.

STEP 1 - Lift mannequin off base and position on floor.

STEP 2 - Tie wire around waist and extend to nail on floor. Secure to nail. For safety, have second person balance mannequin.

STEP 3 - Add a second wire around mannequin waist to balance figure. Secure to floor.

STEP 4 - Apply marker or paint to wire to match window background.

Figure 12.6 Striking a mannequin is typically a two-person task done in four steps.

Tip 2 Select props that make sense with the theme. Think about what goes naturally with the merchandise you are presenting. Prop choices must be limited for the sake of impact and clarity. Select props that call up strong, clear images. In the postage stamp example earlier in the chapter, kids go with cartoons and kids' play clothes go with the active images portrayed by the four stamps.

Tip 3 *Merchandise is always more important than props.* Take a long, hard look at your window. Subordinate props used as risers should blend into the scene and not distract from the theme. You don't sell props and you don't sell risers; you sell clothing. It's a matter of balance and emphasis in the right place.

Tip 4 Use silk flowers or foliage instead of plastic flowers unless you are presenting a retro theme. Don't ever mix plastics with silks. Lighting picks up the differences, and the whole effect suffers.

Techniques for Buildups in Windows

Historically, large display windows have featured smaller accessory displays known as *buildups, laydowns,* or *setups* on the window floor. These were often packages of fragrances, toiletries in bottles and jars, and accessories—handbags, shoes, jewelry—that enhanced the fashion image of the larger, featured display items but lacked stand-alone size. Massed in a miniature presentation of their own, a buildup suggests "go-with items" that can add to the value of the sale. That tradition exists today, although it has taken some appealing twists along the way.

Some large windows are actually masked and sectioned off into mini-windows to accommodate special accessory presentations. Others establish a second focal point off to one side of the main attraction with the use of special graphics and, in some cases, special fixtures to show subordinate themes. In all cases, the goal is the same—adding interest to the presentation and value to the customer's purchase.

The following guidelines will help you create a traditional buildup presentation in a fashion window:

1. Select a small, neutral riser unit—a small plaster column or a clear polycarbonate cube, for example—to anchor a buildup. The riser could also be an item of merchandise tied directly to the window's larger theme. For example, an elegant French Provincial jewelry box matching the antique Louis XIV chair and ornate picture frame that prop a window mannequin in an elaborate ball gown might be an effective choice for a riser. In this case, dazzling jewelry, evening bags, long gloves, and expensive perfume might cascade from the open drawers of the jewelry box, suggesting additional items for add-on purchase.

2. Select a location for the buildup. Imagine that the display window is a picture frame. Using optical weight, position the buildup so that it balances "in the frame" with the mannequin and other props.

3. Select the appropriate related accessory merchandise.

4. Compose a "still life"—formally or informally balanced—that uses all the appropriate art and design elements—height, depth, color, contrast of shapes, textures, and sizes. The buildup must stand on its own, yet relate to the larger items in the main window display. Use one larger focal piece and an odd (3–5) number of subordinate items. Triangles are ideal buildup formats. The line of the composition should draw the eye down, through, and out of the "frame." See Figures 12.7 and 12.8 for examples of buildup compositions.

Techniques for Lighting

Window lighting has a theatrical goal: to create mood, build drama, and heighten excitement. In fact, many lighting terms, tools, and techniques come straight from backstage:

285

Figure 12.7 Tables in a variety of heights create a buildup for handbags in Wilson's, Mall of America. For additional selling suggestions, the tallest table could be replaced by a ¾ mannequin wearing a jacket and scarf.

track-lighting hardware, spotlight "cans," PAR spotlights and floodlights, pin spots (narrow spots), dimmers, attachable colored gels, and spotlight filters. Several national retailers even employ freelance theatrical lighting specialists for window production in their major locations.

The rules that apply specifically to window lighting are useful for all aspects of store lighting as well:

1. Show merchandise in its true colors. Unless your company's window policy is more about dramatic impact than profitable sales, the danger of distorting color is to mislead shoppers. Ideally, what they see in the window is what they should get in the store.

2. Focus on merchandise. Special effects are wonderful, but merchandise is the reason for turning on the lights.

Figure 12.8 This open window display uses a graphic backdrop to isolate it from the selling floor and fixture buildups to enhance the message with related merchandise. Williams-Sonoma, Miami.

3. Make the lighting devices a discreet part of the presentation. Focus on *what* is presented rather than on *how* it is presented.

In a March 2000 article titled "Points of Light," *Visual Merchandising and Store Design* lighting editor Lois Hutchinson presented useful tips from well-known window professionals. From among their best practices for windows, she selected the following:

● Incorporate [open] window displays into the interior architecture of the store. Because most mall stores have no dividing walls behind their window display areas; dramatic lighting using high color gels is usually not feasible. On the other hand, the "clean" look is easy to maintain. "Every time you change the display, the whole window changes," says Tracy Coppicotto, visual merchandising manager for Liz Claiborne, New York City. "But you can't forget the lighting!" To optimize lighting's effectiveness, visual merchandisers need to pay close attention to maintenance issues—not only changing burned-out lights, but refocusing lights as merchandise changes seasonally so that luminaries don't wind up shining onto blank walls or walkways.

- Using multiple beamspreads is another trick in the display lighting toolbox, but visual merchandisers often don't take advantage of it. Lucy-Ann Bouwman of Seitgeist Design, New York City, likes the PAR46 narrow-spot for its controllability. "It's a big lamp, but I get just a small point of light when it hits the merchandise," she explains. "Say I want a flood in the background, and then I want to just target a diamond ring or a pearl necklace. A narrow-spot will allow me to do that." Bouwman adds that she always uses fixtures that can hold color gels and diffusion material. In smaller windows there's the danger of using lighting equipment that's too big for the window and puts out too much light to define and emphasize merchandise. "It doesn't look special if everything is lit up," cautions Bouwman. "The lighting should make the merchandise gleam rather than scream."

- Jim Call, a window proper for Nordstrom Westside Pavilion in Los Angeles, uses gels to create theatrical effects. "I look at the window like it's a set and the mannequin is the actress," Call explains. "Light with white light and then shadow her on the side with dark blue, so it looks like she has a rim light. You still have the mood, but you're not losing the real merchandise color quality and texture." Call also uses colored light to make colored merchandise pop, or to mute the color somewhat. He prescribes a light-blue gel to make black look richer. "First of all, figure out what the center point of the window is. Look at the window as a whole and choose what things are important. You're the one who makes them important with light."

- Domenic Metta, principal of Windows and Interiors, Wayne, New Jersey, recommends that track fixtures be placed carefully, in front of merchandise displays and as close to the window line as possible. "Very often, architects will drop the lights in the center of the window wall or ceiling," he notes. "They forget that you lose a lot of depth for the placement of merchandise. You end up lighting the top of the merchandise rather than the face."

"Good lighting can guide the customers' eyes, reveal the color and cut of the merchandise, show the styling and tailoring details, and emphasize the qualities of the outfit, helping the merchandise to be pre-sold to the customer."

Boyd Davis, on-line editor, **www.fashionwindows.com**

You can even find professional window lighting tips on the Internet. One particularly good Website is **www.fashionwindows.com,** where visual merchandisers can read articles excerpted from trade publications, view window photographs from all over the world, chat with others in the field, search for used props and mannequins, or look for employment.

Techniques for Ledges and Display Cases

Ledges and display cases may be thought of as small windows, especially when it comes to composition and propping. These atmospheric presentations add visual interest to store areas that primarily stock packaged goods in secured showcases (cosmetics, small leather goods, jewelry, watches, etc.) They may be used to create focal points in select areas throughout a department, including perimeter walls. Choose locations carefully and edit the number of ledge and countertop displays, or they will add clutter instead of emphasis.

The same is true for the interiors of display cases. If a department has a center island display case for stock surrounded by a perimeter counter over glass-front stock cases, select one space per side for decorative displays that incorporate stock, props, and graphics. From a distance, these small displays can break the visual monotony of row upon row of packaged merchandise and highlight certain important products. They focus shoppers' attention and are very useful reminders about advertised items. Display case interiors should be reset when advertising changes or when new products arrive.

When you analyze the display illustrated in Figure 12.9, you'll note that the display uses risers to achieve height. Simplicity is the key to effective display work.

Housekeeping

Begin any display in windows, on ledges, and in showcases with a thorough dusting and glass cleaning. As you complete a display, seek out and remove any loose threads, staples,

Figure 12.9 A center island display case featuring merchandise on mannequin forms and risers. It is a strategy for making use of the "air space" above the display case. Marshall Field's, Chicago.

wire trimmings, and so on. Check to ensure that fashion items have no tags or threads showing. Step outside store windows and inspect displays for minor details.

Daily, before the store opens, revisit displays that are accessible to shoppers and reposition merchandise that has been handled. Walk through all of your areas; dust and clean as you go. A display, even in an enclosed showcase, gathers dust. Remember that shoppers' first impressions are lasting impressions. They reflect on the store's image and your professional reputation.

Don't forget the safety and security aspects of this housekeeping tour. Be sure that mannequins aren't tipped precariously, that their hands are properly positioned, and that accessories are still in place. If visual merchandisers are not available during all store hours, sales associates may have sold items from your editorials and not had time to replace them before the store closed.

Windows as an Art Form ....

An amazing thing happened in May of 1999. Store windows were elevated to an art form and all of New York City saw it happen. From the Cooper-Hewitt National Design Museum, Smithsonian Institution at 91st Street, to Paul Stuart at 16th Street, fashion windows in 15 prestigious stores became an off-site exhibition—*The Window Show.* The weeklong show was dedicated to the memory of legendary Tiffany & Co. window designer Gene Moore, who died in 1998. One year prior to his death, Moore donated 39 years of window archives to the Cooper-Hewitt, where they can be studied. Tom Beebe, former creative director of Paul Stuart (a New York City retailer) and a good friend of Moore's, served as the project's design liaison.

New York window designers created 15 unique presentations based on artifacts from the Cooper-Hewitt's departments of textiles, wall-coverings, applied arts and industrial design, drawings and prints, and its library of archival material from American manufacturers and designers. Their mission was to tie in the artifacts with their store's brand image and merchandise.

Retail Ad World (October 1999) had this to say about the show:

The show demonstrated the museum's mission to explore the important role of design in daily life by focusing on an area that is often taken for granted—window as design, and window trimmers as designers. By turning store windows into "satellite galleries," the exhibition also served to showcase the breadth and scope of Cooper-Hewitt's distinctive collections.

The show was notable for several firsts—adding a new chapter to the history of window display:

- The first time a museum has recognized window display as a decorative art with an outside show.

- The first time stores recognized each other's displays.

- The first time designers from "competing" stores met together for a common purpose.

The Cooper-Hewitt's program brochure added this note:

Leonard Marcus (*The American Store Window*) saw the "scene behind the window" as a reinforcement of the theatrical nature of store windows and the city itself as a "sphere of public performance." The opening credits for the 1960s TV sitcom *That Girl* underscore the author's point. While the show's opening theme plays, the main character (actress Marlo Thomas) stands before a store window where she is startled to meet the gaze of a mannequin that seems to have turned into her double. The mannequin winks at her. That wink, "acknowledges the complicity between the passerby as audience and the window as the stage. In this psychodrama, reenacted every day in cities around the world, the mannequin serves as our double, representing the impulse to pass through the glass and step into the store window's realm of drama, fantasy, and desire."

See Colorplate 16 for photographs of windows included in *The Window Show.*

Shoptalk
· ·

The Window Show

By Tom Beebe
former creative director, Paul Stuart, New York City

There have been some wonderful, magical moments in my career—the timing has been right and the project was in line with the stars and the moon—when I've been able to create energy and maintain the momentum. I hope that doesn't sound too worldly for you, but honestly, I think that's what happens sometimes when things go 100 percent right for me. You'll find other words to describe those moments, I'm sure, but I hope you have lots of them in your creative life.

The Window Show was one of those moments for me. In a nutshell, I was a player in a tribute to the art in our profession and an homage to the genius of Gene Moore. We were working on the project just prior to his death, and so he knew it was going to happen. I was so glad he understood that the Cooper-Hewitt wanted to recognize display as a design field and wanted to acknowledge Mr. Moore's 39 years in the Tiffany windows, helping to elevate all of our work to artful status.

I've had fine role models and mentors as I worked my way up—the best of them all was Gene Moore. And, as famous as he was, he always called himself a "window trimmer." As we scurried around and convinced 15 stores and as many window designers to participate in The Window Show, each window keyed off items and artifacts in the Cooper-Hewitt's extensive design collections, people asked, "Why go to all this work for something that's going to last only a week?"

I hope my answer was loud and clear: Why should we *not*? That's what we *do!* As others do their day-to-day work and live their lives, we "window trimmers" do our passion. We create work that is our craft—work that has developed deep in our hearts and souls and is transformed through our minds and hands into the windows, the stage, and our street theater, for all to see.

We don't feel able to think fast enough or move fast enough or have enough patience. Whether we fill our space with merchandise and props upon props or create the most minimal of minimal presentations, when the wires are cut, the pins are nibbed, and the lights come up, the curtain is drawn away, and the time has come for "ooohs" and "ahhhs." That moment never fails to make me think of Mr. Moore, who was always waiting to do his best window . . . time after time.

I hope that my craft continues to develop (and my mind and soul along with it) and that I can keep after more of those magical moments when the timing is right and the spark of an idea is in harmony with the universe. That's when, as Mr. Moore would say, "I am my window and my window is me!"

Out-of-the-Box Challenge
· ·

Window Review

Look

Visit three to five stores with enclosed windows and evaluate each window. Take notes on the categories of merchandise, color scheme, theme, props, mannequins (if any), product accessories, and housekeeping, using the form in Figure 12.10. You may make as many copies of the form as you need.

Compare

Compare the presentations.

Innovate

What would you do to improve each of the presentations? Be prepared to discuss and justify your critique in a class discussion.

Critical Thinking
· ·

Develop a window theme and compose a line of sign copy for each theme based on each of the following idea sources:

1. Current directions in fashion design, popular color palettes

2. Recent or upcoming local events

3. Influential cultural directions

4. Historical perspectives

5. Retail image decisions

6. New developments in props or decorative items available from the display industry

Case Study
· ·

Design Challenge

The Situation

You have applied for a position as the visual merchandising director of a local department store. Until this time, you've worked exclusively as an independent contractor in the men's wear area. One of your pre-employment challenges is to prepare window presentation concepts to be executed by the staff. The interview committee asks you and the other two finalists to complete an impromptu design challenge that you will present during your second interview on the day after tomorrow.

Your Challenge

The bulleted items that follow are your tasks. The numbered items represent four specific challenges—with specific design requirements.

- Identify a theme for the window that could also be used as a sign copy headline.

- Write sign copy (or specify a lifestyle graphic to be placed in the display as a means of communicating the window's contents).

- Specify colors, props, and style of mannequin (if used).

- Sketch a front view of your window concept.

- Label any figures or items necessary for committee members to understand the concept.

- Be prepared to present all four concepts, although time may permit you to discuss only one of them with the committee.

1. Design a *fashion window display concept* for the fall season that does not rely on a single autumn leaf or pumpkin for its props.

2. Design an *institutional window concept* that celebrates the opening of a new exhibit at a local art museum.

3. Design a *white sale window* concept for a department store using large banners announcing the sale. Assume that you have state-of-the-art display props and materials.

4. Design a *"tween" trend window* to appeal to a back-to-school audience in August.

STORE WINDOW REVIEW

Window Function

1. Function is fashion, promotional, institutional, sale, or other?

   _____

Merchandise

2. Merchandise theme is seasonal, fashion, trend, dressy, casual, or other?

   _____

3. Merchandise category is: _____

4. Merchandise includes accessory items.	Y	N	NA

5. Merchandise color scheme is bright, pastel, or other?

   _____

6. Merchandise is wrinkle free.	Y	N	NA

Mannequins (if used)

7. Mannequin used is appropriate for merchandise.	Y	N	NA
8. Mannequin pose is natural.	Y	N	NA
9. Mannequins appear to relate to each other.	Y	N	NA

Props

10. Props selected for the window relate to theme.	Y	N	NA
11. Props do not dominate the window display.	Y	N	NA

Signing

12. Identifies trend, designer, brand, or item features.	Y	N	NA
13. Directs shopper to selling area in store.	Y	N	NA
14. Signing type is large enough for easy reading.	Y	N	NA

Housekeeping

15. Window glass is clean (inside and outside).	Y	N	NA
16. Window floor is clean, lint-free, dust-free.	Y	N	NA
17. Fixtures, buildups, mannequin bases clean, dust-free.	Y	N	NA

Figure 12.10

Chapter 13

MANNEQUINS AND MANNEQUIN ALTERNATIVES

After completing this chapter, you should be able to

Explain how the mannequin is used as a communication tool

Identify resources for mannequins and mannequin alternatives

Evaluate criteria for matching mannequins to store image

Follow guidelines for dressing and maintaining mannequins

Develop strategies for placing mannequins in departments

"Mannequins are the high-octane
gasoline that fuel the throbbing of
my window-dressing Lincoln
Continental. No matter how
groovy your window concept is,
a dreary mannequin can reduce it to
the level of suburban dinner theater."
Simon Doonan,
Confessions of a Window Dresser

Communicating Self-Image and Fashion Image

The mannequin is regarded as one of the retailer's most powerful communication tools. Used strategically, it speaks volumes about fashion trends and a store's brand identity. In order to communicate effectively, we know that a store mannequin must relate to the shopper's self-image. When shoppers follow current fashion—read about it, talk about it, look at it, buy it, and wear it—they are defining "self" and describing who they are through the clothing they wear. In fact, more than one industry writer has suggested that visual merchandisers would gain valuable insights into shopper self-image by observing and studying shoppers in stores as if they were the ones on display rather than the mannequins.

Mannequin Evolution

To trace the history of the mannequin as a medium for communicating fashionability, you may also want to consider the evolution of the human body. Bodies have changed over time, as indicated by a discovery made in preparation for a 1997 Christian Dior retrospective show at the New York Metropolitan Museum of Art.

As the Metropolitan's Costume Institute designers prepared to dress mannequins in costumes spanning Dior's haute couture career, they found that many of his garments didn't fit their exhibit mannequins well at all. The Museum's principal mannequin supplier, Pucci International, needed to design and fabricate an entirely new series of figures to fit the Dior costumes.

From his early career as a fashion illustrator to the 1947 introduction of his revolutionary "new look," and his death 10 years later, Dior's fashions were constructed for his ideal client body of that era—a figure evidently a bit shorter and thicker-waisted than the Costume Institute's longer, leaner mannequins.

Pucci mannequin sculptor Michael Evert said, "For the Dior show I'm having to create a mannequin to fit the clothes, because it's as if there's an idea of what people's bodies are *supposed* to look like that really does not correspond to what most people do look like."

What Evert and his colleagues on the Dior project discovered was that bodies have changed. These changes are partly due to improved nutrition, better health care and medicines, and clearer understandings of how our bodies work and must be maintained. The last century saw people growing taller, living longer, doing more. Those factors all contributed in some way to the changes currently taking place in the fashion industry and the mannequin industry.

Today's mannequins are designed in response to anatomical trends as well as current events, social trends, and value shifts in a global fashion market. If haute couture decides that tiny waistlines are in and full bosoms are not, then the current generation of mannequins will reflect that trend as designer fashion trickles down. It may take a year or so to arrive in U.S. stores, but if fashion designers and global media make these decisions, it may be time to order new mannequins.

Mannequins have stood and sat, smirked and smiled, or plumped up and thinned down to match the fashions of the day for centuries. If bodies evolve in the next several centuries, you may be certain that mannequins will, too.

Reflecting the Times

No one is positive when the first mannequin appeared, but most agree that the dressmaker's form is its basis. Historically, that could have occurred as early as the time of Egyptian pharaohs. Small design models known as fashion dolls were utilized in Europe and Colonial America in the 1700s. Like a cabinetmaker's scaled furniture models, these remarkable costumed miniatures served as portable displays for skilled seamstresses, showing potential clients what hand-stitched fashions are available to order.

In April 1991, *Smithsonian Magazine* published an important feature article titled "Mannequins, the Mute Mirrors of Fashion History," by Per Ola and Emily d'Aulaire, that explored the mannequin's origins and evolution. "Most experts agree that the succession of stages set in motion during the Industrial Revolution—the manufacture of large, steel-framed, plate-glass windows, the invention of the sewing machine, the electrification of cities—cleared the way for [the mannequin's] arrival."

It makes sense. Larger store windows made it possible for passersby to view merchandise inside the store. With the development of the electric light bulb, genteel people strolled and "window shopped" as entertainment after an evening meal. Progressive merchants began lighting store windows during evening hours to take full advantage of the new custom.

By 1885, a British manufacturer of wax dressmaker forms (Gems Wax Models and, today, Gemini Mannequins) and a French company, Siegel and Stockman of Paris, were making and exporting wax mannequins and some "articulated figures" with wooden hands and bendable fingers to the United States. Later on, American companies like The French Wax Company of Milwaukee entered the competition. On both sides of the Atlantic, the collective design challenge was the creation of features and poses that both represented and flattered the shoppers whose attention they were meant to capture.

Some advanced wax mannequins, like those created by another French maker, Pierre Imans, were strikingly accurate *and* artistically beautiful forerunners of today's realistic action figures. They were posed to "interact" with other mannequins on display, participating in fashion vignettes—a novel idea at the time. Imans's work, while prophetic, was not universally approved and the conservative retailers continued to display fashions on their stiff, staid, and more or less upright pillars of the wax community. (See Figure 13.1A.)

According to mannequin historian Marsha Bentley Hale, World War I and its necessary rationing brought about changes in perfection standards for women's body shapes. "Sugar rationing had trimmed down the figure in contrast to the buxom ideal prior to the war." Working in factories and businesses while the male workforce fought, eager younger women put aside cumbersome fashions for higher hemlines—exposing legs for the first time—and headed straight into the Roaring Twenties "flapper" era after the war ended. In response, the mannequins of the day began to reflect the more active and energetic roles that women were assuming. (See Figure 13.1B.)

As a result of new technologies developed during the war, mannequins made of less volatile (meltable) materials like plaster replaced fragile wax figures. The "down" side to that was a loss of the delicate facial sculpting possible with the wax medium. As a result, more abstract mannequin features evolved, which were in sync with postwar modern attitudes and experimentation in all aspects of design.

The 1929 stock market crash forced the next generation of mannequin development in the form of one-dimensional poster art forms and wooden cutout alternatives. During the subsequent Depression of the 1930s, when people escaped to fantasy lives in Hollywood's spectacular movies, stars sang, danced, skated, skied, sailed, and did all the things their audiences couldn't in real life. Mannequins—including some of the first designed to replicate famous fashion models—became equally active, creating lifestyle fantasies in stores and windows where people who were experiencing tough economic conditions could window-shop in another world and hope for better times. (See Figure 13.1C.)

World War II brought an end to the grinding poverty of the "Dirty Thirties" but also brought the European mannequin market to a near halt. This allowed talented American mannequin designers and manufacturers to market their products unhindered in the United States. In Denmark, Hindsgaul, a firm known primarily for store fixturing, geared up to supply the European market for fashion mannequins and survived the war years to establish an international reputation that remains strong today.

Plastics and fiberglass were the war technologies perfected during the postwar era. The female form, camouflaged for years under war factory coveralls, emerged victorious as the

A Retail Reality:
Have you ever heard a mannequin referred to as a "clotheshorse?" This term comes from the historic practice of storing elegant (and voluminous) upper-class men's and women's costumes on dressmaker forms or "clotheshorses" to protect lavish trimmings and preserve appearance between wearings. The only other storage option was an armoire or a "clothespress" suitable for less elaborately structured garments.

country's young soldiers returned from Europe and the Pacific. Women were back in style. (See Figure 13.1D.)

Pinup actresses Marilyn Monroe and Ava Gardner were icons of feminity. Movie star mannequins, sexy and glamorous, went up on pedestals. And during the 1950s, live runway models attempted to look and act like the postwar window mannequins—emulating New Look exaggerated bosoms and nipped in waists; vamping on spiked heel pumps. During this decade, more sexuality than ever before was evident in female and male mannequin collections, and once again, mannequins seemed intentionally interactive, telling stories and setting mood with aware-of-each-other poses.

Reflecting the Trends

"The idea of bringing to life the fashion models from the magazine was Adel's groundbreaking idea. Outdated fifties mannequins looked the wrong age and the wrong shape modeling the new Mary Quant miniskirts."

Kevin Arpino, creative director, Adel Rootsein and Co., London, speaking about the company's late founder.

Some say that the realistic mannequin styling we take for granted today began, or at least speeded up, when Adel Rootstein's Twiggy mannequins and Mary Quant's 1960s miniskirted "mod" English fashions roared across the Atlantic and radically changed American fashion. (See Figure 13.1E.)

It isn't unusual for fashions to change abruptly several times during a decade if the communication that puts fashion-conscious people in touch with markets and products all over the world functions efficiently. In the 1960s, we weren't aware of the personal potential of the computer, but we became a nation of jet setters, and we traveled freely. Society's pace accelerated, and shoppers often complained that they were stressed-out from trying to keep their lives from unraveling. Americans were into wash-and-wear clothes, wash-and-wear hairstyles, instant foods, and anything else that they could buy to streamline their lives. Many began to look inward.

Other, very real, shadows appeared in American culture, and waves of change brought another evolutionary turn to mannequin design. You can see the results in styling showing liberated female body forms. Some mannequin breasts developed nipples, belly buttons were bared, postures and poses became more aggressive—mirroring what was happening in society during the tumult of the 1960s, carrying over to the early 1970s.

By the 1970s, fashion windows and their inhabitants were deeply into "telling it like it is," and relating to each other in scenes that depicted the bumpy ride that much of post-Vietnam-era America was experiencing. If you were to compare the facial expressions on mannequin faces, in the 1970s, to those on the faces of Depression-era mannequins, you'd have to ask yourself who was really depressed. The 1970 figures often seemed troubled, tense, and even tired. Add to that an emerging counterculture and increasing interest in life in galaxies far, far away, and you had an interesting mix of mannequins on the menu, because mannequin manufacturers responded to nearly every trend.

In the 1980s, mannequins became citizens of the world, and more realistic, flattering, and beautifully rendered ethnic mannequins came to live in retail stores in major shopping areas all over the country. At the same time, abstract mannequins without any distinct features emerged with the ability to cater to shoppers of any ethnicity (see Figure 13.1F). In addition, higher levels of activity and vitality and color and excitement came to the abstract action figure category. Name a sport; there was a mannequin prepared to compete.

In the 1990s mannequins came out of their windows and off their platforms to be seen shopping, waiting for friends near an elevator, relaxing against display tables, looking over the escalator railing to watch shopping activity on the floor below. Their collective message to shoppers were: "We're not remote, set apart, or untouchable; we're just like you. In fact, we're out here with you, enjoying the store, taking in the ambience." Call it "open display" if you will; this disarming strategy really predated the movement toward open sell in the late 1990s. (See Figure 13.1E.)

Another decade of evolution challenges us now. In February 2000, *VM + SD* associate editor Randi Holm-Bertelsen identified increased demand for mannequins with heads as one of the most identifiable trends in the earliest part of 2000. Her article "Mannequins Get Real: A softer realism and heads prevail," spotlighted California mannequin manufacturer George Martin who wryly observed that everyone in the last decade had "headless mannequin disease, thinking 'it's all about merchandise.'" Martin felt that there was more to it than that: "Aside from the fact that heads give a display more proportion, they have also become important commodities because retailers are more 'ethnic conscious.'" Essentially, retailers are taking closer looks at their markets and communicating awareness of their diversity back to consumer groups.

Holm-Bertelsen added preadolescent and adolescent markets to the list of strong groups that will affect mannequins in the decade: "We're noticing more young body images packed with plenty of attitude. And New York City illustrates another trend clearly: From the elegant romantics seen in such upscale windows as Bergdorf Goodman to the fascinating motion of animated mannequins at Old Navy, realism is in."

In 2001–2002, a new trend emerged that is continuing—a virtual mannequin explosion. Gap relocated on Michigan Avenue in Chicago and opened with more than 500 mannequins. Simple to dress, smooth-finish mannequins with magnetic arm fittings and no heads were displayed in mass with amazing impact. Victoria Secret opened a store in New York City with more than 300 mannequins and forms. In 2003, Burberry opened its Soho store with ten abstract mannequins lined up on a red acrylic runway down the center of the store. Also, in 2003, Prada installed 24 mannequins at the store entrance, and another 30 on its stadium stairway. (See Figure 13.2.) The Chinese vintage mannequins were part of Prada's tribute to China, which provided the proper setting for its Asian influence fashions. This is just part of a story that reaches far beyond the limits of how mannequins have been used historically. What it holds for the visual merchandising industry and its practitioners remains to be seen. The exciting part is knowing that you may be part of it and may have an impact on it. Practitioners and students of visual merchandising could be talking and reading about *your* work 10 years from now.

Sourcing Mannequins

Among the skills you'll use and value most as a visual practitioner is knowing where to look and how to find the products you need, or **sourcing.** Today, you can source, or search, globally, nationally, and locally on the Internet to save yourself (and your company) long-distance phone charges as well as time and travel expense for initial research on fixtures, props, or mannequins. In the information-gathering phase of sourcing, you'll also want to acquire hard-copy promotional materials from manufacturers that will build your knowledge base and a library of reference materials. Later, when you get into the markets, you'll see firsthand what your sources have in store.

Sourcing is a term coined in the 1990s to describe the process of finding resources for use in a business.

Internet Sourcing

To start your work in this chapter, visit **www.fashionwindows.com** to see and source mannequins. Clicking on the button labeled *mannequins* will give you access to many articles published on the topic that you may read on-line or print for future reference. Clicking on the word *companies* when you get to the mannequin page will take you on a fully illustrated tour of the current leaders in mannequin design and manufacturing. You may also view stunning full-color examples of the latest models in all categories from infants to plus-sized specialty mannequins and every age, gender, posture, and position possible.

However, it's important to understand that Websites are edited down to essentials. The text is short; the descriptive portions are spared. To gather the background information and develop a feel for the lore of the industry, the talents of the people in it, and the way it

A A wax mannequin by Pierre Imans, vintage 1911

B A more active and energic posture in a Siegel and Stockman mannequin from Paris, circa 1920

C A Depression-era mannequin of the 1930s by the U.S. producer Cora Scovil, which provides escapist fantasy and glamour

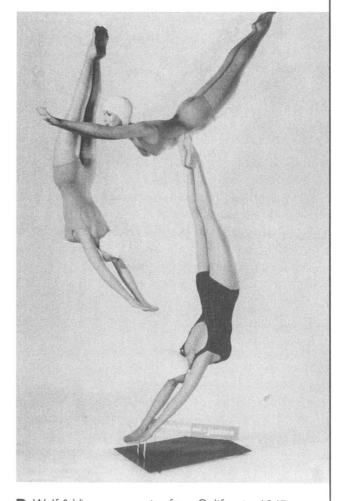

D Wolf & Vine mannequins from California, 1945

Figure 13.1 Fashion mannequins, like the clothes they wear, have changed over time. Examples from the twentieth century.

E A Twiggy mannequin by Adel Rootstein, 1966, exemplifying the inspiration of Mary Quant's Mod designs

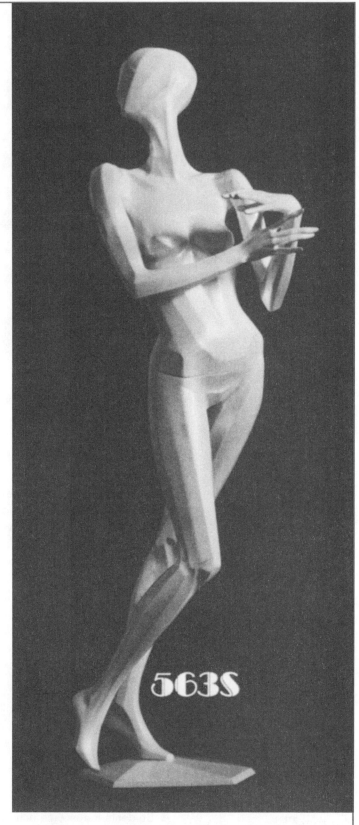

F An abstract mannequin of the 1980s from the Prismatic Profiles series by Decter Mannequin Company of Los Angeles, adaptable to displaying fashions for shoppers of any age or ethnicity

Figure 13.2 Prada in Soho, New York City, filled its store with Asian-featured mannequins in its "Tribute to China" installation.

operates, more in-depth printed publications are the next logical items to add to your visual merchandising tool kit.

Trade Publications

One of the most familiar sources of trade information for the visual field, a feast of new products and articles between two covers, is the monthly edition of *VM + SD* (*Visual Merchandising and Store Design*) magazine. Introduced as *Display World* in 1922, this publication now has a Website (**www.visualstore.com**) with an abbreviated selection of photographs and articles from the magazine. However, Web pages change frequently, and you can't build a permanent reference library from back issues, which is what many visual merchandisers like to do, so a subscription to the magazine is a wise investment.

Display and Design Ideas (DDI) magazine is another leading trade resource that is essential for any visual merchandiser. DDI's Website (**www.ddi.com**) features links to mannequin manufacturers including on-line catalogs in men's, women's, and children's mannequins and mannequin alternatives.

Trade Shows

Display markets are generally held in March (locations rotate to major cities like Chicago, Las Vegas, Orlando, etc.) and during December in New York. Both *DDI* and *VM + SD* preview these domestic markets and include pictures of new items being featured for sale. You'll learn more about trade shows in Chapter 14.

Field Trips

"When you think about mannequins as tools, each is as expensive as a digital camera. Why wouldn't you thoroughly research an investment like that?"

Anne Kong, Fashion Institute of Technology Display and Exhibit Design Department.

Students in resource-rich market centers like New York and Los Angeles can visit mannequin showrooms during seasonal markets to learn mannequin resourcing from the ground up. Anne Kong, Display and Exhibit Design department chair and instructor at Manhattan's Fashion Institute of Technology (FIT), occasionally takes her students behind the scenes as well, to mannequin manufacturers' design and production areas. If your program conducts field trips to market centers, you could ask that a similar tour be added to the trip itinerary. It's an important learning step.

Even if your present store doesn't use mannequins, your next employer may, and then you'll need to know about them. As a display manager or director, you will at least have to compare the value of mannequins to the effectiveness of mannequin alternatives. As a display practitioner, you will have to know how to choose mannequins and how and when and where to use them. As is true of any major purchase—for yourself or an employer—it's wise to do extensive research and comparison shopping before you buy.

Choosing and Buying Mannequins

Mannequin Trends

Before mannequin buyers commit significant amounts of money, from $700 to $1200 per figure, it is important for them to study the trends affecting the marketplace. Granted, they've already done a lot of homework by sourcing. They know what's available in the marketplace. Their next questions must be: *How long will these mannequins be fashionable? How long will these mannequins communicate our image and fashion message to our customers?* In trend-driven marketing, visual merchandisers must anticipate trends and respond to demand. No retail division can afford to tie up resources in tools that fail to produce results. The mannequin market is no exception.

An increasing reliance on abstract forms reflects far more than a fashion trend, according to one mannequin manufacturer. Ralph Pucci, president of Pucci International, a premier supplier of mannequins for fashion figures as well as museums and exhibits, sees the adoption of abstract mannequins as a business trend. "I think realistic mannequins are becoming dinosaurs, even when they are very well done. When you consider the frenetic pace of trend retailing and look at the practicalities of mannequin upkeep—current hair and makeup styling—more retailers are beginning to opt for the fresher characteristics offered by abstracts. They can be more reflective of the times and evoke important feelings and spirits without being too specific."

He points out that it has been nearly a decade since his firm produced a realistic mannequin collection in the image of a specific fashion model or celebrity. "If realistic mannequins can be done with a truly unique slant, they're great to do, but I feel that trying to duplicate someone without capturing the individual's 'essence' is a mistake."

Pucci now prefers to create figures and forms that are both a reaction to and a reflection of the moment—the art, music, and architecture that influence people's lives. As a result, he enlists designers from those realms to reinvent the mannequin. This strategy is evident in a collection by architect Patrick Naggar that has female torsos, vaselike bottoms, and metallic and earth-toned finishes.

Illustrator Ruben Toledo's "shapes" collection in petite, plus-sizes, and tall female forms have the artist's trademark tiny hands and feet on bodies that are full-blown in tribute to voluptuous femininity no matter the garment size. "The larger sizes were amazingly successful," Pucci says, "We took a chance because we believed that size range doesn't limit anything, including being attuned to art, fine dining, good music—things that everyone enjoys. Shoppers responded very positively to seeing mannequins in their sizing, but even more, they appreciated the art Toledo brought to the project."

Pucci's "yoga" mannequin collection, first introduced in 2002 and modeled after Christy Turlington, and the Robert Clyde Anderson collection designed exclusively for Marshall Field's in 2003 illustrate the broad range of mannequins available from this very innovative mannequin designer-manufacturer. (See Figures 13.3A and 13.3B.)

303

A Yoga mannequins, designed in the likeness of Christy Turlington, at Marshall Field's, Chicago.

B An exclusive series of mannequins for Marshall Field's by Robert Clyde Anderson.

Figure 13.3 Two very different styles of abstract mannequins from Ralph Pucci, New York City.

Designing and Manufacturing Mannequins

As the mannequin industry is reaching out to other art forms for its design work, it is spending more time on conceptualizing—thinking out of the box—to capture the flavor and pace of the era.

Ralph Pucci describes the manufacture of a mannequin as a process that begins with imaginative ideas from those new resources. "From the conceptual directions, we work in-house with artists and models to sculpt a miniature prototype. If that seems promising, we move ahead to full-size bodies, creating molds, fabricating bodies in fiberglass and heads in plaster."

Although mannequins are created in a series of poses or collections—groupings of mannequins that appear to be related by styling, gender, age grouping, size, ethnicity, positioning, or other characteristic—they can be used singly, in pairs, or groups. The overriding trend is storytelling.

Pucci's "brownstone" collection is a story in itself: "We had discovered the magazine illustrations of Robert Clyde Anderson and were struck by his style—the way his characters had an aristocratic, sort of 'uptown' feel to them. We began to call them 'the brownstone people,' because they looked like people you'd see on a city street in a typical residential area of brownstone buildings, and, as we fleshed out the concept, we began to tell a story."

The company commissioned Anderson to create a collection of figures that would evoke six such individuals. One of the company's goals was portrayal of age and ethnic diversity that would widen the collection's ability to communicate with more shoppers. The characters took on special individual identities. "One was a [white] 'wanna-be' actress; another was an African-American woman. We also wanted to have an older couple and wound up with a woman in her sixties, very chic and modern, who was probably an art gallery owner. Her companion, a man we call Hamilton, is a former Ivy Leaguer, in very good shape—he probably plays handball—and he works in the financial world."

Before the new figures were launched in Pucci's Manhattan showrooms and photographed for promotional catalogs, they were dressed by fashion designer William Calvert and positioned interactively before a brownstone streetscape mural done by Robert Clyde Anderson. All that remained was an opportunity for the brownstone characters to silently tell their stories to mannequin buyers. (See Figure 13.4.)

Each mannequin's posture, makeup, hairstyling, facial expression, height, weight, stance (position), and so on are designed to send out attitudinal "messages" that the store hopes will be perceived and received by the targeted shopper. Some mannequins are purely fashion mannequins and are meant to represent a sort of chic but neutral "everywoman" persona that will speak to the average shopper with a particular self-image and level of fashion awareness.

Some mannequins make very strong statements reflecting currently popular lifestyle trends, and they project "attitude" to match. One immediately thinks of "counterculture" or youth culture trends that have influenced clothing for an entire age group, like "grunge" fashions. (See Figure 13.5.)

Many stores choose a "signature mannequin" that will appear in every window and in every in-store editorial. One such signature collection was Dayton Hudson's Workday Casual series commissioned from Pucci in 1994 by Andrew Markopoulos for the company's department stores. Ralph Pucci said, "They selected one mannequin style to represent their

Figure 13.4 Pucci International's "Brownstone People" are city-smart and fashion-savvy.

Figure 13.5 Alu's contemporary mannequin collection projects a specific attitude.

merchandise throughout their stores, from one department to the next. They took a stand on their image, a look that describes what they're all about, and they acted on it. When they commissioned us to do their Workday Casual rollout, they went all the way with more than a thousand mannequins for their stores. Where they couldn't place mannequins, we created busts and cutouts for shelves and ledges that restated the workday theme. If shoppers didn't 'get it,' they simply weren't going to at all." (See Figure 13.6.)

Matching Mannequins to Images

Deciding on a series of mannequins—essentially, hiring your store's silent sales force—is as important as hiring the right individuals for a selling staff. Both ought to *look* like your store's image, represent your product lines appealingly and effectively, and both need to *sell merchandise*. The decision process involves establishing some criteria for mannequin selection, and that can be accomplished by matching the right mannequin to store image and/or current trends.

Interpreting Store Brand Image

Store brand image is the visual merchandiser's first criterion for mannequin selection since many fashion stores believe they have developed niche positions and do not offer "flavor-of-the-week" fashion innovations to their clientele. If they're committed to classic fashions or a client lifestyle, some retailers may prefer the more abstract, more neutral display figures that can carry fashion without locking into a distinct mannequin persona or fashion statement.

Figure 13.6 Ralph Pucci's Workday Causal mannequin collection was designed exclusively for Dayton Hudson's department store division.

A store that responds more quickly to contemporary fashion trends may think that it can be chameleonlike, poised to become whatever its customers want it to be. In that case, it will embrace mannequin stylings more in keeping with recent fashion directions, lifestyle trends, and current social attitudes—even if it means changing mannequin styles more frequently to keep pace.

Large department stores frequently own multiple series of mannequins that portray the variety of fashion images necessary to serve the multiple market segments that make up their customer base. With more room and larger budgets, they also have the luxury of choice. They can use one series or another to match the form and function of the merchandise to be shown.

A department store might own hundreds of mannequins, for example, a series of elegant mannequins, a series of active mannequins, a collection of juniors, misses, men, children, infants, and special sizes (tall, petite, and plus-sizes). It might also have both realistic-looking and abstract (stylized) mannequins in its collection. Since every display begins with products, it simply has to decide which mannequins will show them the best advantage. Smaller stores (with smaller visual merchandising budgets, fewer windows, and less floor space) may have fewer mannequins to choose from, have to use them longer, and do more with them, so they must be extremely selective as they plan purchases.

Interpreting Merchandise Image

Since merchandise is *always* the focus of an editorial presentation, choosing an appropriate mannequin or a series for a particular display is critical to its success as a selling vehicle.

Determining "the Look"

When you have your store's identity clearly in mind, do you see yourself using realistic mannequins, action-posed abstract forms, or custom-designed mannequins that look like a popular model? Mannequins are manufactured of fiberglass, resin, foam, metal, wood, glass, fabric, or cardboard. Many full-figure mannequin bodies are frequently molded of fiberglass layered with resin-reinforced plaster "skin." Realistic mannequin heads are molded, then sculpted in plaster and painted before hand-painted finishing makeup is added to reflect a current fashion look. Abstract heads are detailed (or not) to match their design specifications.

Recently, translucent and transparent abstract mannequins have been fabricated out of space-age plastics. Such is the pace of change in visual merchandising.

Today's realistic mannequin heads are mostly topped with stylable wigs of the same synthetics used for human wigs retailed in stores and salons. Permanently styled vinyl "hard" wigs (once secured with bank pins in cork inserts in mannequin skulls) are practically a thing of the past unless a very definite or very complicated hairstyle is integral to a realistic figure's fashion image.

Abstract mannequins, not dependent on realism, are frequently smooth-headed creatures with minimal facial detail. Some abstract models may have molded hairstyles that can be modified with plug-in ponytails, chignons, or other add-ons for variety's sake, and others may sprout wigs of rope, yarn, raffia, wood shavings, or something yet to be devised, as part of their unique designs. Let's look at what's available today.

Realistic Mannequins   Realistic mannequins replicate human anatomy and facial features and may be modeled to portray any age, size, ethnicity, or attitude. A collection usually contains several head styles that can be mounted on a variety of standard body poses. Buyers may also specify anything from upright to seated to reclining and any number of action poses—in full stride, with legs apart to straddle a backward-facing chair, or with a raised, bent leg suitable for posing with one foot on a cube or chair, for example.

Hair styles and makeup are generally contemporary, but special collections may be quite avant-garde portraying counterculture or other unorthodox fashion looks. High fashion (haute couture) mannequins frequently mirror makeup and hairstyles popular on designer catwalks worldwide, some of them more extreme than "normal-for-streetwear." In fact, some buyers term them semirealistic or stylized. This is especially true if the mannequin has all human features except colorful makeup or natural skin tones. The more extreme or fadlike hair, makeup, posture, and "attitude" are, the shorter the lifespan for the mannequin. (See Figure 13.7.)

Abstract Mannequins   Not particularly true to human anatomy in an everyday sense, these figures are about impact and effect. They will have a normal torso to carry fashion garments, but facial features, arms, and legs may be elongated or otherwise exaggerated, and sometimes heads or arms are absent altogether. You'll find them in any color or finish that's appropriate to store décor and image. If these fashion statements fit your store's image, they may have greater longevity than realistic forms, particularly if they create a signature look for your store. (See Figure 13.8.)

Soft-Sculpture Mannequins   Soft-sculpture mannequins are covered with fabric or leather rather than paint and frequently have little facial detail. Some are serious, formally posed figures; some are purely novelty figures designed to communicate a decidedly informal mood. Soft sculptures may portray either gender or any age group although children's

Figure 13.7 Realistic mannequins designed and manufactured by Patina-V, City of Industry, California.

forms are probably the most popular. Built over a flexible wire infrastructure to keep their foam-padded extremities in place once posed, these figures can be positioned almost anywhere a retailer needs them—atop a fixture, on a ledge, or flying through the air like trapeze artists. They may be very obvious in bright colors or dazzling white coverings, or they may seem to disappear into scenes made in colors that match backdrops. Again, as long as they fit a store's image, these are less expensive mannequins with indefinite life spans. (See Figure 13.9.)

Figure 13.8 Abstract mannequins designed and manufactured by Patina-V.

309

Figure 13.9 Soft sculpture mannequins designed and manufactured by True Visual, San Francisco.

Puppet Cutouts   Puppet cutouts can be fabricated of corrugated cardboard, Fomecore, plywood, plexi, metal, or any other stiff material and articulated with bolts and wingnuts or other hardware fasteners to create entertaining, informal two-dimensional action figures. Toylike in appearance, they adapt well to children's fashion and merchandising. They can be purchased, commissioned, customized, or built in your own prop shop. Versatile and novel alternatives to three-dimensional mannequins, these are not for every store image but, for the budget-conscious, they can brand the store as well as entertain.

Animated Mannequins   Some day animated mannequins may come to fashion windows. That's a prediction, not a reality. The Santa's elves and Easter bunnies that fill major retailer's windows every holiday are animated *figures*, not mannequins.

Animated mannequins wear merchandise for active lifestyles, and the technology to set them in motion has emerged. One new sports-oriented line, Animated Cyberquins from Europe, can mimic slow-motion human activity—walking, sprinting, or cycling—in a store window or on a selling floor. These high-technology figures may eventually find homes in sporting goods store interiors and other retail stores. You may see one novel application of this concept strolling midair in Old Navy stores.

Mannequin Alternatives

In Chapter 5, you read about mannequin alternatives designed specifically for wall system merchandising. The alternatives described here are designed for selling floor use, on or near fixtures. Alternatives may be simple and very utilitarian, or they may be more elaborate, in designs that reinforce other aspects of store fixturing and décor. Mannequin alternatives are economical for four reasons:

1. You can focus shopper attention on merchandise fashioned for specific parts of the body without having to dress the rest of a form.

2. You do not have to pay for an entire mannequin in order to have a dimensional display.

3. You can place alternatives in display areas and strategic spaces that cannot accommodate a full figure.

4. You add brand identity and visual interest for shoppers at minimal cost.

Hosiery Forms

Hosiery forms may be right-side up or upside-down; they may be one-, two-, or three-dimensional in design (flat, half-round, and fully round). To show fashion from the toes up, there are

"We focus on creating *systems* of body forms rather than whole-body mannequins in order to offer clients more flexibility and economy with each of our form designs. With a system of alternatives depicting various sections of anatomy—separate but visually coordinated torsos and leg forms, for instance—that can be combined or reconfigured to fit the merchandising goal, retailers are able to maintain a strong look without limits on the ways they may be used."

Erwin Winkler, past president, Alu.

- Shoe and foot forms
- Sock forms
- Knee-high forms
- Stocking leg forms
- Pantyhose forms

Innerwear Forms

Fashion is not limited to outer garments. Underwear and intimate apparel mannequin alternatives are available in varying sizes and skin tones, fabrications and finishes, for both genders and all ages. (See Figure 13.10.) You will find

- Brief and boxer forms
- Panty forms
- Corset forms
- Lingerie forms
- Swimwear forms
- Bra forms

Ready-to-Wear Forms

To accommodate layering and accessorization for ready-to-wear, these alternatives are designed for both genders and all ages. They may be mounted on flat bases for table- and fixture-top presentations or on bases and pedestals for floor display. You could purchase

- Shirt forms
- Blouse forms
- Bust forms
- Swimwear forms
- Suit forms

Figure 13.10   Forms designed and manufactured by Seven Continents, Toronto, Ontario, Canada.

Dressing a standard men's shirt form is one of the more challenging tasks of a visual merchandiser. Jeff Spizale is a store planner, fixture designer, and manufacturer, and principal of Duffy Creative, Inc., in Minneapolis, Minnesota. He grew up as one-fifth of a father-son team of visual merchandisers, respected in the Minneapolis-St. Paul metropolitan area as expert menswear visual practitioners. Here, he offers step-by-step instructions for basic dress shirt or sport shirt "rigging."

1. Select a shirt with a standard 16-inch neck size. (All menswear bust forms are standardized to measure 16 inches at the neck, 42 inches at the chest, and 36 inches at the waist.) The fabric-covered form is padded so that you may push common straight pins into it, anchoring the shirt to its contours. Some shirts are meant to fit more loosely than others. Ask the department buyers or an experienced associate about the ideal fit before you begin.

2. This is the most important step—properly press the garment. For a dress shirt, reverse the collar and iron this portion on the underside (underpress) so there will be no wrinkles pressed into the collar's front. Repeat with the cuffs; press the body of the shirt and the sleeves last. Wrinkles are never an option.

3. Slip the shirt over the torso form so that the shirt buttons form a vertical line. To hold everything in place, push a common pin near the collar's top button and then pull the front of the shirt taut, placing a pin near the bottom buttonhole. Now the shirt is securely anchored to the form and the placket lies straight.

4. At this point, smooth the shirt front toward the side seams, placing pins through the side seams at the armpit and waist to lock the shirt in place and minimize any slack fabric. You should now have a smooth shirtfront that reveals the body contours of the form underneath. Whenever you pin into fabric, work in the seams or double the fabric over itself. Then, if a sales associate tries to remove the garment from the form, there will be less chance of damaging the fabric. A well-rigged form should have only ten to twelve pins in the total presentation.

5. Forming the sleeve attractively is the next step. Take four sheets of white wrapping tissue and form two cylinders of the same general shape and size as the shirtsleeve and slide them gently into the sleeves of the shirt. Then, insert a Styrofoam coffee cup (upside down) into the cuff of each sleeve. This gives the cuffs shape and keeps the tissue in place. The stuffed sleeves can simply hang naturally, or you could bend one sleeve at the elbow and pin the cuff to the side of the form with the shirttail draped over the cuff—a technique that mimics a person with his hand in his pocket—in a casual pose. The style and fabrication of the garment will determine whether the shirt's presentation should be formal or casual.

6. In this last step, you may add a necktie or drape a sweater, coat, briefcase, book bag, or other accessories that seem appropriate to the look you're after. These items help complete your display, adding colors and textures. Accessorizing builds multiple sales.

A Retail Reality:
Jeff Spizale urges visual merchandisers to "follow the logic of the garment." He says that a formal oxford cloth dress shirt should look crisp and "squared-away," while softer, more casual garments ought to call attention to luxurious fabrics and textures with less formal rigging.

Lead time is the amount of time it takes to complete products from receipt of order to production.

Purchasing Mannequins

Once you've decided on a mannequin style or collection, you must think about **lead time.** You won't be able to order one day and receive your shipment the next week. Ordering mannequins from stock rather than having them custom-made requires less lead time, but even then more and more manufacturers are producing "to order" rather than maintaining large inventories waiting to be sold. It's not unusual to wait as long as 16 weeks for a mannequin shipment to arrive on your loading dock. Custom orders, especially commissioning a design for a mannequin that will belong solely to your company or have an unusual finish, may take even longer because of the design and approval phases that precede other production steps.

Receiving and Unpacking Mannequins

Mannequin support rods are bent at specific angles to support the mannequin properly. When you unpack a new mannequin, use a sharp permanent marking pen to indicate the support rod's *back* side and its *bottom end.* If you don't do this immediately, the figure may be damaged in setup. In any event, you will not be the only person handling it in the future, so this is an important step toward protecting the store's investment as well as ensuring safety for the mannequin, you, and your customers.

Each torso section plus any removable parts should also have an identifying number or symbol already marked on both locking plates so you can reassemble parts correctly when you're dressing multiple figures. If not, do so yourself. Label hands right and left as well.

Sometimes brand-new mannequin joints fit rather snugly. To make it easier to position arms and fit the male-female connectors more easily, you can swipe the connecting plates and connectors with an absorbent cloth lightly sprayed with a lubricant like WD-40. Spraying the joint and plates is not advisable because of potential damage from oversprays and drips that will damage the mannequin's expensive finish.

Learning Sizes of Mannequins

You already know that a mannequin has to fit a store's image. It is equally important that it fit the store's apparel. While mannequins are designed to meet more or less standard sizing specifications across the garment industry, they are not all created equally.

For example, the catalog description of the "Prismatic Profiles" collection from Decter will tell you that these abstract forms wear garment size 6/8 (some of the more active poses may require the larger size) and shoe size 6½ B with a 2½-inch heel height. Standing 5 feet 11 inches tall, the mannequins average 62 inches high at the shoulder; and they measure 33–24–33.

Having learned that, however, you cannot assume that all Decter mannequins follow suit. In fact, Decter's "W25th St. Girls" are 5 feet 11 inches tall but their shoe size is 8½ B and heel height can be 2½ or 3½ inches, depending on your specifications. W25s wear size 8 garments and measure 34–24–34 with a 62-inch average shoulder height.

Then contrast Decter's two types of "missy" figures, with their half-size series wearing garment size 18/20 and measurements of 44½–34–44½ at 5 feet 10 inches tall, and you can see that mannequins can be as individual as real people.

Trial and error wastes time when you've steamed and prepared garments for mannequins only to find they don't fit well, so this aspect of mannequin dressing is an important one to master. With practice, you'll learn each mannequin's unique fit requirements. You may want to write the sizes on the mannequins waist or hip plates as a reminder of each figure's garment size.

Selecting Garments for Mannequins

Here are some suggestions to help you in selecting garments for mannequins:

1. Choose garments for a single end use, by fabrication, style, and then color for each grouping of mannequins you plan to use. Example: A group of mannequins wearing garden party prints in bright cottons or a group of mannequins in pastel cashmere holiday sweaters. Choose garments that make just one statement. Fashion impact comes from repetition and congruity. You'd never want to confuse shoppers with mixed messages in a single display. Instead, *underscore* each statement with a *strong* presentation, endorsing that specific end use.

2. Choose items that are stocked in quantity, so that the mannequin will not have to be redressed immediately. If an item is already selling down without your help, it's time to move on to the department's incoming merchandise.

3. Select the proper size of garment.

4. Write down the sizes of all the garments and accessories you will be using and post it for the sales staff. Most stores operate with a duplicate copy sign-out book that accounts for any merchandise you're taking off the selling floor for use in the windows. One copy is placed in a secure location in the window with the merchandise. The other copy stays in the department—usually at the wrap desk so that sales associates can easily refer to the list when a customer is waiting for information. The sign-out book is an important security safeguard for both you and the store.

5. Repeat the colors in the garments with appropriate accessories for a tied-together, coordinated look. Choose accessories to clothe the mannequin from head to toe. Think of this task as dressing a live model for a fashion show or photo. Effective presentation of earrings, watches, hats, handbags, briefcases, day planners, hosiery, shoes—even eyewear—can teach shoppers how to accessorize fashionably and trigger additional purchases for the store. At the same time, you must practice restraint. Accessorize the mannequin according to your store's seasonal fashion message or follow trend directions you see in current media. Eventually, you'll develop a feel for an appropriate level of accessorization for your store's fashion image.

Dressing Mannequins

Most stores have a protocol for mannequin dressing that says when and where this will be done. Some stores require mannequins to be dressed and undressed away from the selling floor or that the work is completed before or after store hours. Many stores cover their windows so that passersby don't see mannequins undressed or even partially assembled. These safety concerns and aesthetic concerns are more important to some retailers than others. Be sure that you understand your store's mannequin policies before you dress one for the first time.

Preparation makes this task easier. Here are some general guidelines related to necessary housekeeping, record keeping, and safety practices:

- Wash your hands before handling mannequins or garments. Oils and dirt from your hands can damage the value of both.

- All merchandise must be steamed or pressed.

- Remove any price tickets and extra buttons that cannot be tucked out of sight and reposition them with a ticket gun to the inside of the garment's fabric label, *not* to the garment.

- String tags for jewelry must be removed and stored in an envelope along with a description of the item. Earring cards must also be saved along with a brief descriptor for reticketing and return to the department. If earring backs do not fit the mannequins ear, place them in the envelope with the card. Staple the envelope to the sign-out sheet corresponding to the merchandise.

- Sticky labels that can't be hidden by turning them away from view can be peeled off and placed on a piece of waxed paper along with a brief description of the item. Save the SKU number so the item can be reticketed if necessary.

- Before you start dressing your mannequin, choose a place to work that keeps walkways clear and safe for shopper traffic.

After these important preliminaries—work space cleared and all materials assembled—follow this step-by-step dressing procedure:

1. Remove mannequin arms, hands, torso, and wig. Place them in a cart, rather than on the floor, as a safety precaution. Remove the legs from the base and slip on pantyhose, thigh-high stockings, socks, or anklets, if the mannequin is a realistic version. (See Figure 13.11.)

2. Slip pants on the form. Skirts are not put on until step 5.

A Retail Reality:
Thigh highs are less prone to runs since the base rod doesn't have to puncture the pantyhose brief. However, their elastic edging cannot show through garments or create distracting lines, or you'll have to switch to pantyhose. Another drawback to thigh-high hosiery is that it doesn't come in a complete selection of current fashion colors.

314

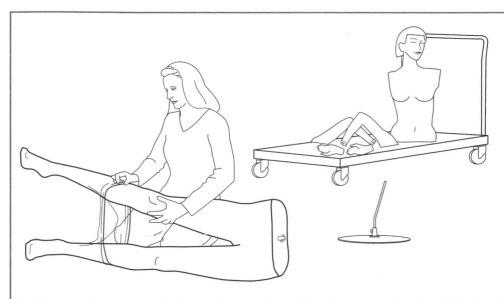

Figure 13.11 Pantyhose and slacks may be easily pulled onto a mannequin's legs while you are seated on the floor.

3. If the mannequin is going to stand on its base, you have two options for placing the mannequin back onto it without slitting the back seam. (See Figures 13.12 and 13.13.)

    Option 1: If the pant leg and hem or cuff are wide enough to accommodate the space between the leg and rod, you may simply lift the mannequin up and settle it onto the rod at the square fitting in the mannequin's butt. Then tighten the set screw connecting mannequin to the rod. Some mannequin dressers work in pairs to do this step and may also fit the shoes onto the form at the same time they stand the form back on the base.

    Option 2: Remove the rod from the mannequin *and* the base. Then fit the rod back down the leg after the mannequin is back on its feet. Tighten the set screw at the butt and then tighten the screw into the base plate.

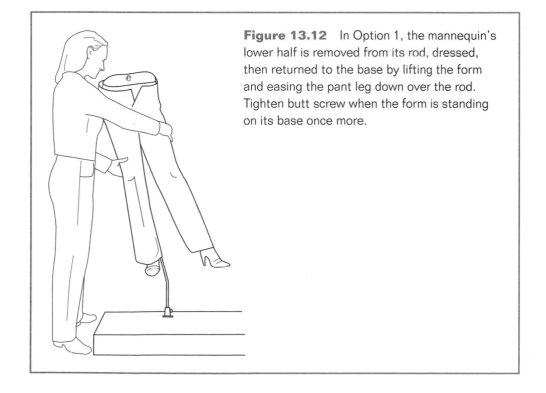

Figure 13.12 In Option 1, the mannequin's lower half is removed from its rod, dressed, then returned to the base by lifting the form and easing the pant leg down over the rod. Tighten butt screw when the form is standing on its base once more.

315

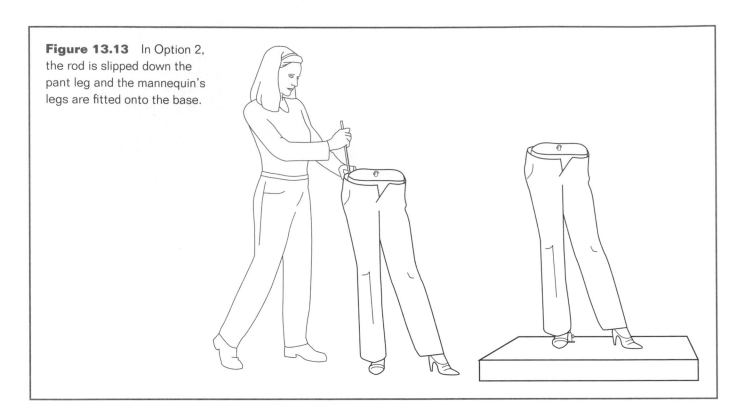

Figure 13.13 In Option 2, the rod is slipped down the pant leg and the mannequin's legs are fitted onto the base.

If you're using a standing or striding mannequin, the pant leg may not hang properly with the rod in place. (Figure 13.14.) If the pant leg is pulled taut by the rod, don't use that pant. Or you can carefully slit the back seam and insert the rod through the opening.

Action figures and mannequins with longer strides generally have one bent leg that must be removed for dressing and undressing. Treated like an arm, it is inserted through the waistband *before* the straight leg attached to the hip section has been inserted. Holding the bent leg and pant in one hand and balancing the inverted form between your feet, you'll slide the empty pant leg over the straight leg's foot. As the pant slides nearer the hip section, you'll be able to snap or lock the bent leg in place. This task is easier for two people to accomplish.

Because of all this maneuvering, you may decide to select a larger size than the mannequin usually wears and pin any excess fabric away after the garment is on the figure. There is no simple way to describe this procedure, you'll simply have to do some hands-on experimenting until you know the mannequin well.

4. Slip on the mannequin's shoes. Be sure that the shoe you've chosen has the proper heel height. Measure the mannequin as shown in Figure 13.15. If the heels are too low, the mannequin will tip backward; too high, it will tip forward.

   Be sure that the shoe is properly fitted to the mannequin's foot. Shoes with gaping sides or shoes that slip off the figure's heel are never acceptable because customers won't buy or wear shoes that look as if they will fit poorly. Ill-fitting shoes left on mannequin's feet for long periods of time in hot windows tend to form in position, causing damage that makes the shoes unsalable.

5. Slip a skirt over the waist or hip, but do not zip or button.

6. Twist torso back onto waist or hip section. (See Figure 13.16.)

7. Slip front- or back-closure tops onto mannequin (pullovers must slip over a wigless head) torso and leave garment open to accept arms (with hands removed) in the next step. If you are layering tops (i.e., a turtleneck under a sweater, or a blouse under a jacket), slip the sleeves together so that you can insert the arms, wrist first,

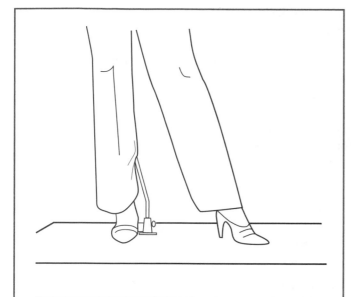

Figure 13.14 This pant, is too narrow for the rod to be fitted through and, the pant is pulled taut in an unnatural manner.

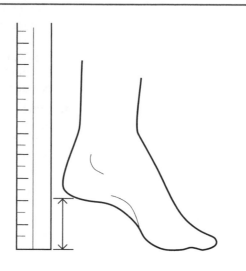

Figure 13.15 The heels of shoes must be the correct height to ensure that the mannequin will stand properly and safely. Measure the space between heel and floor and write it on the bottom of the mannequin's foot for future reference.

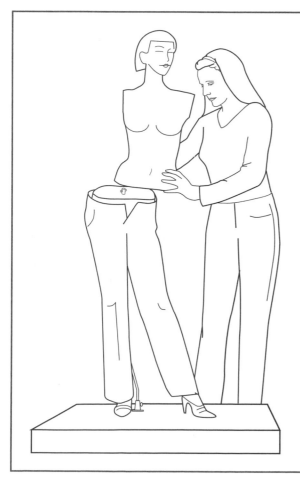

Figure 13.16 Grasp the mannequin torso firmly when fitting it back onto the hips. Slide it over the hips until the peg on the bottom of the torso slips into the hip fitting. Twist it until it locks in place.

through the neck opening into both sleeve layers at once. Guide the arm to the locking plate and gently slip it into place. (See Figure 13.17.)

Use care when layering garments so that you don't create more bulk between the mannequin's arm and torso than it is meant to accept. The clothes will look bunched-up, and the stress on the mannequin's arm joint will eventually loosen and damage the arm locking plate.

8. Button top garments and tuck them into waistband. Adjust to create a smooth and natural "blousing" of fabric at the waistline if that's part of the fashion look. Be sure that all buttons are buttoned and all zippers are zipped. Add belt if appropriate. Tug on sleeves and hems to smooth the fit.

Check that hosiery doesn't "ghost" through outer garments. Gaps and misfit areas of a window mannequin's costume may be pinned discreetly. Your goal is to smooth the lines, not remanufacture the garment. Pinning isn't done on the selling floor mannequins because shoppers may be handling the garments. If the garment is the correct size for the mannequin, pinning will not be necessary.

9. Replace brushed and styled wig. Be sure the hairline fit is natural.

10. Accessorize neck and ears. Mannequins have pierced ears, but some models are too rigid or their ears are set too close to the head to accept French wires and some hoops without bending them badly out of shape. Posts aren't always long enough to accept their backs. Clips generally do not stay on at all. Tacky gum (the kind used to hang posters) will hold pierced and clip earrings in place. If you can't hook the French wires or hoops correctly, avoid them for that particular mannequin. You'll soon learn which figures can wear certain accessories.

Figure 13.17 Carefully slip the mannequin arm through the garment stretching the garment's fabric as little as possible. Slide the arm over the locking plate until it slips into place; then adjust the arm to a natural position.

Figure 13.18 Adjust mannequin arms and hands into natural positions, as shown in the correct example. In the incorrect example, one hand is backwards, and one arm is pulled forward so that the hand is suspended in the air.

CORRECT   INCORRECT

11. Adjust hands and arms to natural positions. Add any handbags or bracelets before twisting hands into place at the wrist joints. To make the handbag seem more a natural part of the mannequin's costume, it should be tucked under an arm or held by the mannequin in the same way that a model might carry it on a fashion show runway. (See Figure 13.18.)

12. When the mannequin is in place and properly lit, step away (outside if this is a window mannequin) and check the figure from head to toe. Make any necessary adjustments. All mannequin bases, risers, and window floors or pedestals must be dust free.

Safety Concern:

In-store mannequins placed on pedestals or riser platforms must be removed from their safety glass or metal bases and bolted directly to the units where they'll stand. This prevents them from being bumped or tipped accidentally by curious shoppers.

Maintaining Mannequins

Mannequins are among your store's most visible fashion fixtures. They are also among the most frequently handled. The fact that they attract attention is good, but the fact that they may be disturbed by customer handling is not—unless you maintain their appearance and grooming daily.

Watch for

● Exposed price tags

● Improperly positioned wigs, hands, and accessories

● Missing accessories or items of clothing

● Substitutions (resulting from sale of the original garment)

- Shopworn garments
- Dirty-looking "skin"
- Hosiery with runs or sagging wrinkles
- Dusty risers
- Trash on the riser or in the area of the display

Scheduling Changes

Shoppers should never have to search out selling stock for merchandise that they've seen on editorial mannequins. Since editorial mannequins should always be positioned with adjacent two-way or four-way selling fixtures with stock of the displayed garments, sell-down will often dictate your schedule for changes.

Other retail practices also require the visual department to change the store's mannequins frequently:

- Management's expectation that regular weekly shoppers will see something new each time they come to the store.
- Strategies that schedule quick, significant markdowns to keep stock turning through a department.
- Aggressive weekly advertising schedules that include backup floor displays in key editorial positions.
- Transfer and consolidation of groupings to facilitate sell-through.

Positioning and Propping Mannequins

A Retail Reality:
Place departmental two- and four-way fixtures hold in the selling stock next to fashion mannequins on editorial platforms. Customers want to take a closer look at garments in their sizes immediately after they see them in eye-catching displays. Don't make them search through an entire department for the garments you have featured.

Positioning mannequins with props in a triangular shape is more effective than positioning them in a straight line. If you look at Figure 13.19, you'll see a mannequin grouping in a triangular format that creates a three-dimensional presentation with more depth and greater visual interest than would have been accomplished if the mannequins were all at the same height.

The triangle is also a useful way to analyze the positioning of fixtures, props, and mannequins arranged on a floor or platform. Used as you see illustrated in Figure 13.20, the triangle forces mannequin and prop into better optical balance with the prop and sign relating more closely to the form after repositioning.

Probably the most important thing to realize is that grouped mannequins, frequently used in odd-multiples (3 or 5), must relate to each other in theme, in color story, *and* in physical proximity. The group must also relate to the props selected in exactly the same ways. They should all touch somewhere—either physically or *optically*. The correct view in Figure 13.20 shows an optical relationship. The potted plant isn't really touching the mannequin; she is positioned behind it. But the two elements appear to touch; lending depth and texture to the composition, causing it to feel "tight," or closely related.

If you use two mannequins in an editorial platform grouping, a single larger prop will probably be all that the space can carry. Try to work in odd numbers if you can, because they are more pleasing to the eye.

Mannequin positioning, with or without props, can tell stories and set tone. Multiple window mannequins can be positioned so that one is standing alone while the others are positioned in a conversational grouping—causing viewers to wonder what's going on.

Mannequin positioning can also focus attention precisely where you want it. Imagine mannequins lined up in military file diagonally across a window floor, all wearing purple garments, except for one mannequin dressed in brilliant red. A dramatic presentation with a point of emphasis is created without the use of a single prop.

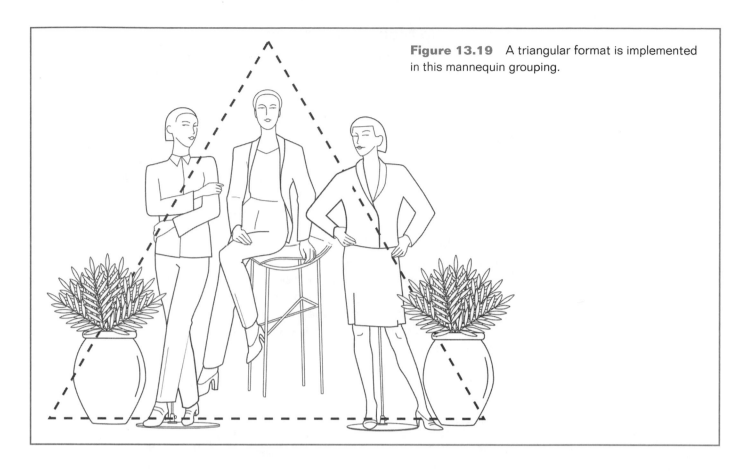

Figure 13.19 A triangular format is implemented in this mannequin grouping.

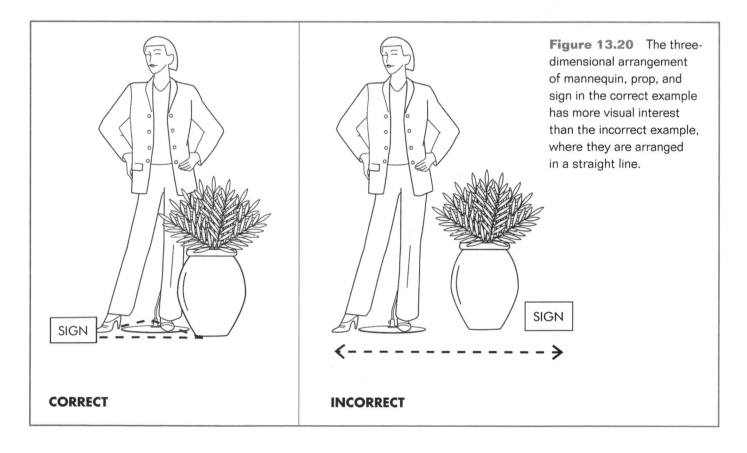

Figure 13.20 The three-dimensional arrangement of mannequin, prop, and sign in the correct example has more visual interest than the incorrect example, where they are arranged in a straight line.

CORRECT

INCORRECT

SIGN

SIGN

Maintaining Mannequin Image

In an industry that has as much visual change as fashion retailing, mannequins are going to become outdated after a time and will have to be replaced. Expensive as they are, mannequins are still the best way to help customers visualize garments. Sometimes you can update a mannequin series with new wigs and prolong the inevitable need to update.

Cycling

Some retailers cycle their mannequins, saving their newest, trend-right figures for prime window presentations and rotating last season's mannequins into the store for interior editorial and departmental use. Finally, outdated mannequins are either sold, sent to the mannequin factory for refurbishing, donated to a school or a thrift store, or discarded.

Refurbishing

Mannequins don't always age gracefully, and some are accident-prone. This gives rise to an important visual merchandising support system that can extend or restore a mannequin's usefulness—"remanufacturing," as Ruben Esparza calls it. His Ontario, California, business provides mannequin services for retailers and for photo production and movie studios. The company has even created celebrity look-alikes to stand—not in the windows—but *outside* Las Vegas casinos.

Ruben's technicians also make emergency "house calls" to repair mannequins that have fallen or broken before department store openings and top-management walk-throughs.

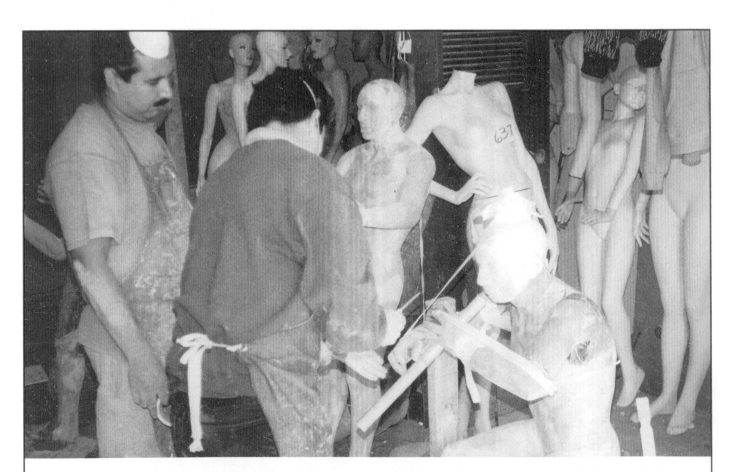

Figure 13.21 Repairs and cosmetic updates by professionals like Ruben Esparza's skilled refurbishers can extend the useful life of a mannequin.

They have also visited movie and commercial sets to makeup mannequins used for special effects and as stand-ins for movie "extras"—pointing up several additional career possibilities in the field, both for you and for "retired" mannequins.

Speaking about his mannequin "clients," Esparza says: "Some have old and garish makeup; the paint can be old, outdated, or chipped. Others are missing fingers or limbs. The head may have a hole in it, or worse yet, it might be missing altogether!" (See Figure 13.21.)

Repairs begin with reinforcement of cracks and replacement of missing or severely damaged parts. "The task that proves most difficult," says Esparza, "is replacing limbs or heads. They must be positioned to conform to the existing muscle structure and posed to give a natural appearance."

The next phase of the refurbishing process involves sanding and sculpting, followed by a coat of primer and at least two coats of paint to which are added a formula that increases scratch resistance. A portrait artist applies fresh makeup. Oil paint is the medium of choice for its durability and lasting qualities. If an update is part of the order, a new wig may complete the makeover.

Shoptalk

Innovation Grows a Business
By Ralph Pucci, president, Pucci International, Inc.

In spite of differences in generation and location, I think that you, the reader, and I probably have much in common. When I started my career in this industry, it was with an established company that had an interesting history, rich traditions, and exacting quality standards. It was a business dedicated to serving its customers beyond their expectations.

I started out in my family's business, and you may be starting out in one that belongs to someone else's family. As I once did, you may feel alternately challenged and hemmed in by the company's traditions and standards. But at the heart of it, you'll probably end up doing those things that best serve your company's mission and its customers, just as I did.

I helped grow the business I'm in today. From exclusively doing mannequin repair in the 1950s, we turned to mannequin design and manufacture in 1976 when it was my turn to lead the firm. We set ourselves apart by anticipating trends and doing things that differentiated Pucci from its competitors.

First, we took a rather innovative approach and let our mannequins recline and relax on the job. Then we painted them brilliant colors. Having done all that, it was necessary to keep our vision fresh in other (and sometimes surprising) ways. I came to believe that display mannequins can (and should) do more than simply wear clothes. In Pucci's reach to lead the industry, we've commissioned well-known people from other creative fields—a pop artist, an interior designer, a fashion designer, an architect, and an illustrator—to push the parameters of mannequin design for us. Our vision is to create an identity for our products that will help you do the same for yours in whatever retail business you join.

Would you agree that a mannequin ought to communicate with customers, whether they be young, trendy, sophisticated, or chic? Do you think a mannequin should enhance the total visual environment and be your company's most efficient salesperson? Do you want the mannequins you use to add a unique point of view, a certain freshness, and a creative element to an item traditionally made purely with function in mind? If you're nodding your head "Yes," we *do* have a lot in common.

I want what you want—to have people lined up on the sidewalk to see your windows and to see shoppers throng the aisles to view fashion in your selling departments where art and fashion have come together to create history, tradition, and high, high quality.

I wish you well in your work.

Out-of-the-Box Challenge

Window Review

Look

Make six copies of the mannequin checklist in Figure 13.22. Take the forms with you as you visit three stores with enclosed windows showing mannequins and three stores with interior mannequin displays. Fill out the charts with all the required information.

Compare

Compare the presentations—windows to windows, displays to displays.

Innovate

Choose the one presentation from each chart that you believe needs the most improvement.

- What changes would you make?
- Explain why you think your changes will improve each presentation.

Critical Thinking

Sourcing and Selecting Mannequins

Directions: This exercise will help you make the important connections between store image, merchandise, and mannequin selection and send you off into cyberspace to source mannequins.

1. Select three designer costumes or three trend designs from a fashion publication that you'd like to put into your favorite store window. The threesome should have some connection in theme, season, color story, and/or attitude. Cut them out and mount them on a sheet of typing paper. Add appropriate accessories to the page. Don't worry about the size or scale of the pictures. Just be sure that the "look" meets the text's general requirements for selection—end use, fabrication, style, and color.

2. Describe your favorite store's fashion image and explain how the fashions and accessories you've chosen fit that image.

3. Visit several mannequin manufacturers' Websites and scan recent issues of *DDI* and *VM + SD* to select the mannequin (or series) that would be most appropriate to wear the garments you've chosen for your store window. Print a photo of the mannequin or series that you've chosen.

4. Describe the types and kinds of mannequins that you saw and rejected. Explain your reasoning.

5. Collate your report. Justify your mannequin choice using criteria from this chapter, and present your findings in a group discussion.

Case Study

Choosing Mannequins

The Situation

Assume that you are a sales representative who is going to represent a consortium of mannequin manufacturers at a national visual merchandising market. Your company's mission is offering one-stop mannequin shopping for retail merchants no matter what size or style of stores they have.

Your Challenge

Prepare a brief presentation using appropriate mannequin (or mannequin alternative) photographs or drawings for *six* of the following clients:

- The Club—an upscale exercise enthusiast shop for men and women
- Just Like New—a consignment shop featuring infant and children's clothing
- The Pantry—a kitchen and cooking enthusiast's shop that carries chef's garb
- Stagebrush—a Western-themed clothing boutique chain operating in Arizona, Colorado, and Montana ski-country resort areas
- Artisan Alley—a wearable art apparel shop and gallery
- T'ween Scene—a national trendy clothing chain for girls aged 9 to 13
- CEO—a conservative menswear apparel store specializing in high-quality suits, shirts, shoes, leather goods, ties, and other accessories
- Fairchild's—a national moderate-price department store chain specializing in clothing for the entire family
- Getaways—an upscale resort wear boutique for men and women
- Expeditions—an adventure sport clothing and gear store for men and women, which also carries camping, climbing, and diving gear
- Underworld—a specialty shop that sells natural fiber underwear for men, women, and children
- Abondanza—a women's clothing shop that specializes in business apparel and special-occasion dressing for larger women

Assume that each of these stores has a display window. Go to any of the following Websites (or other Websites or trade magazines) to find photos or drawings of *at least one* appropriate mannequin or alternative to fit each store's image and justify your choice in a written paragraph. You may add any necessary details about the store's image to strengthen your presentation. If possible, include budget figures for purchasing two or four mannequins and explain why you might prefer to have more than one.

Mannequin Websites:

- True Visual **www.truevisual.com**
- Alu **www.alu.com**
- Bernstein **www.bernsteindisplay.com**
- Decter **www.decter.com**
- Greneker **www.greneker.com**
- Hindsgaul **www.hindsgaul.com**
- John Nissen **www.new-john-nissen.com**
- Patina-V **www.patinav.com**
- Rootstein **www.rootstein.com**
- 7 Continents **www.sevencontinents.com**
- Vogue **www.vogueinternational.com**

MANNEQUIN CHECKLIST

1. Mannequin fully dressed?	Y	N
2. Garments properly adjusted?	Y	N
3. Garment tags hidden?	Y	N
4. Mannequin fully accessorized?	Y	N
5. Accessory tags hidden?	Y	N
6. Exposed "skin" is clean, fingerprint-free?	Y	N
7. Wig is brushed and styled?	Y	N
8. Arms and hands positioned properly?	Y	N
9. Hosiery in good condition, properly fitted?	Y	N
10. Shoes in proper position, fitted properly, dust-free?	Y	N
11. Mannequin base clean, dust-free?	Y	N
12. Riser/platform clean, dust-free?	Y	N
13. Mannequin secure on base or platform?	Y	N
14. Supporting stock of merchandise nearby (if interior display)?	Y	N
15. Signing in place and current?	Y	N

Location: _____

Date: _____

Observer: _____

Action Required: _____

Figure 13.22

Chapter 14

BUILDING A VISUAL MERCHANDISING DEPARTMENT

After completing this chapter, you should be able to

Setup a visual merchandising office with basic supplies

Organize tools for visual merchandising tasks

Develop a visual merchandising resource center

Plan a productive market trip

Write a purchase order

Plan a visual merchandising budget

Create an idea board for presentations to executives

"I will try every day to never say, 'What difference does it make,' remembering that no detail is small. I want to tolerate less mediocrity, laziness, incompetence, excuses, lateness, lousy execution, relaxation, uninspired efforts, punishments, rewards."
10 Years of Peter Glen: One Hundred Essays for the Improvement of Work, Life and Other Matters of Consequence

Organizing Your Professional Work Environment

Attention to detail makes the difference between a good visual merchandiser and a great one. The way you handle detail on the job determines your working "brand identity." Whether you're presenting mannequins in windows or presenting yourself in the way you dress and act, you are expressing your personal identity. When a visual merchandising executive can look at a display you've done and know that *you* did the work, you'll know that you've established a trademark—a reputation—for a certain performance level. That trademark should stand for excellence and a regard for detail.

Retail observer Peter Glen, longtime writer for *VM + SD* magazine, often offers astute, career-level advice in his monthly columns. In one, he offered two powerful ideas that have direct bearing on establishing your working brand identity and putting its indelible stamp on your career in a fast-paced industry. Glen wrote that concentration cuts through chaos and changes it to clarity, and then he added, "A composed mind is a confident workshop." Glen's remarks seem apt because you may not have much more than concentration and a composed mind in your toolbox as you get started in the fast-paced field of visual merchandising.

Glen's topic was "multitasking"—a word coined to describe people routinely attempting (but not always succeeding) to juggle many tasks at once. With a ringing telephone as his example, Glen advised, "Finish what you're doing. The assumption here is that whatever you are doing when the phone rings, you are already doing *something*. You have decided what is most important, which gives you clarity and concentration, and presupposes order and even planning. So with that in mind, when the phone rings, keep doing what you are doing. Do it right. Do it until it's finished and then go on to the next (predecided) priority and concentrate on that. Answer the telephone when it's the highest priority, not when it rings. . . . You have to believe that without control you'll be multitasking helplessly, and that only concentration leads to your best effort at anything."

If you're going to be a visual merchandising manager—and the assumption here is that you will be—you'll need a strong resource center to back up your work. Your powers to prioritize, to organize, and to pay attention to detail will be critical to your success. Being focused and operating efficiently will lead directly to increased productivity, and productivity is what's going to get you noticed. Something as simple as having the right supplies within reach will free more of your time for activities that will build your visibility and reputation (your working brand image) in your department and your store. Never forget that the first product you'll ever market on the job is yourself!

This chapter is dedicated to providing you with survival strategies, effective practices, and useful tips that organize the environments in which visual merchandising professionals labor—their workshops, toolboxes, offices, suitcases, briefcases, and appointment books.

Becoming the "Go-To Person"

Visual managers need well-organized workspaces with accessible, easy-to-find information—contact names and phone numbers for product line vendors, up-to-date and accurate budget reports, idea files, resource files—to support their work routines. Maintaining a professional, well-planned workspace, and becoming the person others go to for information, can lend credibility to your working brand, or style, and the ideas you express. When people in your department begin to say: "Go to [insert your name here] for that," you'll know you're on your way to wherever it is you plan to go in your career.

In the book, *Be Your Own Brand, A Breakthrough Formula for Standing Out from the Crowd,* authors David McNally and Karl Speak believe that everyone has a brand: "Your brand is a reflection of who you are and what you believe, which is visibly expressed by what you do and how you do it. It's the doing part that connects you with someone else, and that

---

"You have to be able to walk and chew gum. . . . The term 'multitasking' must have been coined after following visual people around for a day. It requires diving into many disciplines and pulling them all together with too little time and too little money. It's also what makes the work so challenging and exciting.**"**

Christine Bellich, executive creative director, Sony, New York City.

A Retail Reality: Competitive retailing exists behind the scenes in the office as much as it does on the selling floor or out in the mall. Just as stores compete for business, departments in corporate offices compete to gain company resources for their projects. The more professionally visual merchandisers present themselves and their work environment, the easier it will be for them to gain credibility and secure positions as essential and productive elements in the retail operation.

"I knew I'd arrived as a 'go-to person' when I had to put a padlock on my toolbox.**"**

A visual merchandiser.

connection with someone else results in a relationship. In reality, the image of your brand is a perception held in someone else's mind. As that perception, through repeated contacts between you and the other person, evolves and sharpens, a brand relationship takes form."

Setting Up Your Toolbox

If you've accepted a position as a visual merchandiser with display responsibilities, don't be surprised to discover that the only place you have to call your own is your toolbox. After all, if you're doing what you were hired to do, you'll be out on the floor or in the windows doing your job, not behind a desk.

If that's the case, that toolbox will be your first resource center, holding everything you'll need to work efficiently and effectively. At the same time, you'll need to be able to lift and carry your "office" from place to place, so it can't literally hold everything an office usually contains. Start assembling your toolbox by reviewing your job description. Knowing what the company wants you to do will tell you what you'll need to do it.

An inventory of essentials for a fashion *window* toolbox might include:

- Large, lockable toolbox with lift out tray/drawer
- Padlock
- Striking wire (20 gauge)
- Monofilament thread (50-pound test)
- Heavy sewing thread and needles with large eyes (yarn size)
- Diagonal wire cutter
- Pliers, adjustable and needle-nose
- Adjustable wrench
- Allen wrenches, hex wrenches
- Tack hammer
- Tack claw/staple puller
- Awl or hole punch
- Pin-pusher (brad driver)
- Assorted small screws, common nails, and brads
- Screwdrivers (Phillips and straight slot)
- Bank pins (#17), T-pins, dressmaker pins (#20)
- Wrist cushion or pin cushion
- Staple gun and staples
- Fabric scissors, small and large (very sharp)
- Paper scissors, not for fabric
- Razor blades, single edge
- Exacto knife, blades, safety cap
- Retractable utility knife
- Clear tape, masking tape, double-face tape
- Floral adhesive or foam tape tabs
- Velcro adhesive tabs
- Wood glue, rubber cement, epoxy glue
- Straight edge/metal ruler
- Measuring tape, steel and cloth
- Seam ripper and safety cap
- Whisk broom, disposable dusting cloth
- Assorted bandages, antiseptic
- Premoistened towelettes
- Prepackaged "dry cleaning" product

The list is extensive . . . and could be expensive as well. If you work for a corporation, your tools will be supplied, but if you have your own business, you will need to purchase tools. Before you buy every item, ask an experienced visual merchandiser for a guided tour of his or her working toolbox. Display routines vary, and reviewing someone else's survival kit may help you edit the list to purely essential items.

Here you can borrow a letter from the SCAMPER model (see Chapter 1) and "minify" at every opportunity. For instance, elect to carry a reversible head screwdriver that stores one head in its handle when the other is in use; or carry three or four bandages and a small tube of antiseptic in a resealable bag or container, rather than full-sized packages.

A Retail Reality:
Many creative individuals work best with their work spread out around them. If you are one of them, remember to put everything back in its place after your projects are completed. An organized office is the sign of an organized individual, a quality that is critical for handling a large number of projects and people. In short, if you want more responsibility, prove that you can handle what you already have.

The same toolbox for an interior fashion display person may not require striking wire, or wire of any kind. Instead, that person's toolbox may require a bag of ceiling clips compatible with the store's ceiling grid system, or a rubber mallet rather than a tack hammer. It may also require all of those items plus some that are not on the list. After a few days on the job, you'll learn exactly which tools you will need for your work.

Remember the padlock on the list? If you want to maintain a reliable set of personal tools, you will need a lock and a secure place to keep your tools overnight. Some seasoned merchandisers even color their toolboxes and hand tools with fluorescent paint so they can spot them when they've been left behind.

Setting Up Your Office

Basic Office Supplies

When you progress to the point where you have a space to call your own, you will need to think about your office setup. Your office, an expression of your working self, will eventually reflect your working style, so you may as well accommodate that right away. Know your work habits. If you're a spread-it-all-out person, you'll be happiest with a fair-sized work surface. If you're a filer and don't work well in clutter, you'll need filing cabinets, tote boxes, and open shelving. Try to provide yourself with a comfortable chair and the type of lighting that helps you work efficiently. Whatever size, customize your workspace for function and comfort.

Your office fittings may be divided into priority tools that you use daily, like pens and pencils, and those that you use occasionally, like manufacturer resource catalogs and price lists. You may find it helpful to have a small reserve of these items on hand and replenish them regularly. You'll soon discover other indispensable tools and develop a list of your own as your responsibilities become more defined.

Priority Office Tools

- Desk or wall calendar
- Business card file
- Pens, pencils
- Art gum erasers
- Rubber cement
- Spray mount
- Pencil sharpener
- Ruler
- Steel and cloth tape measures

- Stapler and staples
- Tape and dispenser
- Paperclips
- Push pins
- Bulletin board
- Scissors
- Calculator
- Highlighters
- Markers

Basic Desk References

There are additional essential and extremely useful priority supplies you'll need to keep your brand identity strong. Among the more important ones are the references that can guide your written communications and oral presentations. Rely on them so that your skills will grow stronger with each project.

- *Writing reference books:* A dictionary, a thesaurus, Strunk and White's *The Elements of Style* or *The Chicago Manual of Style* for authoritative assistance with spelling, punctuation, and writing style issues.

- *Graphics references:* Pantone color specifiers (coated and uncoated "chips" for universally understood color choices) and International Paper's *Pocket Pal: A Graphic Arts Production Handbook.*

- *Company references:* Policy and procedures manuals for signing and fixtures, and any additional proprietary guidelines for presentation.
- *Professional references:* Every visual professional has favorite dog-eared and much used sources for expert opinion. This textbook has been designed as a practical reference that you can take with you to your workplace. Then add the *Advertising Age Handbook of Advertising,* by Herschell Gordon Lewis and Carol Nelson. *Wake Up Your Creative Genius,* by Kurt Hanks and Jay Parry, is a refreshing paperback that can renew your energy and recharge your creative batteries.

Basic Organizer Systems

You will need in/out baskets for internal company mail; in/out baskets for postal service mail; and a "hot file" for important requests and projects. A "planner" of some kind is essential. The workplace is too fast-paced for a manager to operate efficiently without a management system to organize time and activities. Franklin Planners (**www.franklin covey.com**) represent one such system and are available in a variety of sizes and configurations, including interface with electronic Palm organizers. Another well-known planning system is from Filofax (**www.filofax.com**), a British company.

The really useful system will be portable enough to carry with you all the time. It should have some means of breaking your day into units of time. Most systems show you at least one day on a page, and you may be more comfortable if you can see at least a full week (if not an entire month) at a time. A prioritized daily "to-do" list, where you can check off completed tasks, is a good feature. For one thing, it forms a diary or record of what you've done to date.

Ideally, your planner will have a cover that snaps or zips plus a ring-binder format, so that you can add blank pages for note-taking, sketching, or capturing ideas. This resource will travel everywhere with you, so it's worth investing in a format that's sturdy, looks professional, and functions well. For example, you'll want an editable alphabetical directory section for key names, phone and fax numbers, and e-mail addresses because you'll be updating it constantly. A business-card holder and a calculator are a plus, and a pen holder is a necessity.

In your office, you'll have to maintain a few files in a nearby cabinet for materials related to company operations, general information, and user information for company communication tools like e-mail and voice mail. If you manage a staff, you'll need to establish a file folder for individual staff members with information on their weekly projects, concerns, and requests. Any personal staff-related information, from performance reviews, for instance, must be kept in a locked file.

"Palm pilots are one of the many organizing systems that allow you to travel with everything you need to know about your business, from calendars and contacts to task lists to drawing pads for creative thinkers to e-mail, and even an alarm to remind you where you need to be when your calendar gets crazy! Just remember to back up the information because without it you may be lost."

Tony Mancini, vice president, Global Retail Store Development, Walt Disney Imagineering and Walt Disney Parks and Resorts

Maintaining Your Office

The work in any retail organization moves at a fast pace. Sometimes multitasking without multifiling results in near-avalanche conditions. It is all too easy for project files to stack up, mail bins to overflow, and desks to become overrun (if not totally obscured). The appearance of your desk and office is part of your "brand."

Don't let paper and piles keep multiplying, says Ronnie Eisenberg writing in *Priorities: The Journal of Professional and Personal Success* on the Franklin Covey Website (**www.franklincovey.com**) "Process each paper as it comes in, and get it off your desk."

It is a matter of establishing better desk-work habits, says Eisenberg. She advises, "Make it a rule to refile things." Maybe current projects get their own standing file on your desk but everything else needs to be put away at day's end. Set aside a daily quiet time (early in the morning, before staff arrives, or late afternoon, when they've all gone for the day) to handle your paperwork. Then she says, "Clean up your desk every night so there's no chaos when you begin the next morning."

"Clutter diminishes clarity. It occupies space, both physical and mental. It impedes movement and progress, and detracts from efficiency and effectiveness."

Stephanie Denton, a Cincinnati-based organizing expert who travels the country uncluttering the desks and lives of CEOs.

Building a Multimedia Resource Center

Capturing Ideas

There are resources and ideas everywhere you go, and you must be prepared to capture them, even if you are not on the time clock. If you remember only one idea from this text, it should be this: Look (take a picture or do a sketch); compare; improve. There are five key items you should never be without so that you are always ready:

- Camera (loaded, plus one extra roll of film)
- Tape measure
- Calculator
- Pen
- Small notebook

If you see a great storefront in your travels, you'll want a photo to remind you why you thought it was so effective. If you discover a good-looking fixture, you may want to sketch its features and record its dimensions accurately. If you need to figure prices or square footage in a hurry, you shouldn't have to do the math in your head. These are the subtle tools of the comparison shopper. Be a discreet observer.

The sketches and photographs, along with things you make note of, become the basis for building a multimedia resource center in your office that will support your work (and the work of your department) for years to come.

Gathering Insights and Inspirations

Sometimes we simply need to look to others for fresh or unusual perspectives on our industry. Visual merchandisers and retail observers are beginning to write about their craft, their views on retailing, their "take" on consumer issues or the way art, science, current events, or economics affect our work as marketing practitioners.

This has been more of a *doing* industry than a *writing* industry, so the shelves are just beginning to fill with insightful books geared to our business concerns. However, an excellent starting place would be the following books:

- Paco Underhill, *Why We Buy* and *The Call of the Mall*
- Peter Glen, *It's Not My Department* and *10 Years of Peter Glen*
- Faith Popcorn, *EVEolution: The Eight Truths of Marketing to Women* and *Clicking: 17 Trends That Drive Your Business*
- Gian Luigi Longinotti-Buitoni, *Selling Dreams*

If you're looking for something outrageous and funny and often inspiring, you might try

- Simon Doonan, *Confessions of a Window Dresser*
- Greg Gorman, *Visual Merchandising and Store Design Workbook*

Reading about the Industry

You can begin to build a visual merchandising resource center by subscribing to trade magazines specific to the visual merchandising industry. Purchase plastic or corrugated magazine files to store back copies of your magazines. Keep 2 years' worth on file and after that recycle them.

Display and Design Ideas and *VM + SD* are magazines that relate directly to your work in visual merchandising. *Style Guide* is a German retail publication. The other publications are mentioned here because they relate to manufacturing trends, product developments, retail operations, merchandising specialty areas, and specific merchandise categories that you'll be working with during your career. Understanding the factors that affect retail businesses in general will be a real advantage in your work. Once you know what's available, you can decide which publications will give you a competitive edge in terms of product knowledge and other insights that can advance your working identity and your position with your company.

You may subscribe to these magazines by phone or electronically

- *VM + SD* (Visual Merchandising and Store Design)
  1 (800) 421-1321
  e-mail: customer@stpubs.com

- *Display & Design Ideas*
  1 (800) 241-9034, ext. 218
  on-line: www.edimagazine.com

- *Style Guide*
  on-line: www.style-guide.biz

Chain Store Age magazine is known as "the voice of retailing" among retail decision makers. A monthly publication, it provides readers with critical information on the retail industry. Departments include: retail technology, payment systems, real estate, e-retailing, and store planning, including operations/facilities management. Its Website is **www.chainstoreage.com.**

Women's Wear Daily (*WWD*), a Fairchild publication, is a daily newspaper for the fashion industry. The newspaper covers the entire gamut of fashion: business issues, fashion trends, retailing developments, international ready-to-wear, couture presentations, and market overviews. *WWD* is written for retailers and manufacturers of women's apparel, accessories, fibers, and textiles. Go to **www.wwd.com** for a look at its Website.

U.S. *DNR*, also from Fairchild, is the men's wear industry's trade paper. Its Website (**www.dailynewsrecord.com**) offers abbreviated versions of its key stories and news articles. Published three times a week, *DNR* offers up-to-the-minute news and in-depth features on men's wear retailing, apparel, fiber, and fabric.

Children's Business (*CB*) is a monthly trade magazine covering the entire spectrum of children's products, fashion coverage of apparel, footwear, and entertainment for infants through preteens, boys and girls. The Website is **www.childrensbusiness.com.**

Footwear News is the leading publication in the international shoe industry. A weekly news magazine, it focuses on the fashion, retailing, manufacturing, and financial segments of the market, spotlighting the hot designers, newsmakers, and business leaders, as well as style trends in all aspects of men's, women's and children's dress, sport, and athletic shoes.

Home Furnishings News is the leading weekly newsmagazine serving the home products industry with "need to know" news about furniture, housewares, textiles, consumer electronics, and computers. The Web address is **www.hfnmag.com.**

InFurniture magazine provides furniture retailers a forum to exchange successful and innovative merchandising, sales, and operational strategies to assist them in growing their business. Each month, *InFurniture* features the leaders and innovators in furniture retailing and focuses on all aspects of the furniture business, including case goods, upholstery, lighting, and area rugs.

WWD/DNR: The Business Newsletter for Specialty Stores is a specialty retailer's survival guide, providing valuable and pertinent information for specialty stores only. It is designed to increase sales, decrease costs, and help retailers compete against category killers. Each issue addresses hot topics for specialty retailers and provides answers and ideas from industry experts about such topics as customer service, merchandising, hiring and turnover, promotion and advertising, inventory control, and technology.

Supermarket News is the only national weekly newspaper serving the supermarket industry. It covers such industry issues as format development, information systems developments, retail marketing, market profiles, and consumer trends.

Brand Marketing is the only magazine that provides its readers with news, trends, and analysis about the marketing and sales of packaged goods through the food, drug, and mass-market trades. These fast-moving consumer goods are being promoted to consumers using a variety of new, sophisticated techniques, such as in-store marketing, scan-based frequent shopper programs, and electronic couponing.

There are many other exceptional industry magazines and publications to round out your library, depending on the merchandising style and the product focus of your store. Ask your supervisor or the store's trend department about the magazines and newspapers the company relies on for its market and trend information. You may request to be added to the in-house circulation list for these publications. You may also want to subscribe to popular newsstand magazines for the general public or special focus magazines that have editorial content focused on your area of responsibility.

In addition, you may want to use the readers' service cards in magazines such as *VM + SD* and *DDI* to order brochures and other promotional materials about products that interest you in those magazines' editorial articles and advertisements. Each product mentioned or advertised will be listed on a numbered index located in each issue's last pages. Simply circle the appropriate number on the cards, stamp, and mail. Within weeks, you'll be receiving the requested sourcing material for your files.

Building a Manufacturers' Library

Setup a manufacturer's product file to organize and store the materials you receive. First, purchase clear file tabs in a variety of colors. Choose a different color for each category you would like to include in your sourcing file. For example:

- Red for mannequins and mannequin alternatives
- Orange for display props
- Yellow for fixtures
- Green for sign holders, printing processes, photography
- Blue for lighting fixtures
- Purple for design resources

Create file labels with manufacturers' names. Arrange them in alphabetical order in your file cabinet. If the manufacturers build *fixtures,* insert the name in a *yellow* clear tab. If they produce and sell *mannequins,* insert the name in a *red* clear tab. If they sell both, insert both a yellow and a red tab. By the time your resource file grows to several drawers and cabinets, you will enjoy the convenience of being able to quickly pull out all of the red tabs in the file for an in-depth mannequin search. When you've finished, they can easily be slotted back into the alphabetical system.

A few manufacturers and distributors provide their clients with large binder presentations that encompass all of their product lines. You'll need a bookshelf to store them in some orderly arrangement, so that they are readily accessible when you need them.

Building a Photo Library

There are professional people in our field who have faithfully photographed every window, documented every major rollout, cataloged every holiday animation, and logged every major promotion as proof of their endeavors. They have bulging file cabinets and slide boxes to prove their claims. They are the meticulous record keepers and archivists of our field. We are lucky to have them. Many of their works appear in this book, and they have both lengthened and widened our view of visual merchandising.

334

Where will *your* archive come from? Where will your *portfolio* come from? Photography can record how you've grown professionally and remind you of theme ideas you've tried, fixturing techniques that worked well, and props, mannequins, color stories, and lighting tricks worth remembering. You can become your own press agent and your own historian.

At the same time you're photographing things that relate to you personally, you must document your professional work for the company. Remember, as a company employee you're not just marketing yourself. You're part of a team. Later on as a manager, you will be marketing your department and its projects, too. Here's how to do it:

● Build a photo library of every project your group completes. Don't overlook the value of "before" and "after" to show improvements.

● Date each project and include notes on the store location where the project was tested, its costs, and a list of stores where the project was adopted and installed.

● Archive proposals and supporting materials that didn't receive initial approval. Ideas that are not accepted the first time they are presented may be successfully resurrected at a later date. Bits and pieces may inspire even better projects.

● Preserve project pictures to document what you and your teammates in the department have accomplished. This builds a departmental track record—a graphic history. At some point, you may need to justify your department's expenses, demonstrate its effectiveness to the company, or document a body of completed work to gain new resources. Photographs are also helpful during progress reviews, to remind your supervisor of your accomplishments.

Building a Materials Library

What's the latest trend in floor coverings for heavy traffic areas? Where could we buy spray paints that will look the same on plastic lettering as they do on wood? Is there a local upholstery fabric store that will match the wallpaper we found in the antique store in New York? These are the kinds of questions that you may be asked in visual merchandising. They are also the kinds of questions that take valuable hours to answer if you do not have a materials library. How to build your library:

● Setup a system of clear boxes to hold samples of trend materials such as laminates, plastics, fabrics, paint, and carpet samples, showing the most recent product entries available to planners and designers.

● Setup a system of clear boxes to document materials and sources currently in use in the store. Label each sample to show its vendor and style number, where the materials are being used, and date of installation for each. This facilitates reorders in the event of damage or excessive wear.

Building a Travel or Market Library

One of the benefits of retail employment is travel, provided you make a point of developing familiarity with the cities you visit. If you work for a national or international retailer, travel may be a part of your basic job description.

Building a travel library that includes information about cities where your company currently does business—or plans to open stores in the future—is a career-booster. Companies send confident, competent people to represent them away from home base. By doing some research up front, you'll be better prepared to be that representative.

If you hold a management position and your budget allows, plan to attend all of the visual industry's markets, and any other conferences or conventions relevant to your company's retail business.

In addition to EuroShop, which is held in Germany, there are several U.S. markets, trade shows, and exhibitions that offer a wide range of visual merchandising products.

Generally, attendees at these major markets and exhibitions are retail and point-of-purchase design professionals, visual merchandisers, store designers, contract designers, and brand marketers.

The following ideas can get you started on a resource library that can either help you build a case for attending major market events or ease your transition from inexperienced work-related traveler to seasoned frequent flyer:

- Setup a travel file for each city you visit or plan to visit. Whenever you travel, collect informational guides, brochures, and maps from local tourism organizations.

- Contact convention and visitors' bureaus for the cities you'd like to learn more about and request materials and maps. You can usually find a Website and "tour" its links to points of interest and make inquiries about materials at the same time.

- *Where* magazines are targeted exclusively to the visitor market, providing timely local information on the best shopping, dining, cultural attractions, and entertainment that cities have to offer their guests. On-line, you'll find Where at **www.wheremagazine.com.** Make notes of favorite restaurants and hotels, and add all of these to your travel file.

- *Mapeasy's Guide Maps* are exceptional. Hand-drawn, they include landmarks that really give you a feel for the particular city. They are color-coded with hotels, restaurants, retail stores, and attractions. You can find these maps at your local bookstore.

- To check specific dates and look for other shows that may have meaning for your particular visual merchandising specialty, visit The Tradeshow News Network (TSNN) at **www.tsnn.com.**

Markets, Trade Shows, and Exhibitions

Descriptions and approximate schedules follow for the most popular trade shows and exhibits.

GlobalShop

GlobalShop is produced by *DDI* magazine and is traditionally held in Chicago in March or April although the show sometimes travels to other cities. In 2005, for example, it was held in Las Vegas. It is the world's largest annual store design and in-store marketing show. It includes the Store Fixturing Show, the Visual Merchandising Show, Retail Operations and Construction Expo, and P-O-P Marketplace. More than 15,000 people from the industry attend to see fixtures, visual merchandising products, mannequins, display accessories, lighting systems, and signing systems. The show offers many relevant workshops and conference sessions where experts from a variety of retail sectors offer information and lead discussions aimed at current issues in the industry. The Website is located at **www.globalshop.org.**

STOREXPO

STOREXPO is produced by *Visual Merchandising+ Store Design* magazine and is held in New York in December. The Website is **www.storexpo.info**. STOREXPO offers programs built around resources and creative solutions for store design, visual merchandising, and in-store marketing professionals. Its mission is to assist its retailer visitors to enhance store designs, build retail brand identity, attract and retain new customers, develop powerful merchandising programs, and create environments to boost sales. Over 25 Manhattan showrooms are also open concurrently with STOREXPO. They are not to be missed, because they are often dramatic, theatrical showplaces.

EuroShop

EuroShop is the largest international store design, visual merchandising, and retail equipment show in the world. It is held every three years during the month of February in Düsseldorf. The Website is **www.euroshop.de**.

Planning a Productive Market Trip

Always plan to spend a minimum of 3 to 5 days at any market. Anything shorter is not cost-effective. If you do not reside in the city where the market or convention is being held, prepare a list of new retail stores or remodels that you can tour while you're there. Provide your supervisor with your schedule. A sample schedule might look like this:

- Thursday: Arrive city a.m., check in, visit new retail stores afternoon and evening
- Friday: Continue tour of new retail stores
- Saturday: Convention seminars and booths; opening night reception
- Sunday: Convention seminars and booths
- Monday: Convention seminars and showrooms

Planning a market trip well in advance of the actual show date assures you of both hotel availability and the best rates. Many market and exhibition producers hold blocks of rooms for attendees and may even have arranged for reduced airfares, but all of these should be booked as early as possible.

Reserving Rooms

It's probably wise to make hotel reservations for STOREXPO in Manhattan up to 1 year in advance. This show is held during the holiday season. If you don't reserve until a few weeks before the market, your only option may be a room priced at $350–$450 per night. You may find accommodations in New Jersey, but you'll spend more time commuting than attending the market. Manhattan is especially busy during the holidays, and at times it may take as long as a half-hour to move a single mile in traffic.

Reserving Workshop Seminar Tickets

Most market registration is free if you preregister (except for EuroShop, which charges a fee for each day that you attend). You may register to attend markets by mail and, in most cases, also on the Internet. One of the most attractive features of the markets is their educational and professional development programs with timely topical seminars and special speakers. These are events but require tickets because of limited seating. They should be booked early because many of the sessions are "sold out" at show time.

Networking

Opening night receptions and other hospitality events are networking sessions with the bonus of entertainment, food, and drink. Book these important tickets in advance. There is usually a fee, but these dollars are well spent. Receptions provide relaxed opportunities for visual merchandisers to get to know manufacturers and suppliers personally rather than as voices on telephones. An important function of your position, even if you didn't see it in your job description, is developing cordial working relationships with reliable vendors. This ability is critical to your advancement in the field. Free of the pressure to sell and buy, you can both enjoy each other's company.

Manufacturers' showroom parties are by invitation only, but there is no charge. You may be invited because your company is a good customer of the manufacturer. You may be invited simply because you requested information from a manufacturer on a Reader Card or through a Website. You may be invited because your company has been identified as a po-

A Retail Reality:
A great deal of networking takes place immediately before and after seminars. Other excellent opportunities for networking are round-table discussions facilitated by industry leaders who are always interested in meeting talented young professionals.

"Equal in value to the information generated by those who exhibit is the information generated by those who attend. Trade shows also provide an opportunity for you to tell vendors and the show's organizers about your needs, opinions, and experiences. Your input can result in products and services that better meet the need of your profession."

Allen Konopacki, president of Incomm Center for Research and Sales Training.

tential customer for the manufacturer. Go. It's another opportunity to get acquainted with people in the industry.

Dressing the Part

By day, business attire, workday casual, or unique trend looks are appropriate apparel for the market. Keep in mind that your business is fashion and that your own personal identity is reflected in your appearance. Take advantage of the opportunity to present yourself as a fashion industry professional.

By night, depending on the fashion season and the occasion itself, trend looks are fine. You'll find that many market-goers wear travel basics that can be dressed up with accessory changes. If you are planning to attend a manufacturer's showroom party, ask in advance about appropriate attire. Although business attire is always acceptable, many dress in cocktail attire, especially in New York City, where there may be multiple types of events to attend in one evening.

Comfortable shoes are a necessity no matter what else you wear. Bring at least three pairs of comfortable (not brand-new) shoes so that you are able to change each day, or even twice a day. Athletic shoes are too casual; a lower-heeled or flat shoe with support is recommended. You may be on your feet for 10 or more hours each day.

Packing

Be sure to take along the following items to make your trip and your information gathering easier and more productive:

- *Business cards.* Bring at least 100 for your first trips. If you are just beginning to build a resource center, you will be collecting a great deal of information and will be asked for your business card in return.

- *Shoulder bag with a wide carrying strap or a backpack.* Catalogs and brochures are heavy, and a thin shoulder strap will become uncomfortable. A shopping bag on wheels is a good alternative.

    Manufacturers will offer to send brochures, but it is always best to collect them yourself, so that you will have a complete presentation to show to your colleagues when you return to your office.

- *Ministapler.* You can use it to attach vendors' business cards to their brochures, to locate them easily when you want to contact someone about a particular product. A small stapler is a simple tool, but it is critical for organizing your materials.

A Retail Reality: Since booth space is limited vendors show only small portions of their lines, usually their newest products. Most have binders with photographs that you may ask to review in the booth. If you find an item that interests you, ask them to send you a copy of the photograph. You may also ask to purchase a sample of an item you need immediately.

Shopping the Trade Shows

The Center for Exhibition Industry Research posts extensive trade show attendee information and strategies on the Trade Show News Network's Website **www.tsnn.com.** Some of its guidelines include

- Look at the show as an essential opportunity to learn firsthand about your fast-paced industry—new technologies, new materials, new ways to do business.

- Make trade shows part of your business plan, not a perk of your job. You need the networking, the fresh perspectives, and the in-person look at products you've only read about. Keep an on-going information "shopping list" on your desk all year, and do the research in person during the show.

- Exhibitors participate in trade shows to sell; you attend to gather information and make purchases. It's your responsibility to gather information from a variety of sources before you make decisions about buying. Preplanning your buying agenda will help ensure that your company's needs are met.

- Plan your shopping strategy. Refer to your shopping list of informational needs and identify four or five must-see exhibitors. Prepare a short list of questions to ask each one. Make a list of would-like-to-see booths for your second pass through the exhibition halls. The "golden hours" for really good contacts are the first hour of the show and the last hour before it closes for the day. You'll have a better chance to speak directly with the exhibitor and to handle the products that interest you.

- Network before, during, and after the show. When you enter an exhibit hall, look for colleagues who are exiting the show. Ask, *"What exhibit should I be sure not to miss?"* When you return home, be sure to share the information you've gathered with your staff and peers. The interest and enthusiasm you communicate to them helps ensure that you'll be thought of as a "go-to" person.

- Come equipped, mentally and physically. You should start with the must-see businesses before you start picking up samples and literature from other vendors. Use your floor map and mark your priority visits first. Wear a watch; budget your time. If must-see vendors are busy when you get there, move on and come back later. Keep asking questions and writing down answers. Revise your questions in response to what you learn during your vendor visits. Keep working at your priority list.

- Take advantage of trade show extras. Special events, promotions, and incentives may flow freely. Look into the "good deals;" they may actually *be* good. Since trade shows are showcases for new products, you may see some launched there. You might get a chance to speak to the technicians and designers who've been directly involved in the formation of the new product or line.

- Follow up after the show. Go back to the office and confirm any deals you might have put into motion, record the names and phone numbers of new contacts you've made, sort your information and samples. Make three piles. One for action, one for future reference and reading, and one to pass along to colleagues in the store.

- Prepare a report for your supervisor. Get on her or his next staff meeting agenda. Start an information shopping list for the next trade show on your calendar.

Setting Up Visual Merchandising Projects

Being a go-to person means that you have developed a reputation for being organized and being able to produce accurate documentation when it's called for. As your career develops, you will need to discipline yourself to become a respectable record keeper. Whether you work for a large corporation or have your own visual merchandising business, you will need a systematic method for recording and tracking information related to projects, contacts, deadlines, and the like. (See Figures 14.1.)

Here is a format used in one effective project filing system:

- Write the project's name or title with bold marker on a white label and position it on the upper-left-hand side of an expandable pocket folder. Add a sticker with a project number.

- Develop a project planning form that lists information like the project name, its objectives, strategies, names of contact people, and due dates on its header. If the project involves fixture development, include a safety engineer as a contact. Under that, provide spaces to write consecutive, brief updates on all meetings related to the project. Then, if someone else must fill in for you at a meeting, that person can refer to the meeting updates and report on current project status.

- Place the project planning form at the front of the expandable file in a manila folder labeled "Project Planner."

- Label two more manila folders and title them: "Illustrations/Photos," and "Budget/Costs." Place these inside the expandable file to organize project paperwork.

- If a number of different people need access to project files, arrange them by number in an open file so that they are easy to find. Develop a multiple project master form that lists each current project, its current status, due date, and the name of the person in your area responsible for overseeing each one. (See Figure 14.2.)

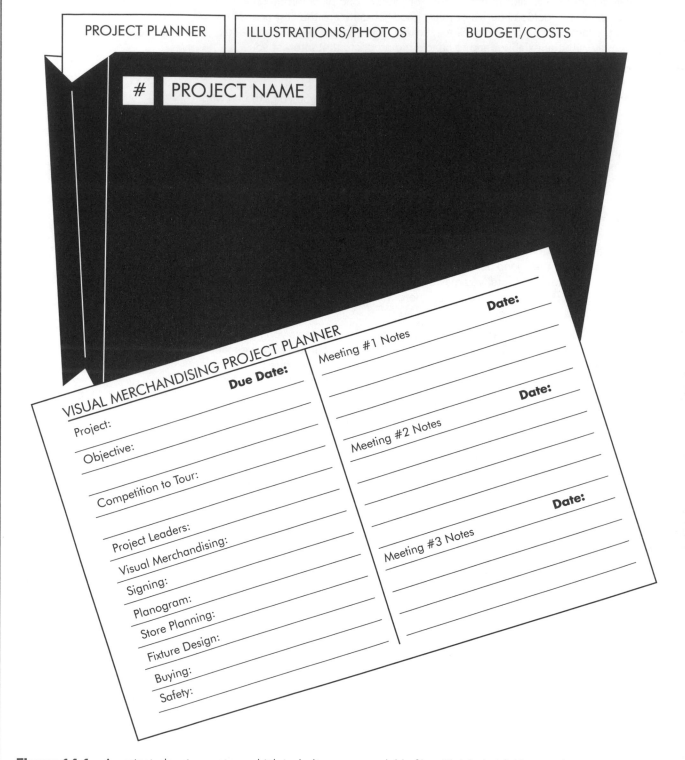

Figure 14.1 A project planning system which includes an expandable file with labeled folders and a project planner form.

VISUAL MERCHANDISING PROJECTS

#	PROJECT	DUE DATE	CAPTAIN	STATUS
1	Valentine's Day Windows	January 15	Tracy	Waiting for design approval, need 10/15.
2	Private Label Cosmetic Event	November 15	Cheryl	Props due to arrive 10/30.
3	Cruisewear Kiosk	November 15	Jenny	Written instructions for stores due 10/15.
4				
5				
6				

Figure 14.2 A multiple project list which may be reviewed weekly to ensure accountability of project leaders and timeliness of tasks.

Setting Up and Managing a Visual Merchandising Budget

Tracking and Reporting Systems

In a business environment, creative ideas must always have strong financial backbones. Even then, creative projects must do more than merely pay for themselves. They must generate income and contribute to profits.

To be considered a credible business manager as well as a creative merchandiser, you'll need to develop resource management skills that demonstrate your ability to use the company's resources wisely and bring resulting profits back to the organization. To accomplish that goal, you must be able to control your budget: You must know the exact dollar amount available in your budget at any time. Before you make purchases or hire any outside agencies or consultants, you have to know how many unencumbered dollars are available for spending.

Your working relationship with your company controller's office or its bookkeeping department is very much like your relationship with your personal bank. You trust the bank to handle your money correctly on your behalf. It knows how to do it, and you let it. However, you also keep a check register, record the checks you write, and once a month, you compare your version of expenditures to the bank's monthly report (statement). Where there are discrepancies, you work with the bank to explain and correct (reconcile) the differences between its records and yours. Tracking and managing your department's finances is really no different—at least from a record-keeping perspective.

A Retail Reality:
Ability to maintain a balanced budget is an important criterion for advancement. It is a straightforward way to demonstrate your skills and business sense to your employer. It is also a great selling point for your résumé as you move on to other positions or companies. Employers value positive results.

If you're working in an established business, the mechanics of the company's financial system are already in place through the controller's office or the accounting department, but you must still keep your eye on the purchase orders you write from your department's account. In your personal checking account, although the bank has no control over your spending (the checks you write) it can refuse payment on your overspending or warn you that you're exceeding your balance. In business, when you overspend your budget, you can count on hearing from the controller or your supervisor. Ideally, neither happens, but both scenarios depend on your paying attention to vital details.

Like any other system, an effective budgeting system is one that you actually use to guide your work. (See Figure 14.3.) It will be a record-keeping system (like your personal check register) that accurately describes and allows you to track:

- The total amount (in dollars) available at the beginning of your department's fiscal year (or specific reporting period)
- The total amount already spent (bills that have been paid)
- The total amount outstanding (dollars already encumbered or bills that have not yet been paid)
- The total dollar amount that remains available in the budget

Writing Purchase Orders

To track what is being spent, your department will probably use a purchase order (PO) system. Most companies have these systems in place and expect you to use them and to following guidelines for working with the established purchase order system. Many of these systems are accessible only through an in-house computer network. If you operate your own business, you may purchase a software spreadsheet system that tracks spending, generates purchase orders, and writes checks. If you're keeping your company's books manually, you can buy generic accounting books and purchase order forms at an office supply store.

Purchase orders should have consecutive identifying numbers to facilitate orderly record keeping. You will want to track each document and, in many companies, you are responsible for each numbered form. Missing forms, or gaps in PO sequence, will alert you to a possible problem. It could mean that you've spent money that you haven't accounted for or assigned to your budget, or it could indicate a security problem. Look at the purchase order in Figure 14.4.

As you fill out the description of items on a purchase order, be sure all of the information is accurate. These documents are legal contracts between you and the supplier. If you are hiring consultants or creative agencies, clearly describe each task they have agreed (contracted) to do. Place one copy of the purchase order in the project file for reference as shipments arrive or creative projects are delivered.

Creating an Executive Presentation

One of the most challenging aspects of any corporate visual merchandiser's job is selling creative ideas to the company's internal clients and upper executives. Independent contractors also sell ideas to retail clients. To gain support for your ideas and the use of resources in either situation, your presentation skills are very important. You may only have one chance to make a favorable impression.

Your ideas and plans must always be presented concisely and clearly, and they must generate excitement and enthusiasm. Graphic presentations add power to your spoken words—especially when you want listeners to visualize the finished project—since people aren't always visual thinkers.

VISUAL MERCHANDISING BUDGET REPORT   Date:

DESCRIPTION	BUDGET AMOUNT	PAID	OUTSTANDING	BALANCE
Agency, Creative	$500,000.00	($20,000.00)	($20,000.00)	$460,000.00
Photography	100,000.00	(5,000.00)		95,000.00
Prototypes	100,000.00	(50,000.00)		50,000.00
Travel, Competitive Shopping	50,000.00	(20,000.00)	(5,000.00)	25,000.00
Samples	50,000.00	(5,000.00)		45,000.00
Special Projects	100,000.00	(80,000.00)		20,000.00
Freelance	100,000.00	(30,000.00)		70,000.00
TOTAL	$1,000,000.00	$210,000.00	$25,000.00	765,000.00
			Balance	$765,000.00

BUDGET WORKSHEET/AGENCY, CREATIVE

PURCHASE ORDER #	VENDOR	DESCRIPTION	INVOICE DATE	PAID	OUTSTANDING
0 01	Hovel Group	Valentine Signing	10/15	($20,000.00)	
002	Chute Gerdeman	Private Label Shop Concept	11/25		($10,000.00)
003	Smart Associates	Private Label Shop Concept	11/25		(10,000.00)
TOTAL				($20,000.00)	($20,000.00)

Figure 14.3   A budget report that includes both paid and outstanding invoices and a budget worksheet.

PURCHASE ORDER

Carolyn's

PURCHASE ORDER NUMBER
5480

ORDER DATE	SHIPPING DATE	ARRIVAL DATE	PAGE OF PAGE
10/25/06	1/25/07	2/03/07	1 of 3

ORDER PLACED WITH	PHONE NUMBER
Peggy Egan	(516) 555-7311

F.O.B. POINT

FREIGHT ALLOWANCE	PARTIALS ALLOWED
10%	No

TERMS
your standard instructions printed here

BILL TO

Carolyn's Inc.
4590 Broad Street
Carmichael, CA 95608

SHIP TO

22 locations
(see attached)

VENDOR

Bernstein Display
7 Harbor Park Drive
Port Washington, NY 11050

SHIPPING INSTRUCTIONS
your standard instructions printed here

SPECIAL INSTRUCTIONS

Mark each box to the attention of the individuals noted on the attached sheets.

ITEM NUMBER	QUANTITY	U/M	DESCRIPTION	UNIT PRICE	TOTAL	SHIP TO
MA-SAM-B-1	220		Samantha mannequin Size 8 Hands on hips Molded shoes Translucent fiberglass (10 mannequins to each location, as per attached)	$550.00	$121,000 + tax and shipping	

	TOTAL

ORIGINATOR'S REPRESENTATIVE	PHONE NUMBER	APPROVED BY
Carolyn Holland	(916) 555-1000	TSA

Figure 14.4 A sample purchase order.

Presentation boards, accompanied by samples or actual models, are powerful selling tools. Giving the viewers something to visualize and touch engages them in your presentation. Your presentation boards may be any style, provided that they are uncluttered and easy for your viewers to see from their positions in the room. Ideally, they should be sized at about 22 × 28 or double that size, in order to make a more dramatic, significant presentation.

What you present and *how* you present it are expressions of your working brand identity. They should reflect your standards for a quality project and a quality presentation. More than anything, you want to direct attention to the important concepts you're presenting. If you make many presentations to the same audience, you may find it helpful to change your board styles and layouts to create new visual interest. For example, a standard plain black foam core presentation board may be updated with a computer-generated border or sidebar for a fresh look.

Each presentation should feature one board that lists the project's objectives and strategies. Your idea boards will feature renderings or photographs. Photographs look best when they are enlarged to *at least* 6 × 8 inch size. Professional-looking boards never have photographs mounted directly on them. Each item should be mounted separately on white paper or card stock with no less than a quarter-inch border before being positioned squarely on the board, grid fashion, in clearly horizontal and vertical lines. Do not position photos and renderings at angles. (See Figure 14.5.)

Display your idea boards on floor easels in the presentation room. If you have samples or models, easels may be setup on tabletops with the samples displayed in front. If you are making a sizable presentation with several exhibits, prepare a brief agenda outlining key points and hand the agendas out to your audience as they enter the room. Do not post financial information on presentation boards. State it clearly and simply on 8½ × 11 paper, and hand it out only if your audience is interested in the project, after you have made your presentation.

A Retail Reality:
Do not turn presentation boards backward with the intention of turning them around one by one as you present. Today's executives know at a glance if an idea is good. You risk alienating them with what they may interpret as time-wasting theatrics. Perception is reality. No amount of presentation will save ideas they do not accept.

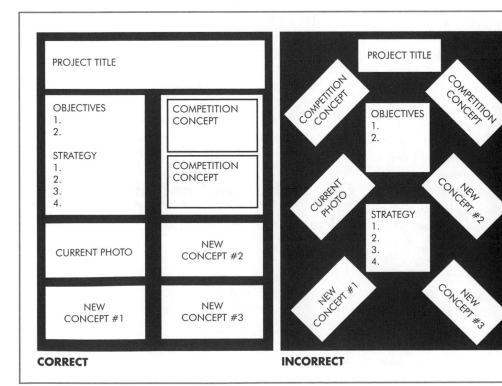

Figure 14.5 A project presentation board. In the correct example, all photographs and information sheets are laid out in a grid fashion. In the incorrect example, the items are pasted on at angles, resulting in an unprofessional, grade school look.

Shoptalk
●●●●●●●●●●●●●●●●●●●●●●●●●●

Letter to the Reader
Organization, Administration, and Credibility
By Eric Feigenbaum
president, Global Arts
(A Retail Design and Visual Merchandising Consultancy)

Retail is the showplace for new ideas, new concepts, and new products. As such, the store environment becomes a selling stage for the merchandise offerings of the day. The essence of retail is the ability to compel the prospective customer to stop, look, and buy. The question that confronts every retailer is: What encourages a customer to shop in one store rather than another? The answer: A well planned, coordinated "team effort" that includes marketing, merchandising, store planning, store operations, and, of course, visual merchandising. Every endeavor that you undertake in the retail world will be a team endeavor. Every team member's contribution must be in sync with the established company image and stated company goals. Long gone are the days when a "display man" would emerge from a back area of the store with a multitude of props to present a single item. Today, the visual merchandiser is an integral member of a holistic "selling team." The retail formula is simple: "Buy It, Show It, Sell It." Our role as visual merchandisers is to interface with all members of the "team" in order to "show" the merchandise to its best advantage.

Each team member has a defined role, bringing specific contributions and insights to the overall team effort. Beyond the obvious—creativity—the successful visual merchandiser will possess and consistently demonstrate the following three attributes and/or skills: *organization, administration,* and *credibility.* Visual merchandising is a 24-hour-a-day, 7-day-a-week occupation. You must be a sponge—soaking up all stimuli whether they are visual, literary, contemporary, traditional, popular, or offbeat. Read anything you can get your hands on, see movies, visit museums, and listen to music. All of this collected "information" is applicable to the art of visual merchandising. Remember, retail is a mirror of society and visual merchandising is the reflected image of life and culture within that society. The ability to have information, inspiration, and sourcing at your fingertips is essential. You must develop you own "filing" system for this information. Upon building a visual merchandising department, you must organize your workplace both physically and mentally.

As you ascend the organizational ladder, your administrative abilities will be called upon as often as your creative abilities. The running of a visual merchandising department is a multifaceted endeavor. You will be asked to manage multiple tasks and meet strict deadlines. A good administrator knows how to prioritize responsibilities. Moreover, documentation of what needs to be done, what was done, and what will be done is essential. The development of your *administrative* abilities will complement your creative energies and creative sensibilities.

You are an integral part of a team. As such you have specific responsibilities. Your teammates will depend upon you. Each teammate's performance and deliverance is vital to the success of the whole. Complete your assigned tasks in a professional and timely fashion. If you declare that a particular task will be complete by the first Tuesday of the following month—be sure that it is. Your team and your supervisors will soon know that you are reliable. You will become a go to person. This is *credibility.* Don't drop the ball!

During the course of your visual merchandising career, you will make numerous trips to the various visual merchandising and store design markets. You will experience a change of roles—you will be the customer. What will compel you to shop one vendor rather than another? As any targeted customer, you will be inundated with a blizzard of stimuli and messages. Employ your organizational skills. Walk the entire market once for an overview, then a second time with focus. Zero in on what is important to you, on what will make your job easier, and on what will make your company more successful. Be a sponge, but a selective sponge.

With a professional sense of organization, administration and credibility, you are now positioned for the "center stage." The store environment is a critical medium in the selling mechanism. The store itself is the fulfillment of the customer's expectations. It's the delivering of every promise that was made to the customer through marketing and advertising campaigns. Visual merchandising is the "icing on the cake." It's the first tactile representation of projected merchandise that the customer will see. You've worked with the merchants, the marketing, with store design. You've interfaced with store management. Now is the time to execute. Be organized, be a leader, and deliver what you promised and what is expected. With a well-developed sense of OAC (organization, administration and credibility), you will now be able to let your creativity loose.

Out-of-the-Box Challenge
●●●●●●●●●●●●●●●●●●●●●●●●●●

1 Planner or Palm Pilot?

Look
Visit an office supply store and a Franklin Planner store if one is near you, and look at the varieties of planners and Palm Pilots near you. List a few pros and cons for each time management system.

Compare
Compare the systems.

Innovate

Which system would you choose to try? Are there any ways you could improve on the suggestions for its use that would better fit your needs?

2 Creating a Resource Center

Look

Take a picture of your current "office" space (at home or at work) and describe how it functions as a resource center for you today. If you do not have a camera, purchase an inexpensive disposable camera with a flash. You need a photo to capture details (clutter) that you'd naturally edit out with a sketch.

1. Does your workspace meet all of your current needs? Describe what you actually do in that space.

2. What are its strengths? (What works well for you?)

3. What are its more challenging aspects?

Compare

Visit a store that sells and displays office organizers or desk and storage systems. Find one additional source on the Internet, too.

1. Select a "system" that seems to combine strong positive features that you already have in your present setup with solutions to some of the challenges you noted in Question 3, above.

2. Create a picture of the comparison system and identify and label the improvements.

Innovate

1. Design an improved workspace or resource center for yourself based on your comparisons of your present-day reality and an improved, custom-designed ideal.

2. Present your picture of your current workspace and compare it to your new design. Share your findings and results with classmates in a small group discussion.

Critical Thinking

Discussion Questions

1. If you had to describe your working "brand identity" to someone in a job interview, what would you say about yourself? Pair up with someone in class and do this exercise together.

2. Is your working brand identity different from your personal brand identity in any way? Note: It isn't unusual for people to think that the two are different.

3. Describe what you think about the chapter's premise that being the go-to person is advantageous to career advancement. Do you share that sentiment? Disagree? Explain.

4. Describe your current time management system. Use an example to demonstrate how it currently works or does not work to keep your life operating smoothly.

5. Assume that you and some of your classmates are going to present a time management workshop. As a group, create a list of ten useful ideas that you'd present at the workshop. Provide a real-life example to accompany each idea. Present your workshop in class.

6. Assume that you are planning to go to GlobalShop for the first time. Go to the Website **www.globalshop.org** and do the following:

- List participating manufacturers that you would like to visit.

- Find a way to rationalize or justify your attendance at GlobalShop.

- Prepare a presentation that could be made to a group of "executives" who control the funding for your first trip to GlobalShop to get their endorsement of your venture. Show them your proposed itinerary.

Case Study

Setting Up a Professional Toolbox

The Situation

You have been employed as a visual merchandiser in a large department store for nearly 5 years and feel that you are ready to strike out on your own as an independent contractor. There are a number of interesting shops, galleries, and restaurants opening in a revitalized section of a former warehouse district near the river that flows through your city, and you want to be part of the excitement. Your business cards and brochures are at the printer, and the only remaining item on your to-do list revolves around equipping yourself with a professional toolbox. You know that leaving your present position means leaving behind the tools that have been supplied for you up to this point.

Your Challenge

Option 1—Use the tool list in this chapter and price the items to discover a bottom-line figure for a practical tool and accessory assortment that will prepare you to work independently.

Option 2—Invite an experienced visual merchandiser to bring his or her toolbox to your classroom.

1. Ask your guest to compare the items in his or her toolbox to the items on your list and comment about the tools that person finds indispensable.

2. Prepare a list of questions you might ask relating to your guest's training and experience as a professional in the field. Possible topics:

   - The creative process in day-to-day work
   - All-time favorite or least favorite display project during career
   - Sources of inspiration and fresh ideas
   - The role of competition in the company's visual strategies

   - Required (or helpful) technical skills or background (art, drafting, theatrical lighting, stage carpentry, electricity, etc.)
   - Sources of product and technology information
   - On-the-job training, mentorship, potential for growth, and advancement on the job
   - The role of teamwork in the department
   - The department's place in the corporate culture
   - The politics of the department and corporate culture
   - Networking opportunities, employment opportunities

Part Six

CAREER STRATEGIES

Chapter 15

VISUAL MERCHANDISING CAREERS

After completing this chapter, you should be able to

Identify many visual merchandising career options

Build a professional résumé and visual portfolio

Prepare to be interviewed effectively for a visual merchandising position

Discuss constructive interpersonal strategies to advance your career

Use networking skills to establish yourself in the retail community

"Visual merchandising has infinite opportunities. At one time it was mainly in retail. Today, it's how companies communicate their brand, and who they are—galleries, magazines, automotive showrooms, restaurants, architectural firms, etc. It's about how you pursue the options. Get out there and make a difference!"
Tony Mancini, vice president, Global Retail Store Development, Walt Disney Imagineering and Walt Disney Parks and Resorts

Beginning a Career in Visual Merchandising

Do what you love. As you begin to think about your professional career, consider that you want your work to bring you a psychological reward as well as a paycheck. If you are going to spend 40 or more hours each week in the workplace, why not spend it in a career that is engaging and fun? Why not get involved in something that you have a passion for, and enjoy?

Since you are just beginning, you may not know *exactly* what you want to do. Sometimes hobbies and leisure activities are accurate career indicators because they represent things you enjoy. Let's assume that you've already narrowed the field to retailing. If you enjoy indoor and outdoor sports, you may want to look for employment at stores like Galyan's, Niketown, or Sportmart. If you are happiest when you are entertaining in your home, you may want to check into opportunities at stores like Crate&Barrel, Pottery Barn, or Williams-Sonoma. If you read fashion apparel magazines and stay in tune with the latest trends, a position in your own favorite fashion specialty or department store may be a good place to start.

If you live in a larger metropolitan area, try to connect with a major retailer for your first full-time job. At least aim as high as you can go in the community where you live. The better known your earliest employers are, the better your chances are of moving up. For example, **Fortune 500 companies** frequently hire people trained by other industry leaders, knowing they will benefit from the new hires' experience with those companies. Another plus is that companies of this stature usually provide the best benefits and opportunities for growth. A job with such a company will help you build a more impressive résumé and make you more marketable.

Retail Forward, a consulting firm that specializes in retailing, is an excellent source for determining the dominant retailers. It's list of the top 100 retailers in the world for the year 2003 was led by these ten:

1. Wal-Mart
2. Carrefour Group of France
3. Home Depot
4. Metro AG (German retailer)
5. Kroger Co.
6. Tesco (United Kingdom)
7. Target Corp.
8. Royal Ahold (Netherlands grocer)
9. ITM Enterprises SA (French grocer)
10. Costco Companies Incorporated

August 2004 *www.retailforward.com*

No matter where you begin your career, each path you try is part of your journey, not your destination. In other words, there is no need to think you are "stuck" in any one position or that you have gotten off to a "bad" start. If you discover that you are not well suited to a position that you were initially excited about, you have still made progress. The only way to find your professional niche is experimentation. Looking back, you'll find that no single experience was a waste of time because you learned something from each situation. Experienced people will tell you that figuring out what they *didn't* want to do eventually lead to discovery of what they wanted to do passionately!

There are countless stories of interests that grew into great career successes. Here are four of our favorites:

A Retail Reality:
You can accelerate career progress by starting out with a national retailer. Later, when you compete for positions in other companies, your early connections may be determining factors in your being hired.

Fortune 500 companies are the 500 largest companies in the United States ranked by revenue (gross sales). *Fortune* magazine publishes the list annually.

Ken Albright, President, Seven Continents

"After high school graduation with an honors diploma and college scholarship, I left home, finished a year of college, and then worked a summer with four overlapping jobs. Along the way, I discovered that I was 'tapped out' on conventional education. At age 20, I took my winnings, bought a motorcycle, and hit the road to experience life.

"After a year in the cultures of Central America, Mexico, the U.S. and Canada, I took a two-month break for more self-evaluation. That accomplished, I liquidated the bike and took two years more to see Europe, North Africa, Central Asia, India, Southeast Asia, Japan, and Hawaii. Now 24 years old, it was time—to take stock of my global interests, to choose an economic course for my life, to have fun, and to stay stimulated.

"My business began with a parasol—found in my travels. In Northern Thailand I noticed a cottage industry fabricating decorative parasols of handmade paper with painted patterns. I bought some and they sold very well at retail for residential interiors, but they quickly migrated to furniture store windows. The parasols were serendipitously spotted by people in the visual industry—and my vision was realized!

Seven Continents was named for the places I'd been during that journey of self-discovery. It began as a firm retailing antique textiles and artifacts from Thailand, Indonesia, and Japan. Our focus was creating reproducible products using the indigenous materials and techniques from these locales.

"We had barely broken into the Canadian market when America beckoned. Bloomingdale's bought in, and Saks Fifth Avenue followed. We were in business. We were a hit! We discovered the NADI show and booked the last available space. . . .

"Fast forward 20 years: We have 250 on staff in Toronto, 150,000 square feet, sales of $35 million. My risk became my reward and perhaps will be my legacy—$10 million—I sold the firm but still run it. We are chameleons. We continue to invent new proprietary products twice per year, and the rewards keep coming. From seed to reality, it's great! They call me Mr. Ken."

Christine Belich, Executive Creative Director, Sony

While studying art at Kent State University, Christine Belich, executive creative director of Sony Style in New York, landed a part-time job at a local department store, a branch of the May Company known today as Kaufman's. She says that the only apparent criterion for that job was to be "a fashionable looking art student. In the 1970s and in the Midwest, I must have stood out in my vintage wardrobe."

On the job, Christine learned the basics—stapling pads, dressing mannequins, and rigging forms. "I learned some on my own (out in my little branch store) and some from the 'road crew' that visited me once a month supplying me with endless bolts of felt and piles of dried foliage. When I had learned enough, I joined that traveling team." Eventually she moved on to Texas and Neiman Marcus in Houston. "I spent years there, then continued with Neiman's in Westchester, New York. I learned so much about display excellence—how to make the merchandise stand out and on its own without the clutter of props. There is an 'old Neiman's' way of doing display that everyone who was part of it is still so proud of . . . It's almost like a secret club. The standards I learned at Neiman's are with me today. They are what I try to teach to everyone else."

The teamwork theme is still strong with Belich: "I came to Sony when the company was just getting into the retail business and was part of a team that created and marketed the retail brand Sony Style. I have had many exciting opportunities at Sony that go far beyond the traditional role of visual merchandising. I was part of the team that created several retail venues for Metreon, a Sony Entertainment Center in San Francisco—a huge and challenging project. Now we are in the process of reinventing the Sony Style store and connecting it to e-commerce and our *Sony Style* magazine."

353

Tony Mancini, Sr., Vice President, Global Retail Store Development, Walt Disney Imagineering and Walt Disney Parks and Resorts

"I started my career as a stock boy for the Anderson Little Company. One time I was in this store shopping for a suit for Easter, and someone asked me whether I worked there. Little did I know a couple of years later that I would indeed work there.

"After stocking the store, I became involved in sales and suddenly had an opportunity to display product in the store. I loved it! That led to a regional merchandise position, to assistant director, to divisional director. Anderson Little was once owned by the Richman Brothers Company, a division of the Woolworth Corporation. I was promoted to corporate director, visual merchandising and store design for the Richman Brothers Company. After 17 years, I moved on to Herman's World of Sports in New York as director, and within 6 months became vice president VM & SD. Then, the most exciting call of my career came from the Walt Disney Company. After one and one-half years as a director, I was promoted to my current position, where I am responsible for store design planning, merchandise presentation, retail project services, special events display, fixture manufacturing, and the sculpting production division.

"Along the way I have met the most incredible people and established friends and personal relationships in this industry. I am involved in four boards of directors. Still, there's so much more to do! You can absolutely have a phenomenal career in this industry. It takes creativity, business savvy, courage, and most important—passion!"

Richard Stolls, President of Trimco, President and CEO, Trim Corp. of America

"Actually, visual merchandising is my second career. I was 35 years old, running a chain of women's shoe stores, and was very, very bored. We had a display department (it was called display in those days), and I started to attend the NADI [National Association of Display Industries] shows. I loved the excitement, the creativity, and the passion that was part of the industry and began to meet some of the players. I felt that I wanted to be a part of this industry. One of the suppliers we bought from was a small company called Trimco. On January 3, 1979, I joined Trimco as its general manager. Three years later Buddy Stein and I bought Trimco, and the rest is history. We built our company to become the largest visual company in the nation. Twenty-one years later, I still love coming to work, and I've never once been bored."

Twenty-One Visual Merchandising Careers

There has never been a better time to begin a career in visual merchandising. Once limited to "trimming" windows and in-store displays in apparel stores, the visual merchandiser's role has dramatically expanded—in the *level* of positions, in the *scope* of positions, and in *earning capacity*.

Today, someone who began as a display specialist might become a vice president of visual merchandising in almost any retail-related environment—a grocery chain, a group of automobile showrooms, a shopping channel on television, or a Website.

Trends indicate that consumers appreciate and expect good design in the products they bring into their lives and their homes, no matter what their income or spending capabilities. As a result, employment potential for someone with a "good sense of design" increases proportionately.

As design-related positions and responsibilities evolve, their exact titles and types vary among retail-related companies. A look at the following 21 job titles and job descriptions—plus interviews with people who hold some of those positions—will give you an idea of what's available today:

354

1. Visual Merchant/Trimmer/Visual Presentation Specialist

This person is primarily responsible for the hands-on construction of displays and product arrangement on fixtures. Department stores often employ two or more visual specialists. Depending on sales volume and size, specialty stores may have one visual position per store, or a single visual specialist may be responsible for weekly or biweekly visits to a group of stores. This is an excellent entry-level position.

2. Corporate Visual Designer

A visual designer creates new presentation techniques, develops fixtures for product displays, and may also do graphic design. The designer, who works with manufacturers and printers to build prototypes to be used in the corporate stores, is responsible for testing them before they are adopted companywide. The visual designer presents testing results to management to facilitate corporate decision making. When the fixtures or techniques are rolled out, the designer works with a visual communication specialist to write simple instructions for installation and use of the fixtures. This position requires a seasoned visual professional, often with 5 or more years of experience, including attendance at national markets.

3. Presentation Specialist/Adjacency Specialist

These specialists work closely with store buyers to develop planograms and floor layouts showing placement of products and fixtures. This position requires excellent written communication and computer design skills. In some retail organizations, walls are "set" in one store, then photographed. With an accompanying set of directions (identifying specific products and suggested placements), the photographs are sent to the other stores, ensuring uniform implementation chainwide. Other stores do graphic schematics on paper and list products to be placed. This is largely an "inner office" (corporate) position, but it is essential that specialists have had hands-on experience merchandising wall and floor fixtures in a store environment.

4. Visual Training Specialist

Visual training specialists train sales associates in multi-unit chains to coordinate and present merchandise with brand identity and visual image in mind. They use videos and compact discs, visual merchandising guides, and update bulletins provided by visual communication specialists. Training specialists may travel from store to store or use video conferencing and company television broadcasting. An outgoing personality with excellent interpersonal communication skills is required because a large part of the job is motivating sales associates to follow company standards and create effective presentations. A teaching or training background is desirable, but not necessary. A clear sense of the company's vision, mission, goals, objectives, and strategies is essential.

Interview   Jenny Phillips is senior training team specialist for the Target Corporation in Minneapolis, Minnesota. After 4 years with Target, she was promoted to this senior position. She came to the company with a bachelor's degree in marketing and took extended fashion merchandising courses along with her other work. She credits internship positions with a strong focus on fashion as her lead in to employment after graduation. "I interned as a fashion show stylist and as a photo stylist and in Dayton's special events office working on short-term projects. Based on my work there, I secured a full-time position in the special events department."

Her position at Target involves traveling for the corporation, in total, about 9 weeks a year. Her greatest challenge? "Reinventing ways to continually convey the importance of attention to detail." What does she enjoy most about her career? "That I am able to use creativity. I enjoy fashion and I love when something sells because of how I put it together." Her advice for visual merchandisers who are beginning their careers? "Expose yourselves

355

to as much of the industry as possible—especially through internships—just to get the experience."

Phillips had two important mentors who supervised her early work during internship. They allowed her the freedom to explore alternatives and take chances in unfamiliar territory. "They were always supportive." Perhaps even more important, Jenny Phillips says, they asked questions . . . "and they listened."

5. Visual Communication Specialist

This individual writes copy for the visual merchandising guides and visual merchandising update bulletins and develops the videos and CDs that corporate visual training specialists use as communication tools to support training efforts. In addition to being effective in a "directive" sense, this specialist's writing must be as descriptive and imaginative as any ad copy and must motivate as well. Moreover, because the work requires so much attention to detail, this person's organizational skills are critical for successful employment.

6. Visual Art Director

Art directors sketch graphic designs or develop layouts on computers, hire photographers and models, and oversee photo shoots. They also select the photos to be used in graphic signing and pass them along to the production department. The visual art director also supervises any technicians supporting the art department's work.

7. Visual Merchandising Manager

This individual manages a corporate creative team representing a variety of positions, which vary according to the corporation's organizational framework. In addition to strong organizational skills, an ability to direct and motivate creative people is required. Because orchestrating interaction among other store departments is a key part of this manager's role, excellent "political" skills will make this manager's role easier to perform.

Department stores often employ a visual manager in each branch store to coordinate and oversee the activities of its visual merchandisers. In the corporate headquarters environment, this manager may supervise visual designers, visual merchandisers, visual trainers, and communication specialists.

8. Visual Merchandising Director/ Creative Director

The individual in this corporate position directs teams of managers for visual and point-of-sale departments. Visual directors must have keen awareness of industry trends and must be able to act as expert advisers for the vice presidents to whom they report. In addition to the organizational skills that go with direction, presentation skills, and ability to sell ideas are critical. Visual directors often have to present their ideas to the highest levels of upper management at corporate meetings.

Interview   Tom Beebe, for many years creative director of Paul Stuart, New York City, began his career thinking he wanted to go into advertising. Instead, his father suggested that he look into display as a creative field that was growing at the time. He began at Gimbels, assembling fixtures and gathering as much product knowledge as he could from the retail side of the store. From there he traveled uptown to Bergdorf Goodman, then Nieman Marcus—each time moving into increasingly responsible positions until he was named regional display manager for Nieman's East Coast stores. Beebe found a "home" in Manhattan's Paul Stuart store windows in 1986, and remained there for 14 years.

9. Vice President of Visual Merchandising

The vice president of visual merchandising leads a team of directors for visual, point-of-sale, and, in some organizations, the store planning and advertising departments. This top management position requires excellent leadership, political savvy, and negotiating skills, in addition to strong communication and organizational skills. Vice presidents attend a multitude of meetings and are frequently asked for their opinions; therefore, they must be able to think objectively, clearly, and quickly in this important consulting capacity.

10. Senior Vice President of Visual Merchandising

This individual has a visionary role. As leader of other vice presidents in the corporate lineup, the senior officer develops concepts and spearheads strategies for both short- and long-range projects. At this level, the senior vice president must have an extraordinary ability to think out-of-the-box and motivate others to lead their departments to the cutting edge of design and presentation. The senior vice president usually attends the corporation's higher-level meetings, often reporting directly to the corporate CEO.

11. Independent Visual Merchandising Consultant

This seasoned professional usually has had 15 to 25 years of experience in the visual merchandising industry in a variety of management-level positions. Consultants may have developed specialties as a result of their extensive experience, including visual fixture design, graphic design, store design concepts, and training. Most consultants contract for hourly work or bill companies on a project-by-project basis.

12. Independent Visual Contractor

Visual contractors (formerly known as freelancers) are equivalent to visual merchandisers who function at a middle-management or senior-management level. They specialize in hands-on production of displays, working with independent specialty stores or corporate retailers on special projects. Depending on the size of the project and its scope and timing, they either work with staff from the contracting store or hire their own visual merchandisers or laborers to accomplish the projects. Here, the ability to manage and market a small business is critical. Working independently calls for self-motivation and a strong entrepreneurial spirit. Visual contractors sign contracts with retailers that often include confidentiality agreements that protect project details and marketing strategies.

Interview   New York contractor Steve Platkin, a 30-year visual merchandiser, has his roots in men's window displays. "I learned my trade through apprenticeship with the (now defunct) Men's Display Guild. In menswear I worked my way to upscale apparel boutiques and then to women's and accessories. Along the way I did some photo styling and now I do trade show exhibits."

Asked about the unique challenges of contracting, Platkin replies, "Contracting can be a grueling and stressful career at times, working with one client one day and preparing for another client the next." He says that dealing with schedule changes and last-minute cancellations can add to stress levels, too. The pace is hectic. "If you carry enough independent stores to make a living, you have to do at least three stores a week, leaving little time to buy and prepare for each one." Contractors cover their own business overhead: salary, studio/shop rent, additional labor costs, travel, display materials, insurance, and so on. "These are not small expenses, and retailers don't always realize that my fees have to cover more than my own time." Platkin thinks newcomers should know about these factors, but he's quick to add that there is an upside, too.

He advises newcomers to the field to remember that "The merchandise is the focal point," and then adds his personal mantra—"Image is everything."

13. Visual Merchandising Corporation President

A visual contractor sometimes chooses to legally incorporate his or her growing business in order to employ a permanent staff of visual merchandisers, adequately insure against liability, and provide additional services for retailers. No one should start such a venture without consulting an attorney about incorporating options available, the prudent and necessary requirements for business operation, and liability insurance. Unless the new business already has an operational infrastructure in place, the attorney may recommend firms specializing in business start-ups that can provide support in those areas.

Interview   Tracy Tommerdahl, founder of Tommerdahl, Inc., has been involved in her own visual services business for 5 years. A generalist, Tommerdahl's company specializes in "what needs doing" for corporate visual departments—designing visual fixtures, writing installation instructions and merchandising guidelines for fixture implementations, creating planograms, constructing presentation boards, photo styling, and testing prototype fixtures. In short, Tommerdahl has created a niche business built on the things she has liked best about her work: "The creative process and unlimited opportunity for variety."

To sample this entrepreneur's résumé is to sample the opportunities she has sought out for variety's sake: "I have 2 years of college credits and 25 years of experience. I have been a sales supervisor and a display coordinator for two Midwest specialty stores, Braun's and GiGi, a sales associate at The Limited, an area display manager and merchandise manager for Casual Corner, and a visual merchant for Target's Everyday Hero."

Today her greatest challenge is "Trying to keep one step ahead of the newest trends and creativity on a stop watch." To students who would like to have their own visual merchandising companies someday, she says, "Get as much hands-on experience as possible. Leave your ego at the door!" Then, she says, "Learn to produce creative ideas that are customized for your clients needs yet maintain a practical application."

14. Independent Stylist

An independent stylist works as a contractor for a corporate art director. At her or his direction, the stylist purchases props and prepares home fashion products or fashion apparel for advertising or graphic photo shoots. This involves polishing glass, removing labels, coordinating decorative accessories, pressing out wrinkles, basting hems, and sometimes applying clamps to cinch in garments from behind to ensure that each item fits the model as if it were custom-made. Stylists pay close attention to details during the photo shoots, and they readjust items as needed between shots. For home products or fashions photographed without models, stylists actually display the product in buildups or on layout boards. A background as a visual merchandising specialist with experience in handling both hard and soft lines is essential for this position. Another means of gaining experience is serving an internship with guidance from an experienced stylist.

Interview   Minneapolis stylist Lisa Evidon has all of the necessary background, from college training as a design artist and part-time retail sales jobs and internships to her professional start as a full-time visual merchandiser. "In college, I learned by trial and error that I was more of a three-dimensional hands-on artist than a two-dimensional drawer and painter. The people with a future seemed to be out there *doing* something, so that's where I went—to find a job where I could start *doing* things. That took me to retailing."

Evidon says that it's quite rare to move directly from visual merchandising into photo styling despite the fact that that's exactly how she got her first position. "It's harder to get started today. Department stores used to be 'little colleges' that helped people explore work in other areas. Today I'd say figure out how to hold a flexible job that pays the bills while you make yourself available as a stylist's intern or helper. What's the best training for a position like mine? Being on the set as a helper or intern with your eyes open—steaming, pressing, reticketing, packing up, and unpacking—that's where to start. Work your way up, building skills and building your portfolio. Study trends and looks because you never want your work to look dated."

Evidon sees the biggest difference between the photo stylist's job and that of the visual merchandiser this way: "The visual merchandiser seems to have greater freedom to be creative within the store image than the stylist does interpreting the art director's vision. I have to put much of my artistic independence aside when working in the studio for an art director. Then it's all about the client and the product image."

15. Visual Merchandising Creative/Architectural Design

This visual merchandiser expands the typical scope of architectural firms, after the store interior is complete, using her or his professional display and presentation skills to enhance the total look of the store. There are a variety of titles for this position, ranging from visual merchandising director to vice president, depending on the firm. Firms usually employ a few visual merchandising specialists inside or outside of the firm, to call upon as projects need to be dictated.

Interview   Robb Cook, currently director of visual merchandising for Shea, Inc., a Minneapolis architectural firm, began his career as a "trimmer" at Sears, moved on to become a visual manager for J. C. Penney, and was parkwide visual designer at Camp Snoopy in Bloomington, Minnesota's Mall of America. Working for Shea in a newly created position, Cook believes that architectural firms will hire more visual merchandisers in the future because "they are finding that it enables them to offer additional services to their clients."

What does Cook enjoy most about his new job? "I love the variety. I've worked on everything in softlines and hardlines from A to Z, cosmetics to haute couture, shopping centers to pet stores." He advises visual merchandisers beginning his or her careers to "take every opportunity that is presented to you to express your individual creativity. Keep a photo library of all your visual projects as a foundation for your portfolio."

Cook is thankful to those who have mentored him through the years. Early in his career during his internship at Sears, a mentor noticed his work and offered him a position in special projects at the corporate offices. "He continued to offer support and guidance throughout my career at Sears." Cook later found another mentor at Mall of America's Camp Snoopy. "Even though I did not have an entertainment background, he offered me a visual position which enabled me to make an indoor theme park come alive."

16. Manufacturer's Designer

This person designs visual props, store fixtures, signing, and graphics for a manufacturer who sells to retailers through catalogs, brochures, permanent market show rooms, and trade shows. Sometimes the designer has an engineering and manufacturing background, sometimes a retail background, and sometimes an architectural background that brings him or her into contact with retail businesses and leads to a specialized design connection.

17. Manufacturer's Representative

This is a sales position in which an individual may represent one or more manufacturers. A single manufacturer may employ a team of professional business-to-business salespeople who will represent only that company's products nationally and internationally, or an individual may work as an independent representative showing noncompeting products for several store fixture manufacturers on the same basis. In either scenario, sales representatives are typically responsible for a specific region of the country and travel to meet with retailer customers on a regular basis. They may also present their line(s) of products at regional and national markets.

Interview   Ed Shilling, who is a sales representative for Niedermaier, based in Chicago, and Pucci, in New York City, began his career as a "window trimmer" at George Muse Co., a men's store in Atlanta. He traces his career path from there: "Following that, I was an assistant director of display at Saks in Atlanta, then a visual merchandising director at August Max in New York City. After that, a creative director at Winkleman's in Detroit, and finally vice president of visual merchandising and store planning at Ivy's, Florida." If you charted Shilling's work history graphically, you'd see a career ladder.

359

Shilling also knows visual design work, having served as vice president of design at Niedermaier in Chicago, where the international manufacturer makes custom products for retailers, the hospitality industry, Fortune 500 companies, architects, and designers. Now a full-time sales representative, Shilling spends about 40 percent of his time on the road covering coast-to-coast sales territories. "It used to be 80 percent, but due to better communication [technologies], I can travel less. The increased number of business mergers means there are fewer clients to see."

His greatest challenge seems to fall in the category he calls "time frames." He most enjoys "the creativity . . . and the people." Shilling advises newcomers to the visual field, "Don't be afraid to move onto the next step, don't be afraid of challenge, and don't follow the rules!"

18. Visual Merchandising Specialist/Advertising Agency

A creative position within an advertising agency specializing in retail environments, the specialist devises and implements advertising strategies to support the retail effort. This person needs to know a great deal: the demographics and psychographics driving the retail economy overall, retail trends and climate nationally and locally, and what the client retailer's competition is doing. In addition, this person must understand current retailing practices in general and client retailers' visions, missions, goals, and objectives specifically. He or she must be able to think out of the box and present ideas effectively as the agency "sells" clients on the agency's proposals and visuals.

19. Magazine Editor—Visual Industry Trade Magazine

Interview   Steve Kaufman, editor of *VM + SD* (*Visual Merchandising and Store Design*) magazine explained how he got his start in visual merchandising communications. "I'd been a writer and editor long term, when I saw an ad in *The New York Times*, answered it, and became the editor of *Display & Design Ideas*." He later joined the staff at *VM + SD* as editor.

Kaufman earned a journalism degree from the University of Illinois. In college, he had planned to be a sportswriter, which might explain the advice he offers to people starting out in their careers: "Don't view life as a linear experience. Don't assume that if you start *here* you are going to get *there*. Life is full of curves and turns and even reversals, and you can't always plan for them, nor should you try to.

Although Kaufman didn't grow up in retailing, it didn't take him long to get to know and like his target audience. "The [visual merchandising] industry is filled with creative people who are on a mission. It's fun to spend time with them. I find it fascinating to see how they fit their creative impulses and ability into the business of retail." These same people pose Kaufman's greatest professional challenge: "Writing to people who know more about the topic than you do. It's a huge responsibility—you want to provide a service; offer them help in some way."

20. Visual Merchandising Instructor

The visual merchandising instructor is usually licensed and/or holds a degree in education, marketing, or a related art field. Courses are offered in vocational-technical schools, community colleges, and four-year institutions as well as high schools and proprietary colleges. The instructor should have previous professional experience in visual merchandising. In fact, in some states, licensure is based on having a specific number of full-time hours of related employment. The instructor needs to be able to teach hands-on display skills and know current trends, retail operational practices, and marketing strategies, as well as understand the retail climate locally and globally in order to prepare students for employment in retailing in general and visual merchandising in particular. Ideally, the instructor will have networking connections to the local retail community and be able to facilitate internships and student employment. The instructor's biggest challenges usually relate to teaching in an environment that lacks store space, merchandise, and up-to-date equipment and fixtures, thus making it difficult to apply skills in a realistic setting.

21. Internet On-line Store Designer

Up to now, you've read about people whose early work as visual merchandisers led them to new positions where they have built on their previous experience. Now you're going to read about someone whose career started somewhere else and led him to the visual merchandising industry as an on-line site developer.

Site design and development is a career area that's still evolving. Understandably, there is not a long tradition to describe exactly what this job entails. Until the end of the last century, there were few sophisticated e-commerce sites, let alone a community of on-line retail stores. The pioneers in this field generally came from backgrounds other than visual merchandising, and many of them arrived without much sales or business experience at all. Instead, many were computer experts—formally trained engineers or self-taught "hackers" and everything in between—innovators who recognized the commercial potential of the Internet and World Wide Web as creative communication media.

Interview   John Tymoski, director of ST Online, is one of those individuals. His story is typical of the way many people worked into their positions as on-line developers. He started out as a freelance journalist while he was still in college. Today, he oversees all of ST Publications' industry-leading e-commerce and Internet efforts, including: SignWeb (**www.signweb.com**) the on-line version of *Signs of the Times* for the sign industry; ScreenWeb (**www.screenweb.com**), a site for screen printers and screen-printing suppliers; BigPicture.net (**www.bigpicture.net**) for large format digital graphics printers and buyers; and VisualStore (**www.visualstore.com**), for store designers, visual merchandisers, and retailers—the on-line version of *Visual Merchandising and Store Design*.

John's job description includes responsibilities for development of additional electronic products for ST's revenue growth and adding value to each current site, plus the maintenance, marketing, and management of each of the company's business-to-business portals. The technical tools John uses are HTML, FileMaker Pro, Microsoft Office, and Photoshop. He also has a working knowledge of applications ranging from WYSIWYG (What You See Is What You Get) HTML editors, Flash, Illustrator, ImageReady, and GIF Builder to basic UNIX commands. This list tells you what skills you might need to add to your professional portfolio if you want your career to head in this direction.

"I started freelancing when I was working on my college newspaper where I had learned pasteup and key-lining skills. I got a few jobs writing and putting pages together for publications. I started with ST Publications with a job that was purely writing. Later, I took over a family-owned printing business and eventually worked for a small advertising agency that needed copywriting as well as campaign ideas and project management."

Tymoski says, "About this time, desktop publishing was taking off, and because I understood the production process from all sides, it was easy for me to communicate with vendors. By then, I was back at ST and was able to convince them that it was time to take our printing technology digital. As that was happening, the Internet was starting to take off, and I was in a great position to launch a site for the ST magazine I was working on, *Signs of the Times*. We wound up buying the technology firm that put the site together and rolled out sites for our other publications, too."

John Tymoski's career path points out the fact that prior knowledge and training can help you carve out a niche for yourself in a surprising number of related industries. All you need are wide-ranging skills that can be adapted to current trends and demands—sometimes in ways you never suspected possible.

"The best way to have a good idea is to have lots of ideas.**"**
Linus Pauling

Retail Organizational Structures

The organizational structure for all of the listed in-house positions varies greatly within retail corporations. In some, visual merchandising stands alone, performing only creative, hands-on functions. In other organizations the creative functions may be combined with the presentation, point-of-sale, and store planning departments that actually execute the creative department's plans. The charts in Figures 15.1 through 15.4 show some typical organizational structures. A chain of 100 specialty stores might operate with a small team of ten for visual, point-of-sale, and advertising, while a group of 500 department stores may have a staff of 200 performing these functions, in addition to a large team of outside contractors and consultants.

A quick glance at the organizational charts in Figures 15.1 and 15.4 shows that the visual staff may not report to the same senior executive. In the first example, training is a component of human resources, so visual people in charge of developing others' skills report to personnel, while visual teams involved in designing presentations report to store operations. In the fourth scenario, visual merchandising may be a more integrated function with all visual teams reporting to the same individual.

Whatever the structure, visual merchandisers, presentation specialists, fixture designers, point-of-sale, and training departments must actively communicate with one another to create a profitable retail operation, whether it's one store or a thousand stores. Every project requires highly productive brainstorming and strategy development sessions, with ideas coming from many business perspectives. This is where visual merchandisers can bring their trend awareness and design skills to encourage their colleagues to push the envelope, so to speak, and ensure their organization's leadership position.

Visual Merchandising Career Strategies

Career Tips

Once you've decided that you want to pursue a career in visual merchandising, strategic thinking can expedite your progress. If you're already employed, there are some things you can do immediately. Otherwise, you will have to wait until you've had experience. Let's begin with some things you can do right now:

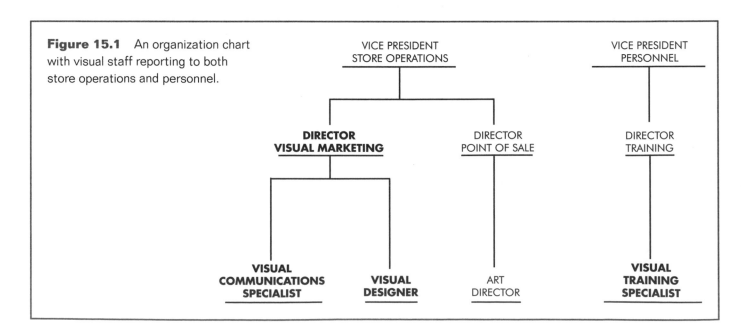

Figure 15.1 An organization chart with visual staff reporting to both store operations and personnel.

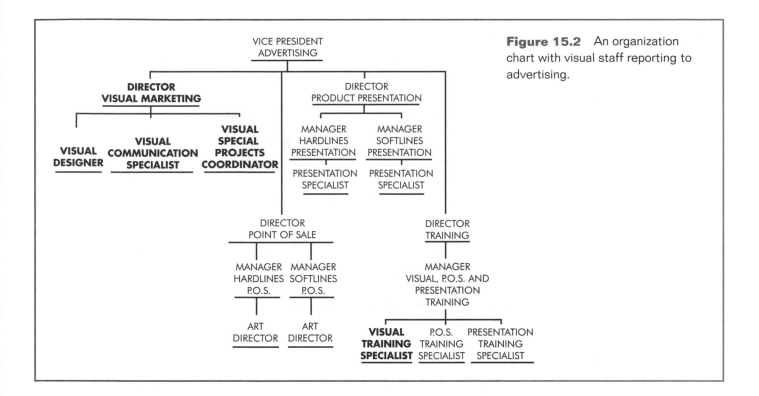

Figure 15.2 An organization chart with visual staff reporting to advertising.

Career Tip 1   If you already work in a store but have ambitions to move into visual merchandising, you are in a good position to make your ambitions known. However, while you're reaching for the next rung on the career ladder, you must continue doing exemplary work at the rung you're on now. Don't let your ambitions for the future translate into a lackluster performance today because that's the first place a visual merchandising executive will look for a recommendation of your work.

Career Tip 2   Sales associates are occasionally asked to execute displays in their departments. This is a great way to develop your visual presentation skills. Experimenting with a product display, tracking the difference it makes in sales, and documenting the results is a good practice. Positive results are concrete, bottom-line items that demonstrate that you

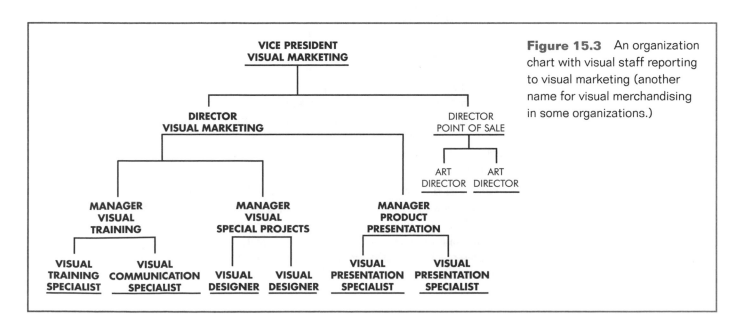

Figure 15.3 An organization chart with visual staff reporting to visual marketing (another name for visual merchandising in some organizations.)

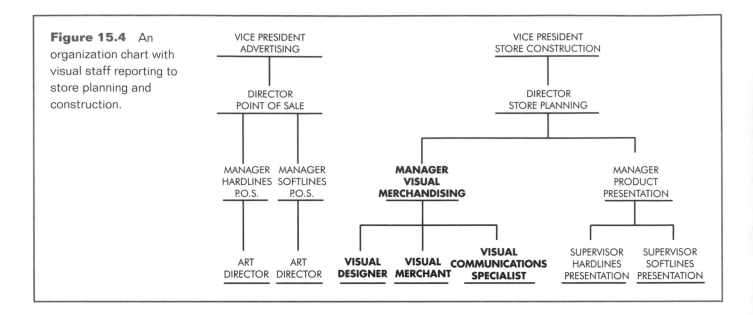

Figure 15.4 An organization chart with visual staff reporting to store planning and construction.

A Retail Reality:
Photograph your work. It is the best way to record the professional displays you've done and sell your design skills to future employers. It also shows that you have ambition, determination, and initiative—all good things for a job candidate to have.

understand the connection between effective presentation and sales results. Be sure that it's okay to do displays before you go off on your own. Follow company policies and presentation guidelines.

Career Tip 3   Whenever you have an opportunity to create a display, photograph your work for your professional portfolio. Center the display carefully in the viewfinder and take several photos from different angles and various distances. The best shot can be enlarged to a 6 × 8 inch size, or an 8 × 10 inch photo. Anything smaller is not suitable, because details are not visible.

Career Tip 4   If you can, work for a retail organization that will expose you to a variety of responsibilities. You may be able to sample several facets of the visual merchandiser's role in the store by watching what others do. In an organization with fewer than a hundred stores, a visual department may perform many functions in addition to window and departmental displays: visual fixture design and development of presentation planograms, fixture concepts, point-of-sale, and training.

Career Tip 5   Seek out internship or volunteer experiences where you can practice visual merchandising techniques. Volunteering to work in nonprofit gift shops operated by hospitals or museums may help you experiment with merchandise displays and build your experience base. Goodwill, Easter Seals, and the Salvation Army operate thrift stores and desperately need volunteers who can do extra things like attractive wall and window displays, floor merchandising, and sales training for their employees-in-training. Volunteer to coach DECA (Distributive Education Clubs of America) retail competitors at your local high school. Volunteer to judge their competitions. These activities are credible and valuable on a résumé, and they are never overlooked by companies that encourage their employees to volunteer in the community. It shows that you value what they value.

Career Tip 6   You are a lifelong learner. Build your skills by attending seminars, trade shows, training sessions, discussion groups, and classes that interest you. Even if they are unrelated to your industry or current employment, these extracurricular activities will help you gather information, develop interpersonal skills, and meet new people. You never know when an employment opportunity may evolve out of a connection made through someone you meet at one of these activities. These professional development efforts belong on your résumé as well.

364

Getting Along in the Workplace

It's a fact that more people lose jobs because of poor interpersonal skills than because they lack technical skills or talent. Failure to get along in the workplace equates with failure to hold onto a position or advance in a career.

Being creative simply isn't enough to guarantee success in the visual field any more. With all of the changes taking place in the retail industry, use of interpersonal skills accounts for at least half of any visual merchandising position. Creative people who once worked alone or in very small teams now interact daily with key corporate managers and routinely conduct visual training programs for groups of 25 to 75 store employees.

Professionalism and political savvy are interwoven with survival skills and success on the job at all levels. In other words, how visual merchandisers present *themselves* and *their ideas* is now just as important as how they present products.

Here are ten tried-and-true strategies to work with as you develop a more marketable image of yourself in your workplace:

1. Look at yourself in the mirror. How are you presenting yourself? "Arty" clothing, for instance, is fun to wear but may not send the right message to others in your organization. Pay close attention to what's going on in the corporate culture and dress accordingly. No matter what you wear, groom yourself impeccably. You can maintain your own unique look, but accomplish it subtly. Communicate your skills and abilities in ways the company understands and values.

2. Look at the "big picture," both the creative and business aspects of retailing. You represent the vision of your department as it interacts with others in the corporate setting. Think of people in other departments as your departments internal "customers" and give them top-notch service. In truth, they are the end users of many of the services you and your colleagues provide.

3. Become a student of the world. Read the newspaper and keep up-to-date on current events, especially in the "business" section. Not only does it help to keep conversations going at business lunches; you will be perceived as a person who is in the know (and therefore, credible) when you present information on trends or new concepts and merchandising strategies. If you don't have a newspaper subscription or can't afford all the trade papers and magazines, go to the Internet on your breaks. Excellent publications to read are *The New York Times, USA Today, Women's Wear Daily, Forbes, Business Week, Wallpaper,* and *New York* magazine.

4. Learn to listen to all sides of any discussion. Even if you go into a situation with strong beliefs, keep an open mind, look at the big picture, and be prepared to negotiate. You may not have been "born" a negotiator but you can learn to be one. Negotiation is a powerful professional tool.

5. Think before you speak. You don't always have to give an immediate response. It's acceptable to gather your thoughts and give yourself time to think things through before you commit yourself or your coworkers to major ideas or projects. If you're being pressured, simply say that you need time to consider all the points and do some research before you reply.

6. Accept challenges that will make you and your coworkers visible in the organization. Be prepared to deliver and then over deliver! If challenges aren't given to you, invent your own. What is good for you must also be good for the rest of your department and the organization as a whole. If you want to be viewed as a potential manager, give others credit for contributing; someone will notice that you have an attitude that strengthens teamwork.

7. Don't burn bridges. If you decide to leave a job because of personality clashes or other differences, leave on a positive note. With the constant movement in the industry, there's a very good chance that you will find yourself reconnecting with the

individual(s) you thought (or hoped) you'd left behind. Never criticize a former colleague. You never know who has network connections with people in your former company.

8. Develop and maintain contacts with key people inside your organization. Instead of working through lunch at your desk, have lunch with a coworker in another department or with a sales representative or a designer from an outside agency. The up-and-comers you network with today are tomorrow's organizational influentials. Opportunities that you never dreamed possible can develop through informal conversations.

9. Seize every opportunity to speak to key people in your organization. Some of the most important conversations take place in elevator banks. If they ask how you are, you may want to mention how much you are enjoying a particular project you are working on. Let them know you are an enthusiastic member of their organization. Remember to "edit" your conversations; speak succinctly.

10. Learn the names and positions of all of the executive management people in your company. Whenever the *appropriate* opportunity arises, introduce yourself. You'll stand out from the crowd and be remembered if you make yourself visible at the right time.

Getting Ahead in the Workplace

The ten tips and hints you've just read can be put into practice from day one in your career. You may also need some management-level strategies immediately. It isn't unusual for a fairly new visual merchandiser to start managing a department after only 6 months to 1 year of training, especially in a smaller retail operation where staff size is limited. Here are additional strategies to use as you enter the next natural phase of your career:

● If you are in a management position, hire people who appear to be practicing the same ten strategies you've just learned about. They are exactly the kind of workers you'll need on your team. They can carry the department (and you) to great achievements.

● Make it your goal to build a strong identity for your department within the company. If you put the department's progress high on your priority list, your career will take care of itself.

● Invite your entire team to write a mission statement that describes what your department has to offer the larger organization. For example, "We turn ideas into reality." Your department is a part of the corporate culture, but it's also a microculture of its own. Ask yourself what kind of culture you want to work in and what kind of culture will foster the results you want for the larger organization.

● Invite your entire team to develop goals for your department. For example, "Our goal is to train all of our stores to use the latest presentation techniques in order to increase sales." Retail goal statements should always include the words "increase sales" or words to that effect. If there are no profits, there is no company. If there is no company, there are no jobs. If your team understands that, it will have little trouble embracing the goals it has set for itself.

● Market your department to the rest of the company. Consider developing a logo and a tagline for your department. Use them on printed interoffice memos and other tools to help familiarize the rest of the company with your departmental goals. Treat your department like an important product and sell it to your internal customers.

● Once you launch a "visibility" campaign (or any other internal program), revisit it regularly and reinforce its value to the group. If the campaign fails through of lack of support from you, your team will question your leadership credibility and be skeptical about other motivational techniques you use.

- Visit stores in your organization on a regular basis, even if the majority of normal working hours are spent in a corporate office. In addition, *work* in the stores occasionally. Associates will understand that you're accessible.

- Model behaviors you want store associates to use, and establish standards for performance. Demonstrate something you want them to do in a certain way—how to set a floor according to a planogram, for instance. Then ask them to set the floor in another area. Next, ask them to train others to do the task they've just completed successfully. The "see one, do one, teach one" strategy accomplishes several useful tasks for a manager:

    1. It communicates to associates that you're a real working partner.

    2. It sets standards for acceptable performance.

    3. It shows associates that the tasks they're being asked to do can be accomplished and worth doing well.

    4. It helps associates internalize (learn) an important task and empowers them to take ownership of it.

Working with Right-Brain and Left-Brain Personalities

All individuals are not motivated in the same way. Whether managing a group of creative, dominantly right-brain thinkers or working along side them, this is critical to understand. Anneli Rufus in her book *Party of One,* explains:

> "Some of us appear to be in, but we are out. And that is where we want to be. Not just want, but need, the way tuna need the sea. Someone says to you, "Let's have lunch." You clench. What others thrive on, what they take for granted, the contact and confraternity and sharing that gives them strength leaves us empty. After what others would call a fun day out together, we feel as if we had been at the Red Cross, donating blood."

Many companies impose "voluntary fun" on their employees. When one U.S. retailer opened stores in Europe, some employees were found hiding in the restroom to avoid doing the company cheer at the start of the business day. We do not all respond to the same stimulus.

Creative individuals are by nature not followers of the pack. This is what gives them their edge and ability to think outside the box. Understanding this, giving them the space and freedom to work in their own style, at their own pace, will generate creativity at its best. And if you are the creative individual with a stomach that churns when you see others "follow the flock" and join in with company cheers, respect their need for a different kind of motivation. Left- and right-brain personalities working together, allowing each other to operate with their own personal style, will create the most amazing innovations of all.

Networking

Networking is the all-important human connection. Whether you know it or not, each time you interact with another human being and exchange even the smallest bit of information, you are building your network and expanding your world.

You already have active networks in your life:

- Family, friends, and acquaintances plus all of their friends
- Coworkers, fellow club members
- Teammates, fellow volunteers, church members
- Accountants, attorneys, doctors, dentists
- Former workmates, classmates, roommates

What binds you to these people is some common interest, concern, opinion, or some mutual connection. It can be a now-and-then, "Hi, how are you?" sort of relationship, or a

A Retail Reality:
One of the most effective ways to network is to join a professional group or a service organization, like a downtown council or mall merchant's association. You can become your company's ambassador to the retail and creative community. (Never leave work without business cards.)

A Retail Reality:
The Planning and Visual Education (PAVE) partnership holds an annual student design competition judged by leaders from the visual merchandising industry. Winners travel to national markets for formal recognition and an opportunity to meet executives from nearly every retail operation in the United States. Check out PAVE **www.visualstore. com/pave** for details on the competition.

"PAVE's mission is to approach and embrace the students of today, the future designers, architects, planners, and visual merchandisers of tomorrow for the retail design industry. Exposing these fresh minds and new talents to the life beyond the school classroom is both priceless and rewarding, opening their eyes to optimal career paths."
Greg M. Gorman, PAVE chairman.

A Retail Reality:
What goes on your résumé and into your portfolio must be the absolute truth. Always. No exaggeration of skills, no bending the truth, no stretching of salaries, no embroidery of titles, honors, and degrees. No fudging. No kidding! They check.

A Retail Reality:
Employers *do* check on previous employers and references. Be sure to ask the person's permission before using anyone as a reference.

A Retail Reality:
"Professional" is the key word for any résumé. An overdesigned, overillustrated résumé may cost you an interview. Keep the font readable, with no italics. Use plain paper, no colors. If you want to do something "extra," create a simple business card with your name, occupation, address, phone number, and e-mail address. (Be sure that your online e-mail provider has a professional sounding name.)

long-lasting thick-and-thin friendship. Each person you know is part of your "circle of influence"—maybe a hundred people or more. Each of them has a circle, too, so you can imagine how far your networking may reach.

There are as many ways to network as there are interactions between humans in a day. To make networking strategies effective in your professional life, however, you really have to keep your goals and your specific needs in mind all the time—just in case. After all, you're managing a career, and networking is a great way to give and receive, to build your reputation as a person who is always "in the loop." Your company has resources and you're one of them. You can use other people's resources, and you can be one of theirs.

There are global networking possibilities for you in the message boards on pertinent sites on the Internet. For example, **www.visualstore.com** has a message board feature that invites visual merchandisers from all over the world to discuss relevant issues, new products, and emerging technology. Perhaps the best thing about this Internet function is being able to post a professional dilemma on a professional bulletin board and see who responds. Someone with years of general experience might answer with a tried-and-true solution. Someone with really inventive ideas might provide an unexpected alternative. Someone with specific expertise might direct you to a technological link. Someone with a sense of humor might convince you it really isn't a dilemma after all.

The same Websites frequently serve as informal employment agencies, inviting employers to post available positions and job seekers to post résumés or make inquiries. A note of caution: Be careful how much personal information you post in any public place, the Internet included. Get company names and mailing addresses so you can check out the sources before you become more involved.

How do you get started as a networker? You communicate. First, you need to really look at people you pass in the halls. If you say, "Hi! How are you?" to each person you see and then move down the corridor without waiting to hear the answer, you've just wasted an opportunity to network. Of course you can't stop and visit at length with every person you pass, but you can stop asking empty questions of people when you have no intention of listening to their answers. Smile and nod, say "Hi!" but save extended conversations for networking and make them meaningful. Networking is not about a popularity contest. Networking is about engineering your outcomes. That must begin with *listening*. When you listen, you become important to the speaker. Be selective. Keep your goals and specific needs in mind when you seek out the people who need to know you're alive and a contender. If you want to market your department, build a network of people who can help you do it. If you want to market yourself, build a network that can help you do that. If you want to enhance your resources, become an expert networker.

Getting Your Foot in the Door
Informational Interviews
Once you have identified positions that you want to learn more about, you can try to setup brief, informational interviews with industry professionals. Because most of these people are extremely busy, you may only be able to get in by "networking." If you know anyone working for the company, for instance, ask for help connecting with someone in the visual department. Encourage your school to invite a panel of professionals working in the visual industry to answer questions during a class session.

Internships
An internship is an excellent way to take a step inside a company and learn more about it. Many college programs offer credit for school-term internships; some allow them only during breaks, interim sessions, and summer vacations. Internships often lead to permanent positions. Treat each opportunity very seriously because it could launch your career.

Independent Contracting

Many companies will hire a visual contractor to work on a specific short-term project. A permanent position may be created if the need for the contractor's work extends to a longer period of time. Even if the new position has to be posted for all applicants, the experienced contractor has an excellent chance of securing the permanent position. This is often the easiest way to make your way into an organization, even though it may mean spending some time as an independent contractor.

Documenting Your Professional Qualifications

You are preparing for a career in a visual industry, so you will eventually develop a **portfolio** with examples of your professional work. Until then, a good cover letter and a simple but professional looking résumé are all you need. Simple is better. It is the style most business executives say they prefer to the fad versions that stream across their desks every May and June. There is a certain amount of ritual to job seeking. You do not need to reinvent the process.

A **portfolio** is a visual résumé, a portable case for presenting photographs, drawings, graphic designs, certificates, letters of recommendation, and other documentation of a person's professional experience.

Résumés

A simple résumé means *one* sheet of paper, listing your name, where you can be reached, your education, awards, and job experience to date. Spelling and grammar must be perfect, so it's a good idea to have someone else proofread your final copy. Fresh eyes will catch things you've missed because you're so familiar with the document. Needless to say, that reader must be a reliable speller and have good grammar skills. Don't trust your word processor spell-checker because it doesn't read minds and may misinterpret word choices (for example, *there* for *their,* or *too* for *two*).

The famous career objective statement on your résumé is optional, more applicable to a beginner who is applying for an entry-level position than to an experienced employee. A good interviewer will ask you about your long-range plans and goals later on.

Cover Letters

First, you have to *get* the interview. That's what the cover letter is all about. An effective cover letter will sell the reader on giving you a chance to discuss the position in person. The cover letter should link your training and work experience to the tasks required by the position. State the specific position you are seeking. Stress your strong work ethic and your ability to get along with people. Show how a part-time job you've held or a course you've taken convinced you that you belong in the field. Keep it short, keep it simple, and keep it focused on what you can bring to the company, not what you hope it will do for you. No one expects a beginner to have a huge list of accomplishments or experience. (See Figure 15.5.)

Portfolios

No portfolio at all is preferable to a weak one. Do not include photographs of your work from fine arts or any other projects you have done in school unless the work is *truly* exceptional and has won national awards or has appeared in a national publication. Photos from retail displays you've executed are acceptable. In any case, when you are just starting out, keep the portfolio presentation brief. Editing your own presentation is as important as editing any visual presentation you'll do. If you're not sure about the quality or effectiveness of a display photograph, ask someone from the visual merchandising department to analyze its merit as a portfolio item. This is just like asking another person to proofread what you've written in your résumé and cover letter. You need an objective opinion.

Invest in a simple black portfolio case with clear pages and a zipper closure. Place your résumé in the first sleeve and follow it with all of your favorite displays and floor or wall fixture presentations. If the photographs don't completely fill the sleeve, mount them on good quality paper. Slip thin cardstock into the sleeves between paper documents to give them

Jody Williams
22 Sheridan Street, NW
Washington, DC 20000

(202) 555-4418
JodyW@email.com

June 6, 2002

Ms. Simone Havel, Manager
Make Yourself at Home
333 Linden Hills Blvd.
Columbia, MD 21000

Dear Ms. Havel:

At the suggestion of Terry Romano, I am writing to inquire about the opening for a position as assistant manager at Make Yourself at Home. Mr. Romano was my advisor at the University of Maryland, where I recently earned my B.S. degree in marketing with a concentration in retailing.

For the past four years, I have been preparing for a career in the home fashion industry. In college, I completed courses in interior design, visual merchandising, fashion merchandising, advertising and promotion, marketing, and management. During this time, I worked at Crate&Barrel on weekends, and for several summers I was a sales associate at Restoration Hardware. I also volunteered as a visual merchandiser at the National Symphony thrift shop during the holiday season.

Interacting with clients, co-workers, and vendors in all three environments has convinced me that I have found my niche in home fashion retailing. The combination of my formal education and work experience has prepared me to begin my career in a management training position.

As a consumer, I have always enjoyed the unique range of products at Make Yourself at Home. The intimate size of the store, the inviting environment, and the knowledgeable sales staff make shopping there an enjoyable experience. I'm sure that it would be an equally pleasant place to work.

I would like to arrange an interview to learn more about the position, and I will phone you early next week to schedule an appointment. My résumé is enclosed for your consideration. I am looking forward to meeting you.

Yours truly,

Jody Williams

Jody Williams

Enclosure

A

Figure 15.5 A cover letter (A) and professional résumé (B).

Jody Williams
22 Sheridan Street, NW
Washington, DC 20000

(202) 555-4418
JodyW@email.com

EDUCATION

1998 – 2002

University of Maryland – B.S. in Marketing awarded May 2002

Concentration in retailing including courses in visual merchandising, advertising and promotion, fashion merchandising, marketing, and management

Grade point average 3.8

Honors
- Dean's list, four semesters
- Member of marketing honor society

Activities
- Set design for campus productions of *Porgy and Bess, Evita, Brighton Beach Memoirs*
- Decorations committee for Parents' Weekend dinner, 1999, 2000
- Advertising sales manager for college yearbook, 2001

EXPERIENCE

Sept. – May, 1998 – 2002

Sales associate
Crate&Barrel, Takoma Park, MD
- Customer service
- Cashier service
- Phone service
- Stock keeping, housekeeping

May – Sept., 1999 – 2002

Sales associate
Restoration Hardware, Silver Spring, MD
- Customer service
- Cashier service
- Phone service
- Stock keeping, housekeeping

Dec. 1998 – 2001

Volunteer visual merchandiser
National Symphony thrift shop, Washington, DC
- Helped to design and maintain holiday window displays
- Set up displays of incoming apparel and home fashion donations

INTERESTS AND ACTIVITIES

- Computer skills – Microsoft Word, Excel, Photoshop, Internet
- Photography
- Travel
- Yoga

B

A Retail Reality:
Common sense says that you should be appropriately groomed and dressed when you present yourself for interviews, but you'd be amazed to know how many applicants arrive chewing gum and wearing wrinkled clothes and unpolished shoes. Interviewers just shake their heads and slip those applications into their circular files. It's true: You have only seconds to make a good first impression.

more body. As your career progresses, edit your photographs to a dozen of your best. Also include any awards or recognition certificates that you receive.

Interviewing Effectively

You can prepare yourself for your interview by learning all you can about the company, by learning what to do at the interview, and by planning answers to the questions that you may be asked at the interview.

Preinterview Strategy

Candidates who've done their homework impress interviewed. Plan a preinterview strategy. Here are a few ideas that have worked for others:

- Research the organization's Website. You'll find company history there, and often its mission statement, lists of products, locations, and other information that you can later use in conversation with the interviewer. Print the pages and insert them into the notebook that you'll be taking to the interview. Invest in a professional looking cloth or leather-covered version rather than the usual college spiral or three-ring binder.

- Pay a visit to the store where you will be interviewed. This special trip will help you become familiar with the company's current promotions and strategies. Bring your notebook along and make a note of the store's strengths.

- During your store visit, analyze how the employees are dressed. Take your clothing cues from them, but plan to take it up one level for your interview. There is a wise old saying: "Dress for the job you want, not the one you have."

- Next, visit the company's competitors, so that you are able to have a discussion if the interviewer goes in that direction. The more knowledgeable you are, the greater your level of confidence will be. If the topic comes up during your interview, describe competitors objectively, never negatively.

- Select clothing that is appropriate for the environment where you would be working. Even if the company is having a "casual dress" day on your interview date, dress in business attire. Clean the outfit, if necessary, and always press it. Check the heels on your shoes; they should not show wear. Clean and polish them. This is the fashion industry. Dress as if you understand that. Look in the mirror, at least twice. You're the one on display today!

Your Interview

Here are some suggestions for a successful interview:

- On the day of your interview, arrive at least 10 minutes before your appointment. Turn off your cell phone and put it away. A few minutes at rest in the waiting room will help you to compose your thoughts.

- Excellent posture is a plus; it helps you radiate confidence—and allows more air into your lungs, which will send more oxygen to your brain and help you to think clearly.

- Make eye contact. Smile. Let your interviewer offer his or her hand to shake. When you respond, your grip should be brief and *gently* firm.

- Wait to be offered a seat. Once seated, do not handle anything on the interviewer's desk or help yourself to the candy dish.

- Answer questions thoughtfully and clearly. If you don't know the answer to a question, say so. See the list of typical interview questions that follows.

- Let the interviewer know you are interested in the job and excited at the prospect of working for the company.

- Once the interviewer has had the chance to ask you questions, indicate that you also have a few and open your notebook to your list of questions so that you can take notes. Not only will you have a record for yourself, but the interviewer will perceive that you are serious about the job opportunity.

- After the interview, shake the interviewer's hand again and thank her or him for the opportunity to learn more about the company.

- Send a thank-you note the next day and again express your interest in the position and the organization.

Typical Interview Questions

You should be prepared to answer these typical questions:

- Why are you interested in a position with our company?

- What are your short-term career goals?

- What are your long-term goals?

- What are your strengths?

- What are your weaknesses? (Neutralize the negative in that sentence and rephrase it by responding with something like "My greatest challenge is. . . .")

A list of questions you would like your interviewer to answer might include

- What are the most critical responsibilities for this position?

- May I see a written job description?

- What positions could someone working in this area grow into?

- What are the company's expansion plans?

- How would you describe your organization's culture?

- What benefits do you offer to your full-time employees? (Save this question for after you have been called back for a second or third interview, if this will be one of your first positions in the field.)

Connecting with the Industry

Some professional organizations act as employment clearinghouses as a service to their members. The National Association of Store Fixture Manufacturers (NASFM) welcomes résumés from people interested in connecting with the fixture design and manufacturing companies that belong to the organization. When you go to NASFM's Website (**www.nasfm.com**), you'll see a Member Only section marked "Personnel Available," where the organization posts job seekers' résumés. You may also fax your cover letter and résumé to (954) 893-7500 for inclusion on this secure site, or e-mail to **nasfm@nasfm.org** and attach your documents. NASFM's street address is: 3595 Sheridan Street, Suite 200, Hollywood, FL 33021.

The National Association of Display Industries (NADI) offers a similar service. This association was founded in 1942 and has always been a leader in the visual community. It is composed of retailers, manufacturers, and allied disciplines of this industry. It is "dedicated to fostering the growth of the visual merchandising and store design industries." You may send a résumé via e-mail at **nadi@nasfm.org,** fax it to (954) 893-8375, or mail it to NADI, 3595 Sheridan St., Suite 200, Hollywood, FL 33021.

Future Career Goals

The visual merchandising Industry has a wonderful history of recognizing leaders in the retail design field. There are two prestigious awards offered each year: the Markopoulos Award and the PAVE Lifetime Achievement Award.

A Retail Reality:
Now that you have a sense about your interviewer's style, you can be creative with your thank-you note. If your interviewer was strictly professional, your thank-you note should be the same. If the interviewer was casual and creative, respond accordingly. One candidate for a graphic design position sent his interviewer a pair of work gloves with a computer-designed label that read, "Ready to Work." His name, phone number, and "Thank You" were also imprinted on the label—and yes, he got the job!

The Markopoulos Award was established in 1996 by *Display and Design Ideas* magazine, in honor of the late Andrew Markopoulos, who was the senior vice president of visual merchandising at Dayton Hudson's department store.

The award recipient must exhibit an unwavering commitment to design excellence, with demonstrated creativity, innovation, leadership, and mentoring.

Markopoulos Award and PAVE Award Winners

- 1996: Andrew Markopoulos, senior vice president of visual merchandising, Dayton Hudson
- 1997: Ignaz Gorischek, vice president, visual planning and presentation, Neiman Marcus
- 1998: Tony Mancini, vice president, global retail store development, Walt Disney Imagineering and Walt Disney Parks and Resorts
- 1999: Judith Bell, corporate manager of visual merchandising, Target
- 2000: James Mansour, founder, Mansour Design
- 2001: Linda Fargo, vice president, visual merchandising, Bergdorf Goodman
- 2002: Chuck Luckenbill, founder, Luckenbill Design
- 2003: Simon Doonan, creative director, Barney's
- 2004: Christine Belich, executive creative director, Sony
- 2005: James Damian, senior vice president, Experience Development Group, Best Buy

The PAVE awards are presented by the Planning and Visual Education Committee. Following are recent winners:

- 1996 Federated Department Stores
  Mercantile Stores
  Greneker
- 1997 *VM + SD*
  Nieman Marcus
  Nautica
  The Walt Disney Company
- 2000 Martin Pegler—lifetime achievement
  Larry Israel—lifetime achievement
- 2000 Martin Pegler—lifetime achievement
  Larry Israel—lifetime achievement
  Wayne Visbeen—chairman emeritus
- 2003 Richard Stolls, president, Trimco—lifetime achievement

Shoptalk

By Janet Groeber, former associate publisher/editor, CSA by Design (Chain Store Age)

I can't ever remember a time that I wasn't involved in some kind of publication. My family still laughs about the newspaper I started, *The Groeber Gazette,* which was designed to inform my mom and dad, brother and sisters about our activities.

I guess I got the idea from my dad—a reader of several daily newspapers, myriad magazines, and editor of a union newsletter. I had a rubber stamp set; he had a typewriter. From grade school through college, I worked on newspapers, yearbooks, and magazines.

In college, I took a job doing layout for the student newspaper, which helped pay for expenses. My coursework as a communications and journalism student included news reporting, writing, editing, and law, and I rounded out the communications portion to include art and theater history, mass media, stagecraft, music appreciation, literature, public speaking, psychology, politics, geology, geography, and business. In short, a liberal arts education. As an upperclassman I landed an associate editorship on the quarterly student magazine—and that cemented my desire to work professionally for a magazine.

Interestingly, I was working summers in a local department store as well as between breaks at the same time. There, I was exposed to visual merchandising, formerly called the display department. And, though I was working in the bargain basement, another young college part-timer and I put together our first presentation. It was a fully ensembled outfit pulled together from merchandise on our floor and presented in the bottom half of an old wooden showcase. I was hooked! I can remember visiting the store's attic filled with fixtures, displayers, and props and thinking "What a world."

After college, I worked for a textbook publisher. My job was to research photography for business textbooks for high school and college students. Among our references and resources were publications such as *Stores* and *Visual Merchandising and Store Design*. Later, I learned *VM + SD* was based in Cincinnati. Eventually I met someone who worked at the company, and that person introduced me to the right people. When I was hired as an assistant editor, my friends and family thought I'd died and gone to heaven. I was working my two favorite passions! Within eight years, I was named editor and later took on the additional duties as associate publisher.

Next, I did a stint on the other side with two retail interior design and architectural firms. I helped gain new business for one and handled media relations for the other. I actually got to see another side of the process that I'd only been reporting on, and, of course, it was a wonderful addition to my professional education. And, when I could (and it was appropriate), I accepted assignments with other retail and design-oriented trade magazines. Just recently, I returned to publishing to help launch a new section on design, planning, and visual merchandising with the editors of *Chain Store Age* magazine. Once again, I am using both my newfound and long-term experience and skills in my chosen profession.

Out-of-the-Box Challenge

1 Personal Presentation

Look

Name two people you admire in the business world. List the traits you find admirable.

Compare

Compare their traits with your own.

Innovate

How can you improve the way you present yourself? What are you doing to sell yourself?

2 Informational Interview

Look

Setup an informational interview with a visual professional. Assess the traits and interests this person possesses that contribute to his or her success in the visual field.

Compare

Compare this person's traits and interests with your own.

Innovate

How can you improve on the skills that are necessary for success in the visual field?

3 Leadership Skills

Look

Examine the culture of your classroom. Which students seem to be most successful at getting their ideas implemented? Who are the class leaders?

Compare

Compare the techniques they use with your own current leadership skills.

Innovate

What do you think you need to do to further develop yourself as a leader? This could become an action plan for you.

Critical Thinking

Department Identity Building

The text suggests that you could start an internal marketing program for your own visual merchandising department as a motivational tool for people working there and also to raise your group or team's corporate visibility (stressing your department's potential to contribute to the company's bottom line). Create an identity for your department by completing these two projects.

1 Identity Building

1. Design a logo that a visual merchandising department might use as its marketing symbol.

2. Write a tag line (motto) to accompany the logo: for example: "Creative Solutions That Increase Sales."

3. Write a departmental goal statement in 25 words or less: for example: "To train store teams to execute the latest techniques in product presentation."

4. Design an interoffice memo form using your logo.

2 Building Your Own Brand Identity

Use the following questions and assignments to develop a strategy to market yourself:

1. What do you want to do with your visual merchandising career?

- List your *long-term* career goals: for example, what do you want to be doing 5 years from now?

- List your *short-term* employment goals: things that must happen in the next year or sooner in order for you to reach those long-term goals.

2. Name two potential employers in your area.

3. Whom do you know right now who might be able to help you connect with those potential employers?

- Name the people you know right now.

- Describe your *networking plan* to meet more people connected in some way with the employers you've identified.

4. Write a brief script that you could use for calling each company to arrange an informational interview.

5. Describe your plan of action for a preinterview on-site visit. List the elements that you would be looking for as you visit each store prior to an informational interview.

6. What would you need to know in order to determine which company might have the better opportunity for your career development and employment goals? Write down at least five possible interview questions to ask each potential employer. Include questions about working climate, work ethic, and so on.

7. Think about the things you know about yourself and what you've learned about the visual merchandising field that would make you a good "fit" as an employee for each company. Envision each of the potential employers you've identified for this activity as "shoppers" and yourself as a branded "product." Write a short paragraph that explains why either of them would want to hire you? Describe the unique talents, interests, and skills that makeup your personal brand identity and make you a truly value-added individual.

Case Study
The Next Step

The Situation

You have graduated from your training program, and you are ready to look for work in a retail setting as an entry-level visual merchandiser. You realize that you don't have a great deal of (or, perhaps, any) experience in the field. Nevertheless, you are determined to work for one of the following types of stores:

- A large national chain with hundreds of stores. You'd like to explore several parts of the country before settling in one area.

- A mom-and-pop operation in the city where you live. This company doesn't have a visual merchandising staff, but you'd like to create such a position.

- A retail company selling merchandise that you've purchased to pursue your favorite outdoor sport. It has a number of regional stores in the five-state area and also has a very busy Internet site that reaches out to specialized shoppers all over the world.

- Any store that has a bank of closed display windows. You want as much experience as you can get to build a portfolio for a position in New York City a few years from now.

Your Challenge

Working with your present résumé and educational experience, design a job strategy that will give you the experience you need to take your next professional step and then do the following:

1. Modify your current résumé to emphasize the skills, work experience, work habits, and personal accomplishments that you currently have.

2. Set long-term and short-term goals.

3. Examine your interests and experiences outside of work.

4. Think about your personal characteristics in terms of strengths to capitalize on and weaknesses to overcome, as you set about this task.

Capstone Case Study
Creating and Communicating a Brand Image

This case problem concerns a fictional retail opportunity that has many real-world counterparts. In the introductory stage, you're asked to think about the store concept and imagine what you might do to bring it to life. Have fun with the assignment. Let your imagination take you away.

The Situation

You are an owner, store designer, or visual merchandising executive in a new stand-alone retail store that will be located in a midsized metropolitan area with a well-developed downtown business district. You have a long-term lease on the main floor of a modern-looking brick-front retail building that has 3500 (50′ × 70′) square feet on its main floor. It has a set of two (8′ × 7′) windows on either side of a generous double-door entry. The store's interior is completely open and undecorated—literally a blank page for a store owner to work with in developing a retail concept.

Step One

Select a merchandise category that you will enjoy researching and working with for this capstone project, which will challenge you to use information and ideas from all of the chapters in this textbook. You may select your own store type or "look, compare, and innovate" on the following ideas:

- A bridal and special occasion shop
- A men's business wear or specialty sport, clothing, and equipment shop
- A women's size, women's tall, or women's petite fashion shop
- A "tween" shop aimed at girls from 9 to 13 years of age
- A specialty bookstore—selling only mysteries, travel books, poetry, or cookbooks
- A tabletop store—featuring merchandise for setting a table and serving food products
- A luggage store—with everything needed for travel from carry-on bags and pet carriers to footlockers and wardrobe trunks
- An antiques store specializing in lighting fixtures and lamps
- An ethnic design shop featuring textiles, needlework, art, and handcrafts from the Tibetan culture
- A plant store or floral design shop
- A greengrocer, artisan bakery, or other food specialty shop

Step Two

Select a name for this new store and explain how the store's name will help you communicate the image ideas you've generated to a potential customer—for example, what does the name communicate about the owner, the business, or the merchandise.

Step Three

Before you commit anything to paper, challenge your imagination and think outside of the box about the following ideas as you begin your work:

1. List any trends that you might recognize from current events, literature, entertainment, or other lifestyle elements that you might tap into or that might have an impact on the way you approach an overall plan for this store's merchandising.

2. Think about this book's views about brand image and write your preliminary vision statement describing what the store is going to be like.

3. What kind of mental image do you want your customers to have of this store?

4. What kind of physical image do you want this store to communicate?

5. With your target customers in mind, name some of your "must haves" in terms of store layout.

6. Describe how your layout will affect customers' mental images of themselves and your new store.

7. What communication goals will you consider when displaying merchandise and signing it?

8. What kinds of opportunities do you think you'll have to teach your customers about your merchandise?

9. What role could merchandise presentation play in teaching customers about the use of the products your store carries?

10. List as many presentation possibilities as you can imagine. For example, you might specify "interior windows" on sightlines.

11. How important will the role of the salesperson be in your new store?

12. Would a salesperson in this store need any special qualifications? How would a salesperson interact with the store's visual presentation strategies?

13. Does the salesperson have to "match" your store's brand image in any way? Do you see any particular opportunities to make a statement about your store's brand image by hiring a certain type of salesperson?

14. Now that you've completed the preliminary thinking for presenting this novel store to the buying public, do you think there is any special "promotable" angle to this store's image, its mission, its merchandise? Explain what that angle might be and how you'd use it to communicate image to your targeted customer.

Step Four

Describe store merchandise (use photographs or illustrations from other sources and include items from all categories you intend to sell).

Step Five

Describe your target customer in a customer profile. Prepare a fully developed paragraph about age, education, gender, interests, lifestyle, occupation, income, and the like.

Step Six

Compose a mission statement that explains the store's purpose; list at least five marketing objectives and a number of related strategies to meet each objective. Include the visual merchandising component.

Step Seven

Describe the store's brand image or how you want customers to think of the store. Include examples from the store's proposed physical look.

Step Eight

Design its exterior look and its exterior signing to describe how the store will "greet" customers who approach the building and what it will "say" to passersby.

Step Nine

Design the store's interior in terms of its atmospheric elements—sounds, lighting and lighting levels, displays, traffic patterns, directional signing, informational signing.

Step Ten

Choose colors for the walls and floors and, if possible, include paint chips, samples, and so on. Explain how these materials support brand image and the atmospherics for your store.

Step Eleven

Choose fixtures that carry out the brand image message to present the merchandise to customers. Design your own fixtures or use photographs and illustrations from published or Internet sources. Explain why the fixtures you've chosen are a good match for facilitating both merchandise presentation and store image.

Step Twelve

Devise a planogram to show locations of fixtures throughout the store. On it, locate office/storage space, restroom(s), and fitting rooms (if appropriate). You may add space for these items along the store's back wall if you need the space.

Step Thirteen

Write sign copy for five items of merchandise (see step four) that enhances your store's brand image and demonstrates the "tone of voice" you intend to use when you communicate with customers.

Step Fourteen

Describe the type of display window treatment and interior editorial displays you intend to use, and indicate where they go on your planogram.

Step Fifteen

Select mannequins or mannequin alternatives (if appropriate) for your store's image.

Step Sixteen

Complete a wall elevation and merchandise display like the planograms in Chapters 5 and 7.

Step Seventeen

Describe an in-store special event appropriate to the merchandise and the store's image.

Step Eighteen

Present your project to your class or your instructor.

GLOSSARY

accent lighting describes lighting effects designed to emphasize certain wall areas, merchandise displays, or architectural features in a retail setting.

adjacencies are thoughtfully planned layouts that position same "end use" products next to each other. A logical adjacency, for example, would be to position shoes and hosiery side by side.

ambient lighting describes general, overall lighting.

atmospherics is a word coined by retailers to describe the elements (lighting effects, sound-levels, aromas, etc.) that appeal to our five senses and contribute to the overall environment of a store.

bid is an estimate of manufacturing costs to produce a fixture or perform a service and a formal offer to do so. Once the bid, and all its terms, have been accepted, a contract is awarded. This formal agreement between the buyer and the manufacturer becomes the official basis for actual production, delivery schedule, and terms of payment.

brand image is the retailer's identity in the shopper's mind. It encompasses not only merchandise brands and types but also store environment, reputation, and service. In some cases, the retailer employs the store's name or another exclusive title on its private-label merchandise; for example, Bloomingdale's "Bloomies" label, Macy's "INC.," or Sears' "Craftsman."

capacity fixture holds large quantities of merchandise, usually showing a single style in several colors and in a complete range of sizes.

catwalks are narrow walkways. In theatrical production, they are the bridge over the stage lights up in the "fly" area that allows technicians to reach, change, and aim spotlights. In fashion, it's the narrow runway that extends beyond the stage that allows fashion show patrons unobstructed views of models and garments.

color rendition is the degree to which lighting allows colors to be viewed under conditions that are closest to those offered by natural light. The lighting industry uses the term

CRI (color rendering index) when listing specifications on each lamp.

color story tells customers through a store's color-coordinated or color-keyed product groupings show how to use a season's trend colors.

colorways are the assorted colors or groups of colors a manufacturer has chosen for its line of fashion products. A manufacturer's representative might tell a store buyer that a polished cotton skirt comes in three different colorways: jewel-toned solids, pastel floral prints, and earth-toned plaids.

combination floor plan employs the best features of several selling floor layouts in an overall plan that suits a retailer's specific strategies.

crossbar is a rectangular tubing garment rod used to hang apparel on walls or floor fixtures.

cross-merchandising refers to moving merchandise across traditional department or classification lines to combine elements in a single department or display. For example, books of poetry, romantic novels, candles, bath salts, terry cloth robes, and over-sized bath towels could be brought together in a single display.

endcaps are valuable display and stocking spaces at the ends of gondola fixtures. They may be used to feature a sampling of the merchandise on either side of the gondola, for new merchandise offerings, for value-priced products, or for advertised specials. They may be either pegged or shelved.

étagères are tall furniture units with open shelves. Originally used only as pieces of furniture in homes, these elegant cases adapt well as display fixtures.

face-outs are hardware for hanging merchandise so that the full front of the item is visible. Face-outs may utilize straight arms or slanted arms that create cascading "waterfall" effects.

fashion editorials are displays in strategic locations within a store that reflect retailers' support for merchandise and trends in the form of strong fashion statements. Editorials are always positioned in high-traffic areas like store entrances, department entrances, escalator platforms, main aisles, and at the ends of aisles on sight lines. Other names used by retailers for these locations include strike-points, hot zones, focals, and interior windows.

faux pas a phrase taken from the French for "false step," is an error in fashion judgment or a mistake in coordination techniques.

feature fixtures typically hold smaller merchandise assortments, allowing presentation of two styles (on a two-way) or a coordinate grouping (on a four-way). They are intended to spotlight items rather than show full category assortments.

flagship stores display the highest ideals of a company's brand image. Every detail from fitting room hooks to floor coverings reflect the company's brand. Stores built after the "flagship" is developed are usually modified for cost effectiveness. Examples of flagship stores are Niketown in Chicago, Prada in Soho, New York City, and both Levi's and Old Navy in San Francisco.

fluorescent lamps are sealed glass tubes filled with mercury vapor. Their inner surfaces are coated with a mixture of phosphor powder. When electricity arcs through the gases in the lamps, the gases produce ultraviolet energy that is absorbed by the coating and cause the powder to become fluorescent, emitting visible light.

Fortune 500 companies are the 500 largest companies in the United States ranked by revenue (gross sales).

four-way fixture also called a customer, features a hanging coordinate group or small (24–48 items) quantities of separates presented as coordinated outfits.

free-flow layout has selling fixtures arranged in loosely grouped, informal, nonlinear formations to encourage browsing.

G

garment rod is a length of round or flat metal tubing that fits into wall-mounted brackets and is used to hold rows of garments on hangers. Garment rods are generally cut in 4-foot lengths to allow flexibility in wall design and to avoid overloading.

gondola is a versatile four-sided capacity fixture that may be shelves for folded or stackable products and set with garment rods to show apparel on hangers.

grid layout is a linear design for selling floors where fixtures are arranged to form vertical and horizontal aisles throughout the store.

gridwall is a wall system of metal wire that accepts brackets and display accessories with special gridwall fittings.

H

halogen lamps contain highly pressurized halogen gas that, combined with evaporated tungsten, cycles the gas

back to a filament which, in turn, cleans the glass while maintaining lumen output throughout the lifetime of the lamp.

high concept stores are stores with store design themes that dominate the total presentation. Every detail, from fitting room hooks to fixtures to floor coverings, fits the theme. The Disney Store and Niketown are examples. Overall visual image appears to be as important to the stores' identity as the perceived value of any products they offer.

high craft look describes fixtures that appear to have been made by a cabinetmaker rather than mass-produced in a factory.

home meal replacement (HMR) foods are complete ready-to-eat meals (portioned out in microwave-safe covered serving plates) or prepared entrees like meat loaf or roasted chickens.

incandescent lamps are glass bulbs with interior tungsten filaments that are heated by electric current, producing light. You know them as common light bulbs.

institutional windows are display windows devoted to intangible ideas and causes; they promote an image for the store as an institution rather than feature merchandise.

intensity is the degree of saturation of a color.

kiosks are freestanding selling units, open on one or all sides.

lamp has at least two distinct meanings. In the lighting industry, lamp is another word for light bulb. In common terms, it applies to a lighting fixture complete with a bulb, a power source, a base, and a "shade" that is either decorative or purely functional.

lead time is the amount of time it takes to complete products from receipt of order through production.

leaselines are the boundary lines where store space begins and the mall's common area ends.

leveraging used as a verb, means gaining a mechanical advantage, or adding impact, power, or effectiveness. An example would be leveraging a store's brand identity by using an interactive display window.

minimal floor layout almost gallerylike in its simplicity, shows small selections of handcrafted or very exclusive merchandise.

mom-and-pop store is a phrase that comes from early retailing when many retailers were in family businesses and often lived in apartments above their stores. Today, it refers to small, independent retailers.

multiple sales is a term that refers to a transaction where two or more items have been purchased. For example, a shopper buys a single CD plus a carrying case.

N

niche marketing means identifying a very specific market segment and offering a product or assortment of products that research shows the segment wants or needs and can afford to buy.

O

open sell is fixturing that makes most merchandise (even items traditionally kept in locked cases) accessible to shoppers without the assistance of salespeople.

operational signs are signs that relate to the day-to-day business of a store; listing store hours, return policies, emergency exits, locations of help phones, department locations, and fitting room policies.

optical weight is how important, large, or heavy an object appears to be versus how much it really weighs or how large it is in actual scale.

outriggers are decorative or functional elements mounted to a wall at right angles in order to define, separate, and frame categories of merchandise presented on shelves or display fixtures.

P

pegwall system is a backer panel with a gridwork of holes into which pegwall hooks and other specialty fixtures may be inserted.

pivot pieces are the dominant items that dictate the direction (end-use, fabrication, style, and color) for all subsequent pieces used in coordinated outfits.

planograms are drawings that show how merchandise and selling fixtures should be placed on selling floors, wall sections, or freestanding displays and window displays. They are planning tools that make it possible to communicate consistent store layout and décor directives to multiple locations thereby creating a strong identity for the retailer.

portfolios are visual résumés carried in portable cases (also called portfolios) to present photographs, drawings, graphic designs, certificates, letters of recommendation, and other documentation of a person's professional experience.

price points are the actual numbers (for example, $12.99) used on signs to inform shoppers of prices.

promotional mix is a combination of communication tools—advertising, in-store marketing, special events, and personal selling—that tells targeted customers about stores and their merchandise.

props (stage properties) are items or objects other than painted scenery and actors' costumes that are used on a stage set. The term has migrated to the visual vocabulary to mean decorative items or objects other than merchandise and signs used in a display.

prototype is the original model of a store upon which a series of stores are based. Before rolling out a dozen retail stores, a prototype is built so that design features may be tested and refined if necessary. The same process is used in the development of custom merchandise fixtures and visual fixtures.

R

racetrack layout exposes shoppers to a great deal of merchandise as they follow perimeter traffic aisles with departments on the right and left of circular, square, rectangular, or oval "racetracks."

retrofitting is the act of adding architectural features, fixtures or other elements after the original structure is completed.

riser is a display unit used to elevate merchandise in a composition so that the overall presentation has visual interest and variety.

round rack (rounder) is a capacity fixture fabricated in several diameters and adjustable heights for stocking quantities of basic apparel items on hangers.

S

sell-down also called sell-through, is a retail term for the period during which an item or grouping is on the selling floor, from introduction at full price through the markdown stage.

sightline refers to the area a person can see from a particular vantage point—the view at the end of an aisle, or at the top or bottom of an escalator, for example.

signature fixture is an attention-getting, one-of-a-kind unit positioned at store and department entrances that reflects a stores' brand images.

slatwall is a wall system of horizontal backer panels with evenly spaced slots that accept brackets and display accessories with special slatwall fittings.

soffits are long ledges, permanent arches, or boxes reaching down from a store's ceiling to its top shelves or usable wall space. They are often used to mask nondecorative (functional) lighting fixtures that serve to illuminate merchandise displayed on store walls.

soft aisle layouts are floor sets with fixtures arranged in groups, creating natural aisles without any change in floor covering to designate separate aisle space.

sourcing (or resourcing) is a term coined in the last decade to describe the process of finding resources for use in a business.

straight arm is a perpendicular display arm affixed to a wall standard, slatwall, gridwall, T-stand, or other selling floor fixture to show small quantities of hanging merchandise.

striking a mannequin means removing its support rod and base plate in order to secure it to the floor with wire so that it appears to stand on its own.

strip malls contain side-by-side stores with parking lots immediately outside their doors. Some strip malls may have enclosed walkways, but they are not configured under one large roof as conventional covered malls are.

superquad is a four-armed capacity floor fixture with adjustable height used for showing items purchased in depth or coordinate groupings of pants, skirts, blouses, and sweaters or jackets.

target markets are identified (targeted) segments of the population that research indicates are good "fits" for retailers' products or service offerings. These are the groups at which retailers aim all of their stores' promotional communication efforts.

task lighting is designed to illuminate work areas where strong, bright light simplifies detail work.

two-way fixture also called a T-stand, is a two-armed hanging fixture used to feature 12–24 items of trend apparel or test merchandise.

venues are locations where special events or entertainments take place. The word comes from the Latin verb venire meaning "to come."

vignettes are a condensed version of a larger scene. For example, a home furnishings vignette might establish the mood and the scene of a larger room with only a few elements—a chair, an end table, and a lamp.

waterfall is a set of angled display arms affixed to wall standards, slatwall or gridwall systems, and T-stands (two-way or four-way), or other selling floor fixtures to show cascades of hanging merchandise.

way-finding is a term used by architects to describe any tools that help customers to "find their way" through a store. Signs positioned in highly visible areas—on walls or hanging from the ceiling—are examples of way-finding strategies.

DIRECTORY OF VISUAL MERCHANDISING PROFESSIONALS

The visual merchandising leaders pictured here have shared their thoughts with readers who are considering a career in this field. If you are interested in positions with any of the organizations with which they are affiliated, follow standard procedures with human resources departments. Do not contact these individuals directly.

Ken Albright, President, Seven Continents
NADI Board of Directors
PAVE Board of Directors
NASFM
TEC (The Executive Committee)
"There is a visual message in everything you see."

Judith Bell, Group Manager, MAGIC, Marketing & Guest Insight Center, Target Corporation
NADI Board of Directors-officer
PAVE Board of Directors, past officer
NASFM Advisory Board
DDI Editorial Advisory Board
Fashion Group International
"Do something that you're afraid to do every day."

Tom Beebe, Creative Director, DNR Former Creative Director, Paul Stuart
NADI Board of Directors

"Pins . . . wire . . . thread . . . a career in display . . . fulfilling passion. Dramatic or small gestures . . . a magic world of change. An art form of inspiration . . . imagination . . . originality. I believe in the craft. Full speed ahead!"

Rick Burbee, Creative Director, Sears Full Line Stores
PAVE Advisory Board

"Visual merchandising is the perfect career for anyone with the ability to think creatively, communicate clearly, and evoke continual change in the store environment."

Christine Belich, Executive Creative Director, Sony
NADI Board of Directors

"Make sure that you are passionate and obsessive about details. This separates the true visual 'greats' from the rest. You've got to love the details."

Linda Cahan, Principal, Cahan & Company, Retail Visual Designer and Consultant
SVM

"There are *many* creative people out in the world and no one is the best—but if you want to succeed, learn how to communicate by listening, hearing, understanding, keeping an open mind, realizing that there is more than one right way of doing things, respecting other peoples' opinions, staying calm, breathing, laughing with someone—not at them—and learning how to explain something more than one way, because if someone doesn't understand your idea the first time, explaining it the same way, only louder, isn't going to work!"

Simon Doonan, Creative Director, Barneys
Author, *Confessions of a Window Dresser*
"If you take some risks, you may even create
some trends."

**Eric Feigenbaum, President, Globe Arts:
A Retail Design and Visual Merchandising
Consultancy**
SVM—Chairman
PAVE—founding member and Education Chair
Fashion Institute of Technology, NYC—Adjunct Instructor,
Retail Advisory Board
of the Display and Exhibit Design Department
Laboratory Institute of Merchandising, NYC—
Adjunct Instructor
DDI Editorial Advisory Board
"Absorb all that surrounds you; look, listen, and feel; then
endeavor to move the world."

**John Dougan, President of Presentations
Plus, Inc.**
NADI Board of Directors—Officer
WAVM—past President
"This quote, from George Lincoln, a former Commandant of
West Point, has guided me for the past twenty-five years:
'You have to pick good people and pick them young, before
others get into the competition. Then help them grow, keep
in touch, and exploit excellence.'"

Gareth Fenley, Editor,
Display & Design Ideas **magazine**
IALD, press affiliate member
"Research by Display & Design Ideas magazine shows that
retailers are looking to hire people who can envision and
guide the total development of brand identities. Computer
skills are a must, but most equally valuable is the ability to
make a verbal presentation."

Dan Evans, President, Joint
NADI President
IIDA member
ISP member and past chapter President
PAVE Board of Directors
"Always remember—there is no such thing as a bad
creative idea, only bad timing."

**Denny Gerdeman, Principal, Chute
Gerdeman Design**
ISP
NASFM Advisory Council
"Sometimes genius is purely innovative application. A lot of
times a specific problem has already been solved, but not in
your industry. Remember to look outside your own industry
for solutions."

Larry Gerow, President, Area Code 212 Display
"Feed your creativity constantly—use the arts as fuel for inspiration."

Steve Kaufman, Editor, *VM + SD* **magazine**
"Create goals, but allow for the fact that you will change, the world will change, and opportunities will change."

Ignaz Gorischek, Vice President, Visual Planning and Presentation, Neiman Marcus
PAVE Board of Directors
"If you really want to learn, ride escalators with your customer; you will hear it all!"

Chuck Luckenbill, Luckenbill Design
NADI Board of Directors 1994–1998
DDI Editorial Advisory Board
"Be flexible . . . be curious . . . be honest. Have the courage of your convictions and don't take yourself too seriously."

Greg M. Gorman, Principal, Creative Services, GMG Design, Inc.
PAVE—Chairman
ISP
Landmarks Association of St. Louis
"Challenge the norm, because change is a mandatory partner for survival."

Tony Mancini, Sr., Vice President, Global Retail Store Development, Walt Disney Imagineering and Walt Disney Parks and Resorts
NADI Board of Directors
PAVE—Board of Directors
NASFM—Advisory Board
DDI Editorial Advisory Board
"It's not just your ideas that make a program successful, but how you present and package them—you're selling ideas every day, and remember, practice what you preach."

Janet Groeber, RE:Media
NADI Board of Directors
PAVE Board of Directors—Officer
ISP—honorary member
SVM—media member
"As you follow your desires, see as much as you can, do as much as you are able, make as many lasting friendships as you can, remain open-minded and, always listen, listen, listen to what others have to say."

James Mansour, Executive Vice President, Visual Merchandising Macys East, NYC
"Set the highest standards for your work and compare your work to the best in the world."

Cindy McCracken, Director of Visual Merchandising, Big Lots
PAVE Board of Directors
"Find inspiration in every single thing you do."

Ed Pettersen, Vice President, Visual Merchandising, Circuit City
ISP
PAVE—founding member
"Use your imagination to make a visual statement that refuses to be ignored by the customer."

Ralph Pucci, President and CEO of Pucci International, Ltd.
NADI
VNY
"Don't be afraid to be different or to take chances."

Ed Shilling, Sales Representative, Neidermaier, Chicago, Pucci, NYC
"Don't be afraid to move on to the next step, don't be afraid of challenge, and don't follow the rules!"

Jim Smart, President, Smart Associates
SVM
ISP
President, Board of Directors, Dale Warland Singers
Board of Directors, ARC of Hennepin County
Mixed Blood Theatre, past Board of Directors
Minneapolis Arts Commission
Board Of Directors Minneapolis Children's Theatre
"Learn to Sell."

Richard Stolls, CEO of Trim Corp. of America
Affiliations: NADI—Treasurer, past President
PAVE—founding member, Treasurer
SVM—founding father
"If you plan a career in visual merchandising, be prepared for long hours and hard work, but—if you give it all you have, and you have passion—you will be greatly rewarded."

RoxAnna A. Sway, Editor-in-Chief,
Display & Design Ideas **magazine**
Institute of Store Planners—professional member
SVM—professional member
College Art Association of America—professional member
National Accreditation Board of American Colleges and Universities—professional member
"Your talent, your taste level, your design philosophy—and ultimately the level of success you achieve in life—are all defined (or limited) by the range of your experiences. So get out from behind that computer and get as much experience as you can."

Kate Ternus, Marketing Instructor, Century College

Fashion Group International

IFEA (International Festivals and Events Association)

MFEA (Minnesota Festivals and Events Association)

"As a 'work in progress,' you're a lifelong learner. Don't even think you're finished—there's always something new to try, somewhere unfamiliar to go, someone new to know."

Wayne Visbeen, Founder and President, Visbeen Associates Inc., Architects

PAVE Board of Directors—founding member and Chairman Emeritus

AIA

SVM

IIDA

ISP

NRF Store Planning and Visual Merchandising Board— past Chair

"Absorb every aspect of retailing in the retail environment during your training. The person who is multifaceted is valuable to the success of the retail store from sales to visual merchandising, from fashion to accessorizing, and from architecture to housekeeping."

Ronald Thiele, Visual Merchandising Implementation Director, Nordstrom, Inc.

DDI Editorial Advisory Board

"Take personal pride in what you do. Look at each of your creations (even daily) and don't be satisfied until you feel like you can actually write your signature on it as a true artist would."

Marianne Wilson, Senior Editor,
Chain Store Age **magazine**
"Always put the customer first."

REFERENCES AND RESOURCES

Chapter 1: Albrecht, Karl. *The Creative Corporation.* Homewood, IL: Dow Jones-Irwin, 1987.

Aleinikov, Andrei G. *Mega Creativity: Five Steps to Thinking like a Genius.* Cincinnati: Walking Stick Press, 2002.

Allan, Jerry and Georgina. *The Horse and the Iron Ball.* Minneapolis: Lerner Publishing Group, 2000.

Csikszentmihalyi. Mihaly. *Creativity: Flow and the Psychology of Discovery and Invention.* New York: HarperCollins, 1996.

Eberle, Robert. *SCAMPER: Games for Imagination Development.* Buffalo, New York: DOK Publishers, 1977.

Edelson, Sharon. "Gene Moore, Longtime Tiffany's Window Designer, VP, Dead at 88." *Women's Wear Daily,* November 25, 1998.

Hanks, Kurt and Parry, Jay. *Wake Up Your Creative Genius.* Menlo Park, CA: Crisp Publications, 1991.

Jennings, Jason and Haughton, Laurence. *It's not the Big that eat the Small, it's the Fast that eat the Slow.* New York: Harper Collins, 2002.

Kelly, Tom with Littman, Jonathan. *The Art of Innovation.* New York, NY: Doubleday, 2001.

Loehr, Jim and Schwartz, Tony. *The Power of Full Engagement.* New York: Free Press, 2003.

O'Brien, Tim. "The Value of Foolish Questions." *Saint Paul Pioneer Press,* March 10, 1999.

Ueland, Brenda. *If You Want to Write.* St. Paul, MN: Graywolf Press, 1997.

Chapter 2: www.bloomingdales.com

"Cotton Incorporated's Lifestyle Monitor TM." *Women's Wear Daily,* November 5, 1998.

Levy, Melissa. "Wraps Come Off Lifestyle Center." *Star Tribune,* September 12, 2003.

Lindeman, Teresa F. "Betting bigger isn't better, Kaufmann's shows off smaller Waterfront store that's aimed at giving the public what it wants." *Post-Gazette.com,* October 15, 2003.

Socha, Miles. "Shaking Sameness: Luxury Goes Custom To Rev Up Consumers." *Women's Wear Daily,* January 2, 2003.

Shimp, Terrance A. *Advertising, Promotion and Supplimental Aspects of Integrated Marketing Communications,* 4th ed. Fort Worth, TX: The Dryden Press, 1997.

Underhill, Paco. *Why We Buy: The Science of Shopping.* New York: Simon and Schuster, 1999.

"Designer Stores Go Local." *Women's Wear Daily,* April 2, 2003.

Chapter 3: www.colormarketing.org

Gorman, Greg M. *The Visual Merchandising and Store Design Workbook.* Cincinnati: ST Publications, 1996.

Longinotti-Buitoni, Gian Luigi. *Selling Dreams: How to Make Any Product Irresistable.* New York: Simon and Schuster, 1999.

www.pantone.com

Underhill, Paco. *Why We Buy: The Science of Shopping.* New York: Simon and Schuster, 1999.

Chapter 4: Longinotti-Buitoni, Gian Luigi. *Selling Dreams: How to Make Any Product Irresistable.* New York: Simon and Schuster, 1999.

www.nasfm.org

Underhill, Paco. *Why We Buy: The Science of Shopping.* New York: Simon and Schuster, 1999.

Chapter 5: Gorman, Greg M. *The Visual Merchandising and Store Design Workbook.* Cincinnati: ST Publications, 1996.

Underhill, Paco. *Why We Buy: The Science of Shopping.* New York: Simon and Schuster, 1999.

Chapter 6: Doonan, Simon. *Confessions of a Window Dresser.* New York: Penguin Putnam, 1998.

Chapter 7: Glen, Peter. *10 Years of Peter Glen: One Hundred Essays for the Improvement of Work, Life and Other Matters of Consequence.* Cincinnati: ST Publications, 1994.

Green, Penelope. "Chic Housewares are the New Must-haves with Prices to Match." *Star Tribune,* August 20, 2000.

www.homeportfolio.com

www.living.com

www.marthastewart.com

Underhill, Paco. *Why We Buy: The Science of Shopping.* New York: Simon and Schuster, 1999.

www.williams-sonoma.com

Chapter 8: Glen, Peter. *10 Years of Peter Glen: One Hundred Essays for the Improvement of Work, Life and Other Matters of Consequence.* Cincinnati: ST Publications, 1994.

www.signmuseum.com

Chapter 9: "Consumer Forecast – 2001." www.colormarketing.org.

Green, Marc. "Designing Displays for the Aging Population." *Display and Design Ideas,* July 1999.

Pegler, Martin. *Visual Merchandising and Display,* 4th ed. New York: Fairchild Books, 1988.

Underhill, Paco. *Why We Buy: The Science of Shopping.* New York: Simon and Schuster, 1999.

Chapter 10: Blank, Dennis. "Natural Food Stores Pursue Organic Seals of Approval." *The New York Times,* June 29, 2003.

Cavicchia, Marilyn. "Everybody Welcome." www.ideabeat.com, May 22, 2000.

Callahan, Patricia and Zimmerman, Alice. "Price War in Aisle Three." *The Wall Street Journal,* May 27, 2003.

Collins, Terry. "We Really Are What We Eat, and There's Cause to Celebrate." *Star Tribune,* October 8, 1999.

www.design.ncsu.edu/cud

Egerstrom, Lee. "Growing Naturally." *Saint Paul Pioneer Press,* August 27, 2000.

www.egrocer.com

www.fmi.org

www.fredmeyer.com

Liebmann, Wendy. *Home Furnishings News,* May 1, 2000.

Litwak, David. "Michael Gilland: From Free Spirit to Innovator." www.quip.com, May 30, 2000.

Lofstock, John. "Tracking Eating Trends." *CSP,* March 2000.

McLachlan, Michelle. "Healthy Indulgences." *Display and Design Ideas,* May 2000.

Rosenberg, Matt. "Grocery Stores, Supermarkets and Piggly Wiggly."

www.geography.about.com/education, November 23, 1998.

Supermarket News, February 3, 1997.

Sway, RoxAnna. "Architecture and Artichokes." *Display and Design Ideas,* May 2000.

Troy, Mike. "Publix Supermarket Debuts Apron's HMR Concept." *DSN Retailing Today,* May 22, 2000.

Wahl, Mike. *In-Store Marketing: A New Dimension in the Share Wars.* Winston-Salem, North Carolina: Wake Forrest University Press, 1992.

Chapter 11: "Forbes Favorites: Luxe Shopping." *www.forbes.com,* October 2003.

Niemela, Jennifer. "Bringing Catalogs Online." *Corporate Report,* May 2000.

"Stock Market Isn't Squelching the E-Tailers." www.visualstore.com, April 18, 2000.

Tedeschi, Bob. "Online Retailers Go Public." *New York Times,* October 6, 2003.

Chapter 12: Albrecht, Donald and Livenstein, Barbara. Cooper-Hewitt National Design Museum Program Notes for the Window Show, May 14–21, 1999.

Doonan, Simon. *Confessions of a Window Dresser.* New York: Penguin Putnam, 1998.

Gorman, Greg M. *The Visual Merchandising and Store Design Workbook.* Cincinnati: ST Publications, 1996.

Hutchinson, Lois. "Points of Light." *Visual Merchandising and Store Design,* March 2000.

"The Window Show: A Groudbreaking Exhibition by Cooper-Hewitt, National Design Museum, Spotlights Window Design and Designers." *Retail Ad World,* October 1999.

Chapter 13: Bentley Hale, Marsha. *Visual Merchandising and Store Design,* August 1983.

Doonan, Simon. *Confessions of a Window Dresser.* New York: Penguin Putnam, 1998.

Holm-Bertelsen. "Mannequins Get Real." *Visual Merchandising and Store Design,* February 2000, 86.

Ola, Per and d'Aulaire, Emily. "Mannequins, the Mute Mirrors of Fashion History." *Smithsonian,* April 1991, 61–75.

Pegler, Martin. *Store Windows 10.* New York: Visual Reference Publications, 1999.

Portas, Mary. *Windows: the Art of Retail Display.* London: Thames and Hudson, 1999.

Redstone, Susan. "Adel Rootstein." www.fashionwindows.com, August 8, 1998.

Sipe, Jeffrey. "Adoring Dior's Haute Couture." *Insight on the News,* v12 n47, December 16, 1996, 37.

Tobias, Tom. "I Sing the Body Inanimate." *New York,* June 28-July 5, 1999, 177.

Chapter 14: *The Chicago Manual of Style: For Authors, Editors and Copywriters,* 13th ed., rev. and exp. Chicago: The University of Chicago Press, 1982.

Doonan, Simon. *Confessions of a Window Dresser.* New York: Penguin Putnam, Inc., 1998.

Eisenberg, Ronnie. "Desk Organization." *Priorities: The Journal of Professional and Personal Success,* September 30, 2000.

www.franklincovey.com

www.gesexpo.com/education

Glen, Peter. *10 Years of Peter Glen: One Hundred Essays for the Improvement of Work, Life and Other Matters of Consequence.* Cincinnati, Ohio: ST Publications, 1994.

Glen, Peter. "ADD: Attention Divided Disorder." *Visual Merchandising and Store Design,* November 1999.

Glen, Peter. *It's Not My Department.* New York: William Morrow and Company, Inc., 1990.

Gorman, Greg M. *The Visual Merchandising and Store Design Workbook.* Cincinnati: ST Publications, 1996.

Longinotti-Buitoni, Gian Luigi. *Selling Dreams: How to Make Any Product Irresistable.* New York: Simon and Schuster, 1999.

McNally, David and Speak, Karl D. *Be Your Own Brand.* San Francisco: Berrett-Koehler Publishers, 2002.

Popcorn, Faith. *Clicking: 17 Trends That Drive Your Business.* New York: Harper Business, 1998.

Popcorn, Faith. *EVEolution: The Eight Truths of Marketing to Women.* New York: Hyperion, 2000.

Strunk, W., Jr. and White, E.B. *The Elements of Style,* 3rd ed. New York: Macmillan, 1979.

Underhill, Paco. *Why We Buy: The Science of Shopping.* New York: Simon and Schuster, 1999.

Underhill, Paco. *Call of the Mall.* New York: Simon and Schuster, 2004.

Chapter 15: www.nasfm.com

Rufus, Anneli. *The Party of One: The Loner's Manifesto.* Marlowe and Company, 2003.

Useful Websites

Chapter 1:   Echochamber—http://www.echochamber.com

Retail Interiors—http://www.subscription.co.uk/rimag

Style Guide—http://www.style-guide.biz

Chapter 2:   Bloomingdale's—http://www.bloomingdales.com

International Trend Website—http://www.echochamber.com

Chapter 3: Color Marketing Group—http://www.colormarketing.org

Elle Magazine—http://www.elle.com

M. Grumbacher—http://www.sanfordcorp.com/grumbacher

Pantone, Inc.—http://www.pantone.com

W Magazine—http://www.fairchildpub.com

Chapter 4: Alpha Display—http://www.alphadisplaycoinc.com

B & N Industries—http://www.bnind.com

Betsey Johnson—http://www.betsyjohnson.com

The Center for Universal Design at North Carolina State University—http://www.design.ncsu.edu

DKNY—http://www.dkny.com

Dolce & Gabbana—http://www.dolcegabbana.it

Envirosell—http://www.envirosell.com/articles

Look—http://www.lookonhudson.com

MET Store Fixtures—http://www.metmc.com

National Association of Store Fixture Manufaturers (NASFM)—http://www.nasfm.org

Presentations Plus—http://www.presentationsplus.com

Propaganda—http://www.4propaganda.com

Sephora—http://www.sephora.com/help/about_company.jhtml

Silvestri—http://www.silvestricalifornia.com

Swatch—http://www.swatchgroup.com/group/brands

Chapter 6: *Daily News Record* (DNR)—http://www.dnrnews.com

Women's Wear Daily—http://www.wwd.com

Chapter 7: ABC Carpet and Home—http://www.abccarpet.com

Chiasso—http://www.chiasso.com

Crate & Barrel—http://www.crateandbarrel.com

Eddie Bauer Home—http://www.eddiebauer.com

Home Design Website—http://www.homeportfolio.com

Martha Stewart—http://www.marthastewart.com

Pottery Barn—http://www.potterybarn.com

Restoration Hardware—http://www.restorationhardware.com

Saks Fifth Avenue—http://www.saksfifthavenue.com

Williams-Sonoma, Inc.—http://www.williams-sonoma.com

Chapter 8: American Sign Museum—http://www.signmuseum.com

Boston Proper Catalog—http://www.bostonproper.com

Fishs Eddy—http://www.fishseddy.com

Chapter 9: Adart—http://www.adart.com

Adbox—http://www.adbox.com

American Lighting Association—http://www.americanlightingassoc.com

Color Marketing Group—http://www.colormarketing.org

Display & Design Ideas Magazine (DDI)—http://www.ddimagazine.com

Envirosell—http://www.envirosell.com/articles

Rainbow Signs—http://www.rsigns.com

Visual Merchandising and Store Design Magazine—http://visualstore.com

Chapter 10: Byerly's—http://byerlys.com

Celestial Seasonings—http://www.celestialseasonings.com

Food Co-op—http://www.prairienet.org

The Food Emporium—http://www.thefoodemporium.com

The Food Marketing Institute—http://www.fmi.org

Fred Meyer Stores—http://www.fredmeyer.com

Grocery Service Website—http://www.egrocer.com

The International Co-operative Alliance (ICA)—http://www.coop.org

The Mississippi Market—http://www.msmarket.org

Online Food and Flowers—http://www.greatfood.com

Piggly Wiggly—http://www.shopthepig.com

Portland Public Market—http://www.portlandmarket.com

Publix—http://www.publix.com

Real Simple Magazine—http://www.realsimple.com

Store Equipment and Design—http://www.storequip.com

United States Department of Agriculture—http://www.usda.gov

Web Grocer's Magazines—http://www.ideabeat.com
http://www.supermarketnews.com
http://www.supermarketworld.com

Web Lifestyle/Food Magazine—http://www.epicurious.com

The Wedge Community Co-op—http://www.wedgecoop.com

Whole Foods Market, Inc.—http://www.wholefoodsmarket.com

Wild Oats Markets, Inc.—http://www.wildoats.com

Chapter 11: The Disney Store—http://disney.store.go.com

Forbes Favorite Websites
http://www.banaldesign.com
http://www.dwr.com
http://www.forbesbest.com
http://www.gansevoortgallery.com
http://www.icon20.com
http://www.modernism.com
http://www.modernity.nu
http://www.momastore.org
http://www.newel.com

Chapter 12: Cooper-Hewitt National Design Museum—http://www.si.edu

Display & Design Ideas Magazine (DDI)—http://www.ddimagazine.com

Elevations—http://www.elevations.com

Eviaggo—http://www.eviaggo.com

Fashion Display Website—http://www.fashionwindows.com

GlobalShop—http://www.globalshop.org

Lord & Taylor—http://www.mayco.com

Storeworks—http://www.storeworksinc.com

Tiffany & Co.—http://www.tiffany.com

Trimco—http://www.trimco-display.com

Visual Merchandising and Store Design magazine (VM + SD)—http://www.stpubs.com/VM.html

Chapter 13: Alu—http://www.alu.com

Truevisual—http://www.truevisual.com

Bendies—http://www.bendiesforms.ca

Bernstein—http://www.bernsteindisplay.com

Carol Barnhart—http://www.carolbarnhart.com

Characters Unlimited—
http://www.charactersunlimitedinc.com

Decter—http://www.decter.com

Fashion Windows—
http://www.fashionwindows.com/mannequin_compa

France Display—http://www.manex-usa.com

Greneker—http://www.greneker.com

Hindsgaul—http://www.hindsgaul.com

Patina-V—http://www.patinav.com

Pucci International—http://www.fashionwindows.com

Rootstein—http://www.rootstein.com

Seven Continents—http://www.sevencontinents.com

Silvestri—http://www.silvestricalifornia.com

Chapter 14: *Chain Store Age* Magazine—
http://www.chainstoreage.com

Children's Business (CB)—
http://www.childrensbusiness.com

Daily News Record (DNR)—
http://www.dailynewsrecord.com

EuroShop—
http://www.messe-dusseldorf.de/en/2002/euroshop

Footwear News—http://www.footwearnews.com

Franklin Planners—http://www.franklincovey.com

GlobalShop—http://www.globalshop.org

Home Furnishing News—http://www.hfnmag.com

MapEasy's Guide Maps—http://www.mapeasy.com

ShopEast—http://www.shopeast.com

ShopWest—http://www.shopwest.com

The Tradeshow News Network—http://www.tsnn.com

Visual New York—http://www.storeconcepts.com

Where Magazine—http://www.wheremagazine.com

Women's Wear Daily—http://www.wwd.com

Chapter 15: National Association of Store Fixture Manufacturers
(NASFM)—http://www.nasfm.org

Planning and Visual Education (PAVE)—
http://www.visualstore.com/pave

Visual Merchandising and Store Design Magazine—
http://www.stpubs.com/VM.html

Retailers

Abercrombie & Fitch—http://www.abercrombie.com

Ann Taylor—http://www.anntaylor.com

Banana Republic—http://www.bananarepublic.com

Barney's—http://www.barneys.com

Brooks Brothers—http://www.brooksbrothers.com

Costco Wholesale—http://www.costco.com

Dillard's—http://www.dillards.com

Federated Department Stores—
http://www.federated-fds.com

- Burdine's
- Goldsmith's
- Lazarus
- Macy's East
- Macy's West
- Rich's
- Fingerhut

Gap—http://www.gap.com

J.Crew—http://www.jcrew.com

Kohl's—http://www.kohls.com

Lands' End—http://www.landsend.com

Old Navy—http://www.oldnavy.com

Neiman Marcus—http://www.neiman marcus.com/about

Sears—http://www.sears.com

Sony—http://www.sony.com

Target—http://www.targetcorp.com/index.asp

- Marshall Field's
- Mervyn's California
- Target Stores

T.J. Maxx—http://www.tjmaxx.com

The Wiz—http://www.thewiz.com

INDEX